The Glittering Man
(RISE OF THE KHITAN)

A family historical novel by
Allen E. Goldenthal
(7th Book of the Kahana Chronicles)

The Glittering Man ∽ Allen E. Goldenthal

Copyright © 2025 1st Edition

All Rights Reserve – Allen E. Goldenthal

No part of this book can be reproduced or transmitted in any form or by any means, graphic, electronic, or mechanical, including photocopying, recording, taping or by any information storage retrieval system, without the permission of the publisher in writing.

VAL d'OR PUBLISHING

ISBN: 978-0-6488083-8-1

The Glittering Man ❦ Allen E. Goldenthal

Author's Note

The people and places that you are about to experience in this historical novel all existed and all played a significant role in establishing current accepted history. The events described herein occurred to the best of anyone's knowledge as presented. The Buddhist traveler Hsuan-tsang records how a Chinese princess at the end of the fifth century headed west to marry an unnamed king beyond Khotan (Persia/Iraq), which is described thoroughly in the book, *Zutra*, and the cave paintings at DanDan-Uiliq which depict the events of her life as they happened following the turn of the 6th Century AD. One should question as to how paintings depicting the Princess She-Ping's (Ti-Ping as she was known in Mahoza) journey to the West to meet her betrothed could be painted on these walls, including the portrait of the prince she would be marrying if she was journeying westward and hadn't even met her betrothed as yet to know what he looked like. The answer is actually quite simple, as we learn from the final chapters of the book *Zutra*. These events were painted almost eight years after she made that fateful journey to Mahoza, because at this time she was fleeing eastward, back to Northern Wei, in order to preserve her own life and that of her young child, Mar Yanqa.

Piecing together the next chapter of the lives of those that had been entangled with Mar Zutra took some time. Time for the research into Chinese history, time to visit Inner Mongolia and explore excavated tombs and past civilizations, and time to assess the impact that a man like Mar Yanqa, holding dear the same beliefs and customs as his father, would have had on the nomadic tribes of the region known as the Mongolian steppes. Once you have visited the steppes with what appears to be infinite grasslands and an equally infinite sprawling desert, the vastness of the region, as well as the harshness of the surrounding environment, will have an impact that imprints upon your consciousness forever. One can only imagine what the effect would have been on a young boy who had been torn away from the splendor of royal life that he had enjoyed for the entirety of his first eight years in the city of Mahoza.

He was equipped with only the knowledge of his father being a great king and a more phenomenal warrior, but more importantly, he had a mother with the spirit of a tiger and the formidable nature of a dragon. What his father had passed on to him would only take him so far in life, but the indomitable spirit of his mother would take him to heights that a half Chinese warlord could never have imagined. Mar Yanqa changed history in Asia by achieving the inconceivable. The empirical powers of China had felt safe for over eight hundred years behind their massive stone walls and technologically superior armed forces, considering an invasion by the nomads of the West an impossibility. After all, the barbarians on their rugged steppe ponies, armed with bows and arrows could never mount a serious attack on China for two reasons; the first being their lack of any military strategy, and secondly, but most important, their inability to cooperate for any length of time because of their tribal rivalries. That is until a stranger from Persia came into the domain of these nomads and changed the balance of power forever.

We know from Chinese historical records that the 6th to the 12th Century, oversaw the establishment of the Khitan kingdom, later to be renamed the Liao dynasty. The Khitan leaders were able to put an end to the conflicts that long existed among the peoples of different ethnic groups that inhabited the Mongolian steppes and integrated the nomadic and agricultural economies that existed in Northern China into a single sustainable economy. The implementation of traditional etiquette institutions of the Central Plains, the construction of many cities, the popularization of the agricultural economy and the influence of a cultural philosophy, bound the Khitan tribes into a unified multicultural nation. Meanwhile, the smooth Grassland Silk Road, the lifeline of China's diplomatic and economic future, was now dependent on appeasing the Khitan nation to guarantee the thousands of caravans safe passage though their lands.

What had begun as northern step nomads, the Khitan originating along the banks of the Xilamulun River and the Laoha River of Inner Mongolia, the descendants of the Yuwen tribe of the eastern Xianbei had grown into a loose affiliation of eight tribes during the Northern Wei Dynasty, that spent most of their time attacking and pillaging each other, unable to unify into a singular fighting force in order to defend themselves against the Turkomen and Rouran raiders that destroyed their homes and stole their womenfolk. That is until a young princess and her red-haired, green-eyed teenage son, accompanied by a cohort of western looking infantry entered into their lands, and suddenly, the world changed forever.

Dr. Allen Goldenthal

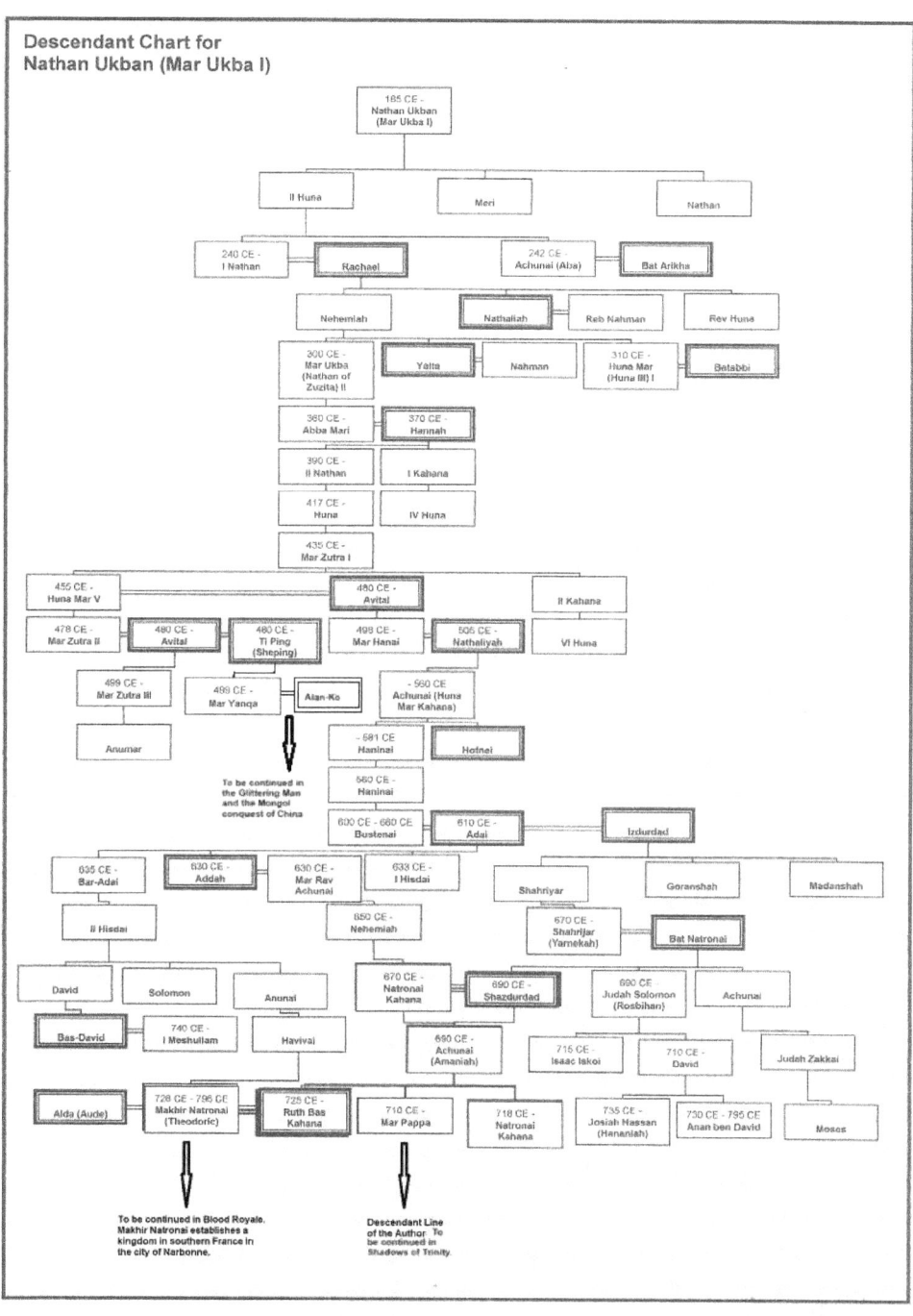

The Glittering Man ⊗ Allen E. Goldenthal

PROLOGUE
Winter 506 AD

Approaching the third bell of the afternoon, the Great Shah's generals had assembled their forces on the Ctesiphon side of the bridge. The winter sun had already begun its descent and the air was feeling slightly chilled. Standing alongside Pharazman, Zutra commented upon the state of the Shah's army assembled, appearing much smaller than the expected complement of fifty thousand men.

"That is because the other half has gone north to the bridge at Baghdad and will try to circle us from behind," the captain suggested.

"How do you know?"

"It is what I would do," Pharazman replied modestly.

"So how do you see our chances," Zutra asked.

"Chances?" Pharazman let out a burst of laughter. "There are no chances!"

"I know we have no chance to survive," Zutra agreed. "What I want to know is what will be our chances to write ourselves into the pages of history?" Zutra winked at the Persian Captain. "Surely we want this to be our finest moment."

"The longer we survive the more of them we will take into the netherworld with us. If we slaughter enough of the bastards, then their historians may have no other choice but to record the battle. That's when we will make history."

"I'd like my sons to know what we've done here," Zutra said wistfully.

"Then it doesn't matter whether we kill a thousand or even ten thousand today, that won't make any difference in the end. Your sons will know what you have done, not for what you do this day but for what you have done for the past seven years. You have given men, all men, a taste of freedom. Today we die as free men!"

"Thank you Pharazman. I will remember your words in the afterlife."

The captain was no longer listening to Mar Zutra, transfixed by a cloud of dust showing movement in the distance. Approaching from the south a force measuring no more than half a legion marched at a double step, rapidly closing the distance between their armies.

"Surely they do not intend to drive us from the bridge with so few units," Pharazman indicated his disdain at the paltry attempt by curling his lip. "What manner of trickery is this that they could have crossed the northern bridge and circled around us so soon?"

"No trick," Mar Zutra held him back. "Those men aren't attacking us. I recognize some of them, especially the golden armor of the one in front. Take a better look!"

Pharazman squinted his eyes to get a better look against the glare of the sun. "By Ahura Mazda, what in God's name is he doing back here? The fool had a chance to live. Why bother to return to certain death?"

"Why does any man do what he does?" Zutra waxed philosophically, his heart beginning to pound excitedly at seeing them approach. Anxiously, he waited for the leader of the force to jog towards them.

"Am I too late?" the Commander puffed.

"I don't understand. Why aren't you with my son?" The sudden appearance of Patricius with several cohorts of soldiers caught Mar Zutra completely by surprise.

"Your son is safe. Everyone is safe," he reassured him. "You have the word of the Empress Ariadne in that regard. She has promised to see him safely to Holy Land where she will have him instated as the western Exilarch. My duty was done there!"

Zutra was still shaking his head in disbelief. "So, you came back here in order to die. Are you crazy? That makes no sense at all."

"There were extenuating circumstances," was all that Patricius would say on the matter of his return.

"And where did you get these men?"

"Courtesy of the Emperor Anastasius. They were all condemned to die for crimes they committed while in the military. He gave them a choice, fight under me and have their slates wiped clean and their family's honor restored or watch their children be executed before they met the same fate."

"Not much of a choice." Zutra mused. "So, all of them were prisoners?"

"Not exactly all," Patricius revealed. "I bought the services of about a thousand mercenaries. I figured whatever money I paid would be replenished by you if we win, and if we don't, then money is really of no concern to me afterwards," the General laughed at his own joke.

"But why?" was all that Zutra could think of saying, "You could have gone anywhere, started over, and lived!"

"I don't know," the Commander commented as he gazed upward into the cloudless sky surveying its brilliant blue hue. "Didn't want to miss what looks like a fine day for dying."

It was the same old commander that had returned and Zutra could not help but laugh at his nonchalance. "Yes, that it is my friend, a mighty fine day for dying."

"Plus, who was going to look after you if I didn't return?"

"Well, you won't be doing that for long," the Exilarch remarked with a huge grin across his face.

"Long enough to keep my promise to your wife."

"Which one?" Zutra jested.

"Actually both." It was the second surprise that Mar Zutra had received within such a short period of time.

"So, you've come to fulfill your pledge to two women." The king still couldn't believe that his Vizier would be so willing to make the ultimate sacrifice.

"That and an attempt to gain your forgiveness," the Commander confessed, his smile turning quickly into a frown of regret.

"I don't follow you?"

"This was the only way of gaining back my honor for betraying you. There was an episode in the past involving the Lady Avital and myself that I have suppressed all these years that I need your forgiveness for." Patricius awaited the anticipated angry outburst but none was forthcoming.

"I know," was all that Zutra said.

"You know?" Patricius's jaw dropped to his chest.

"Yes, Avital told me all about it when she tried to make me separate your head from your shoulders years ago."

"But you said nothing! Why would you not have said anything?"

"What was there to say? I knew whatever happened would have been manipulated by her own hand. Hers alone! She betrayed no one but herself. You were never guilty of betrayal."

Patricius felt extremely humbled by the forgiving nature of his monarch. "But you said and did nothing," he stammered. "Why would you have not slain both of us?"

"What and lose the best friend I ever had? Don't be ridiculous. Moreover, Avital proved to be a much better wife afterwards as well. I can only pray that you have forgiven me for having led you into such a predicament."

"You had nothing to do with it," Patricius objected to the king's inference.

"But I did, my friend. If you were to examine the scenario carefully, you would see that it was the Lord's way of punishing me. I coveted another man's wife and my sins had to be paid for. Foolish pride but at least I fared far luckier than my ancestor David was when he took Bathsheba. I didn't have to kill the son I loved most because of my weakness."

"You are a very strange man," was all that Patricius could say.

"That may be the case but you're still the one who has led over a thousand men across a continent only to face certain death. That to me is even stranger. And in case you didn't notice, Kavad still outnumbers us five to one."

"Couldn't let you hog all the glory to yourself. Not to mention, I'm not the only one lacking any sense. You could have left at any time as well. No one would have faulted you. I'm certain the Princess is making my cousin's life a living hell for not going back and retrieving you."

"Common sense and love," Zutra commented, "Two things that rarely work in harmony."

"You definitely are the strangest man I have ever had the honour of serving."

"Actually, the Princess did beg me to leave with her. But how could I ever defy the manifest will of God? My survival was never a consideration. Now I must give my sons much more than a father, I need to leave them a legend to live up to."

"While you two reminisce about better times, let me remind you that we have thirty thousand men on the other side of this bridge waiting to tear us to pieces," Pharazman quickly filled in Patricius of the situation, bringing both men back to reality. "And within two hours, there will be another twenty thousand circling behind us."

"Are you asking for my opinion?" Patricius countered. "If so, then I think this rivals the Greek legend of King Leonidas and his Spartans at Thermopylae. If this doesn't make us legendary, I don't know what will."

"Perhaps some military advice you wish to offer," Pharazman smirked upon listening to Patricius's comparison to Herodotus.

"Yes, attack before the other twenty thousand arrive."

"Shall you lead the charge or shall I," Zutra inquired of his Vizier, the smile on his face indicating that he was definitely enjoying their last moments together.

"You, of course! After all, it is your legend we are inscribing today."

"Well then, shall we?"

"No, wait!" Patricius raised his hands to stop his king from running towards the bridge. "Not yet. There's one more thing we must do." Drawing his sword, Patricius raised it high above his head and paraded back and forth in front of their soldiers assembled on the eastern side of the bridge and then brought the flat of the blade down repeatedly to beat against his shield. "Zutra, Zutra," he started to chant in unison to the hammering blows, the contagion of his enthusiasm spreading through the rank and file until all of them chanted and beat their shield in harmony. A resounding, earth-shaking chant that sent a shiver of fear through their enemies, especially to those that could remember the last time they heard that particular chorus. "Zutra, Zutra," the words sailed to the heavens, on the wings of a prayer. "Zutra, Zutra," it echoed through the alleyways and homes of the twin cities until the mortar began to crumble from the vibrations. "Zutra, Zutra," as a few drops of rain fell mysteriously from a cloudless sky, the tears of angels saying farewell to a favorite son.

The King laughed with delight on hearing his name rolling off every one of his soldiers' lips.

Turning to his king, Patricius placed his sword in front of his face and saluted his comrade farewell. "Now we're ready!" he shouted.

"Alright men let's do it," Zutra raised his sword in a return salute. He shouted his final order to begin the charge, leaping fatefully on to the bridge, "For God, for glory, for freedom! Attack!"

From the book Zutra

Chapter One: 510 AD

Mar Yanqa sat cross-legged on the wooden floor of the quiet study room, his back straight but his expression clearly displaying boredom, as his teacher, Master Huan, droned on about the Analects of Confucius. The room was dim, lit only by the flickering shadows of candles that burnt brightly beside the few students attending the class; a class only for the most privileged children of the aristocratic families living in the city. Master Huan was considered one of the most erudite authorities on the teachings of Kong Fu Zi. Outside, the sky above Kaifeng was heavy with the haze of early spring, but inside, the air was thick with the musty scent of ancient scrolls and parchments. Like any young boy, Mar Yanqa dreamed about playing outside with the other children, those of a lesser social standing, rather than being confined to a school room with a teacher as old as the documents he was reading from.

As for Master Huan, he was an elderly man with a slightly hunched back and greying hair, but he lectured with a passion that had not dulled with age. "Confucius said that the ruler must act as a role model to his people, that to lead is to follow the Way. Only through virtue can an emperor guide his nation."

Mar Yanqa listened somewhat dispassionately, his green eyes fixed on the teacher's face, his expression thoughtful but not distracted. At just under twelve years of age, the boy already understood the weight of the words, but something deeper stirred in his heart, something his father, Mar Zutra, had taught him in the quiet of their home back in Mesopotamia before he died. Mar Zutra, the great warrior, had taught him of a higher authority than the emperors and kings of this world. An authority that no man could defy, no matter how high his standing may be in society.

"Master," Mar Yanqa interrupted, his voice soft but steady. "If the emperor is to be a model of virtue, then who teaches him? If there is no one greater than him, then who will the emperor learn from?"

Master Huan paused, blinking at the sudden interruption. It was unusual for a student to question a statement from the Confucian texts, but Mar Yanqa's curiosity was never easily curbed. The boy had always been different — not just because of his red hair and green eyes, which set him apart in a court that valued conformity, but because his mind worked in ways that were both extraordinary and unsettling. To a teacher in Confucianism where all followers must adhere to uniformity for the sake of society, questioning the teachings was not permitted. Mar Yanqa was setting a bad example for the other students.

"The emperor is the highest authority," Master Huan replied, his voice a little cautious. "He is the son of Heaven, a man chosen by the heavens themselves to rule."

Mar Yanqa tilted his head, his eyes narrowing as he considered the words. "But does not even the emperor answer to the invisible God, the Great Creator? The One who reigns from beyond the clouds, who gives life to all things and to whom all kings must answer? You implied such when you said the emperor is chosen by Heaven. My father taught me that there is a power higher than any throne, a master who cannot be seen, but whose presence is known by all who seek truth and his name is Yahweh."

A ripple of laughter spread though the students upon hearing mention of some foreign god of the heathens. Master Huan stiffened, his brows furrowing at the mention of this "invisible God" and the boy's use of the name "Yahweh." It was a completely foreign concept, one Mar Yanqa's father had instilled in him through stories of the Jewish faith, an ancient belief that had crossed paths with China with many merchant travelers but which was totally rejected. The idea that the emperor might not be the ultimate authority in the universe was dangerous and bordered on insurrection. In the royal court of Luoyang, where loyalty to the emperor was sacred, such thoughts were considered to be a seed of rebellion. The teacher tried to mask his unease with a smile, but it faltered and his disdain for such thinking could not be easily discarded.

"You speak of things not suited to a child of this class," Master Huan said softly, his voice betraying his discomfort. "It is wise to remember your place."

But Mar Yanqa, so much more than a child, saw no danger in his words. To him, it was simple truth. "Is it not Confucius who said that a ruler must be virtuous, must lead with the Way? But how can one follow the Way if one does not recognize a higher master that taught him the Way? The emperor, no matter how great, cannot be greater than the source of all life. My father said this to me, before he died. He told me that kings and emperors are like any other man, no more, no less."

Master Huan opened his mouth to respond, but hesitated. There was an unspoken warning in the air now, a tension in the room thick enough to choke the words from his throat. The children nervously fidgeted with their writing boards, fearful of what might occur next. Instead, the teacher let the silence stretch out for a moment before gathering his composure.

"Perhaps your father was a great man in his own kingdom, but you must understand, Mar Yanqa, that such words have consequences in this kingdom. The Emperor must never hear of this. You must be cautious in your thoughts and in your speech. Do you understand?"

But Mar Yanqa was already lost in thought, the words of his father and the teachings of Confucius swirling together in his mind. He didn't mean to upset anyone; he only sought greater understanding. His father's death, though a heroic one by sacrificing himself on the battlefield to protect the people of his land from the Sassanid king Kavad, had left a void in Mar Yanqa's life. His father's principles, though harsh and practical, had instilled in him a sense of justice and honor. Yet now, under the weight of his mother's royal title, he was becoming more aware of the dangerous game of politics that shaped the world around him.

But he had more questions that needed to be answered, and even though his teacher had warned him not to pursue this avenue, such a warning would do little to dissuade him from his pursuit of knowledge.

"Master Huan, if Confucius only lived a thousand years ago, and Yahweh gave mankind his laws and rules of behavior two thousand years ago, could it not be said that Confucius based his philosophy on what had already been written in the Hebrew scriptures?"

"Don't be impertinent child! There are no similarities between the two on which someone can build such an argument. Remember your place. Your mother may be a princess of Northern Wei, but only as a guest of the Emperor. Here you will abide by the rules of the Empire and not seek to undermine them." It was evident that Master Huan was quickly reaching his limits with the boy.

"But Master Huan if it can be shown that Kong Fu Zi's statements of honoring parents, not stealing from others, or committing adultery, or lying unnecessarily, not murdering, and being benevolent rather than covetous are identical to the Ten Commandments on human behavior, then how can you make the statement that there are no similarities. In fact, the concept of 'Ren' which is central to Confucian ethics, advocating for kindness, compassion, and respect in human interactions is not only similar, it is identical." Mar Yanqa was quite proud of his argument, thinking that he had outwitted his teacher. The smiles on the other students' faces suggested that he may have done so.

Master Huan was growing furious. "Just because Confucianism and Judaism both recognize the significance of family and social harmony does not mean they are the same. In Confucian thought, the family is considered the fundamental unit of society, and filial piety is a key virtue. Confucius believed that a harmonious family life would lead to a harmonious society, as individuals learn to cultivate virtues within the family setting."

"As does Judaism, Master Huang," Mar Yanqa quickly rebutted. " In Judaism peace in the home underscores the importance of maintaining harmony and mutual respect within the family. Therefore, it can be said that both traditions view the family as a cornerstone of social stability and moral development. And since the Hebrew scripture came first, then there is a high probability that Kong Fu Zi merely recorded what he had heard from the foreign traders."

"To say such a thing is heresy," the master warned the boy. "Let's end this fruitless discussion now. We have no concept of God in Confucianism. Your father's entire system of belief revolves around your central concept of God. That shows you they are fundamentally different. Now enough of this. Let us get back to your learning what is proper in the society you now live in."

"Although one might think Kong Fu Zi makes no reference to God, then how do you explain his numerous references to a heavenly body?" Mar Yanqa continued to challenge his teacher and didn't heed the warning.

"Did I not say this was over!" Master Huan bellowed as he banged his cane angrily against the floor but the young prince did not even flinch, though the other students practically jumped though seated.

"Master Huang, if a man let himself be influenced by his anger, then his conduct will not be correct." The tone obviously suggested Mar Yanqa was mocking his teacher.

"You dare to quote the teachings of Kong Fu Zi to me?" Now the teacher was outraged as he raised his cane in the air as if to strike.

"If you let your anger rise, think of the consequences," Mar Yanqa repeated another of the Confucian lessons. At that point the young prince stood up and though he was only twelve he was already taller than most of the men in Norther Wei, and that certainly made him a couple of heads taller than Master Huan. "If I was to be emperor, I certainly remember that any power that I might wield was only through the grace of God."

The other children gasped upon hearing his proclamation. Master Huan remained silent and barely moved. Whether because he was intimidated by the boy that towered over him, or the fact that he had lost face, being schooled by one of his own pupils in front of the other students on the essence of Kong Fu Zi's teachings, he didn't utter a word as Mar Yanqa turned and walked silently from the classroom with perhaps a tinge of a smug smile upon his face.

The news of Mar Yanqa's words spread quickly. It was not long before Master Huan was summoned to appear in Luoyang, to the imperial palace of Emperor Hsuan Wu Ti, She-Ping's brother. The Emperor, seated on his golden throne, listened as the teacher relayed the boy's statements — ideas that not only challenged the teachings of Confucius but undermined the very foundation of imperial authority.

"Your nephew, the boy," Master Huan said cautiously, "he speaks of a power greater than the Emperor. He speaks of Yahweh, a god of a foreign people, as though this invisible master rules above all, even above you, my Emperor. I fear his mind, though brilliant, may lead him down a dangerous path."

Emperor Hsuan Wu Ti's eyes narrowed as he took in the information. Mar Yanqa was his sister's son, but the boy's words were unsettling. The Emperor had always kept a tight grip on his throne, ensuring that no challenge to his rule went unpunished. The idea of a boy, a foreign-born misfit with his red hair and striking green eyes, challenging the established order was something that could not be ignored.

"How old is he now?" the emperor asked, his voice low and calculating.

"A little under twelve," Master Huan replied.

"You let yourself be bested by a child," the mocking tone of the Emperor's voice was quite noticeable.

"He is much more than a mere boy," Master Huan attempted to defend his reputation.

"Too young to be dangerous, perhaps," the emperor mused, "but too old not to be taken seriously. If his mind is as sharp as you say, then he may become a threat sooner than we think."

Hsuan Wu Ti's thoughts swirled like a storm. His sister, She-Ping, had always been a woman of honor and grace, but her son… The emperor had long tolerated the presence of his half-Caucasian nephew, but now, as Mar Yanqa's intellect began to reveal itself, the emperor could not ignore the possibility that this child might one day pose a threat to his throne.

In the grand halls of the Kaifeng palace, as Mar Yanqa sat alone in one of the garden courtyards, surrounded by the serene beauty of the koi ponds and willow trees, he had no idea that his words had already begun to stir a tempest. His green eyes reflected the calm waters of the pond, but in his heart, there was a yearning for something greater. He had never truly fit in with this particular court, a child of two worlds, caught between the empire of his mother's blood and the legacy of his father's warrior past. He was a boy of brilliance, yes, but also of innocence, unaware that the same brilliance that set him apart was the very thing that could lead to his undoing.

Hsuan Wu Ti's court saw him as a misfit, a foreigner with his red hair and his unorthodox ideas. But in his heart, Mar Yanqa simply sought to make sense of the world he was thrust in to. He sought truth. And the truth, he would soon realize, in the eyes of an emperor, was often the most dangerous threat of all.

Chapter 2: 510 AD

The streets of Luoyang were lined with banners in gold and crimson as Princess She-Ping's entourage entered the city. The air was heavy with the scent of incense and the promise of a spectacle. She-Ping, poised and regal, glanced at her son, Mar Yanqa, who sat silently beside her in the carriage, his striking green eyes gazing out at the bustling city. His red hair, too bright for the Chinese court, shimmered like a flame in the sunlight, and he looked every bit the foreigner he was said to be, even if his bloodline spoke of a kingship extending back fifteen hundred years.

She-Ping, though proud of her son's intellect, was troubled. Her brother, Emperor Hsuan Wu Ti, she knew had invited them to Luoyang under false pretenses. He had claimed it was to discuss matters of the kingdom and her inheritance from her father, the late Emperor Hsiang Xiaowen, but she knew better. This was no mere diplomatic visit…this was a test. A test of her son's mind and his loyalty to the empire. And perhaps, a test of her own thirst for authority as both a mother and a princess.

The palace was a breathtaking sight, its towering white walls gleaming in the evening sun, like a fortress of jade and marble. The doors to the banquet hall swung open with an elegant flourish, and the air seemed to shift, electrified by the entrance of Princess She-Ping and her son, Mar Yanqa. A collective breath was drawn, as if the very heartbeat of the gathering had paused in reverence. The Princess herself was a vision of regal grace, her long black hair cascading like a waterfall of midnight silk, her robes of jade and gold shimmering in the soft lantern light. At her side, Mar Yanqa with his sharp, inquisitive eyes glowing green with excitement, walked with a carefree, youthful energy, his curiosity pulsing through every step. They were escorted past the door of the grand hall, where a lavish banquet awaited, the long table covered in dishes of exotic fruits, meats, and fine wines. The flickering light of lanterns cast a warm, golden glow over the gathered nobles, their faces a mix of curiosity and quiet excitement.

The Emperor sat at the head of the table, his sharp eyes scanning the room with a ruler's practiced detachment. His regal attire, a deep purple robe embroidered with gold dragons, shimmered in the candlelight, and his high peaked leather cap was as black as the night. Beside him were his many wives, each seated according to their rank, their eyes trained on the emperor's every word and gesture.

When She-Ping and her son moved towards the central table, the room fell silent for a moment. The Emperor rose to greet his sister, but his gaze lingered on the boy who was standing at her side. The guests, all of whom had been discussing the boy's brilliance in whispers before his arrival, looked eagerly to see what the child would do. Everyone knew this was a test but none were aware of what would be the outcome.

The Emperor's voice, deep and sonorous, rang out above the quiet hum, "Welcome home, She-Ping, and welcome to my nephew, Mar Yanqa. The night is yours." The crowd, caught between awe and excitement, parted to allow the Princess and her son to make their way forward. With every step, the carpet beneath them, woven with intricate scenes of golden lotus blossoms and silver cranes in flight, seemed to glow even brighter, as though the very earth beneath their feet recognized their royal presence. The people around them whispered in low tones, but the buzz was quickly overtaken by the sounds of the festivities resuming.

"My dear sister, welcome," the Emperor repeated, his voice dripping with feigned warmth. His eyes turned to Mar Yanqa. "And my brilliant nephew, the one everyone is speaking about. You have grown so much in the two years when you first returned to the palace with your mother seeking refuge. But now I am told you are the second coming of Kong Fu Zi."

The guests murmured in awe at the recognition for Mar Yanqa's unusual appearance had already made him a subject of curiosity and speculation among the nobles but to imply he would be comparable to one of the great philosophers was a rare tribute, indeed. To them, he had become an enigma, a foreign child of a legendary warrior but with a Chinese intellect. But what they didn't realize was that he carried the brilliance of his father's mind along with his father's ability to rule, and that was what worried the Emperor the most.

"Everyone please take your places," the Emperor commanded. "It is time to begin these festivities in honor of my sister."

The hall was a vast expanse of opulence with its lush tapestries of dragons and phoenixes, their colors deep and rich like jewels, adorning the walls. The soft murmur of voices hushed, replaced by the delicate rustling of silk and the subtle creak of fine lacquered chairs as noblemen and women shifted to better catch a glimpse of the newcomers. Even the musicians stilled for a moment, their hands hovering over their instruments, before a long, harmonious note spilled into the air to announce the beginning of the entertainment.

The moment they were seated at the high table, a cascade of music, light, and laughter swept through the hall as if the floodgates had been opened. A wave of sound crashed into the room, with flutes and lutes intertwining in a melody so enchanting, it felt like the air itself was alive with magic. The musicians, some clad in imperial red, others in pure white, played with a fluidity that seemed to stretch the very limits of what the human ear could comprehend. Each note rang in perfect harmony with the next, like a celestial conversation between strings and wind.

And then, the dancers entered. Exotic girls, dressed in nothing but sheer veils of glistening silk, spun and twisted like ethereal phantoms, their movements hypnotic, weaving in a trance-like rhythm that echoed the pulsing beat of the drums. The music shifted, and their bodies followed suit, contorting and undulating with the grace of serpents, each flick of the wrist and dip of the waist a mesmerizing dance of fire and water. Their skin, glowing in the soft candlelight, seemed to shimmer with the promise of a forbidden beauty, and the crowd gasped in unison, utterly captivated.

Not far behind, a group of acrobats, their faces painted with intricate designs, leapt and somersaulted from one end of the hall to the other. Their movements were a blur of grace and strength, as if they had unlocked the secret to defying gravity itself. One performer vaulted high into the air, twisting and spinning in a perfect arc, before landing with a roll that carried them into another flip. The entire hall erupted in wild applause, the sounds of excitement reverberating off the stone walls like thunder.

In the background, the animal acts unfurled like a parade of wonders. A troupe of white cranes, their wings spread wide, circled the room in an almost ceremonial procession, the swish of their feathers a delicate whisper against the louder notes of the orchestra. Suddenly, a troupe of monkeys appeared, their small hands flitting over drums and cymbals with surprising dexterity. They juggled oranges, somersaulted through hoops of fire, and mimicked the guests, causing an uproar of laughter that filled the air like music itself.

But it was the food that was the true star of the night. A seemingly endless parade of dishes arrived, each one more lavish than the last. Bowls of steaming, fragrant rice wine broth, rich with spices and herbs, arrived first, the steam curling in delicate tendrils that seemed to beckon the guests to take a sip. Plump dumplings, glistening with savory fillings of shrimp and mountain mushrooms, were served in trays of lacquered bamboo, their aroma intoxicating. Platters of tender roasted lamb, glazed with honey and sprinkled with crushed walnuts, gleamed under the soft light, sending waves of hunger through the crowd.

But it didn't stop there. Crispy golden fish, so fresh it seemed to have just been pulled from the waters, were served with sprigs of mint and lime. Plates of delicate noodles, spun from the finest wheat, glistened with the oils of garlic and ginger, their scent a tantalizing promise of more pleasures to come. Silver bowls of fruit, containing pomegranates bursting with crimson jewels, melons that dripped with the sweetness of summer, were passed from hand to hand, each bite a burst of delight.

And then came the wine. The rice wine flowed in endless streams, a river of amber that filled goblets, beakers, and porcelain bowls, the liquid so fine it shimmered in the candlelight like molten gold. The guests drank long and deep, their laughter growing steadily louder, their words becoming warmer as the wine loosened tongues and quickened hearts. Every sip brought a wave of euphoria, the warmth spreading through their limbs like a gentle fire, coaxing smiles, laughter, and secret glances.

At the head table, Emperor Hsuan Wu Ti raised his goblet high, as the entertainment was coming to an end, his voice ringing out above the celebration. "To family, to friendship, and to the endless joys of life!" he declared, his words carrying the weight of centuries of tradition. The crowd responded in unison, their cheers filling the hall like the roar of a great river. And for a moment, it felt as though time itself had forgotten to move. The room, the music, the laughter, and the indulgence all swirled together in a timeless dance. They could taste the sweetness of the wine on their lips, feel the rush of excitement as the dancers spun by as they exited the room, all of them regretting that such a superb night must eventually come to an end.

The Emperor beamed at his guests, a proud smile curving his lips. He raised his goblet of wine. "This child, my nephew, is said to be even more intelligent than all of my sons. A mind far beyond his youthful years. And tonight, I shall let him prove it to you all." His voice carried the weight of a ruler's confidence, but beneath it, there was a hint of something darker. A challenge. A sinister manipulation to expose the threat the young boy represented to the throne.

Mar Yanqa, ever composed, met his uncle's gaze. His mother's hand rested lightly on his shoulder, a silent gesture of support. He was old enough to know that his words tonight would either confirm the Emperor's admiration or seal his fate. His mother had warned him in advance that this moment would come. The room was heavy with expectation.

"Come, my nephew," the Emperor beckoned him forward, his eyes gleaming with a mix of pride and competition. "Answer me this: what is more powerful? The legends surrounding a dead king, or the power and majesty of a living one?"

The question was simple enough on the surface, but it was a cleverly devised trap. The Emperor's own sense of power was wrapped up in his imperial title, his living presence. But Mar Yanqa, though young, had learned much from the stories his father had told him. His father, Mar Zutra Kahana, the mighty warrior who had fought against the might of the Persian Empire, had often spoken of kings who cared more for their own grandeur than the welfare of their people.

Mar Yanqa stood tall, his red hair gleaming in the light, his green eyes steady. "A dead king, of course," he began, his voice calm but piercing, "because he leaves behind a legacy. A king who fights for the people's freedom, for their right to live without the weight of tyranny, will live on forever in the hearts of those he protected. My father, Mar Zutra, was such a king. He fought against King Kavad of Persia, leading in the end a small army of no more than eight thousand men against an army of forty thousand. He fought for the people of Mahoza, for their freedom. And though he died in battle, betrayed by those who should have been his allies, his memory lives on and is amplified with each telling of his story."

The room fell into a heavy silence. Mar Yanqa's words, though not shouted, carried the weight of a truth too deep for most to willingly comprehend. He had not just spoken of his father's strength; he had spoken of his father's sacrifice, his commitment to justice, and his enduring legacy.

"Whereas a living king," Mar Yanqa continued, "Who thinks only of his own power and magnificence, is forgotten as soon as he dies. His reign is marked not by the strength of his rule, but by the emptiness of his heart. Too often the people need only to look upwards to see a king living among the clouds, while they slog through a daily existence of squalor on the ground. To rule the people, a king must be one of the people. If not, in time his legacy fades as if he never existed."

The guests stirred, exchanging nervous glances. The Emperor's face darkened. His eyes flashed with something between anger and disbelief, but he kept his expression composed, for the moment. He had expected brilliance, but not this. This as far as he was concerned was nothing more than insolence.

"You dare speak of a living king in such a way?" Emperor Hsuan Wu Ti's voice was icy, his grip tightening around his goblet. "I am your Emperor, your ruler! And you insult me with this talk of legacy and betrayal."

Mar Yanqa, undeterred, met his uncle's gaze. He did not flinch or lower his eyes. "I spoke only of a king that did not take care of his people. I made no reference to anyone living or dead. I surely did not intimate my Lord that you were such a king. No one in this great hall would ever think such a thing."

The Emperor's lips curled into a thin smile, but the anger in his eyes was unmistakable. Perhaps the boy could convince others he was not speaking of his uncle but the Emperor knew better. "Let us move on to the next question, then. This one is simpler. Who is the most powerful being in the Empire?"

Mar Yanqa's brow furrowed, but only for a moment. His father had taught him that an empire was but a small piece of the world, that even emperors were just men, and their power was fleeting, like the morning mist on a warm summer's day. He spoke with the conviction that only a child who had known loss could possess. "The most powerful being in the Empire," Mar Yanqa began slowly, "Is not an emperor, nor a king, not even a general. An empire is but a small piece of the entire world, a fleeting moment in the grand span of time. Empires will rise and they will fall. The real question is: who rules over the entire world? Who controls the heavens, the earth, the waters, and the fire? Only one being reigns above all and tha is Almighty God. Even kings and emperors must kneel before His throne, for they too will be judged by His hand."

The room was silent. The air thickened with tension. The Emperor's face turned pale, then red with fury. His hands clenched around his goblet, the veins standing out on his knuckles. He had expected a clever answer, but not this. Not the blasphemy of a foreign god, one whose name could not even be spoken in the halls of power.

"You... you dare speak of a god who is not the Emperor?" Hsuan Wu Ti hissed, his voice low and trembling with a barely controlled rage. "You would challenge the very order of the Empire? You would bring foreign ideas into the heart of my court?"

With a violent gesture, the Emperor threw his goblet to the ground. The wine spilled across the table in a golden flood. "Enough!" he shouted, his voice booming through the hall. "This banquet is over! All of you, leave! Leave now!"

The guests, shocked and terrified, scrambled to their feet, their chairs clattering against the marble floor as they fled the hall. The Emperor's tantrum was so sudden, so unrestrained, that even his most loyal subjects did not dare to speak. The room, once filled with the chatter of nobles and diplomats, was now a scene of chaos.

She-Ping, her heart pounding in her chest, grabbed Mar Yanqa by the arm. "We must go, quickly," she whispered urgently, pulling him toward the door. The boy's face was calm, but his eyes shone with the weight of what he had just said. He had done nothing wrong in his mind, but he knew, deep within, that he had crossed a line that could never be uncrossed.

As they hurried back to their quarters, the sound of the Emperor's furious shouts echoed behind them. Mar Yanqa, despite his brilliance, was now seen as a threat, a dangerous voice of dissent. And as She-Ping closed the door of their quarters behind them, she realized that their lives had just changed drastically, once again.

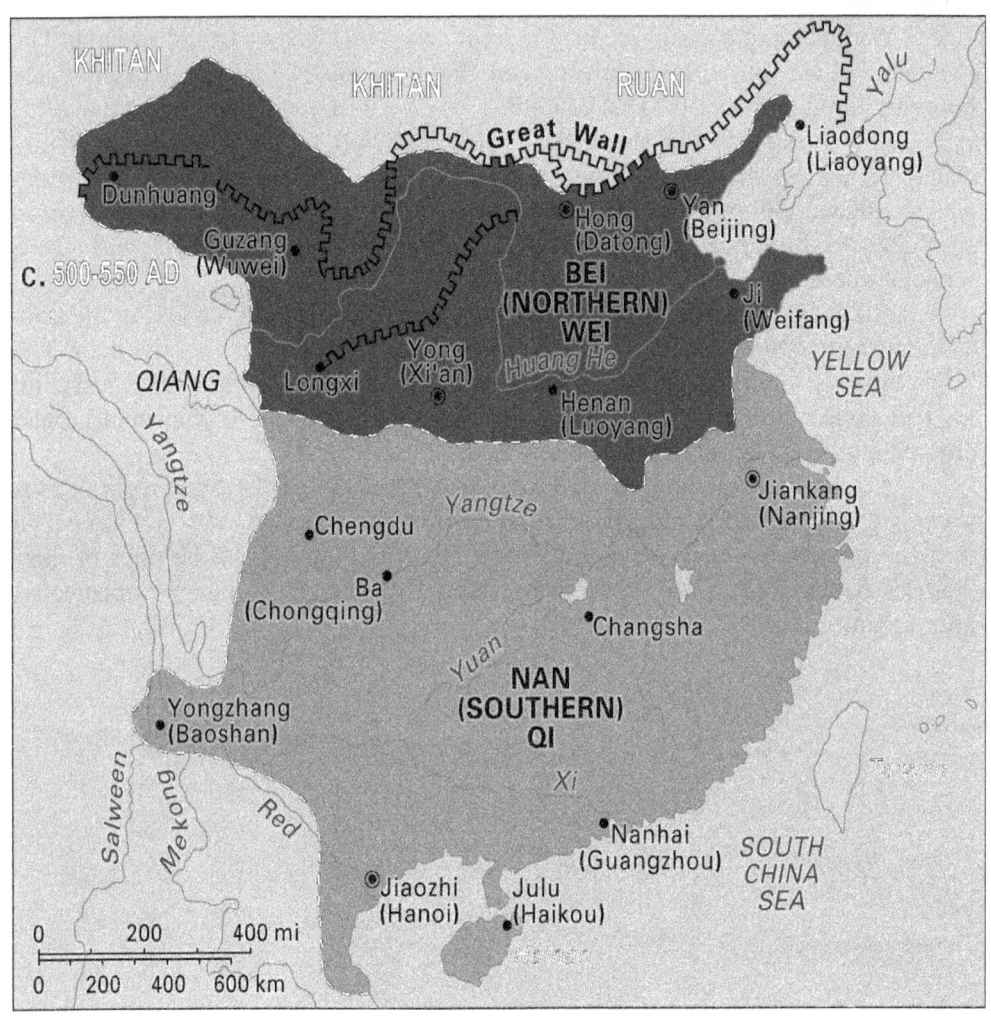

China in the Early Sixth Century

Chapter 3: 510 AD

The morning after the banquet, the palace of Luoyang was relatively quiet. The furious echoes of the Emperor's tantrum still hung in the air, rippling through the corridors of the imperial palace like a storm that had since passed but left wreckage in its wake. As the sun began to rise, casting long shadows across the marble floors, Princess She-Ping sat alone in her private quarters, her eyes lost in thought. The events of the night before weighed heavily on her mind. Her son, Mar Yanqa, had spoken truths that no one in the court dared to utter, but in doing so, he had sealed both of their fates. She could not fault her son, because he was very much like his father, Zutra. Never deceitful, always saying what was on his mind despite the consequences. If she loved and admired her husband for those qualities, how could she possibly find fault in her son for sharing the same traits and characteristics.

A soft knock broke her reverie, and her heart skipped a beat. She recognized the rhythm of the knock. It could only be official business, a summons that could not be ignored. She rose from her seat, her robes brushing the floor like the whisper of the storm yet to come. She-Ping straightened herself, as regal as ever, but her mind raced with dread. She had anticipated that the Emperor would retaliate for her son's words, but the message was about to be made much clearer now. No one was immune to the Emperor's authority, not even his own sister.

As she opened the door, one of the Emperor's most trusted servants stood there, a man who was known as little more than a shadow in the palace. "His Majesty requests your presence immediately," the servant said flatly. The words felt like a decree, not an invitation.

She-Ping followed him down the palace corridors, her footsteps quiet against the polished stone. The weight of the silence was suffocating. She knew this meeting would be about her brother demanding retribution. What the exact price she would need to pay was unknown. When she arrived at her brother's chambers, the doors were opened by the imperial guards, revealing Emperor Hsuan Win Ti seated at his grand desk, surrounded by official looking scrolls and maps. His face was calm, yet there was a steely edge to his gaze that spoke of calculations and decisions that had already made. He motioned for her to sit, but his tone was dismissive, as if their shared sibling history meant nothing in this moment of imperial authority.

"I'm certain you've heard of the troubles we face in the north," the Emperor began, his voice cool and detached. "The Shu and Wu forces in the south are gaining strength, and now the people of the peninsula have sided with them, seeking their own independence. The situation is dire, and my forces are stretched thin."

She-Ping nodded, though her heart sank, knowing that his talk of military situations usually meant someone was about to be sent to the front in order to fight alongside the troops. It had been the easiest way to dispose of the emperor's enemies in the past, without necessarily having to bear in any guilt when reports of their death at the hands of the enemy were reported back to the palace. She could feel the weight of the conversation, the power dynamics shifting all towards one direction before her very eyes. It would not be the first time that someone as young as twelve years old fought in he Imperial army. She had always known that her brother's jealousy would eventually cost her, but the thought of sending her young son to war was intolerable.

The Emperor finally got to the point. "I need your general, Hermantius," he continued, his gaze fixed on the map of the northern provinces. "I understand that your husband assigned him to you because he was one of the bravest and smartest tacticians in his army. Now he must serve in mine. He and his men are to be reassigned immediately to Manchuria. They'll be under my command for the duration of the war. It's no longer about your protection, She-Ping. It's about the survival of the empire. So don't bother to even attempt to argue with me."

She-Ping felt relieved but also as if the ground had shifted beneath her. The two conflicting feelings made her head spin. General Hermantius, her bodyguard, her most trusted protector, and the only security she had left, suddenly taken away in an instant. Hermantius, the man who had served her loyally since her husband's death, would now be sent to the farthest reaches of the empire, leaving her with nothing, rendering both herself and her son vulnerable. She attempted to comfort herself by telling herself at least her son would remain with her, but the loss of Hermantius and his cohort of men was a severe blow.

"I understand," She-Ping whispered, though her words tasted bitter. "But who will guard me now?"

The Emperor's eyes glinted with cold calculation. "You are no longer needed here, She-Ping. The empire has more pressing concerns than your safety. You'll have to make do with what you have. As for your son..." His voice trailed off, but the implication was clear. "He's a liability. You both are."

She-Ping's throat tightened, her heart pounding in her chest. She wanted to speak, to defend her son, but she could already see the finality in her brother's eyes. He had already made his decision, and nothing she could say would change it. Words were a weapon, but she was unarmed in this fight.

The Emperor's eyes softened, just for a moment, and he placed a hand on the table. "I'm not without mercy, She-Ping. You'll be sent back to Kaifeng with a small escort. Your son on the other hand will remain here and stay under my control. I have no intention of harming you, but you must understand the danger he represents." His voice was sharp, cutting through the tension like a blade. "You may go now."

With that, She-Ping was dismissed, her mind swirling with a thousand fears. Her brother was no longer her protector; he was her captor. And her son, the boy she loved, had become a pawn in a game that could no longer be ignored.

Later that night, after the echoes of the Emperor's orders had faded, She-Ping paced back and forth on the floor of her quarters, her mind still reeling from the encounter with her brother. The drone of her Hsuan Wu Ti's words resounded in her ears. She had been stripped of her protection, her general, her bodyguard and now, she feared for what would come next. Would they come for her tonight? Would they take her son away immediately? The thought of losing him was unbearable.

Her quarters were dim, the light from the lantern casting long, flickering shadows across the room. She sat by the window, staring out into the courtyard. She could feel the presence of the palace guards, the watchful eyes that were always present, always there. But tonight, the feeling of danger seemed closer, more imminent, as if her brother had spoken in only half-truths and had not revealed all of his intentions. Having finally exhausted herself by her continuous pacing, she was about to return to her bed, when a sudden movement caught her eye. A shadow flickered across the room, too quick to be a servant, too deliberate to be a mistake. She became aware that she was no longer alone.

Instinct took over, and She-Ping's hand slid under her pillow, grasping the cold hilt of a long knife. She didn't hesitate. The blade was immediately an extension of her body, honed over years of training. She was no stranger to danger, no stranger to the violence that had shaped her life. But this time, the danger wasn't outside her walls as had been the case in Mahoza; it was within her own private room.

The intruder made his move, and She-Ping was ready to strike. But before she could bring the knife to bear, a familiar voice echoed in the darkness.

"Hold, Princess. It's me."

She froze. The voice was deep, rough, but it sent a shock of remembrance through her. It had been years since she heard that voice. She knew that voice. She knew it all too well.

"Valentius?" Her heart skipped a beat as the figure stepped into the light. The man who had once been her protector, the captain of her guard, when she first traveled to Mahoza. The man who had fought beside her husband, the man who had disappeared after he was sent to her father to ask for troops in her husband's war. She had heard rumors that he had been killed in service to the Emperor, but now, standing before her, was proof that the rumors had been false. Valentius, still as imposing as ever, stood in front of her. His broad shoulders filled the doorway; his eyes narrowed with concern.

"I'm sorry to intrude, Princess," he said, his voice low, "But I have news. Hermantius sent me. He's heard of your brother's plans, and he's worried. He fears the Emperor will be coming for you by tomorrow, perhaps even later tonight.

We need to get you and your son out of here immediately and take you to a safe place."

She-Ping's breath caught in her throat. Her heart hammered against her ribs, and for a moment, she felt paralyzed with shock. She had no choice but to trust him, her old captain, the man she thought was dead, back among the living.

"How many men do you have?" She-Ping asked, her voice shaking, trying to hold on to her composure.

Valentius's eyes darkened. "Only twenty. But they're some of the best fighters in China. We're your only chance. We must hurry!"

Only twenty men. She-Ping's mind raced. Hardly enough to make it past the palace guard in case of a fight. It was a dangerous plan, one that would make them fugitives instantly. But if Hermantius's fears were true, and if the Emperor was about to come for her, there was no other choice. "Where could we ever find a safe place?" she questioned the captain.

"We head to the wilderness, Princess. It is our only chance of survival."

"Hardly a chance," she responded, knowing there was practically no chance to survive if left to the elements and the dangers of the forests.

"Better than a guaranteed death if you stay," he appealed to her, "Now please hurry! I have horses stationed outside the city walls. You do remember how to ride?"

She-Ping looked at him as if saying what a foolish question. "Does a koi ever forget how to swim?"

Her response brought a smile to his face. It was the same young princess he had remembered from long ago.

She quickly gathered her son, Mar Yanqa, bundling him in warm clothing as she prepared for the escape. The plan was simple: get out of the palace, get to their residence in Kaifeng, grab whatever belongings she needed, and then disappear into the wilderness beyond. As terrible as it sounded, it was their only hope.

Valentius led the way, his men moving silently through the shadows. They transitioned like ghosts, their steps light but quick, their eyes scanning every corner, every passageway for any sign of danger. As they neared the palace gates, the first obstacle appeared: the palace guards, who had been stationed to keep watch and prevent traffic either in or out of Luoyang at night.

"Hold," Valentius whispered, his voice barely audible. His men froze on the spot.

The guards were blocking their path, their presence too numerous for a stealthy approach. There was no choice now. Valentius turned to his men, nodding only once but they all clearly understood the message.

In an instant, what had been a quiet night was shattered by the sound of iron meeting flesh. The guards, caught off guard, were easily pushed backward as they were no match for the precision of Valentius's squadron. Within moments, several guards had fallen, their bodies sprawled across the cobblestones, their cries cut short. The rest of the guards, now fully aware of the danger, scrambled to defend the palace gates. But Valentius's men were quick and ruthless, giving them an unfair advantage.

As the last of the guards fell, She-Ping's heart pounded in her chest. They had done it. They were free, at least for now. But freedom at what price? The sounds of the struggle would echo through the palace corridors, and what had been an escape, would soon be turned into a capital crime. They were no longer just runaways, they had become criminals, wanted for the murder of the palace guards.

Shouts of more guards approaching rang through the streets, but the Princess, accompanied by her son and Valentius's squadron were already racing their horses through east along the road. At best, Valentius calculated they would have at least a thirty minute advantage on those that would be chasing them. Under the shroud of darkness, the air felt thick with their desperation as Princess She-Ping, her son riding close to her side, rode furiously into the night, leaving the East gate of Luoyang behind them. Captain Valentius, resolute, led their mad race along the road, his twenty riders forming a tight, disciplined circle around their precious charges, their hooves a cacophony of dread and urgency.

Behind them, the walls of Luoyang, towering and immovable, began to shrink into the distance. Yes, it would take at least half an hour to assemble a unit to give pursuit, but every second was precious, a ticking clock of doom that threatened to turn the night into a blood-drenched nightmare if they did not make it to Kaifeng safely.

The road ahead was treacherous, winding through ancient forests and craggy terrain, where the only light was the dim glint of moonlight breaking through the canopy of leaves. Every crevice, every uneven patch of earth was a potential threat. Their horses, breath ragged, thundered through the dense undergrowth, narrowly avoiding the rocks that could snap an ankle or the deep, unseen ruts that could send them tumbling into the unknown. The sound of the wind whipping past their ears was deafening, their world reduced to the constant, rhythmic pounding of hooves, the crackling of branches, and the steady shouts of Captain Valentius urging them onward. "Faster!" he commanded, voice harsh with the strain of the chase. "Do not falter! They will not be far behind!"

The princess, her face pale but set in a grim mask of determination, felt every jolt of the horse beneath her. Her heart raced, knowing her brother would spare no expense in sending his most elite warriors to hunt them down. They would be followed by the best trackers and assassins of men in the empire, who would not rest until she was captured, but preferably dead. "Kaifeng," she whispered to herself. "We have to reach Kaifeng."

The tension in the air was palpable, as thick as the noose they could all imagine around their necks. The moonlit landscape shifted eerily in the distance, but the riders did not dare look back. To glance behind them was to invite failure. They pushed onward, urged by a primal fear of being caught, but also driven by something deeper, the urge to survive. The road to Kaifeng was long, but it offered a glimmer of hope, a safe haven where they could regroup and then subsequently escape the reach of the palace's wrath.

Yet, even as the hours stretched on and the ground beneath their horses began to level out, a gnawing sense of inevitability gnawed at their resolve. They were close, but so were their pursuers. The palace's finest were known to be swift and relentless. As the shadows of the trees thinned and the distant outline of Kaifeng's outer gates came into view, they imagined they could hear the sound of hoofbeats coming from behind.

Chapter 4: 510 AD

The streets of Kaifeng bustled with the usual buzz of the marketplace, the voices of vendors selling their wares, the clinking of coins, and the sound of carts rolling over cobblestones. Yet, for Princess She-Ping, the city that had once felt like home now seemed like a death sentence if tarried too long. The walls of the palace, where she had spent two years in the shadow of her brother's rule, seemed further away than ever. In the distance, she could hear the faint clattering of soldiers, their presence a reminder that the Emperor's wrath would not be far behind.

The princess stood by the front gates of the palace, her eyes scanning the horizon, the weight of the situation pressing down on her chest. Her son, Mar Yanqa, was playing happily on a pile of hay in the stables, the gentle rise and fall of his laughter offering some solace. But for She-Ping, the cacophony of sounds was deafening. She knew that their time in Kaifeng could be no more than this one night, because by morning the Emperor's soldiers would certainly be arriving, and as such, she had to take whatever was necessary to survive life on the road and be as quick about it as possible.

She had spent the last few hours in a fevered haze of preparation, knowing that they could be forced to flee at any moment. But it wasn't just her own safety she had to consider now. She had no other choice but to take her advisory staff of about a dozen, all loyal to her and for that reason they would pay a terrible price if her brother's men took them into custody. Most had accompanied her from Mahoza when her husband had sent them back to China before his defeat by Kavad. Priests, tutors, cooks, servants, and members of some of the most prominent families from Mahoza had all made the journey to Kaifeng as well, and now, She-Ping was faced with the decision as to who would come with her, while the rest would be commanded to remain behind. It was a decision she dreaded, but one that had to be made. In the end, all those too old or too ill to make the journey she decided would be left behind.

The sun was beginning to dip below the horizon, casting a golden glow across the city. In the quiet moments before dusk, She-Ping concluded her meeting with her closest advisors, those she could trust, those who had been with her since the beginning. She-Ping had made her decision regarding the number that would accompany her for the journey ahead. It wasn't an easy task and inside, she still felt a storm of uncertainty.

By midnight, all those that had been selected were informed to be ready to travel.

"Have you gathered them all?" she asked the Captain, her voice calm but laced with tension.

Valentius, ever the watchful protector, nodded. "Everyone that will accompany you has been advised that they will need to be packed and ready to travel before sunrise. But I must repeat my warning Princess, they will slow us down and reduce our chances of survival."

She-Ping exhaled slowly, her mind racing through the logistics. "It is a risk I am willing to take. It is why I limited my selection so narrowly. My only regret is that I cannot take everyone as much as I wish I could. There are so many that I have sworn to protect. Some must stay. Those who know the city best, and can find safe haven, as well as those who can ensure our escape goes unnoticed I must leave behind. I have reduced the numbers as best I can." It was her personal guilt now talking, knowing that some of those she left behind would likely be tortured and killed by her brother's soldiers.

She-Ping turned away from the view outside the gates, her fingers trembling slightly as she adjusted the folds of her gown. "We are only taking my advisors, the priests, the orphans, the teachers, and the cooks. If they have families, they will come too. As well as those men who are young enough to ride and swing a sword. We will need someone left behind to provide information on the Emperor's movements. Make certain that we take along enough carrier pigeons that we can communicate. We cannot afford to be caught unaware."

Valentius pondered her statements, his expression grim. "All those you mentioned have been advised.

She-Ping suddenly thought about all the other families from Mahoza, and her eyes began to water. Her heart ached at the thought. Those families had trusted her, had followed her across the vast expanse of China, seeking refuge from the horrors of the war back in Persia. "I cannot change my mind now," she voiced her inner turmoil. We can only take those I mentioned," She-Ping said softly, her decision firm. "They will be safer here, than in the wilderness." She tried to convince herself.

Valentius knew that she hadn't spoken directly to him but he responded anyway. "Beyond these walls they will have nothing and if we try to take them, it will only make us a much larger and slower target."

There was a silence as they absorbed the gravity of her decision. She knew it wasn't the easiest choice, but it was the only one that made sense. The road ahead would be perilous, and the fewer people they traveled with, the more chances they had of escaping the Emperor's grasp.

"And what of your maidservants?" Valentius asked, his eyes narrowing slightly. "We haven't discussed them as yet. They are extremely loyal to you, Princess."

She-Ping hesitated. "Most must stay behind as well. Only my ladies in waiting will come with us. The others must remain hidden until the Emperor's soldiers have left Kaifeng. Otherwise, they will be certainly raped by them.

Make certain that we lodge them with certain families in the community that can keep them safe. I still pray that with time cooler heads will prevail and my brother will let us be."

Valentius nodded, understanding the complexity of the situation. "We'll prepare those to be left behind as best as possible. I just hope that those left behind will understand and not become a problem for us. The rest you mentioned will come with us and make their way out of the city quietly before sunrise."

That night, as She-Ping lay in bed, the weight of the decisions lingered heavily on her mind. She held her son close, his body warm against hers, and she closed her eyes, allowing herself a fleeting moment of peace. Knowing that she had sentenced some of those she cared deeply about to death by leaving them behind was a dark cloud that she knew would follow her forever.

In the darkness of the early morning, a sudden knock at the door interrupted her thoughts.

"Princess," Valentius's voice came from the other side. "We have to move now. The Emperor's soldiers are coming."

She-Ping rose from the bed quickly, her heart racing. She did not need to ask how Valentius knew. His network of spies, his skill in reading the pulse of the empire, had alerted him to the movement of the Emperor's forces. Although he initially said they would likely camp outside the city for the night and not enter until morning, something had obviously changed. Speed was now of the essence.

Mar Yanqa was still asleep, unaware of the danger that loomed outside the city walls. She gently shook him awake, brushing his hair from his face.

"Mar Yanqa," she whispered, her voice soft but urgent. "We must leave. Now."

The boy stirred, his eyes fluttering open. For a moment, he looked confused, disoriented. But when he saw the seriousness in his mother's eyes, he nodded and sat up. "Where are we planning to go, Mother?"

"To safety," was all she could say. "We must leave this city before the Emperor's soldiers find us here in the palace."

As the household quickly grabbed their packed belongings and readied themselves for the journey ahead, She-Ping couldn't help but feel a pang of sadness. These were the people who had followed her, who had been with her since the beginning. She had come to rely on them, to trust them with her life. They trusted her. But now, they were giving up everything as she was about to lead them all into the unknown.

The courtyard was filled with the bustle of hurried movement as servants, advisors, priests and the selected families gathered their belongings. A few faces were already tear-streaked, especially those who were being left behind unsure of their fate but had come to wish the Princess farewell. She-Ping remained resolute. She knew that she could not save everyone, but she could save her son and many others, and that was what mattered most.

As they left the gates of the palace, Valentius and his men led them through the narrow alleyways, keeping to the shadows. The Princess's personal guards from the Kaifeng palace remained at the rear of those escaping, defending against any attack from behind. Every step was calculated, every movement deliberate. The city had become a labyrinth of uncertainty, and She-Ping's thoughts were clouded with a thousand questions: Where would they go? How would they survive? The road ahead was shrouded in darkness, but She-Ping knew one thing for certain — there could be no turning back now.

As they reached the outer edge of the city, the sound of marching soldiers grew louder. She-Ping's heart clenched. The Emperor's soldiers were close, too close for comfort. But they had made it this far. With Valentius leading the way, they began the long journey out of Kaifeng, away from the city, away from everything they had known.

For She-Ping, the world and life itself had become a place of endless uncertainty. But one thing was clear: her brother's empire, with all its power and grandeur, would no longer define her. It certainly would not define her son. It would now be necessary for them to carve out their own path, no matter what it took; no matter where it would lead them.

Once outside the city, Valentius moved off the road, leading the pack of about one hundred and fifty souls, in addition to his own men and those of the princess's palace guard loyal to her, directly into the dark cover of the forest, where the shadows of the night swallowed them whole. The morning sun had barely begun to touch the peaks of the trees when She-Ping's ragged column slipped deeper into the dense forests surrounding Kaifeng, a city that was no longer in view when they looked behind. The cacophony of the bustling metropolis that the princess had been listening to, just the evening before, had now completely faded, replaced by the oppressive silence of the woods, save for the rustle of leaves and the occasional bird's cry, sounds that somehow seemed to amplify the tension in the air.

The princess's heart thundered in her chest, each beat reminding her of the precariousness of their situation. Her son, Mar Yanqa, stayed close to her side, but he showed no signs of fear. The young boy's face appeared stern and focused, his eyes wide with concentration and he analyzed every step they took deeper into the foliage. He knew for his mother's sake, he could not afford to show any cracks in his composure. Not now, perhaps never. \

Around them, the once-proud procession of noble families, servants, and advisors had turned into a bedraggled, weary caravan. Their clothes, fine silks and embroidered robes, were now dirt-streaked and torn. Many of those not on horseback were now barefoot. The priests muttered prayers, clutching the white and blue fringes that hung from the corners of their tunics, while the soldiers, including Captain Valentius's elite men, moved with the quiet, practiced discipline of men accustomed to war. The forest felt as though it were closing in around them, the dark trees casting deep shadows, and every creak of the branches made them all imagine the worst.

The air was thick with the scent of damp earth and pine. They had not rested for nearly six hours, ever since the Emperor's soldiers had entered inside the walls of Kaifeng. In the distance, the sounds of pursuit were already on their heels. They could not rest now. The had to move fast, or they would be caught.

The first scout arrived at noon. He was one of Captain Valentius's best men, a hawk-eyed tracker who had slipped behind the group. With a grim expression, he pulled the Captain aside along with the Princess. "Your Highness, the Emperor's men are close. They've started to fan out into the forest, and they're moving quickly. They've got dogs with them."

She-Ping's stomach tightened but Valentius remained unphased. The dogs, trained to scent humans, were an insurmountable challenge. There would be no way to mask their trail in this dense forest. Their only hope now was to keep moving and pray they could outdistance them. "Then we keep on moving," Valentius commanded. His voice was low and steady, but the princess noticed his eyes did betray a degree of worry. His men were already gathering their gear, reloading weapons, tightening straps. "We'll go north. The hills will slow them down," he instructed.

The group pressed on, moving through the darkening woods with renewed urgency. The caravan of people was guided by a silent procession of soldiers, who formed a protective ring around them. Their path twisted between the gnarled trunks of trees, and their feet barely made a sound on the soft forest floor. Yet every moment felt like it could be their last. Hours later, just as the group settled for a brief rest, a faint sound disturbed the stillness of the evening. It was the snap of a twig underfoot. The soldiers froze. The Princess's breath caught in her throat. For a heartbeat, time seemed to stretch. Then, from somewhere to the side, the unmistakable bark of a hound broke the silence.

"They're here," whispered Captain Valentius, drawing his sword.

The priests muttered louder prayers now, clutching their prayer shawls as though they could somehow summon divine intervention. She-Ping gripped her son tightly, her heart in her throat. They were out of time.

Without a word, Valentius waved for the column to move. It was an order delivered without hesitation. His eyes had already turned to calculating the path ahead. The group had to split to avoid being cornered. As the loyal families scattered in different directions, She-Ping's heart dropped. The cries of children echoed in the woods, the panic of the innocent bleeding through the trees. They ran. Her lungs burned, the air thin and cold, but She-Ping pushed forward, the sound of hurried footfalls all around her. She could hear the soldiers behind her, their orders sharp and quick. They were still a step ahead but how long could that last?

The dogs were getting closer now. She could hear them, their incessant barking, getting louder. And then, a scream; a woman's voice. The sound pierced the air like a knife, a chilling, raw wail that froze her in place for a moment. It came from one of the loyalist families. Most likely too slow to keep up. They had been found.

"Move, move!" Captain Valentius bellowed. The soldiers drew their swords, their faces grim. "We can't fight them all," one of them muttered. "There's too many."

"We don't need to fight them all," Valentius said, his voice icy. "Just fight them long enough."

With that, he made a sharp motion, signaling for two of his soldiers to break away. They darted off into the underbrush, heading towards the sounds of the dogs. At the same time, the rest of the column continued forward, now even more frantically. She-Ping stumbled, but was caught by one of the soldiers who helped her regain her footing. She could see the soldiers ahead, taking positions, setting up small barriers in the trees—making a temporary stand. She-Ping's chest heaved, her eyes scanning the darkness. Then, suddenly, the forest erupted with noise—dogs barking, men shouting, and the clash of weapons.

A soldier appeared before her, his face pale. "They're here, Your Highness! The Emperor's men. They've found us!"

"We hold them off for as long as we can," Valentius ordered. "Go! The rest of you, keep moving!"

They had no choice but to keep running. But they weren't safe yet. The soldiers had bought them only a few precious minutes. As they reached a clearing in the forest, a shadow loomed from the trees ahead, more soldiers, more dogs. The princess felt her heart lurch; the end had finally come.

Chapter 5: 510 AD

From the other direction, a flash of light flickered through the trees. Suddenly, a cry broke through the air, echoing across the forest. A deep, guttural roar that shattered the night like a thunderclap. The Princess's pulse skipped. It was not the bark of dogs, nor the shouting of men. It was something altogether different. The soldiers drew to a halt, their senses immediately alert. Valentius stiffened, his eyes scanning the shadows. "What was that?" he muttered, but no one had an answer. The noise came again, louder this time, a rallying call from deep within the trees. And then they appeared, riders, dozens of them, emerging from the darkness as if conjured from the earth itself. They rode with the fury of a storm, their horses dark as night, winding through the trees with ease. Their leather armor adorned with furs and feathers, and their faces painted with tribal markings that made them appear like phantoms in the forest. The Tuoba were a clan known for their nomadic ways and for their endless war with the Northern Wei dynasty. In their blood was the history of a people who had never bent the knee to any emperor, whose arrows and blades had often struck fear into the hearts of even the mightiest generals. Their warriors were swift, lethal, and unmatched in battle. And tonight, they had come not to aid the Princess but to kill the Emperor's soldiers.

With a battle cry that could freeze the blood in one's veins, the Tuoba descended upon the Emperor's soldiers, their horses thundering like an avalanche. The first of the Emperor's men barely had time to react before the Tuoba warriors were upon them, their swords flashing like lightning. The battle was brutal, savage, and quick. Captain Valentius shouted orders, and his soldiers along with the guard scrambled to form a defensive line between the Princess with her people and the ongoing battle, but it was clear they were outnumbered and outclassed should the Tuoba turn their attention on them.

The Tuoba were everywhere, an unstoppable tide that swept through the ranks of the Emperor's men with a savage grace. Their spears tore through armor, their swords hacked through shields, and their arrows found their marks with unerring precision. The Emperor's soldiers, though disciplined, were no match for the wild fury of the Tuoba.

She-Ping's heart leapt with mixed feeling of joy and horror as she watched the chaos unfold. She had expected the worst; the bloodshed, the deaths, the screams of her own people, but as the battle raged, something in her shifted. She now felt something she had not felt in days: hope. The Tuoba were here, and they were not just warriors, they were a force of nature, one that may not have come with the intention to defend her, to protect her son, and to see the loyalists safe, but nonetheless, the outcome would be the same. The battle waged on with fury. One of the Tuoba warriors, a towering figure draped in pelts, cleaved through the soldiers with a mighty swing of his battle axe, sending men flying in all directions. His battle cry could be heard over the din of the clashing swords as he fought like a storm unleashed. Another warrior, lighter on his feet, moved through the chaos like a shadow, his spear striking with deadly accuracy, disarming the Northern Wei soldiers with ease and bringing them to the ground with fluid movements.

Closer by, She-Ping caught sight of Valentius, his face grim as he fought alongside his men, cutting through any of her brother's attackers that still attempted to reach her and Mar Yanqa, with precision.

The Emperor's soldiers faltered. Their discipline, honed for years, began to crack under the pressure of the Tuoba onslaught. The berserker cries of the Tuoba rang out like war drums, and the soldiers of the Emperor began to break ranks, retreating into the shadows, desperate to save their own lives.

The sound of their retreat was a miracle. The surviving soldiers, those who could still stand, turned and fled, scrambling through the underbrush like animals. The dogs, once so sure of their prey, were now cowering, their handlers unable to regain control. The battlefield between the trees was littered with the fallen, their blood staining the earth, the stench of death thick in the air. In the aftermath, as the last of the Emperor's men fled into the forest, their retreat a broken, disorganized chaos, the Tuoba warriors slowed their advance. They surveyed the battlefield, ensuring no soldier remained alive as they thrust their swords and spears into every corpse. Their eyes, cold and calculating, scanned the area, then turned back to She-Ping's group.

Captain Valentius stepped forward, his sword raised in defense of the Princess, despite the overwhelming odds. "We have no quarrel with you. We owe you our lives. And for that we are grateful."

The Tuoba leader, a man with eyes like black stones, regarded Valentius for a moment before laughing and applauding his courage. "Put your sword away. We fight only those who are worthy of our blades." The statement was insulting but at the same time a relief to all of Valentius's men that the battle was over and they had survived.

"The Emperor is our enemy, and though you may dress like his soldiers it is clear that he is not your friend. Any that he would attack, we consider our friends," their leader continued. "So, tell us friend, why are thirty or so soldiers and a horde of civilians being hunted by an entire battalion of the Emperor's army."

At that moment, Princess She-Ping stepped forward, ignoring her captain's attempts to shield her and pull her back. "I am the reason why the Emperor was willing to kill all these people. In his desire to see myself and my son dead, he would send an army to kill these defenseless people."

"And what makes you so important that an entire division would let itself become entangled in a forest and easy prey for us?" he questioned, not recognizing the princess.

"I am Emperor Hsuan Wu Ti's sister. I am the Princess She-Ping. If that makes me your enemy, then do with me as you will but spare my son and these people. They do not deserve to be punished for my brother's deeds."

The Tuobo warlord could not help but smile. "Once we were all Xianbei. Your brother has forgotten that and no longer acknowledges his roots. He made us his enemies long before we swung the first sword against his armies. I have no quarrel with one that has returned to live in the wilderness, which it the true way of all our tribes. You are Xianbei and we will acknowledge those with you as your clan. I will pass on word to the other tribes to let our sister with her red haired child pass safely through our lands. Some will accept, others will do as we have always done and choose to fight you as has always been custom among the tribes."

"A custom that must come to an end," Mar Yanqa spoke up after a long period of silence.

"The child has something to say?" the Tuoba leader was more impressed than angry at Mar Yanqa's interruption.

Standing his ground firmly, the boy did not back down one inch. "I am Mar Yanqa, son of Mar Zutra Kahana, the last king of Mahoza. A king who united the people under his care, even thought they were from different nationalities and variant custom, and together they defeated the vastly superior armies of the Persian Emperor. If you are to have any success in doing the same against the Emperor of Northern Wei, then you must also unite. Not as tribes and clans but as one people. One people with one goal. Only then will you succeed."

The Tuoba leader and those around him laughed at the suggestion. "The boy has courage as well as a vivid imagination, I will concede that," the leader spoke. "But he has much to learn regarding our people. We have never been united. Be grateful that today we saved your lives, even though you are strangers to us. Today we were in a generous and merciful mood. Tomorrow it may be different. But I will tell you this boy. If you were ever to achieve the impossible and unite our eight tribes, I would be one of the first to bend my knee to you." The Tuoba found the exchange by their leader humorous and continued to laugh.

"I accept your offer," Mar Yanqa responded, much to the chagrin of Valentius who worried how the words would be taken by the Tuoba leader.

"By the spirit of my ancestors, this boy has balls of iron," the leader shouted to his men. "All of you, be on your way and know that Liwei Guo has saved your lives this day!"

She-Ping's heart swelled with gratitude. "I... I don't know how to thank you."

Liwei Guo's expression softened, and for the first time, his lips curled into a relaxed smile. "I believe there is something special about that boy of yours, Princess. Keep him safe and let us see what the future holds."

With that, the Tuoba turned and began to withdraw, as silently as they had come, their warriors vanishing back into the trees like shadows. As the last of them disappeared, the silence of the forest descended once more, broken only by the quiet sobs of those who had lost someone during the battle.

She-Ping stood there for a moment, taking in the scene; the fallen, the wreckage, the survivors. It had been a victory, but it had come at a terrible price. Yet, in that moment, as she looked at her son, standing there with a look of both determination and contemplation, as if the twelve year old boy was planning their next move, and she knew then that their escape from death's door was no longer a dream but instead it was a reality; a reality filled with hope.

The moon hung low in the sky, a thin crescent barely visible through the endless stretch of cloud. The road westward was narrow, a jagged trail through more dense forests and rolling hills. Following the battle, the survivors gathered their scattered horses and even some of the horses and dogs that had been left behind by the fleeing soldiers of the Emperor's army.

Ahead of them, nothing but the vast unknown awaited.

The sound of hooves echoed in the otherwise silent night as She-Ping rode at the head of the caravan, her eyes scanning the path ahead, every sense alert. Valentius, ever watchful, rode beside her, his gaze constantly shifting from the road to the tree line, looking for any signs of pursuit. The group moved with quiet determination; the horses' hooves muffled by the soft earth beneath. The night air was cool, carrying the scent of pine and distant rivers. Despite the serenity of the landscape, She-Ping could not shake the constant knot of anxiety twisting in her stomach.

The princess had spent the last several days in a haze, a blur of hurried decisions and secretive movements. Now, as they rode through the thick woods that separated the Empire from the unknown lands to the northwest, the weight of her decisions began to press in on her. What lay ahead? "Valentius," she said, breaking the silence, her voice low but edged with concern. "Where are we going? Where will we find safety?" She already knew the answers but she wanted reaffirmation that she was making the right decisions.

Valentius glanced at her, his face unreadable in the pale light of the moon. "We are headed towards the steppes, Princess," he said, his voice firm but reassuring. "To the land of Khitan. Just as the Tuoba leader suggested we do."

She-Ping's eyes widened, and she nearly jerked the reins of her horse in surprise as if she was hearing of their destination for the very first time. "Khitan?" she repeated, an unusual word rolling off her tongue. "You mean the Xianbei? The people who have no love for our royal houses? The descendants of nomads."

The captain nodded, his expression unchanging. "Yes. Khitan, Tuoba, Xianbei, Rouran, it's all the same thing to me. By any name, they are your kin. They all have the same roots as your family. Considering you are an enemy of the Emperor's court; it is more probable that you will be welcomed by them."

Her thoughts raced, torn between disbelief and the grim necessity of the situation. She began to have second thoughts about her decision, realizing that they may have the same roots but after the passing of countless generations, they were worlds apart. The Khitan were a fierce people, often described as nomadic savages in the court gossip of the palace. Their loyalty to the Emperor had always been strained, and the thought of seeking refuge among them, among those who had always been viewed as enemies of the Empire, made her uneasy.

"Are we making a mistake, Valentius?" she murmured, her voice strained. "What are we thinking? The Khitan have no use for us. No love for my family, my lineage. Why would they even want to help me?"

Valentius turned his horse to face her, his eyes sparkling with the knowledge of experience. "I know it's not an ideal situation, Princess," he said, his tone steady. "But believe me when I say it's our best option. Your family's roots run deep in the Xianbei blood. That is a fact that can never be denied. Like it or not, you are their blood. And now, you are an exile, an enemy of the court. The Khitan will be more sympathetic to your plight than any other people. Your presence among them will become a symbol of their resistance against the Empire. Did you not notice the deep admiration of the Tuoba leader for you?"

She-Ping bit her lip, uncertain. The notion of seeking refuge among the Khitan was both dangerous and humiliating. Yet, as she glanced back over her shoulder, toward the distant lands they had left behind, she realized that Valentius was right, they had no other choice. Nowhere with the Empire's boundaries would they find a safe haven. The Emperor's soldiers would be searching for them, for her, for her son, for all who had defied the throne.

As they continued their journey through the quiet night, the young Mar Yanqa, having remained quiet while riding his horse beside his mother, leaned forward, eager to hear more. "What are the Khitan like, Captain Valentius?" he asked, his voice tinged with curiosity. "I have heard little of them."

Valentius glanced over at the boy, a faint smile rimming his lips. The child had always been sharp, his intellect beyond his years, but the questions he asked now were those of a young man, more mature, seeking answers about a world he did not fully understand.

"They may be nomads but the Khitan are a proud and ancient people," Valentius began, his voice rich with the kind of knowledge that could only come from years of travel and firsthand experience. "They have their own ways, their own customs. They live by the bow and the horse, warriors at heart, always on the move. Their society is built around the strength of their clans, with loyalty to their leaders above all else."

She-Ping, still uneasy, looked at her son. "But they are... savages." she stated softly, hesitant to voice her disdain.

Valentius shook his head. "Savages is a word often used by those who don't understand them. They may live differently from us, but they are not barbarians. They value strength, honor, and the warrior spirit above all else. In some ways, their code is no different from the way of life your husband, King Mar Zutra, once upheld. The Khitan respect those who fight for their people. They respect those who are willing to die for their people."

He then turned to Mar Yanqa, seeing the boy's inquisitive expression. "They are the descendants of the Xianbei, just as your family is. They understand what it means to struggle for survival. They know what it is to face the might of a larger enemy and to fight against the odds. They are filled with the same spirit and desire for freedom that has defined your family."

The boy's green eyes, gleaming in the moonlight, locked onto Valentius as he absorbed the words. "Do they hate the Emperor?" Mar Yanqa asked, his voice quiet but intense, like a spark igniting an idea.

Valentius paused for a moment, his gaze drifting over the darkened forest. "Hate is such a strong word. Let us just say that the Khitan do not respect the Emperor, or what he stands for," he picked his words carefully. "They have always been at odds with the Empire. The Xianbei, from whom they are descended, were often in conflict with the Han. So, being in a constant state of rebellion is nothing new to them. And the Khitan have never forgotten their heritage. To them, the Emperor is but a distant figurehead, a ruler who does not share their values or their lives."

She-Ping swallowed hard, her thoughts churning. The Khitan were a wild and unpredictable force of nature, and they would be a far cry from the sheltering walls of the palace. But overall, she realized that there was little choice in the matter.

The boy's voice broke through her musings. "Do they fight with swords or with other weapons Valentius?" Mar Yanqa asked, the interest in his tone growing.

Valentius glanced toward the boy, impressed by his curiosity. "The Khitan are master archers and horsemen. They fight from horseback, with longbows, short swords, and spears. They are skilled in raiding and ambush tactics, knowing the land better than any army from the Empire."

Mar Yanqa nodded slowly, his brow furrowed in thought. "So, they are like... hunters, stalking their prey in the wild?"

"Exactly," Valentius replied. "The Khitan are like shadows in the night, able to move across the land without being seen. They know the mountains and plains better than any other people. They live off the land, and when they fight, they do it with a sense of purpose, not for glory or riches, but for survival."

She-Ping listened intently for the next answer as her son spoke again, his voice thoughtful. "Do you think they will help us, Captain Valentius? Will they take us in?"

Valentius's eyes softened, and he looked ahead at the dark road winding before them. "The Khitan are not a people who readily give charity. They will expect something in return for their help. But you are of their blood, Princess. Possibly, they may help you because of that, because of the shared heritage between your people and theirs. It's not a guarantee, but it is a possible card to play."

"But they are no different from the Tuoba that we met," Mar Yanqa's mind was wrestling with the theoretical differences between the people of the steppes.

"What we encountered was one clan of one tribe that has lived close to the cities of the Empire; so close in fact that their behavior and customs have been influenced by their civilized neighbors, although they would never admit it. The Khitan, on the other hand, are an entire nation that have had little contact with the civilized world and most likely detest the thought of city life. They claim to be Xianbei but different, saying they are descendants of one particular tribe known as the Donghu that lived in the west Liao River Region for countless generations. They see our civilization as a betrayal of everything their ancestors lived for. Remember that, before you go spouting off about any benefits of living life in a palace,"

The lesson had ended and the journey continued, with the moon slipping further behind them, and the chill of the night creeping in. Despite the tension hanging in the air, Mar Yanqa seemed comforted by the captain's words. The thought of the Khitan, fierce and mysterious as they were, had sparked something within him. The lad was always thinking, always learning, always seeking the next piece of essential knowledge.

She-Ping, however, remained apprehensive. She did not know what awaited them in the land of the Khitan. But with every mile they traveled towards their destination, she understood one thing: there was no returning to the life they had known. She could only hope that the land they were heading toward would offer refuge, and that her family's connection to the Xianbei would be enough to secure their survival. Perhaps, in the wilderness of the Khitan, they would find the safety they so desperately needed.

Chapter 6: 512 AD

The wilderness beyond the Northern Wei Empire stretched both vast and untamed, a cold expanse where only the most resilient could survive. The Sungari River, flowing fiercely through the land of Jilin, offered both a challenge and a lifeline to the scattered clans that called the region home. Here, among the snow-covered plains and jagged mountain peaks, Princess She-Ping, her son Mar Yanqa, and their caravan of followers sought refuge from the Emperor's relentless pursuit that though it had waned, it had not been abandoned over the past two years.

When they first arrived, their community had been little more than a disorganized group of refugees. She-Ping, though once a princess, living the refined life of a court aristocrat, was now both mother and clan leader, her regal poise tempered by the raw realities of survival. With Captain Valentius at her side, the group made camp, setting up tents, rough, felt-covered structures not unlike the yurts of the nomadic Xianbei tribes that roamed the land. Each day in the wilderness was a fight against hunger and the elements. Yet with each passing season, the strangers among the nomads began to look less like refugees and more like an established clan.

Mar Yanqa had barely crossed into his fourteenth year while living in this wilderness, but in the span of those two years, he had grown well beyond his age. Now standing almost six feet tall, with broad shoulders and a frame solid from years of hunting and hard labor, he seemed more like a young man of seventeen or eighteen. His face, still boyish, was framed by the faintest shadow of a beard. Eyes that had once been filled with innocence were now sharp, hardened by the realities of this new life.

His mother, She-Ping, watched this transformation with a mix of pride and sorrow. He was no longer the small child who had clung to her skirts when they first fled from Mahoza. In his stead stood a young man capable of survival in ways she had never imagined. The child of royalty had learned to track game, to fire a bow with precision, and to barter successfully with the other nomads. She knew that Mar Yanqa's strength, his towering presence, would one day lead them, but the thought made her heart ache as she recalled the life lived by her dead husband, who was thrust into power because he had exactly these same traits, only to lose his life on the battlefield. She worried that the same fate now lay ahead for her son.

For all the peace that had settled over them in this remote corner of the world, the memories of the Emperor's army in pursuit were never far. The occasional whisper in the wind, the distant smoke from the fires of a rival tribe, it was all a reminder that their freedom was fragile. Yet, for now, they were safe. The people She-Ping had brought with her were no longer just survivors, they had become something more. They were a family.

The first year had been the hardest. The air was bitter, and the nights cold enough to freeze the breath in their lungs. She-Ping's once-polished hands had become calloused from the labor of setting up the yurts and learning the ways of the wilderness. Though she carried the crown of her kingdom in her heart, it had long since been left behind in the ruins of the past. She no longer ruled in halls of marble and stone; now, her kingdom was one of endless grass and blankets of snow, and the weight of that crown, though invisible, was heavier than ever.

The refugees that constituted the clan had to learn everything anew. They had to understand the patterns of the seasons, the signs of approaching storms, and the tracks of animals they had never hunted before. Captain Valentius, though a soldier in the past of the Empire, had spent time under his old general, Patricius surviving in harsh environments before, and it was his knowledge of the land, along with those of his men, that kept them alive.

"These tents won't keep you warm unless you understand the way the winds work," he would often tell them. "Keep the fire low at night and always keep your furs close. The cold out here is as fierce as any enemy you will face. It cares nothing for you and will slay you just as easily as any blade against your throat."

At first, they had struggled. There had been nights when the cold seeped through their bones, and the sound of wolves in the distance was the only thing to keep them awake, so that they could keep the fires going. They had no crops to tend to, no noble tables to sit at, only the harsh wilderness that demanded their respect and vigilance.

But as the months passed, something shifted. They learned to hunt the game that roamed the plains, deer, wild goats, and rabbits. Though there were plenty of wild boar, Mar Yanqa and the group of priests that traveled with them refused to let them eat any pig meat. The same for any horse that died by accident, the priests ruling that which served you in life must be treated with respect in death. The restrictions made it hard when food was scarce, but they survived the worst of times. They discovered the root vegetables hidden beneath the frost and the berries that grew in the shadow of the mountains. Slowly, a rhythm began to settle into their lives. The elders traded knowledge of the Empire for the ways of the Xianbei, and the warriors learned new tactics for defense, absorbing them from the tribes they encountered, adopting their strategies and blending them into one unified strength.

Mar Yanqa, though still considered a mere youth in years, was quicker to adapt than most. He had grown up in the palace with tutors and warriors, yet none of that prepared him for the hard truths of living in the wild. His first hunt had been a failure, as he missed his mark while hunting a stag. But the second time, when a wild goat crossed their path, he had been quick and deadly, plunging his spear deep into the animal's heart. Death must be quick; it was forbidden to let an animal suffer. If the initial strike did not kill it, then it was necessary to cut immediately across its throat, slicing though the jugulars and carotids. The first successful hunt marked a turning point in his development.

"Your hand is steady," Captain Valentius had said to him, after seeing him bring down a second goat a few weeks later. "There's no fear in your heart. You were born for this."

It was a praise that filled Mar Yanqa with pride, though there was something else in his eyes as he spoke. A hunger. A desire not just to survive but to lead. He had to demonstrate to everyone in their newly formed clan that he had the ability to succeed in every endeavor he undertook.

But there were still moments of doubt. The past was never far from their minds. There were times when whispers of the Emperor's army reached them; rumors carried upon the wind. The scouts sent to the border of the lands near the Empire often returned with news that made She-Ping's heart panic.

"Not yet," she would whisper to herself, even as her son asked what they were still running from. She could not explain it fully, not to the boy who had once been an heir to a throne. How could she explain that in her heart she knew her brother would never stop until he had proof that both of them were dead.

The second year brought about even more stability. What was once a caravan of refugees began to resemble a real community. Trade with neighboring nomads became a regular occurrence. They exchanged furs, dried meat, and tools with tribes that had long since mastered the land. In return, the nomads taught them the ways of the wild, how to mend their own clothes, how to craft weapons, and how to read the unspoken words of the earth.

She-Ping's role evolved, as well. She no longer worried solely about her son's survival or her people's immediate needs. She was a leader now, guiding her people through the complexities of nomadic life. She had the wisdom of a queen, tempered by the experience of a refugee, and she used it to secure the future of her people in this strange, brutal and cold land.

Mar Yanqa was also changing rapidly. His hands continued to become rougher, his shoulders even broader. In height he continued to grow until he now towered over most of the others. His legs, once those of a child, were now powerful, capable of outrunning the fast-moving game he hunted. His face had hardened, and the childish glow in his eyes was replaced with a more distant, determined gaze. He had learned quickly how to navigate the politics of the tribe, how to speak to the elders with respect and strength. To the younger boys, those who had once cowered in fear at the unknown, they now followed him when he led them into the forest to hunt or forage. They were eager to please him, to learn from him, for Mar Yanqa was more than just another boy; he was their future leader. In moments of quiet, She-Ping would often watch him, wondering what the future held for her son. He was no longer a pampered prince. There was no longer a palace from which he would rule. There was no great army that he would lead into battle. That which would have been the inheritance from his father was long gone. But she could see that he was something different now. Something undefinable.

"I wonder what it would have been like," she said to Valentius one evening, as they stood on the banks of the Sungari River, the twilight sky painted with streaks of red and orange. "Had we been allowed to stay in Kaifeng. Would he have been a prince? A king? Did he have such a future?"

Valentius turned his gaze toward the horizon, where the mountains loomed tall in the distance. "Perhaps but I think it was more likely that at some point your brother's sons would have viewed him as a threat and would have tried to eliminate him. But believe me when I say this, here, he is something more than he could have ever been in Kaifeng. Here he is a leader forged in fire and those are the ones destined for greatness. Just like his father."

"In the middle of nowhere," she laughed, "You still believe he is destined for greatness?"

Valentius just smiled as if he knew a secret. A smile that said, "Just wait and see."

Mar Yanqa spent most of his days when he was not hunting, training with Captain Valentius, learning the ways of war, strategy, and leadership of men into battle. The older men never doubted he had the strength of a future leader. Someone who could provide their clan with glory in ways his mother would never be able to. Mar Yanqa's towering presence became a symbol of the clan's strength. The younger boys idolized him, while the older men trusted him with tasks that few his age could handle.

Yet, for all his physical strength, Mar Yanqa often found himself in quiet moments of reflection. The boy who had dreamed of ruling a kingdom now found himself torn between two worlds. He had come to understand that the life he once thought was his was no longer within reach. His father's throne, his birthright, it was all just a distant memory now, fading with each passing day in the wilderness. The priests would remind him of stories from their sacred books of the many who became judges or kings when Yahweh called upon them, even though they never imagined that would be their destiny. It gave Mar Yanqa hope that one day he too would hear that calling.

One night, after a long day of hunting, he sat by the fire with a few of the older men from Valentius's squadron, sharing a meal. As they spoke of battles they had fought in and the lands they had conquered, Mar Yanqa realized that his future was no longer aligned with that of the Empire. His future lay with the clan and the other tribes inhabiting the wilderness. If there was to be a future, it was not about fighting with the Empire but against it. But questions such as how and when weighed heavily on his young mind because he could not see how that would ever come about as long as the tribes remained divided. As the flames crackled and the stars stretched across the cold sky, Mar Yanqa knew the answers were not simple. Perhaps the priests were right. It had nothing to do with his desires or his timing. When the time was right, God would let him know.

The second year in the wilderness ended in relative peace, but there were always whispers of the Emperor's pursuit finally catching up to them. Scouts reported sightings of imperial soldiers moving closer to the borders of Jilin. The knowledge that their freedom was tenuous never fully left She-Ping's mind. She had seen the empire's brutality firsthand and each time there was a warning, she would move the clan up into the mountains where they could not be found, only returning to the riverbank when he all-clear was given.

Mar Yanqa stood by the river one evening after they had come down from the security of the mountain, staring into the distance, and feeling a strange calm settle over him as if words were being spoken to him by the wind. "The threat of the Emperor's army would always loom over them," it said. "Next time they would not head to the mountain, it was time to fight

Chapter 7: 512 AD

The Northwind was particularly harsh that autumn. The dense forests of the west had given up their leaves, leaving nothing behind but barren landscapes, rolling hills and rocky outcrops stretching toward the horizon. It was an early sign that the coming winter would be severe and unless they prepared early, not everyone in the clan would survive to see the following spring.

Despite the open land, the barrenness of the forest, the Princess She-Ping could not shake the sensation that the trees were closing in on them. Her thoughts, like the wind tugged at her cloak, as if she was to pay attention to something she overlooked. Her mind attempted to process all they had been through in order to find the missing piece of the puzzle. Behind them, Kaifeng was nothing more than a shadow of a memory. The throne she had once considered her own, now just a distant and unattainable dream. Had they received word earlier from the scouting party that Valentius had dispatched, perhaps she would have known what it was that she was sensing. The Emperor, growing tired of the endless cat and mouse game that was being played, sent his best trackers and soldiers to chase them down, and they had been closing in, day by day. Those scouts that had seen their approach never made it back to camp to spread the word, falling prey to the Emperor's own scouting parties that were seemingly everywhere. After two years without any success, Emperor Hsuan Wu Ti was not about to tolerate it any longer. His last command to the expeditionary force was to bring his sister and nephews heads back in a sack or don't bother to return.

Valentius, despite his strength and leadership skills, was no seer and without his scouting reports he was acting blind. The night had settled in when Valentius pulled his horse to a halt, signaling the others with him to stop immediately. His eyes darted across the landscape, his senses sharp as a hawk's. "Quickly, back to the camp," he ordered and their horses took off at a thundering pace.

She-Ping was resting in her yurt when her captain came bursting in. "What is it?" she asked, her voice filled with both shock and surprise.

Valentius was silent for a long moment, his gaze trained on the Princess as if his eyes were saying how sorry he was.

"Valentius, you're scaring me. What is it?" she repeated.

"Princess, we've been spotted. There's a force closing in on us from the east," he said grimly.

She-Ping felt her stomach tighten. "How many?"

"I cannot be certain," Valentius replied. "From the sounds I could make out, at least several hundred. Maybe more."

"Do they know where the camp is located?" she pressed, her voice sharp with urgency.

"I believe so. They're moving fast, as if they know the terrain well." Valentius was certain that the Empire's scouts must have spotted them earlier in the day and reported back with their location.

"Hurry, we must tell everyone," the Princess instructed.

Moving to the central forum of the encampment, Valentius instructed everyone to gather around urgently. The clan gathered quickly, sensing that this could only mean they were facing serious trouble.

"We need to move. Now!" Valentius ordered them. "The Emperor's cohorts will be here in likely a matter of a half hour. We must hide up in the mountains immediately. Everyone, get you things and start up the trail immediately."

At the order, they were on their feet, gathering their possessions and preparing to leave. But it was already too late.

Before anyone could even mount their horses and flee, the sounds of galloping hooves and shouted commands reached them from the outskirt of the camp. She-Ping's heart pounded in her chest, as she turned toward Valentius, whose expression had darkened with resignation.

Impossible, Valentius thought to himself. They could not have covered that distance in so short a time. "We cannot outrun them. Prepare for battle," Valentius cried out, his hand already resting on the hilt of his sword.

Valentius's squadron quickly took their positions around the outside perimeter of the camp, joined by the young men they had been training over the past two years. Meanwhile the remnant of the palace guard from Kaifeng surrounded the princess and her son. Valentius, though reluctant to fight, had no other choice but to make a stand. Their chances of survival were slim, outnumbered as they were, but perhaps they could make a stand and fight long enough for the princess and her son to slip away under the cover of darkness. It was his only hope.

Before the first arrow could be loosed, a sharp cry rang out from behind them. There were men approaching rapidly, but they were not the empire's soldiers. Valentius' eyes widened, totally caught by surprise. "What...?" He turned, instinctively lowering his sword as he tried to determine whether it was friend or foe that was approaching.

These new riders, moving in a tight formation, wore strange armor and held weapons unfamiliar to him. Bows with curved, odd-shaped arrows, spears tipped with bone. The riders themselves were not the typical Xianbei warriors they had encountered these past two years and certainly weren't the Emperor's men. Even their features were different—strong, hard, and severe, their faces drawn in the rough expression of men who lived for battle only.

A figure at the front of the group raised a hand, signaling the others to stop. The horses slowed, and the riders immediately spread out, encircling all of them.

The one at front, a tall, broad-shouldered man, dismounted and approached them, his gaze flicking over She-Ping and her company. He spoke in a language unfamiliar to any of the elders in the clan. It was harsh and guttural.

"Who are you?" Valentius demanded, stepping forward with his sword raised once more, his stance fairly aggressive and taking no chances.

The tall man tilted his head, then spoke again, this time slowly, his words no more than a broken Chinese dialect carrying a heavy accent. "You are not from here but nor are you the Emperor's men, I can tell that much," he said, his voice rough but clear. "The real question is who are you, and why are you foolish enough to travel alone through these lands?" He completely ignored Valentius's original request to identify himself.

Valentius, still wary, met the man's eyes. "You are mistaken. We are from here, even though we may look different from other tribes. This has been our camp for almost two years. Two years of fleeing from the Emperor's soldiers but now it would appear that they have caught up with us. We are fugitives marked for death. Have you also come to attack us? If so, I warn you, will not be defeated as easily as you may think."

Their spokesperson's expression remained unreadable, though his eyes flickered toward She-Ping and her son, still standing inside the ring formed by her personal guard. "Fugitives?" he repeated, his gaze lingering longer than it should on Mar Yanqa. He recognized the uniform of the palace guards. These were far more than mere fugitives. Then, without warning, he barked something to his riders, who closed in, their weapons ready.

A tense silence fell over the group, the air thick with the smell of sweat and the metallic taste of fear. She-Ping exchanged a glance with Valentius. There was nothing but uncertainty in his eyes.

"We have no choice," Valentius said to his men, his voice low but filled with determination. "We will fight our way out of this."

"No," She-Ping yelled, her voice cutting through the tension. "Lower your weapons."

She took a step forward, leaving the safety of her ring of guards, her hands raised in a gesture of peace. "We are not your enemies," she said, her words slow but clear. "It is the Emperor that will not let us live in peace. We only seek a quiet home of our own to live out our lives. Please… understand, our fight is not with you."

"And why would the Emperor even be concerned about such as you, unless somehow you were a greater threat than you appear." The man could not comprehend of what value these stragglers could be to the Emperor of Northern Wei but only knew they were important.

She-Ping made it very clear. "My brother, the Emperor, is not a ruler that any of us wish to follow. As such, my existence represents a danger to his rule."

The tall man regarded her for a long moment, his sharp eyes narrowing in thought. Finally, he stepped closer. "Your brother is the Emperor Hsuan Wu

Ti?" he asked, his voice still tinged with suspicion. "You are the traitorous princess he rants about?"

"Yes," She-Ping said, keeping her voice steady. "I am Princess She-Ping of Northern Wei. My brother has turned against his own family. I seek only refuge, not war."

A murmur ran through the group of riders, as the man turned to confer with his lieutenants. She-Ping held her breath, praying that the strange riders would see reason.

Finally, the tall man turned back to her. "I am General Soseong of the Goguryeo Kingdom. I have no reason to doubt you speak truth," he said, though the skepticism remained in his voice. "From your mannerism, you are most certainly a princess. But your people are still not welcome here."

The Princess stood defiant. "My people are the Xianbei, General. It is your people that do not belong here for this is Xianbei land. Your are the strangers here."

The Goguryeo General took a moment to reflect on her words. "You are right, we are the strangers here. My mission is to eliminate any element of the Wei Kingdom that invades these lands. You are still a princess of Northern Wei."

"I do not seek to bring about a war with you," the princess continued to speak. "I have no wish for my people to fight the Korean Kingdoms. I only wish to survive, and to keep my son safe. But if you attack us, be aware that it is Xianbei blood that you will shed this day and not Wei blood. As such, all the tribes that you have an alliance within this land will demand retribution. Blood for blood. Are you prepared to lose your allies because of a very serious mistake you are about to make?"

The general studied her for what seemed ages, his dark eyes unreadable. Finally, he nodded, though the suspicion still lingered. "A fair point, Princess She-Ping. We will not attack you but neither will you be free to leave as you please. You will be my personal guests, and all of you will be watched closely. The Emperor's forces are not the only threat we face and having you within our control may prove useful to us."

"You mean your prisoners," Valentius clarified the General's statement.

"You will be well take care of," Soseong explained. "Those two have too much value not to use them as some kind of bargaining chip in our war against the Emperor. In a few days, we will probably let the rest of you go. You are of no value to us."

"And you expect that we will just leave the Princess and her son behind," Valentius challenged the General's intentions.

"If you're smart, you will," Soseong suggested. "Lower your weapons," he ordered his men. Turning to Valentius, he passed on a warning, "Do as I say and there won't be any problems."

As the Koreans lowered their weapons, She-Ping felt a mixture of relief and trepidation wash over her. They were not dead but they were far from safe.

Technically they had become prisoners of the Korean forces, to be used as some sort of negotiating tool in the Korean's war against her brother. Before Valentius could say another word, Princess She-Ping silenced him with a raised hand. "We will accept your offer to be your guests for now. But I expect you will protect us from my brother's forces about to attack."

"Oh, they will not attack today," the General reassured her.

"You seem fairly certain," Valentius was curious how the Korean general could know what the Emperor's forces planned to do.

"They are aware that my forces have arrived on the scene. That changes their entire strategy. It will take them at least two days to prepare a new strategy."

"Based on what evidence?" Valentius was curious to know.

"Based on my experience," he shot back. "Know your enemy well, If you don't, then you will pay a heavy price. Now if you don't mind, my men will ring the perimeter around your camp," Soseong informed him.

"You're using us as bait," Valentius protested.

"Precisely," Soseong smiled.

Over the next few days, the tension between She-Ping's clan and the Koreans slowly turned into something far more complicated. Valentius and his men, along with the princess's personal escort of palace guards had to surrender their weapons. It was a humiliating, intolerable experience that no soldier would allow himself to suffer, except that the princess had requested it of them, and for that reason alone, they accepted the condition.

Meanwhile, General Soseong was smart enough to realize that he could not separate the princess and her son from the rest of their clan. She was the only voice that could keep them under control and open to following the Korean's orders. Whenever the princess would ask the general about his intentions he would only reply that she need not worry, as long as everyone obeyed his instructions. If they cooperated, then they would all remain safe. She hated the fact that she had no insight as to what was fated for all of them but as long as she could see that her people were not being harmed and essentially well treated she was willing to play along with his game for the time being.

General Soseong, was a man of formidable stature, a master tactician who had brought about the downfall of countless enemies. His eyes were sharp, his mind calculating. He obviously saw something in the Princess, something that could be useful but he refused to tell her his intentions. It became evident when he began to spread rumors, sending his scouts out to speak to the people in nearby villages and encampments, knowing that ultimately the message would be carried back to the palace in Luoyang. "The Emperor is a tyrant," they bellowed, their voices booming across the central square of each village and in the yurts of the elders. "The rightful emperor of China is not the man in Luoyang, but the youth, Mar Yanqa, one of you, one of the Xianbei, and he is under the protection of the Goguryeo. Princess She-Ping is his mother, and the boy is the future of China."

It had become obvious to all what the general's intent was. She-Ping and her son would be used to sow dissent throughout the kingdom. It would only be a matter of time before Emperor Hsuan Wu Ti would have to react, otherwise he risked losing everything to a mounting insurrection. The rumors took root quickly, spreading throughout the surrounding land and then into the cities of Northern Wei. Mar Yanqa was no longer just a fugitive's son but was now proclaimed as the rightful heir to the throne, the true Emperor of the people. As for the Princess She-Ping, she had become a symbol, the figurehead of resistance against the tyranny of her brother.

"What have you done?" Valentius shouted at the Korean General. "What may have only been a few cohorts pursuing us, now he will send a legion. He knows exactly where we are. We're sitting ducks!"

"He now has no choice but to send a real army into these territories," the general answered calmly. "And we will be waiting for them."

"Are you mad?" Valentius wondered. "What do you have at your disposal? A couple of thousand men, perhaps three. He can send ten times that. You have doomed us all."

"Do not take me for a fool, Valentius," Soseong cautioned the captive captain. "As we speak, the messages we have spread across the land are being repeated over and over again. Already I'm receiving reports from the Empire's provinces that there are revolts and skirmishes between the Emperor's forces and break away units of his army that favour a change as to who is sitting on the throne. Not quite a revolution but enough that he has to spread his army across multiple sites."

"Still, he will be able to send north far more men than you have," Valentius disagreed with the general's evaluation of the situation.

"And we will have far more men available when they arrive," the general laughed at his concern. "Do you not think that the Xianbei tribes will not join us in this battle? They are my allies and they are eager to settle a score with the empire. Wait and you will see." Having said that, the general calmly walked away from the surrounded camp.

The days stretched into weeks, and with each passing hour, She-Ping and her son were treated with a mix of awe and fear as their reputations grew among the Korean soldiers. Though from all appearances, they were cherished guests of General Soseong, being provided with food, shelter, and protection, what anyone looking from the outside failed to see was that they were nothing more than the hapless victims caught in a political web, waiting for the spider to pounce.

She-Ping's heart grew heavier with each passing day. She had not wanted this life for her son. She had wanted him to grow up in a world where he could choose his own path, free from the chains of power and destiny that were being pulled by others. But now, he was a pawn in a much larger game. The eyes of at least one Korean Kingdom were squarely upon him, and one could only assume that her brother's soldiers were being amassed during this time, exactly as

Valentius had feared, in order to launch an all-out assault against the Korean army and eliminate the two primary sources of concern that were feeding the emerging rebellion that was slowly taking root within the Empire.

Chapter 8: 512 AD

The plains of Liaoning stretched out beneath the heavy, unrelenting late autumn sky, a grey expanse of nothingness where the wind howled through the grass, and the scent of blood was already thick in the air. The Emperor's army, sleek in their iron armor, moved with the precision of a well-oiled machine, their forces pushing forward against the entrenched Goguryeo defenders. It had been four days since the first clash, and the bloodshed had been unrelenting. Hundreds, if not thousands, of soldiers from both sides lay dead, their bodies littering the once-pristine earth like broken dolls. The battlefield was a swirling mass of dust, smoke, and the clashing of steel. The cold had settled in, bringing with it a sharpness that bit at the skin and made the blood freeze in one's veins. The striking of metal and the desperate shouts of men were the only sounds that dared fill the emptiness of the stale air. And yet, despite all the chaos, despite the carnage that had unfolded, the tide seemed to favor the Emperor's forces. The Koreans, reinforced by Khitan and Rouran riders, held their ground but it was obvious that their numbers were dwindling, their ranks thinning as the Emperor's army pressed harder with each passing hour.

General Soseong, the leader of the Goguryeo forces, stood at the edge of the battlefield, his eyes scanning the fight. His face was a grim mask, hardened by the relentless days of battle. The initial optimism that had filled him when the forces of his Rouran allies arrived had dwindled into exhaustion, and now, as he looked out over the field, he could see the strain in his men's movements. There was no more fight left in them. No more fire. In their minds, they had already been defeated.

"General," a voice called from behind him. It was his lieutenant, his breath short and his face pale from exhaustion. "We've lost the east flank. The Emperor's forces are pushing through. We—"

Soseong didn't need to hear the rest. He turned away, his jaw set. It was the beginning of the end. His mind whirled with the desperate calculations of retreat, but before he could give any orders, a figure broke through the haze of smoke, riding hard and fast. A scout had arrived, waving a flag of distress.

"They're coming," the scout shouted, barely able to catch his breath. "Reinforcements from the north. The Emperor's Manchurian battalion…"

Soseong's heart sank. The reinforcements under General Hermantius were famous for the battles they had fought and won in the northern provinces. The sight of Hermantius' banners flapping in the wind, the distinctive white and red of the Emperor's elite legion, cut across the horizon like a death sentence. The battle had gone on for too long, and now the final blow was about to be dealt. The

Koreans were finished.   The Khitan and Rouran, though powerful, were too few now to make any difference.

In the midst of it all, Princess She-Ping had been carried away and confined to the General's tent, her purpose on the field to inspire the men to fight no longer of value.   Her thoughts, her only concerns at this time, were not for her own safety. It was her son, Mar Yanqa, who occupied her mind.   She had to protect him, had to keep him safe.   But confined to Soseong's tent prevented her from taking any action. There was nothing she could do to stop the inevitable.   As she sat in the tent, a wave of dread gripped her heart.

The flap of the tent opened suddenly, and a soldier, pale and breathless, entered.

"Princess… General Soseong requests your presence.   He is… awaiting you."

Her eyes widened. The tense stillness in the air was broken by her sharp intake of breath.   Why the sudden urgency that he needed to see her, she couldn't imagine.   She panicked at the sudden thought that he might be considering a surrender.   If so, she would need to try and convince him not to give up.   If he surrendered the only thing that awaited her and her son was certain death.

When she arrived, the sight in front of her was nothing like she had expected. General Soseong was kneeling, surrounded by his officers, his hands trembling as they gripped a short sword, the gleaming edge dark with his own sweat and fear.   His expression was grim, and there was no light in his eyes.

"General!" She-Ping cried, rushing forward, her heart hammering in her chest. "What are you doing?"

For a moment, the man didn't respond. His eyes were vacant, lost in the horror of the battle, the hopelessness that surrounded them.   He seemed like a man who had already decided he had no place in this world.

The princess's breath caught in her throat as she reached him.   She knew his mind had turned to despair—she could feel the weight of it in the air around him. "General," she whispered, her voice trembling with emotion, "You cannot do this. There is hope still. You have to listen to me."

He turned slowly, his gaze lifting from the blade. "Hope? What hope is there, Princess?   My men are dying.   We are being crushed.   I have failed. I summoned you here to tell you that you and your people are now free to go. Take them into the mountain passes as quickly as you can. I will try to provide you with enough time to successfully escape."

She-Ping became furious.   "You held us here as your prisoners all this time, only to now tell us to run for our lives, knowing we have little chance to escape my brother's soldiers. My captain warned you from the start that your plan was flawed and foolish.   But you did not listen!," she screamed in desperation.

"Our Xianbei allies were no match for the Emperor's reinforcements. There was no way I could have known that," he excused his miscalculation.

"Did you really think that the Emperor would only send a few battalions once he heard that my son and I were in easy reach?   I could have told you that he would sacrifice his entire army in order to see that we were eliminated. You played into his hands all this time," she scolded him.

"And now... now they come for all of us. I will not allow them to take me alive. I will not. Go now while you may still have a chance."

Her heart clenched. She couldn't bear it. She rushed forward, snatching the short sword from his hands, throwing it aside.

"You still have a duty to them," She-Ping said, her voice breaking as she pointed to the ring of officers. "You are their leader. Stand up and lead! Our survival is dependent on you. You are not alone in this. I will not let you take the coward's way out!"

A long silence stretched between them. Then, Soseong stood slowly, his face hard with resolve. "You are the fool if you seriously think we can win? Do you know who that is coming from the north? You have no idea what this man, General Hermantius is like. He is the butcher of the north. We will all be dead by the end of the day at his hands."

"Hermantius?" the princess repeated the name as if was a magical mantra.

"Yes, Hermantius," Soseong responded. "The man is known as the butcher of the north."

"My Hermantius?" the princess couldn't believe what she was hearing.

Now it was time for General Soseong to sound surprised. "What do you mean by my Hermantius?"

She-Ping's eyes were steady. "Exactly that. He is my Hermantius. I can bring Hermantius over to you. Get me a horse, Valentius and my son, and find a way to get us safely through the line to intercept him. Deliver me safely to his battalion and I can guarantee you will not be losing this battle."

"You are insane!" the General scoffed.

"You must trust me, General. You must have the courage to stand by me just a little longer and let me take care of this. I can do what I said."

Soseong stared at her for a long time, and then—after what seemed like an eternity—he nodded grimly. "It's insanity but I will trust you, Princess. But this better not be some fantasy that you are spinning to give my men false hope. If this is a lie, then I will find a way to cut your throat myself."

The princess nodded, stepping back. "General, why in the world would I have you deliver me to a man you called the butcher of the north. You wouldn't have the opportunity to cut my throat. If I did not believe I could turn his favor, I would not be riding to meet him. I am not that desperate to die. You have no other option but to trust me."

Escorted by a contingent of five Korean riders, She-Ping rode swiftly across the plain to the north with Mar Yanqa and Valentius at her side. The dust swirled around them, and the sound of fighting reverberated in their ears as they made their way toward the northern flank. As they drew closer, she could see the familiar banners of Hermantius' legion, the legion her husband had sent to protect her when she fled Mahoza. Their colors were unmistakable in the distance.

There, leading his men across the bloodstained grass, was Hermantius. His face etched with the same grim resolve that had always marked him, his expression hardened by the increased weight of leadership the emperor had placed upon his shoulders.

She-Ping's heart soared. She had made it. They had made it. As they closed the distance, Hermantius turned his head and saw her, his eyes lighting up with recognition. His horse broke into a gallop, cutting across the field until he reached the approaching party. Both the Princes and Hermantius dismounted simultaneously. He ran towards her swiftly, embracing her without thinking, but unable to resist, saddened by all the years he was prevented from seeing her.

It was then that he realized that his lowly position did not permit him to embrace the former Queen of Mahoza. "Forgive me, Princess," he said, his voice thick with emotion. "I have offended you and I must apologize for my actions."

"I am not offended," the Princess excused his action and then hugged him back, the tears streaming from her eyes.

"You're safe now Princess. Why are you crying. By Yahweh, I knew you would be. I would have slaughtered every last one of the Koreans if they harmed you."

The tears sprang to She-Ping's eyes as she looked up at him. "Hermantius," she cried, "You have been misled. It is the Koreans that have protected us."

Hermantius looked confused. "I think the shock of being their prisoner for so long has addled you Princess," he tried to rationalize her statement.

"No, Hermantius. For over two years we have been fleeing from my brother. He has been trying to kill Mar Yanqa and I and it is only General Soseong that has protected us this last while."

Hermantius felt his head spinning. "I only received a message from the ministry that you were taken prisoner by the Koreans and the Emperor was pleading for me to come and save you and Mar Yanqa. I knew nothing of your fleeing from the palace for the past two years. I never would have fought for your brother if I had known."

"Exactly why they did not tell you anything," She-Ping responded. "But the battle… we need your help. The Emperor's forces are pushing us to the brink. We cannot hold out much longer. If we lose, then my brother will see to it that Mar Yanqa and I also die this day."

Hermantius placed a steady hand on her shoulder, his gaze sharp. "You are safe now, Princess. Even the additional forces that have swollen my ranks are loyal only to me. I will put an end to this. I swear it." It was then that he realized he was touching the Princess again and quickly withdrew his hand.

"Dear Hermantius, you can hold me as much as you want. You are as dear to me as your cousin Patricius was." The two of them shared a moment of silent understanding, the weight of their shared struggle over the past decade settling between them.

Having let his mother make the initial approach, Mar Yanqa now ran to the man he had always called uncle. Hermantius turned to Mar Yanqa, his face softening as soon as he saw the strapping young man approach.

"Mar Yanqa? Is that really you, my boy?" he asked, shocked that they were able to greet each other at eye level. "You've grown much. I see the fire in you, just like your father. How is it possible that you are now this big. Soon you'll be as broad as me and they'll call you the bear."

Mar Yanqa, his face filled with emotion, nodded happily. "I will not disappoint you, Uncle. I will continue to work out until I am as big as you." The two exchanged a look. one of unspoken understanding, of an unbreakable bond that had always existed between them. The world seemed to stand still, the noise from the battlefield fading in the background as Hermantius gave the boy a hug that he did not need to feel ashamed of.

Without another word, Hermantius mounted his horse and gave the signal to his battalion. They rode out, crashing into the fray but to the surprise of everyone on the battlefield they began slicing through the Emperor's legion. The surprise was absolute. The Emperor's forces, caught off guard by the sudden betrayal of Hermantius and his battalion, faltered. They had thought the battle won, but now they were scrambling to regroup and counter the butcher of the north's violent assault.

Seizing the opportunity, Soseong's forces, along with the Khitan and Rouran allies, rallied with ferocity, charging forward with all the might they had left. The tide of battle shifted. The Emperor's forces, which had become overconfident, were now completely disorganized and began to fall back. By nightfall, the battlefield was littered with the corpses of the fallen soldiers from Northern Wei. The remnant of the Emperor's forces had fled in disarray, many deserting the battlefield in fear of losing their lives.

The victory, though resounding, came at a terrible cost. Hermantius had led his men into battle with the fury of a man determined to turn the tide and avenge all that the princess had suffered at the hands of her brother, but in the end, it was his own life that was claimed through the chaos of war. As the battle raged on, Hermantius was struck by a blow from a spear, its jagged edge tearing through his armor. He fell to the ground, blood seeping from his wound.

Once the Northern Wei forces were in retreat, Mar Yanqa rushed to Hermantius's side, kneeling beside him. "Uncle! No!" He cried, his hands clutching the older man's.

Hermantius opened his eyes, the pain evident but his gaze filled with love. "My boy," he whispered, his voice a mere rasp. "I... I did what I could. This is... It is up to you now to carry on."

Tears welled up in Mar Yanqa's eyes as he held the fallen general. "You'll live, Uncle. You must live."

The sounds of battle faded into a distant hum, the shrill of horns and the cries of men dissipating as the cold autumn air grew thicker around them. The heavy weight of war had begun to lift, but for Mar Yanqa, that victory had come at too high a price.

His heart still raced as he knelt beside the fallen body of Hermantius. The man who had been his protector, mentor, and surrogate father when they escaped from Mahoza, whose guidance had shaped him since he was a child, was now fading from this world. Mar Yanqa's hands trembled as he gripped Hermantius's, feeling the last of the life drain from his uncle's body.

The great general, known for his unwavering loyalty to She-Ping and Mar Yanqa, had done what seemed impossible, he had changed the course of the battle. But now he lay on the frigid ground, dying in his adopted nephew's arms, the blood of both friend and foe staining the earth beneath them.

Hermantius's breaths came slower, labored, but his eyes still held that same intensity, the same fire that had burned in them since Mar Yanqa first bounced upon his knee. The boy had watched Hermantius rise through the ranks of battle, witnessed his unwavering devotion to his father's cause, and had seen the quiet love he held for his mother She-Ping.

Now, with death's shadow looming, it was Hermantius's turn to give one last piece of advice to his young ward. The general's voice, though weak, was steady. "Mar Yanqa," he rasped, his breath catching in the chill air. "Listen to me, boy. You were never meant to sit upon the throne of China. You're not meant to follow in the footsteps of your mother's family. The Emperor's seat, that… that crown…it's not for you."

Mar Yanqa's brow furrowed. The words, though softly spoken, struck like arrows. His pulse quickened, his grip on Hermantius tightening. This was the man who had always believed in him, who had fought for his survival, and now he was telling him not to pursue the very legacy that had been laid out for him. "But… Uncle… the throne…my mother… she—"

Hermantius's hand, weak but purposeful, reached up, cupping the boy's cheek with a tenderness that belied the violence of the world around them. "No, Mar Yanqa. Your mother is a princess of China, yes, but you are not meant to be part of that world. You are a child of two worlds, and neither will ever be truly yours. What you need is not the throne of an empire built on lies, betrayal, and corruption. The Emperor of China is not your enemy—your true enemy is what he represents."

Mar Yanqa stared down at his uncle, unable to comprehend precisely what he was hearing. "But… if I do not take the throne, what do I do? What is left for me? All I have ever known is that my destiny is to take my place as a ruler. The throne is my birthright. My mother, my people… they all expect this of me."

Hermantius's lips twisted into a faint, pained smile. "Your destiny, boy, is not to inherit a legacy soaked in blood, lies, and betrayal. Your father knew this too. Your father, my one and only king, did not seek power or land. He carved out a new path for himself, a new world, free of the chains of the empire that sought to tear him apart. His dream wasn't to rule Persia. His dream was to build something better…a place where his people could live freely, without the shadow of imperial rule looming over them. Do you understand?"

Mar Yanqa felt a pang in his chest, a tinge of doubt in his heart. He thought of his father, the king of Mahoza, the man whose death had set all of this in motion. His father had been a symbol of strength, of justice, and of the dream of a better world. But now, the idea of leaving behind the vast, glittering world of the Emperor's throne seemed impossible. "What am I to do, Uncle?"

"You must carve out your own nation, Mar Yanqa," Hermantius continued, his voice growing weaker. "You are not meant to rule what is already broken. You are meant to create something new. Something pure. Something better. Your father did not have an empire, but he had something far more important: A kingdom where all men were free. He built something from the ground up. A new kind of place. A new life for all."

Mar Yanqa's breath caught in his throat. The words cut deep into his soul. He had always thought of his father's kingdom as a distant memory, a far-off place that had been lost to him forever. But now, in the face of his uncle's dying words, that world felt closer, more tangible. Realizing his father's dream could be a real possibility.

Hermantius's gaze locked with his. The fire in his eyes all but extinguished, but enough was still there. "You don't need China, Mar Yanqa. You need to make a place for your people, a kingdom that will stand on its own, free of the corruption of the old empire. Build a home for those who have been lost, those who have nowhere to turn, a sanctuary for those pure of heart. Do not be tempted by power, my boy. A real king never seeks power. Instead, it is given to him by the people he protects."

A tear fell from Mar Yanqa's eye as he looked at the man who had given his life to protect him and his mother, and who had now given him the final gift of guidance.

"But how?" Mar Yanqa whispered. "How do I build something new? How do I start? I'm just one person. I'm hardly more than a boy."

"You are more than just a boy, Mar Yanqa," Hermantius said, his voice growing fainter. "You have the heart of a king. You have the will to fight. You have the loyalty of your people. Those are the qualities that will make the people follow you anywhere. You will find a way. Build something different. Build something worthy of your name."

Hermantius's grip on his hand faltered as his breath slowed. "Do not be a puppet to the throne of China. Be the master of your own destiny, Mar Yanqa. You have the power to shape the future of this world. I believe in you…" With a final, lingering sigh, Hermantius closed his eyes, his hand falling limp in Mar Yanqa's. The boy's heart shattered. The man who had been his guide, his protector, and one of the few remaining members of his family was now gone. With what appeared to be his last lingering, peaceful exhale, Hermantius passed from this world.

Though surrounded by all of Hermantiu's men, Mar Yanqa felt alone.

Alone but not without purpose. As Mar Yanqa knelt beside the fallen general, the weight of Hermantius's final words settled over him like a mantle. The throne of China was not his. It had never been his. It was never meant to be. What was his, what he would build was something that could not be found in the cold, blood-soaked halls of the imperial palace of Luoyang. He understood that now. His father had initially carved out a life in a distant land, far from the reach of Emperor Kavad's corrupt grasp. And now, it was his turn to carry that torch forward. His kingdom would not be one of empires and conquests. It would be a kingdom born from the ashes of the old, from the fire of his uncle's sacrifice, and from the dream of a better, freer future. With the dying breath of Hermantius still echoing in his mind, Mar Yanqa wiped the tears from his face. He would forge his own path. Just like his father had done.

For a long time, Mar Yanqa sat there, clutching the body of the man he had always called uncle, his heart breaking with sorrow.

The funeral rites for Hermantius were carried out in a somber, quiet ceremony. His tomb was constructed near Shenyang, in the traditional Judean style that Hermantius had requested; two rooms, one for the living and one for the dead. No images of any living animals were carved into the stone walls or into the monument. Only flowers were placed near the tomb. And only flowers were carved into the exterior and interior walls of the tomb, painted in blues and yellows. There was no plaque or stone to identify who was buried in this resting place. In that way it could not be identified as belonging to the general that turned traitor on the Empire, and the descendants of Hsuan Wu Ti might desecrate the tomb as an act of revenge. By remaining anonymous, it guaranteed Hermantius's resting place would remain unsullied well into the future. It was a humble resting place for a man who had willingly given his life to a cause far greater than himself.

Chapter 9: 512 AD

The smoke from the cremated bodies still hung in the air, swirling around the plains of Liaoning like the ghosts of the men who had fallen there. The clash of steel had given way to an eerie silence in the aftermath, save for the cries of scavenging animals and the dull, rhythmic sounds of shovels digging holes in which to place the ashes. The skirmish had been brutal, a battle without any gain or reward, where neither side had truly won, but instead, both had bled until they had nothing left to give, and one side decided to flee from the field. All it meant was that sometime in the future, the two force would meet again. Korean and Chinese, intertwined in a never ending dance of death.

But in the thickening fog surrounding war and death, a new negotiation had begun. It was no longer about the clash of armies, but the price to be paid for having survived. The Khitan and Rouran, who had descended like a storm upon the Emperor's army, only to suffer losses in numbers that were only surpassed by the Korean forces, had to be repaid for their loyalty. That loyalty was not easily earned and was always costly. The Korean commander, General Soseong, knew this all too well. He had witnessed their volatile nature while negotiating before. Alliances formed under the pressure of necessity, only to be torn apart once the heat of battle had passed. The Xianbei tribes were a powerful people but they were also a proud and mercurial race. Trust, in their world, was a commodity as rare as gold, and now, Soseong found himself in a delicate dance, trying to avoid their ire and to give them what they believed they were owed.

The Rouran appeared satisfied with a chest of gold and possession of a hundred horses that survived from the Chinese cavalry. General Soseong was actually surprised by how easy it was to negotiate with the Rouran. It was probably the fact that they had lost over half of their men that made them eager to accept any reasonable offer and return to their villages as soon as possible. The Khitan on the other hand, it became obvious, were not going to be that easy to pacify.

The remaining Khitan riders gathered in a loose circle, their tall, powerful forms silhouetted against the blood-red sky as the sun began to set. Their horses were the well-muscled ponies of the steppes, their riders unshaven and draped in whatever spoils of battle they could remove from the corpses of their enemy, but their eyes displayed a hunger far more dangerous that would not be easily satisfied.

Soseong stepped forward, his armor heavier from the weight of all the dried blood that clung to it. The prospect of a negotiation that could turn sour at any moment was already on his mind. His men followed behind him, their faces grim, knowing that the Khitan were not a people who could be reasoned with easily, unlike the Rouran, if they already had a price in mind.

The Khitan leader, a gruff looking, tall man with a scar running down the side of his face beneath a helmet adorned with wild turkey feathers, stepped forward. He announced his name as being Tamerlan, a name immediately recognized as his reputation had spread like wildfire across the northern steppes years ago. He was not one to be underestimated even in negotiations. He had led his people into battle countless times, and now, standing before the Korean general, he wanted his men to receive their just reward.

"You've fought well," Soseong began, his voice steady but noticeably laced with the tension of the moment. "Your warriors helped to save us from defeat. You have earned the right to share in the spoils of this victory. But as you can see, defeating an army on the open plains doesn't leave much behind to despoil. What your men have taken already is almost all of what was left behind by our mutual enemy."

Tamerlan's lips curled into a faint, insincere smile. "You think you can now pay us with the bodies of the dead?" he asked, his voice gruff, his accent thick. "Your men fought bravely, but they died as cowards, as fools, believing in the glory of a war that never belonged to them. This is our land. It has always been our land. Not the Emperor's and certainly not yours As such, your army was not welcome to tread our sacred lands either. Your presence here only brought about death. Now you say the only thing left for me to claim are the possessions from your fallen soldiers, their armor, their weapons. That is what you can offer me." His eyes flicked toward the pile of Korean armor and weapons that had already been loaded onto the back of carts.

Soseong swallowed hard. He still had some gold but nothing else to offer. His army was barely holding on as it was. The war chest for his troops had been depleted by the long war, and now that they had won this particular battle, giving up his last bit of gold would leave him with no coin to pay his surviving troops with. The promise of land was an empty one, as the Koreans knew the Khitan considered all of the land theirs to begin with. To make an offer of land on the peninsula to the Khitan would be seen as a betrayal of his own people and bring into question why they even fought this war if they were willing to give up Korean territory.

"You have to understand, we are not a wealthy country, Tamerlan," Soseong said slowly. "Most of the armor of our fallen must be given to the families that have lost a loved one with the hope that their next son will be able to wear it and join the army and fight in the stead of his fallen brother. As for gold, I have the same quantity I gave to the Rouran that I can offer you. As for silver, even if I was to send word back to the capital, it may take months for it to arrive. All we have to offer is what remains on this battlefield and more of the Chinese horses. Take what you will from the Empire's dead, their armor, their horses, whatever food or belongings they have in their kits, but I beg you, do not take this victory from us. Our quarrel is with the Emperor of Northern Wei. This is your land, but you know that it takes both our armies to secure it. If we fail here, then the Emperor will unleash his army next on the peninsula and will take possession of all the land that belongs to Korea. We need you, it is true, but it is also true that you need us."

Tamerlan ground his right toe into the ground, his boots crunching on the frozen earth. His gaze was piercing, and it felt as if he was looking straight through Soseong, weighing his soul, measuring his worth. "Need?" he repeated, his voice almost mocking. "You speak of need, but what you mean is you will not survive without our help. You need us to protect you, to stand with you against the Emperor. What are you willing to give us in exchange for that protection?"

Soseong's mind felt as if it was crashing. There had to be something, something he could offer. The Khitan had long been a thorn in the side of the Chinese empire, and while they were currently allied with the Koreans, the relationship was fraught with instability. It was no secret that the Khitan had their own ambitions. Ambitions that could, at any moment, turn them against their so-called allies. The relationship had always been fragile but never more fragile than at this very moment.

"Your protection is worth more than gold," Soseong said, trying to appeal to the man's pragmatic side. "You know very well that the Emperor will not let this insult stand. He will come for you, and when he does, you will need all the strength we can muster and provide to you. Whether you admit it or not, you do need us too. What we have is a common enemy. All of China could belong to the Khitan and as your allies we would be there to fight alongside you to see that it happens."

Tamerlan was silent for a moment, his dark eyes never leaving Soseong's face. "What makes you think you could help to deliver all of China into our hands if you can barely protect your own kingdom?"

"Because I have something in my possession that could help make the dream a reality," the general grinned, knowing that it would pique Tamerlan's curiosity.

"So, how is it you foresee the Khitan ruling all of China in this future you describe?"

"The same way we were able to stir the uprisings in the cities within the Empire. By offering the people an alternative that they will rise up and fight for. Someone with just as much right to sit on the throne in Luoyang but more attuned to the people's needs and desires. Did you not see how we were able to turn the General Hermantius and his battalion against the Emperor's army? With what I possess, you could achieve that same desertion throughout the empire."

Tamerlan could not help but laugh at the suggestion. "And you think a Khitan leader can lay claim to the throne and the people will accept that by using some trick you claim to have," he sneered.

"No," the general shut down such thoughts immediately. "But a Khitan chieftain married to an Empress, that would make him not only the power behind the throne in Northern Wei but possibly all of China. You could never have the approval of all the people, but she could."

It wasn't clear where General Soseong was heading with this proposal but it did intrigue the Khitan chieftain to hear more. With a sudden movement, Tamerlan drew his sword, held it out before him, and then pointing the tip toward the ground, he slammed it into the soft earth, burying it halfway. It was the Khitan sign that they were meeting on common ground. "What you offer intrigues me, General Soseong. We will talk."

Soseong's heart pounded in his chest. The Khitan leader was clever, dangerous, and he could smell weakness from miles away. He was willing to give up his greatest prize, knowing Tamerlan's weakness was arrogance, his desire to have a stake in the future, a guarantee that one day he might become the chieftain that united all the tribes of the Khitan. He wanted power that stretched far beyond the battlefield.

"Think of it Tamerlan. I'm offering you some gold, Chinese weapons and armor, scores of horses, but most of all, a means by which you can rule over the Chinese empires. And to help deliver this outcome, I will offer you a continuance of our alliance," Soseong said finally, choosing his words carefully. "When the war with the Emperor is finally over and you have won, I will support your people's claim to rule in his stead and I will see that the army of Goguryeo continues to aid you forces in claiming territory until all of China belongs to the Khitan. I will grant you whatever resources it takes to see that it happens. I will make sure the Koreans are loyal to you as a protector of our borders, but you must promise me this, that your people will always fight beside us and not against us, trying to take the Korean peninsula for yourself."

Tamerlan's lips curled into a feral smile, and for a moment, Soseong felt a cold shiver run down his spine. The Khitan were a people who lived for conquest, who sought only to expand their reach. But this negotiation, even if it could be called that, was fragile, fraught with misstep, and guarantees that Soseong had no way of knowing he could deliver.

"You speak of promises, General," Tamerlan growled, his voice low and dangerous. "But promises are like the wind, here one moment, gone the next. If you cannot provide me with wealth, with which I can feed my people through the harsh winters, then you must convince me this something else you offer has real value. I have heard rumor that you have this Princess that you are offering in your possession, but how can you prove she will be capable of providing all you claim? Let us go to someplace secluded where you can prove to me that all you have said is possible. Only then will you have my agreement and my loyalty. But if you can't, then we will see what happens next."

The silence seemed to stretch for an eternity as Tamerlan grabbed the hilt of his sword and pulled it from the dirt. His lips barely moved when he spoke again, his voice thick with mockery, "Promises mean nothing, General. You offered me a kingdom and now that is all that I will accept. Show me how will you guarantee your promise!"

Soseong's hands clenched, frustration boiling in his chest. He had made an offer but there was no way in the world that he could guarantee the outcome. His mind began shifting through countless other scenarios by which he could at least offer some reassurance of the outcome. "Come with me and we shall talk." The two leaders walked together towards the command tent. Soseong ordered everyone else out of the tent.

The lanterns in General Soseong's command tent flickered, casting long, uncertain shadows on the silk-draped walls. While the cold wind hissed outside, rustling the pine trees beyond the ridgeline, inside the tent, the warmth and incense mingled, along with the thick scent of ambition.

Tamerlan stood stiffly, arms crossed, his wolf skin cloak dusted with dried blood. His face, carved from the steppes, betrayed no emotion. His eyes, black and narrow, did not trust what he was hearing.

General Soseong sat cross-legged on a lacquered platform, explaining his plan in more detail. "Princess She-Ping, daughter of the late Emperor Xiaowen. Royal blood of the Wei. A widow, yes, but also with a son who is only fourteen years old. And if she were to marry a man of stature, such as you, we could proclaim her son as the true heir to the throne of Northern Wei and seed an insurrection within the empire. Over time, once they have fought to exhaustion internally, the Wei factions will be desperate for stability, and you would march into Luoyang not as conquerors. but as their savior. You would become regent. The real power behind the throne. Warlord of the frontier. Master of ten thousand riders."

Tamerlan let out a cold laugh. "You think the Han will bow to a Khitan warlord   with a puppet emperor on his lap?"

Soseong's eyes narrowed. "No. I think they'll follow the one who holds the whip.   I would expect that to be you."

The silence that followed was sharp. Tamerlan paced once around the fire brazier, then stopped. "You forget one thing. This She-Ping is not a pawn that will so easily bend to our will."

The general smiled. "Let us ask her if she is willing to cooperate."

He clapped twice.

Moments later, the tent flap parted and Princess She-Ping entered, wrapped in a robe of deep violet brocade, her hair pinned high with jade ornaments. She looked between the men, instantly reading the air.

"General," she said, coolly. "You summoned me."

Soseong gestured elegantly. "Please, sit. Let me introduce the Khitan chieftain that fought so bravely these past few days to protect you and your son. Tamerlan had some questions for you, if you don't mind."

"I am still your prisoner, despite your offer when you thought you were about to lose to set us free, so what choice do I really have?" She arched an eyebrow, then turned to the Khitan warrior.

"Speak, chieftain. But remember if it wasn't for my intercession with General Hermantius, you'd all be dead."

Her frankness and stern attitude made Tamerlan slightly hesitant. He approached her slowly, respectfully. "Princess," he said, voice lower now. "I do owe you gratitude for your swaying the battle. It would appear that General Soseong was negligent in not informing me why the Geneal Hermantius turned against the empire's army. You have been blunt with me, so I will be equally blunt with you. The Korean wish to have me use you and your son to take Luoyang. And use a marriage between you and I to make it palatable. What say you to that?"

She-Ping held his gaze, then laughed; a short, bitter sound. "General, you wish to use me?" she said. "Again?"

Both the Soseong and Tamerlan blinked.

"I was used once, when I was sent westward and married off to cement an alliance. I was young and naïve, but my marriage to Mar Zutra was the happiest time of my life. He was and still is the only man I will ever love. I belong to no man now. Not to the general. Not to you."

Tamerlan's expression hardened. "I never said you did. It was only something the general suggested."

"But you thought it," she snapped. "You all do. You speak of thrones and power and forget that it is I who carries the bloodline you need. Without me, you will never have any claim. And yet you speak as if I am a bridge to be crossed."

Soseong's smile faltered. "Princess..."

"No," she said. "I will not be passed from one ambition to the next like a concubine's comb. If you need my support, then you will negotiate directly with me an ignore this imbecile that almost had us all killed." She pointed at General Soseong as she directed her comment.

The silence that followed was glacial.

Soseong stood and called to his attendant. "I will not tolerate such insolence from you!" he shouted.

Tamerlan looked at Soseong, his voice like gravel. "Sit down or leave general. This matter no longer is up to you."

The general did as he was instructed, returning to his seat and remaining quiet.

Tamerlan nodded curtly to the princess. "You don't know me. I don't know you. All that I know is that you and your son have a claim to the throne of Northern Wei."

Her mouth twitched. "I have both. And neither are yours to take."

Tamerlan shrugged. "The general here seems to think he could marry you off and hand your boy over to me to usc as a puppet. He felt somehow that would pay his debt to my people."

"I will not be used," She-Ping snapped.

Tamerlan glanced at her, now mildly impressed. "You speak like a queen."

"I was a queen," she responded. "And I would rather die in exile than be a pawn in someone else's war. You want something from me, so let's talk."

"Perhaps we should have your son here as well. After all, the matter concerns him as well."

She-Ping nodded her consent.

"Fetch Mar Yanqa," General Soseong ordered his attendants, attempting to maintain some relevance in the discussion.

Moments Later Mar Yanqa entered, his chest bare under a fur-lined vest, sword belted loosely, and his hair unbound "You called for me, General?"

"Here is the youth known as Mar Yanqa. He is still young, but he still has the weight of his lineage hanging on him like a shadow," General Soseong heralded his arrival.

"Come here boy and we will talk," Tamerlan commanded, sensing he was now in control of the negotiation process.

"Do you know who I am?" Tamerlan began the conversation with a question.

Mar Yanqa nodded his head. "You are the chieftain of this Khitan tribe. The one they call Tamerlan."

"The General here has told me you seek to rule. Is that true, boy?"

The lad stepped forward, his presence demanding attention. "My name is Mar Yanqa, not boy!" he began, his voice clear and filled with a quiet confidence that belied his age. "I am the son of Mar Zuta, King of Mahoza and Queen She-Ping, the royal princess of Northern Wei. As such, I am meant to rule, but not in the ways that those that sit currently on their thrones have abused such power. The true power in any kingdom is the people, not the power of armies, nor of riches. True power is built upon vision and loyalty."

Tamerlan's expression softened, just for a moment. He had expected the boy to be meek, afraid to speak up in the face of so much danger, but instead, he was speaking with a command that even Tamerlan couldn't ignore.

"Do you know why I asked for them to bring you before me, Mar Yanqa?"

"If I was to guess, I would say that you have summoned me here because you wish to know about the future of Northern Wei," Mar Yanqa continued much to the surprise of both Tamerlan and Soseong, as neither had given the smallest indication of why they had summoned him.

"I definitely see that you are your mother's son," Tamerlan said more as a compliment than merely an observation.

Mar Yanqa had not finished. "That future does not reside in my uncle's rule. His time on the throne is limited at best."

"Because you intend to take the throne," Tamerlan surmised.

"No," he answered firmly. "Because it is decaying and rotting from within."

"Then it would need fresh blood to assume control," Tamerlan insisted. "Why wouldn't that be you."

"Because General Hermantius made me realize that I have a far greater purpose to achieve. He asked me to consider creating a new empire before he died. A better empire, one that could bring together people from all the different lands and backgrounds. A greater empire that would rise above the others without sacrificing its soul in the process. It is my destiny to bring about a commonwealth of the people and to rule over them by popular demand and not by force of arms."

Tamerlan looked at the boy with newfound curiosity, his brow furrowed as he considered what was being offered. "And where do you think you will raise this commonwealth of people to rule over all of the other empires?" he asked somewhat skeptical.

"This is madness," came the outburst from General Soseong, who could no longer sit in silence. "This is the ravings of a boy, without any knowledge regarding the realities of this world. Utter nonsense, if you ask me."

"I was not asking," Tamerlan shut down the general's protestations immediately. "I said to you general, either sit quietly or leave. It is time for you to leave now."

"But this is my tent."

"Leave!" Tamerlan's tome indicated he would tolerate the general's presence no longer. Grumbling under his breath, General Soseong left begrudgingly.

"And how will you create this new empire," Tamerlan asked Mar Yanqa to explain.

Not me...us," he looked squarely at Tamerlan as he answered his question. "The Emperor has no heirs worth speaking of," Mar Yanqa said, his eyes now focused on the Khitan leader. "Even if his sons do come to the throne, they will not last long. "But there is another path. I offer you this—not as a king, but as a partner in something greater. I do not value the throne of China, as my uncle Hsuan Wu Ti does. I seek to make something new. A new kingdom—a new nation built on respect, loyalty, and freedom. You are a man who understands power. But more importantly, you also understand survival. Join me in this. Help me rebuild this land, not through bloodshed and conquest, but through alliances and respect. First we bring all the Khitan together. Then all of the Xianbei. Help me show the world that the future belongs to those who unite, not to those that continually divide through bloodshed."

Tamerlan was silent for a long while, his piercing gaze never leaving the young prince. How was it even possible that the boy knew exactly what he himself wanted to achieve. It was as if he had read his mind. The boy just wanted to unite all the people. He didn't even care about who rules as long as the people were treated fairly.

"Your son speaks with wisdom far beyond his age," Tamerlan commented to the Princess who sat patiently in the tent.

"He speaks like his father," she stated proudly.

"What you offer, young prince, can be infinitely more valuable than gold," Tamerlan said slowly, his voice quieter than before. "You offer a vision that I didn't believe was achievable before. A vision that I once had but abandoned. And I don't know why, but I believe you may have the ability to make it happen. You offer a chance to build something new from the ashes of the old. Something that might last as an eternal legacy to both our names."

Mar Yanqa nodded, his expression serious. "Yes. Something that will last forever. Will you and you Khitan clan stand by me?"

There was a new fire that shone in Tamerlan's eyes, a fire that mirrored the ambition of the boy before him. For a moment, the chaos of the battlefield seemed distant, as if the promise of something greater had already begun to take shape in the air around them.

Tamerlan stepped forward and placed his hand on Mar Yanqa's shoulder, his grip firm. "Then we will make this bond a reality. Not just with weapons, but with our hearts and our minds. If you speak the truth, young prince, then I will walk this path with you. Together, we will carve a future of our own choosing."

Mar Yanqa, who stood almost as tall as Tamerlan placed his right hand on Tamerlan's shoulder. "Then we are agreed," he declared.

The two of them walked out of the tent together followed by the Princess She-Ping. General Soseong had not gone far after his dismissal, waiting almost at the tent flap for them to emerge.

"General, I will accept you offer but with some added conditions. I take your offer of gold and horses, and the armor stripped from the empire's soldiers. Mar Yanqa and all his people that you have incarcerated will come with me. Those that remain of General Hermantius's brigade, I understand were originally part of the armed escort of the Princess, provided by her husband, they will come with me as well. In return, you have my pledge to continue our alliance. That is my promise to you. Let it be done."

Soseong stood back, his heart suddenly filled with fear. These two working together could prove to be a foe eventually. He had not expected this. An unexpected alliance forged not through gold or land, but through the strength of a vision. It had been his experience that men are most dangerous when they are pursuing a dream. He could only pray that they would not turn their attention to the Korean peninsula any time soon. Tamerlan had left him with no choice in the matter.

Chapter 10: 513 AD

The wind howled through the vast, open steppes, carrying with it the unmistakable scent of the untamed wilderness. The land was wild here, unmarked by the hands of man, yet the Khitan had made it their own, living with the land rather than attempting to conquer it. The sun had risen with a sharp edge to its light, casting long shadows over the rugged cliffs where Mar Yanqa now stood, looking down at the world below with steady eyes.

At fourteen years old, the boy was no longer the helpless child who had arrived in the East five years ago, clinging to his mother's skirts. Mar Yanqa's mastery of horse riding was nothing short of a testament to the rigorous training and fierce discipline instilled in him by the Khitan warriors. In only a year spent among the steppe people, he had transformed from an urban dweller who had barely touched a horse to one of the finest riders the Khitan had seen in a generation. His bond with his horse was one of unspoken understanding, each movement fluid and natural, moving in unison as if the two were one creature.

Something had changed in Tamerlan from the first time he met Mar Yanqa. Though having several wives, none of them had ever produced a son and it was clear to him that the gods had wished it so. Although She-Ping's yurt was adjacent to his own, he never proceeded during the year to pursue the marriage that had been discussed with the Korean general. Instead, his focus had become Mar Yanqa, the son that he never had on his own. The bond between the two became inseparable, and because of Mar Yanqa's extraordinary size for a boy his age, those outside the tribe immediately assumed that the pair were father and son. She-Ping was relieved to see that her son had a role model he could look up to. For a time, Valentius had served that purpose, but as a military officer, he would never have been able to instill into young Mar Yanqa the necessary characteristics to be a ruler. Exactly what Tamerlan, as chieftain of one of the more powerful Khitan tribes was able to do.

It began with mastering horse riding. Tamerlan had watched Mar Yanqa fall many times, his youthful frame initially awkward and uncoordinated on the back of the horse. But instead of discouragement, Tamerlan had only offered encouragement, teaching the boy to respect the animal as much as he respected his own body. "A warrior without his horse is like a hunter without his bow," Tamerlan would often say, a mantra that had become etched into Mar Yanqa's mind. He learned quickly that the horse was not just a mount; it was an extension of himself, a partner in battle, a means of swift travel across the unforgiving steppes.

Soon after, Mar Yanqa learned to sit with the ease of a seasoned rider, his posture straight and strong, but never stiff. The Khitan rode with a sense of fluidity, always in sync with the rhythm of their steeds, and Mar Yanqa was no different. Whether galloping across the plains or maneuvering through the narrow paths of the mountains, his body adapted to the horse's movements without conscious thought. His legs gripped the sides of the horse with the subtle strength of someone who had been trained to ride from an early age, and his hands, the size of bear paws, had grown strong, steadying the reins with the practiced skill of a warrior.

Where many others relied on brute force to control their horses, Mar Yanqa had learned to guide his steed with the lightest of touches, coaxing the animal into obedience with an almost imperceptible shift of his weight. He could make the horse stop, turn, and pivot with a single thought, a motion as graceful as a bird in flight. His movements were always timed perfectly with the horse's, a seamless union of man and animal that looked effortless to anyone who watched, though only Mar Yanqa knew the amount of sweat and discipline it had taken to achieve this harmony.

Next in his training program was the art of wrestling. Every Khitan boy, whether large or small had to learn how to wrestle. It was the chief form of entertainment within the tribe and often it was the way in which they would settle arguments that arose between the families. Tamerlan stood tall and imposing in front of the young Mar Yanqa. But the fourteen-year-old was already a solid mass of muscles and raw determination. Tamerlan's size was certainly intimidating, yet there was something unmistakably eager in Mar Yanqa's eyes, as if he had been waiting for the day when he would finally learn how to wrestle with the skill and grace of the Khitan masters.

Tamerlan grinned, his deep, gravelly voice carrying the weight of years of wisdom. "Strength Mar Yanqa, is not your ally today," he said, slapping his palm against the boy's broad chest. "You're as strong as a bear, but a bear is a clumsy oaf. We're not bears here."

Mar Yanqa furrowed his brow. "Then what do you want me to do, if wrestling isn't about strength?"

Tamerlan raised an eyebrow. "Speed and agility are your true weapons. The power lies in your ability to move faster than your opponent can think."

The boy's large hands flexed, itching for a chance to prove himself. Tamerlan took a step back and motioned for him to approach. "We'll start with the basics," he said. "You're going to try and throw me. Go on, use your strength!"

Mar Yanqa lunged, his muscled arms swinging toward Tamerlan, his eyes blazing with intensity. The older man moved with such speed it was like he vanished when he sidestepped the assault. Mar Yanqa's powerful grip found nothing but air, and suddenly, Tamerlan's leg was behind his knee, sending him toppling over in a heap of confusion and embarrassment.

Tamerlan chuckled heartily as the boy lay sprawled on the ground, blinking in disbelief. "You thought you could just muscle me down like a boulder? Speed, my boy. Speed." He helped Mar Yanqa to his feet with a playful shove. "Now, try again—but remember, it's all in the timing."

Cheeks flushed with both exertion and frustration, Mar Yanqa wiped his brow and took a deep breath. This time, he focused less on his brute strength and more on the agility Tamerlan spoke of. When he lunged again, he was faster, more fluid in his movements, and with a precise twist of his body, he managed to hook Tamerlan's leg and throw him off balance. The older man staggered and tumbled backward, landing with an exaggerated thud that had both of them laughing.

Tamerlan rose, shaking his head in mock surprise. "Well, I'll be. You've learned the first lesson: strength may be your gift, but speed and skill will always be the victor." He clapped Mar Yanqa on the back so hard the boy almost toppled over. "Well done, boy! You've got the heart of a warrior now. Just remember, always move with the wind, not with the boulder."

Mar Yanqa stood taller, grinning wide. He hadn't just learned how to wrestle today, he'd learned how to dance with his opponent. The way to win was to outwit them with speed and precision. It didn't matter how big or muscled he was, his true strength lay in his ability to outthink and outmaneuver. Tamerlan, ever the teacher, knew that this lesson would stick with the young boy for years to come.

While under Tamerlan's private tutelage, Mar Yanqa had also become an expert in the use of the bow while riding, an essential skill for any Khitan warrior. The bow had always been a part of him, ever since the early days of his training under Valentius but now it had become an extension of his arm, as familiar as the reins of his horse. As he rode at full gallop, his body would instinctively lean back, drawing the bowstring taught in one smooth motion. He could shoot arrows with deadly accuracy, his aim unerring even as his horse thundered across the open plains. He had practiced this many times under Tamerlan's watchful eye, learning to shoot over the horse's neck and past its ears, to hit targets at full speed, and to do so with precision.

Tamerlan, in his rare moments of exhibiting the pride he felt, would smile as Mar Yanqa hit target after target without fail. "You've learned well, boy," he would say, his tone gruff but filled with approval. "Not all warriors can ride like a Khitan, and fewer still can shoot like one. You've become something more than your bloodline. You've become a true Khitan."

Mar Yanqa had also mastered the art of the charge, a skill that was deeply embedded in Khitan warrior culture. He had learned to hold his posture firm, leaning slightly forward to add speed to his approach, always aiming for the heart of the enemy. The thundering sound of hooves pounding against the earth, the smell of the wind in his face, and the fierce joy of battle would fuel him as he charged with his comrades, arrows drawn, ready to strike at the straw targets.

But it wasn't just the battlefield that Mar Yanqa had conquered. He had also learned the art of the quiet ride, the moments when the land itself demanded silence and patience. He had ridden for hours, lost in the vastness of the steppe, his thoughts wandering like the endless horizon. His bond with his horse had grown to be something sacred, during these moments of solitude, they were alone in the world, with no one to see their movements, no one to judge their actions. It was in these silent rides that Mar Yanqa often found peace, the rhythmic motion of the horse's gait lulling him into a meditative state.

When he rode now, whether in battle or in peace, he was a reflection of the Khitan spirit: powerful, precise, and unyielding. His mastery of horse riding was not just a skill—it was a way of life. He had become one with the land, the horse, and the bow, and in doing so, he had earned his place among the Khitan, not just as a youth raised by them, but as a warrior in his own right. Under Tamerlan's watchful eyes, Mar Yanqa had been shaped into something else—something strong, something capable. His body had grown lean and incredibly even more muscular, his hands steady and precise, his mind sharpened by years of discipline. The young prince, though still bearing the blood of kings, had become a warrior in the truest sense of the word. And now, he was about to take the final step into adulthood—his initiation into the Khitan tribe, a rite of passage that would shape his future. It was time for the Bekutchi.

The very word was a challenge, a test, one that not only demanded physical prowess but mental fortitude. The ritual was simple but deadly: climb the cliffs, take an eagle's egg from its nest, return with it, and exchange it for a hatchling. In Khitan tradition, the eagle was a symbol of strength and vision, a bird capable of seeing the world from heights few others could reach. And just as the eagle had to be trained to obey its master, so too did Mar Yanqa have to prove that he could master the wilderness and his own body.

He mounted his horse, the great beast beneath him steady and strong. With a nod to Tamerlan, who stood a distance away, arms crossed over his chest, Mar Yanqa urged his horse forward. The cliffs loomed ahead, jagged and imposing. His heart beat with anticipation, and for a moment, he allowed himself to feel fear. But only for a moment. Fear would not serve him here.

The challenge of finding an eagle's nest on the cliff face was not one that Mar Yanqa had taken lightly. The cliff loomed high before him, a jagged and unforgiving wall of rock that seemed to stretch toward the heavens, as if daring him to scale it. He had seen this kind of test before, in the stories of the Khitan warriors and hunters, a rite of passage that marked the transition from boy to man. But the truth of it, now that he stood before it, was more terrifying than any tale he had ever heard.

Tamerlan had told him that this was the moment when he would prove himself, his strength, his resolve, and his ability to command nature itself. An eagle's egg, prized by the Khitan as a symbol of mastery and the bond between man and bird, was a rare gift, but it was also a deadly one to obtain. The eagles of the steppe were fierce protectors of their nests, their talons as sharp as knives, their beaks strong enough to crush bone. Mar Yanqa had to approach this challenge not only with skill, but with extreme caution, for one wrong move would lead to a fatal fall or an attack by the enraged eagles.

The wind howled through the cliffs, its biting cold seeping through Mar Yanqa's clothing as he began his ascent. His hands gripped the rocky ledges with a tension that sent sparks of pain up his forearms, but he dared not stop. The rocks were slick with moisture from the overnight dew, and as he scaled the sheer wall, each foothold and handhold had to be carefully tested before he committed his full weight. The thought of a fall sent his heart into a rapid beat, but there was no turning back. His eyes focused on the cliff's craggy surface ahead, searching for the faintest sign of the eagle's nest. It was somewhere near the top, where the rock face curved inward, a narrow ledge hidden by the shadows of the towering spires around it.

The climb was grueling. Mar Yanqa made his way up the cliffs, his arms burning with the effort, his legs aching from the strain. But he did not stop. Each step brought him closer to the eagle's nest, closer to proving his worth. It was dangerous work, and as he climbed higher, Mar Yanqa had to fight against the vertigo that threatened to overwhelm him. His legs trembled with every movement, his body pressed against the rough stone, yet his eyes stayed fixed ahead. His thoughts were focused on the task, pushing away the fear, even as the wind threatened to tear him from his meager perch.

After what felt like an eternity, Mar Yanqa finally spotted the nest. It was nestled into a crevice, partially hidden by overhanging branches of a stunted tree that clung to the cliff face, its roots digging deep into the stone. The nest was large, woven from twigs and grasses, and within it, there lay several eggs, large and pale with dark speckles, cradled in the soft fibers of the nest. They were the object of his quest, but as he neared it, a dark shadow passed overhead. Near the top, the wind swept across the rocky heights, but Mar Yanqa did not falter. He could see the faint outline of the eagle now perched on the edge, guarding the prize. It would be dangerous. The eagle would not surrender one of its eggs willlingly.

But Mar Yanqa had learned much in his time among the Khitan. He understood that to take what he needed, he must first understand the bird, must show that he was worthy. Carefully, he approached the nest, moving with quiet precision, his heart beating steadily as the eagle watched from its perch. It was his moment now. He reached into the nest and could almost feel one of the eggs with his fingertips. The eagle on the perch let out a sharp cry, but it did not strike. Instead, it was calling out to its mate. Mar Yanqa froze.

A sharp, piercing cry echoed through the air in response to the male's call. The mother eagle was circling above, her keen eyes spotting him in an instant. Whereas the male was large, the female was huge and far more threatening. The wind seemed to stop as the bird began to dive, her wings outstretched, her talons bared for the strike. Mar Yanqa's heart skipped a beat, his instincts screaming to climb back down. But there was nowhere to retreat. The ledge was too narrow, the climb too steep. He had no choice but to keep moving closer to the nest, praying that the eagle wouldn't reach him in time.

His fingers closed around the rim of the nest, and he gingerly reached inside, his body poised and balanced as he tried to take one of the eggs. It was heavier than he had anticipated, its smooth surface cold under his fingertips. He could feel the mother eagle's presence now, her shrill cries growing louder as she wheeled above him. But he could not afford to hesitate. With a steadying breath, he gently lifted the egg, taking care not to disturb it too much, as if the very act of removing it would provoke the mother into a frenzied attack.

Just as he began to withdraw his hand, the eagle struck. With a powerful thrust of her wings, she slammed into the cliffside near him, sending a shower of rocks tumbling down the face. The impact reverberated through his body, knocking him off balance. His heart thundered in his chest as his hand slipped from the egg for a split second, but he quickly recovered, his grip tightening around the fragile object. The eagle swooped again, her talons scraping across his arm, and for a heartbeat, he thought she would tear him from the cliff altogether. The force of her attack left his skin burning with pain, but he held on firmly, unwilling to let go of the prize he had come for.

A rush of wind blasted past him as the eagle made a final, desperate dive. Mar Yanqa ducked, his face pressed into the stone as the bird passed just inches above him. The talons missed, but his nerves were on fire, his body trembling with the sheer intensity of the near-miss. He realized as long as he held on to the egg she would not directly attack, for fear that he would drop her precious egg. He quickly withdrew his arm, cradling the egg close to his chest as he looked up to see the eagle retreating, still circling above in a futile attempt to drive him away. "Do not worry momma," he shouted to the sky, "I will take good care of your baby." The eagle did not launch another dive as if she understood.

Now came the true test. Mar Yanqa had the egg, but his challenge wasn't over. He still had to make his way down the cliff with the precious prize in hand—if he failed, it would be the end. He placed the egg carefully into the sling around his neck. The descent was treacherous. His body ached from the climb, and his fingers were raw from gripping the jagged rocks. Every step down felt more perilous than the last, as his body tensed with the knowledge that a single misstep could send him plummeting to the ground below.

The wind howled again, this time as if mocking him, tugging at his hair and whipping his cloak around his body. His heart was a steady drumbeat in his ears as he moved, inch by inch, lower and lower. Each movement was calculated, each shift of his weight designed to find the safest path down. He could feel his legs shaking from exhaustion, his muscles begging him to stop, but he couldn't. Not now.

Finally, after what felt like hours, he reached a narrow ledge just above the ground. His hands were shaking as he lowered himself down, using his legs for support. As his feet hit solid ground, he let out a breath he didn't realize he had been holding. His heart was still pounding, the adrenaline coursing through his veins. The eagle, for the moment, had retreated, her presence no longer a threat. But Mar Yanqa knew she would be watching him from the skies, ever vigilant for the rest of his life to see if he kept his promise.

His journey down had been just as perilous as his climb, and as he stood there on the solid earth, he could still feel the rawness of the experience. He reflected on how close he had come to falling, to losing everything in a single instant. He had succeeded. The egg was safe, and he was alive. But for a moment, just a moment, he had truly understood what it meant to risk everything for something greater than himself.

As he made his way back to the Khitan camp, the weight of the egg in his hands felt different—he was not just carrying a fragile object, but the symbol of his passage from boyhood to manhood. The lesson had been taught in the most brutal of ways, and it had been earned through blood, sweat, and fear. And now, with the eagle's egg safely in his grasp, Mar Yanqa was ready to face the challenge his father had given him with Hermantius's last breath.

Chapter 11: 514 AD

Mar Yanqa's right hand brushed the smooth feathers of the eagle perched on his left arm. He named it Sepor and the bird had been with him now for six months, its sharp eyes and powerful wings serving as a reminder to remain focused on the singular task ahead. As an eaglet, it had learned to follow his signals, to stay perched on his arm as he rode, to hunt at his command. It was his companion, his challenge, and what would soon be, his test.

Tamerlan had said little as Mar Yanqa prepared for this day. The Khitan leader had always been a man of action, not words but Mar Yanqa knew what was expected of him. This test was not just about strength; it was about connection. A connection to the land, to the bird, to the Khitan way, and most of all to the earth.

He did not hesitate as he mounted his horse and began the long journey into the wilderness. The landscape rolled beneath him in shades of brown and green, the horse's hooves pounding the earth in a steady rhythm. His mind was clear, focused on the mission that all Khitan boys had to perform on their road to manhood. He urged his stallion eastward, where the sky met the endless curve of the grasslands. He was fifteen now and the time had come for his trial as a provider. Not a ceremony necessarily of manhood, but one of bone, silence, and mastering the harsh breath of the land.

Strapped to his box-saddle was a quiver of bone-tipped arrows, a curved hunting knife, and slung across his shoulder, the precious weight of Sepor, resplendent in feathers of burnished gold. Sepor's claws dug into the thick leather epaulet on Mar Yanqa's left shoulder. His golden hood was drawn down to keep his hunger sharp. The boy whispered to the bird perched on his shoulder. "Today we will hunt wild goats, my winged brother." Sepor turned his head slightly, sensing the intent beneath the words.

By the end of the first day, Mar Yanqa had not seen another soul. No smoke on the horizon, no footprints in the soft, moist ground. Only the wind and the long mournful howl of wolves carried across the hills. That night, he wrapped himself in horse-hide and crouched beside the rocks while Sepor perched silently above him, eyes reflecting the river of stars.

The next morning, they ate the few hard cakes and dried berries that were packed for the journey. If he wanted more food, the he'd have to catch it for himself. Hunger clawed at him. The cold licked at his bones. But he was not afraid. He spoke little, conserving his breath, but his eyes roamed ceaselessly, scanning slopes and ridges. He looked for shadow, for movement, for the unmistakable flick of a goat's horn cresting a rise. Sepor, too, listened. His hood remained on during the long hours of travel, but sometimes the bird would shift and tighten his claws when something stirred far in the grass.

That afternoon he saw the tracks. Not fresh, but close. A small herd of ibex, the wild goats of the rocks. They had crossed a distant gully where snow had settled in the creases of the land. Their hooves had cracked the ice.

Mar Yanqa crouched, pulling back Sepor's hood. The eagle stood tall, as if growing larger with the unveiling of his sight. The boy and the eagle shared a long look. It knew exactly what he wanted. Then the bird launched skyward, wings slicing the air, gaining height in spirals. Mar Yanqa followed on foot, careful not to spook the herd. He moved low, light-footed, like the hunters of old whose names had been lost to time.

Then he saw them. Seven ibex, gray and lean, picking their way across a craggy incline. One lagged behind. Limping. A younger male, perhaps injured in a recent fight. Mar Yanqa made the signal with his whistle. From the clouds came Sepor, silent as a ray of moonlight. The young ibex looked up too late. The eagle struck like a thrown axe, talons extended, body coiled, slamming into the goat's neck. The two tumbled in a burst of dust and hooves. Mar Yanqa ran, knife in hand, and ended the animal's struggle with a clean cut across the neck, severing carotid and jugulars.

He knelt. Pressed his forehead to the goat's flank. "Thank you Lord for the food you have provided. Forgive me for taking the life of that which you have created," he murmured. Then, to Sepor, "One. But the wind tells me another waits."

He could have turned back. The first kill was enough to prove his worth. But something stirred in him, a hunger not for meat, but mastery. The sky had begun to close, a storm brewing in the west. His horse was skittish, but Mar Yanqa rode on. Sepor rested on his shoulder, blood still drying on his talons, feathers slightly ruffled.

They found the second herd deeper into the highlands, near a half-frozen stream beneath a jutting black cliff. These goats were larger, older, and twice as wary. For them, a direct approach would not work. Mar Yanqa climbed, flanking from above, pressing his belly to the cold stone. He watched. Waited. Chose a wide-horned male grazing apart from the others. But suddenly the wind shifted. A stone slid from under Mar Yanqa's foot. The goats bolted. He shouted, "Now, Sepor!"

The eagle soared like a hurled spear, this time flying low, threading through boulders, gaining speed. The goat leapt between rocks, trying to evade. Sepor adjusted in midair with impossible grace and struck the beast full in the spine, driving him to the ground. The crash echoed down the cliffs. The animal did not die instantly. Mar Yanqa raced down, breath burning in his chest, and wrestled the goat by the horns. It bucked once, twice, then his knife found its mark again.

Another prayer but this time an apology for taking so long to make the kill. He stood panting, blood on his hands, dust in his hair. Sepor circled overhead once, then descended to perch on a rock, watching his master with something like pride.

When he returned to the camp two days later, the Khitan tribe had already gathered to prepare for the feast. Mar Yanqa came riding into camp with two goats lashed to his horse, his face blackened by the sun and wind. Sepor perched on a high saddle-horn, feathers radiant in the morning light. A few of the elders gathered, whispering. His mother, who was waiting by the path, wept quietly with pride but did not step forward.

Instead, it was the old falconer who approached. "You have crossed the sky and the stone. You have not spoken to men in many days. Who returned today, the boy who left, or someone else?"

Mar Yanqa looked at the eagle, then at the vast horizon behind him. "I returned with Sepor," he said. "But I left my weakness and the boy out there."

And then they feasted. The smell of roasting sheep and rabbit meat was already filling the air, and the sound of the warriors' laughter echoed across the plains. Tamerlan stood near the center of the gathering, a proud look on his weathered face. But there was a new fire in his eyes as he saw Mar Yanqa approach, his eagle perched with pride on his shoulder and two fat goats draped over his horse. From the day they first met, there had always been a connection between the two of them and not even a natural father could have felt any prouder than Tamerlan did at this moment. "You have returned," Tamerlan said simply, his voice low and approving. He nodded toward the goats. "Two. A fine achievement."

Mar Yanqa dismounted, smiling with quiet satisfaction. The challenge had been met, and the tribe would now feast even better. The instruction for his hunt was to bring back one wild goat. Two was seen as a blessing.

But it was not just the feast that had been prepared in anticipation of Mar Yanqa's return. His mother, She-Ping was also busy preparing a very special surprise for him. In the days following the return with the goats, a special event had been arranged according to his father's wishes. A decade earlier, Mar Zutra had explained all the details to his wife, so that when the time came, their son would be welcomed into the embrace of his Judean ancestors as well. The priests who had accompanied him and his mother on their journey had been busy, setting up a podium and preparing the sacred scroll. On the seventh day, Mar Yanqa would stand before the gathered people, not just as a Khitan warrior, but as a man in the eyes of his father's people. It was a rare and exclusive honor, one that none of the Khitan could claim for themselves. The Khitan would feast, and the priests would perform the sacred rites, the sacred jar of olive oil that She-Ping had carried with her from Mahoza would be poured over her son's head, and Mar Yanqa would rise, proclaimed both as a man and the rightful king of his people in the eyes of God. It was already well into his fifteenth year and time for him to become a man.

As the seventh day began, an electrifying sensation filled the camp. No one knew exactly what to expect but that didn't stop the excitement from building towards a crescendo. The morning sun had just begun to rise over the vast steppe, casting a golden halo across the land, the kind of light that seemed to burn with promise and possibilities. It was now officially the seventh day, the day that Mar Yanqa would be declared a man in the eyes of his father's ancestors. The warriors gathered around the podium, eager to see something new, and the women prepared the food. The camp was a sea of life and movement. The air was thick with anticipation of the event, and for the feast that would follow. The flames of the cook fire seemed to dance as Mar Yanqa emerged from his family's yurt, and all eyes which thus far had been drawn to the priests performing their rituals and the carriage of the sacred scrolls were now immediately drawn to him.

The moment he stepped out into the light, time itself appeared to stop. The world paused and took a deep breath. The birds, the wind, the distant chatter, all fell away in an instant. It was as if the earth itself had gasped and then exhaled in astonishment. For Mar Yanqa, who had already become a skilled rider, a fierce archer, and a capable young warrior, today was faced with a different kind of battle. Today, he was not just the boy who had fought for the respect of the Khitan; today, he wore his father's legacy and would now have to live up to an immeasurable expectation.

The robe he wore shimmered, catching the first rays of the sun, and then suddenly burst into a kaleidoscope of dazzling colors; reds, blues, greens, and yellows. All blending together in a wash of brilliance that seemed almost otherworldly. No one gathered around the podium had ever seen a robe like it. It glowed like liquid fire, each gem sewn into the fabric catching the sunlight and reflecting it back with a brilliance that made it seem as though the heavens themselves had descended to bless him. The robe was heavy, as it was made of the finest silk, embroidered with the images of pomegranates and lilies, each thread meticulously woven with golden and silver filigree. But to Mar Yanqa it felt as light as an autumn mist. The stones and jewels, consisting of sapphires, rubies, obsidian and emeralds, seemed to dance and sparkle as if they were alive, each one symbolizing a part of his father's heritage and what he would now claim as his own. This was the sacred robe of the King's of Mahoza, and now it was Mar Yanqa's to wear.

Mar Yanqa stood tall, his chest broad, his shoulders square, the jeweled robe flowing around him in waves of color. The colors were so vivid, so sharp, that they made everything else in the world seem muted by comparison. The robe was a living testament to his bloodline, to his father's legacy and his mother's love. The jewels, ancient, priceless, representative tokens of a ruler's power, seemed almost too perfect. It was the very same robe his father had worn on the day he married She-Ping, the day he had carved out his own destiny as a man of power and dignity. Now it adorned the son who would carry that legacy forward.

To all, it was a breathtaking display. A brilliant cascade of color that filled the morning with its own light. To the Khitan tribe to which he now belonged, it was an event that all present would remember and talk about until the day they died. It was beyond the limits of the Khitan imagination, beyond the boundaries of what they thought was possible. Of course they had heard of such garments, woven by the finest artisans, worn by kings and emperors of distant lands but no one ever imagined that they would see one for themselves. But here, on the rugged plains of the steppe, Mar Yanqa was the living embodiment of all those stories and fables that surrounded ancient kings. He was not just the son of She-Ping, a Chinese Princess, he was also the son of a great man, Mar Zutra. A man the Khitan had never met but could only assume he would have been as great as the robe suggested. This robe spoke of that heritage, that power, and the future they all would inherit together being part of the world to which Mar Yanqa belonged.

  She-Ping stood at the back of the podium, her hands clasped tightly together in a white-knuckled grip. Her heart swelled with pride, but it was a bittersweet emotion. As her son stepped out, so resplendent in his father's robe, a wave of memories washed over her of the man who had worn it before him, the man she had loved deeply and who had shared a dream with her that now seemed so distant. Her Mar Zutra, whose memory had been a steady companion through the years of hardship, had always been a figure of strength, a beacon for her in moments of doubt. So great was her memory of her departed husband that she could never give herself to another man. She knew all this time that Tamerlan had desired to make her one of his wives, but he seemed to understand her inability to love again and never pressed her for a decision.

  Despite what he could have easily interpreted as rejection, he still took Mar Yanqa under his wing and treated him as if he was his own son, for which she would be eternally grateful. But being grateful, and admiring Tamerlan for being the kind, generous and patient man that he was, could still not fill the emptiness she carried in her heart. A hole that she knew she could never fill. But this day was not about her, it belonged to her son and she suppressed the memories of a husband that would never return to her, at least until she left the world of the living herself.

  But here was her husband again, present in the boy standing before her, the boy she had raised alone these past eight years, who had risen to the challenge and was ready to fulfill his destiny. She could hardly contain the surge of emotion that expanded her chest. It was as though Mar Zutra was standing alongside her. She felt him in the weight of the robe, in the glimmer of the jewels that shone like his spirit, as if they were the stars of his soul, burning brightly in her son's heart. It was too much and she could not hold back her tears, though she had tried for her son's sake. A mixture of pride, grief, joy and longing overwhelmed her all at once. Mar Yanqa's face was solemn, but his eyes held the same fierce determination his father had once possessed. The robe, though dazzling, only highlighted the inner strength that had always been a part of him. There was no doubt, her son had become the man he was meant to be.

Mar Yanqa stood for a long moment, the light from the sun catching each jewel on his robe, cascading in flashes of color that filled the air. The assembled Khitan warriors and elders stood in stunned silence, their mouths agape at the sight before them. It was a rare thing for a boy to appear so fully formed, so entirely imbued with power and promise. Yes, he was taller and more strongly built than any other boy his age, but it was as if the very earth had carved him from its bones and clothed him in the riches of the heavens. They had not seen a display like this before, and they did not know whether to bow or shout in awe and praise.

Then, slowly, the silence began to break. Murmurs rippled through the crowd, growing louder with each passing moment. Words like "blessed" and "chosen" were passed between them, and even the most stoic among them, hardened by years of war and life on the steppe, could not contain the fascination they felt for the boy, now a man, that stood before them.

Mar Yanqa looked towards his mother and his gaze softened just a little as he caught her eye. At that moment, he stood still, the proud son, the legacy of his father embodied in his every movement and She-Ping could feel her heart surge with love for him, for this boy who had grown so quickly, so fiercely, and so beautifully. Though she still saw in him the reflection of her parted husband, she also saw the promise of a new era, one that would rise from the ashes of everything that had come before. This was a promise of a new age and Mar Yanqa was destined to be its herald.

As Mar Yanqa stepped forward to the center of the gathering, the wind seemed to grow stronger, as if it, too, recognized the significance of the moment. The sun, climbing higher in the sky, poured down in full force, illuminating his robe, sending sparks of color ricocheting through the air. The earth beneath him seemed to tremble in reverence as the Khitan began their chants, their voices rising in unison, calling him into the next phase of his life, into manhood, into the legacy of his father and the future of his people.

Mar Yanqa then ascended the steps of the podium and stood before the priests that had traveled with them from Mahoza. Dressed in their white robes and turbans, the priests began their blessings in the ancient language of his father, the Hebrew that was written into the very first scroll dictated by Moses one thousand, eight hundred and fifty years before. The priests recited their prayers and blessings and then pointed to the section that had been reserved for Mar Yanqa to read. It was the very first chapter of the first book and it began with 'Bereshith' or in the beginning. Standing tall, he took the sacred scroll in his hands and began to recite the words of his ancestors. This passage from the holy texts of his father's people, a reminder of the sacred duty that bound him to his bloodline, explained that all existence came from God and mankind must never forget to whom they owe their lives. His voice rang out clear and strong, the words filling the air, carried by the wind. The priests situated among the people would translate the words as Mar Yanqa read them into the Khitan language so that everyone would hear the words of God and understand them. The Khitan shamans would then dance and wave their feathered wands, as if spreading the words so that they would shower down upon all the people.

The Khitan listened in silence, with nothing but respect in their eyes. This boy, who had once been a stranger, now stood before them not just as their future leader but as a man in his own right. A man who had been tested by the elements, by the land, and by his people's faith. A man that was destined one day to take over the leadership of the tribe from Tamerlan.

As he finished reading, the crowd erupted into applause. The priests began to chant, their voices rising in unison, while the tribal shamans danced, and the celebration began in earnest.

The meat from at least six goats was shared, fermented milk flowed freely, and the warriors of the Khitan tribe roared with their approval. Tamerlan, standing at the front of the circle, gave Mar Yanqa a quiet nod of approval. "You have become a man among your ancestors, young prince," Tamerlan said, his voice thick with emotion, which he could no longer mask. "Not just in blood, but in spirit. The Khitan now call you brother."

Mar Yanqa smiled, feeling the weight of the moment settle upon him. This was his tribe now, his people. And though the future was uncertain, he knew that whatever path lay ahead, he was no longer to be considered the boy who had arrived in this land years ago. He had emerged from a chrysalis as something far more; a warrior, a man, and the future for what was destined to become a new nation.

As the feast continued throughout the day into the early evening, Mar Yanqa looked around at the faces of those who had become his family. The Khitan had welcomed him, had trained him, had made him one of their own. And now, together, they would forge something new. A future that was no longer defined by bloodshed and old empires, but by unity and vision. It was his father's dream, his uncle Hermantius's last wish and for the first time, Mar Yanqa could actually envision it coming to fruition. More so, it was the first time, Mar Yanqa felt the weight of his father's legacy not as a burden, but as a beacon—a light guiding him toward a future that he would create with his own hands. The land before him was vast, but it would be his now, and with his eagle once again perched upon his shoulder, he felt ready to soar.

The air was thick with the heavy scent of roasting meat, the crackle of firewood, and the murmurs of the Khitan gathered around the bonfires. Laughter and music rang through the night, blending with the rhythmic drumming of warriors celebrating Mar Yanqa's ascent to manhood. The night seemed perfect, bright with stars, the soft hum of the wind, a lullaby against the vastness of the steppes.

Chapter 12: 514 AD

It was close to the midnight hour when the tribe's sentries began to blow their warnings from their outposts, sounding the distinct melody on their ram's horns. Strangers were approaching, a lot of them. The timing could not have been worse. On the steppes, no one approached another tribe in the dark unless it was to take advantage of a night to attack. Drunk on the fermented goat's milk they had been drinking all day, and now only a few of the warriors were in any condition to fight.

From the shadows of the distant hills, a thunderous sound broke the serenity, causing a wave of panic to spread over the partiers. Hooves, dozens, possibly hundreds, pounding the earth in unison. It was a war cry, unmistakable and wild, growing louder by the second. The fires flared higher, casting flickering light as Tamerlan's tribe scrambled to their feet, eyes darting toward the approaching storm.

And there he was. The chieftain of the Borjigin tribe emerging from the darkness—Qatun.

He rode in with all the might of his warriors behind him, a mass of figures clothed in fur and leather, their presence overpowering as they entered the camp like a shadow descending on the moon. The earth trembled beneath their feet, the sound of their horses' hooves rolling like thunder over the land. Qatun's stature alone was enough to silence the crowd; he was a mountain of a man, thick with muscle, twice the size of any ordinary Khitan, his face a jagged map of battles won, his eyes cold as the winter wind. He came not as a friend, but as a conqueror. Already the majority of the Khitan tribes had fallen under his command and those that resisted had ceased to exist.

The tribe of Tamerlan, who had been reveling all day with unbridled joy, suddenly found themselves muted by Qatun's presence. Many of the elders, still loyal to their own ancient ways, knelt before him, recognizing his authority. Qatun's eyes scanned the crowd, his gaze landing on Mar Yanqa. The boy still dared to wear the robe of kings. A robe that glimmered like a thousand stars in the firelight.

Mar Yanqa stood tall, his fists clenched, his eyes meeting Qatun's without flinching. Though Qatun was still larger in size, it was obvious to anyone that even at his young age, Mar Yanqa was also a pillar of strength. A silence swept over the camp as the chieftain's voice cracked through the tension.

"Give me that robe, boy," Qatun's voice boomed, a command as heavy as a stone falling into a well. "It's mine by right, and maybe, just maybe, I will spare your life if you kneel before me."

The words hung in the air like a poison-dipped dagger in the heart of Tamerlan's camp. But Mar Yanqa, his gaze unwavering, opened his mouth and spoke, his voice steady but laced with defiance.

"You are not our king and we do not kneel for the likes of you. My tribe has no king but God," he declared, his voice carrying the weight of a thousand warriors. "We bow before no man."

Gasps rippled through the gathered crowd. It was unheard of, heretical in some ways. But Mar Yanqa's heart beat with the fire of his ancestors, and he was not about to kneel to any man. No matter how powerful, no matter how much force was at Qatun's disposal, Mar Yanqa's faith in God convinced him that everything would be fine. The light from the fire reflected off the gemstones of his robe, making him shine with the glow of a king, only serving to fuel Qatun with contempt and anger.

Qatun's face twisted into a mask of rage. He was a man who took what he wanted, by force or by fear. He had crushed any resistance, destroyed every rival, and now he turned to Mar Yanqa, this upstart, this boy who dared defy him.

"You think you can challenge me?" Qatun sneered, his voice filled with derision. "You would offer your life so easily, little whelpling? You think that robe, those jewels, give you some magical power? I'll take them from your corpse boy, and I'll take all you hold dear as well. I hear there is a Chinese princess in this camp. She will be spreading her legs before me by the time morning breaks."

But Mar Yanqa did not shrink away. Instead, he straightened further, his jaw set, and he spoke, his voice cutting through the air like a blade. "I do not wish to fight you, Qatun. It is not my wish to kill you. I offer you my hospitality. Come, join us in the feast. Share the bond of our people, and let us talk of unity, and of respect. But if you wish to take by force that which is mine by birthright, then I will remind you of the Khitan way. The laws of our people to which you are bound as well."

Qatun's lips curled into a mocking smile. "The Khitan way?" He scoffed. "What could a boy like you know of the Khitan way? You are a stray, a mongrel that Khitan mercy spared, which was not our way."

"The Khitan way," Mar Yanqa said calmly, "is the way of this land. We wrestle. The strongest man takes the tribe. If you are worthy of it, prove it. Or are you afraid?"

Qatun's laughter was like thunder, echoing across the plain. "You want to wrestle me?" His chest shook with mirth. "I am twice your size, boy. I have lived thrice as long. You think you can match me? You want to die that badly?"

But Mar Yanqa's eyes were sharp. "What are you willing to forfeit, Qatun? What are you willing to lose? State it now, so that all will hear and bind us to our contract."

The question cut deep. For the first time, Qatun paused, his eyes narrowing as he sized up the boy before him. Then, with a great, rumbling laugh, he replied,

"If I lose, you will have all the tribes I command.   And... I will give you my daughter, Alan-Ko, as your wife.   She has been widowed too long but no other man has been fit to replace him.   Defeat me and she is yours. The most beautiful woman on the steppes.   Now state what you are willing to forfeit, boy!"

Mar Yanqa briefly looked towards Tamerlan to see if he would be in agreement.   Without any exchange of words, Tamerlan nodded his head.

"If I lose, you will have this tribe to command as yours.   You will have my father's jeweled robe to wear as your own.   And you will have the Princess She-Ping to saddle your cock as your concubine.   Are you man enough to agree? Why do you hesitate?"

The promises hung in the air, reverberating through the crowd, their murmurs rising like a wave. To claim such a prize, the daughter of Qatun, the fairest of them all, Queen of the Borjigin as they named her, would elevate Mar Yanqa to a level of power no one could imagine. Even the most hardened Khitan warriors, who had fought alongside him and watched his rise, found themselves awestruck by the implications of Qatun's words.

But even more so, for Qatun to possibly have a Chinese princess bound to his bed would elevate Qatun to a level almost equal to the Emperor.   The stakes of this match were unparalleled by any that may have come prior and would likely neve come close to being equaled again.

Mar Yanqa looked around the gathered crowd and spoke again, his voice clear, like a bell tolling in the night. "You have heard both his and my promise," Mar Yanqa called out. "If I win, I will take his tribes and his daughter.   Qatun's strength and power will be all mine.   If I lose, you will all kneel to him as your leader and he will take all that I cherish.   That is the Khitan way.   That is the law of the land."

Then, turning to the priests, Mar Yanqa dropped to one knee, a signal to those who shared his faith. "Pray for me," he asked, his voice filled with reverence. "Bless me with the strength of Samson, that I might walk this path of blood and survive."

The priests raised their hands, murmuring prayers in the ancient Hebrew tongue, calling on the one and only God to grant the boy strength and courage. And as the last words of the prayer echoed through the camp, Mar Yanqa stood, his fists clenched, his eyes flashing with determination.   "Shall we begin," he challenged.

Qatun dismounted, his size towering over the boy by at least half a head. His warriors gathered around, forming a solid ring, their eyes wide with anticipation.   The tension in the air was palpable. The firelight danced over Qatun's muscled but scarred frame, but in Mar Yanqa's eyes burned the fire of his ancestors; the fire of those who had built kingdoms, of those who had fought for something greater than themselves.   The night air was thick with anticipation, charged with a crackling energy that made every muscle in Mar Yanqa's body tense with readiness. Around him, the camp fell silent, as if time itself held its breath. Against the seasoned Khitan chieftain, Mar Yanqa still looked like a boy. Large, heavily muscled, but still a boy. The firelight flickered, casting long, dancing shadows across the dirt, illuminating the two combatants—the giant of a man, Qatun, and the boy-turned-warrior, Mar Yanqa.

With a single roar, Qatun lunged forward, his massive hands reaching for Mar Yanqa's throat. The ground beneath them shook as their bodies collided in a grapple of strength and will. Qatun's size also made him slow, and that was to Mar Yanqa's advantage. But Qatun's face, lined with years of bloodshed, twisted into a cruel grin. He knew the advantage he held. He had fought men twice Mar Yanqa's age, crushed them under his overwhelming size and strength. His was the style of the bear, grapple, hold and bury his opponent beneath his overbearing weight.

Mar Yanqa's style was very different. Like that of the wolf. Fierce and far more agile, and his muscles, while large and well formed, they were lean with purpose. He was fast, precise, and above all, he had learned while wrestling with Tamerlan, how to use his opponent's own strength and size against him. The boy's eyes met Qatun's with an unflinching gaze, a silent challenge that echoed through the stillness.

Mar Yanqa twisted, ducking Qatun's grasp, his nimble frame slipping away from the brute's powerful hands. He had anticipated that Qatun's style was simply to win by using brute force, by holding his opponent in his grasp, crushing him into submission. Now that he confirmed his suspicion was correct, as long as he could avoid that grasp he could wear Qatun down, bit by bit, minute by minute. Mar Yanqa was already moving, a blur of speed and precision in constant motion. He darted sideways, his body light and quick, ducking beneath Qatun's massive arms, feeling the air shift as the brute's fists passed mere inches above his head. Speed was his greatest weapon. He flowed like water around Qatun's heavy strikes, each movement calculated, each twist of his body a deadly dance. As Qatun turned to follow him, Mar Yanqa saw his opening. He dropped low, kicking up his foot and striking with pinpoint precision at the back of Qatun's knee. The strike was perfectly timed, landing with a sickening thud against the joint. Qatun's massive frame shuddered as his knee buckled under the impact, sending a shock of pain shooting up his leg. His balance faltered, and Mar Yanqa, already in motion, spun on his heel, using his own momentum to shift behind Qatun.

Qatun roared, his arms flailing as he fought to regain his balance, but the boy was already there, his feet as light as air, his eyes focused on his target. Mar Yanqa didn't give him the chance to recover. With a swift twist of his body, he brought his knee into the side of Qatun's ribs, driving the air from the older man's lungs. But it wasn't enough. Qatun was too strong, his grip on the earth too solid, and the pain only seemed to make him more furious. Mar Yanqa needed more. He needed to break him physically, mentally, and quickly.

He darted in once more, his hands flashing like lightning as he struck at nerve clusters. A blow to Qatun's neck, just below the ear, sent a pulse of numbness through the brute's arm. The giant flinched, his left arm suddenly useless, hanging limp at his side. Mar Yanqa took the advantage, using the momentum of his opponent's bulk against him, pushing forward, locking Qatun in a hold around his neck that threatened to bring him down. For a moment, it seemed as though the elder chieftain might overpower Mar Yanqa simply by falling backwards, his sheer size and weight crushing Mar Yanqa beneath him.

But Mar Yanqa's grip was iron. His muscles burned with the intensity of the fight, and his mind was sharp, calculating. He knew his arm lock wasn't strong enough to break his opponent's neck so he had a change of plan. He would have to strike from the front. Mar Yanqa moved with purpose, shifting like a shadow, slipping between Qatun's massive limbs. He pressed forward, using his agility to keep out of the reach of Qatun's open fingers, and as Qatun swung his good arm toward him, Mar Yanqa ducked and spun, using the giant's forward momentum against him. He darted behind Qatun, his hands finding purchase on the brute's back, using the leverage to push off with a kick that sent him soaring into the air. In that split second of flight, Mar Yanqa's foot landed on Qatun's neck, a precise, calculated movement that he knew should break any man's spine, no matter how large, if done correctly.

The sound of Qatun's breath rattling in his throat echoed in the night air as Mar Yanqa's foot pressed deep into the vertebrae, pushing down with all the force of his training. For a brief, terrifying moment, the giant's massive frame seemed to freeze in place, his motion seized in time, and then—snap—the crack of Qatun's neck breaking rang through the camp like a drumbeat.

Qatun's body collapsed forward, his massive frame crumpling to the earth, his face a contorted mask of disbelief and pain. The sight was almost surreal. The mighty chieftain, who had ruled with brute force and terror, now reduced to a lifeless heap at the feet of a boy who had mastered the art of speed, precision, and strategy.

Mar Yanqa stood over him, panting, his chest heaving, but his eyes cold and unwavering. The crowd, once tense with fear, now erupted into a stunned silence. They had witnessed a miracle—a true warrior's victory, not through brute force, but through the skill and intelligence of a younger man who had defeated the mighty Qatun not with strength, but with grace, agility, and a deep understanding of what a man could do as long as he had the Sky God's blessing.

As Mar Yanqa stood victorious, his heart pounding from the surge of adrenaline released during the fight, he heard the soft rustle of movement behind him. The priests were suddenly there, watching with reverence and delivering their praise and thanks to the Almighty. They had prayed for him, and now they stood in awe, for this was no longer just a battle for power. This was a moment of divine justice, a victory for those who fought with wisdom, and for righteousness. Proof that God had given this boy his divine blessing. This was the battle of David and Goliath all over again and there could be no denial of God's intervention and His future intentions.

The firelight flickered as the cheers of his people erupted around him. Mar Yanqa had not only won the battle, but he had also won the respect of his tribe, and of the tribes yet to come. The tribal shamans sang their songs of victory and all rejoiced.

Tamerlan, who had been holding Mar Yanqa's glittering robe while he fought rushed forward and placed it over the young man's shoulders. "I cannot believe what I saw with my own eyes," the Khitan leader hugged Mar Yanqa, still filled with disbelief.

"Do you mean you had doubts?" Mar Yanqa questioned.

"No doubts, just concern," Tamerlan smiled.

"You did train me after all on how to wrestle," Mar Yanqa reminded him.

"Yes, but not like that," Tamerlan admitted. "This was truly a miracle." Tamerlan began to shout, "The God of Mar Yanqa is our God. All glory be to Yah."

"All glory to Yah," the members of the tribe shouted in unison.

And at a distance, Qatun's warriors stood in stunned silence, realizing that they had witnessed the fall of a giant and the rise of a new kind of king. One by one they took to one knee and bowed their heads. This night they swore allegiance to their new chieftain. Hence forth the Borjigin would serve under the Khitan. They would be loyal only to Mar Yanqa.

Chapter 13: 514 AD

Great honor was given to the burial of Qatun, once his body was returned to his home encampment. Tamerlan led a special delegation on behalf of Mar Yanqa to return the deceased chieftain to his clan. Along with Tamerlan came several priests, officials from the tribe and a specific set of instructions as to how the funeral rites were to be conducted. Qatun's tribe now belonged heart and soul to Mar Yanqa, and he intended to use this opportunity to introduce this addition to the Khitan population to some of the customs and traditions that would be imposed upon them as part of a united people. He knew that the best way to unite the tribes with their different customs and practices was to provide them with a new set of practices that would be unique to all of them but at the same time act as a common element that would bind them together.

Amongst the Khitan, those considered to be chieftains, noblemen, saints, and shamans had to have proper internment, being entombed in places of special significance. That would be Mar Yanqa's starting point to provide the people with a new set of practices. Unlike the corpses of the common people, which were left exposed in open areas of the countryside the services for the noblemen would be far more elaborate. In this particular case, Mar Yanqa instructed that Qatun's body was to be embalmed with spices, then wrapped entirely with a white linen sheet as was the custom of his father's people. Normally the dead would be buried within a day of their death but because of Qatun's status amongst the tribes, Mar Yanqa instructed there would be three days before internment so that all the tribal leaders would have time to gather and pay their respects. The Hebrew priests that he sent along to oversee the burial kept Qatun's wrapped body in his own ger, where dignitaries, family and relatives could visit, placing him on a slab positioned along the western side of the ger, explaining that because it is the part of the home closest to Jerusalem, it would be the area of the ger considered to be holiest and most secure from evil spirits. Most of Qatun's family never heard of a city called Jerusalem and failed to understand the significance of anything the priests were performing but knew one thing for certain; it was the will of Mar Yanqa and that meant that their family's fallen leader was being granted a burial with great honor and they had no choice but to abide.

The priests then proceeded to cover anything that cast a reflection within the ger with black sackcloth, explaining that the souls of the newly departed can attempt to reach out to the living through mirrors and in turn such an event might drive the living mad. As he priests poured fragrant perfumes an oils upon the linen wrappings, they recited ancient Hebrew blessings over the dead body, which they explained to the people were sacred sutras. Following which, they then permitted the Khitan shamans, according to their own traditions, perform an exorcism upon the home, driving out any evil spirits that might attempt to inhabit the soulless body.

On the third day after entering the ger, the body was finally carried from the residence to the site of the tomb in an elaborate funeral procession. Along the way, family members marched alongside the body as it was carried on a decorated litter towards the internment site, while the people played music and made great fanfare along the way. The priests remained at a distance from the throngs of people that paraded in the procession, having now begun their period of uncleanliness, a result of having been in close contact with the body when it was housed within the yurt.

Those in the funeral procession were forbidden to talk to each other or to look back for fear that they might see themselves being followed by the spirits of the dead. Meanwhile, those not in the procession would throw grain across the path taken by the procession in an attempt to distract the spirits and tempt them to feed upon the grain and leave those marching to the gravesite alone. At the front of the procession marched Alan-Ko, Qatun's eldest child and as he had no sons, she was now considered to be the reigning queen of the Borjigin tribe. The funeral procession of Qatun snaked across the open steppe like a black thread woven through the golden plains. The banners of his clan, heavy with embroidered beasts of conquest, swayed in the wind, their flapping noise a warped response to the silence that hung over the assembled mourners.

Alan-Ko shed no tears for her father. Though she had never been a daughter in the manner most girls dream about concerning their father's love, more a possession of Qatun's that he could wield as an object of negotiation as he had done in her previous marriage, she still felt something regarding the passing of her father but she could not pinpoint exactly what that feeling might be. Sadness, remorse…perhaps, but mostly she felt relief and that in turn made her feel guilty for having such feelings. Her braided hair, coiled tightly under a stiff headdress, bore the white ribbons of mourning. Her expression, however, was as unreadable as a cloudless sky, and that did not go unnoticed by the onlookers. She neither wept nor raged, neither mourned nor celebrated. Now, in death, Qatun was nothing more than a burden to be carried on the shoulders of others to his grave.

Behind her, the elders of the clan walked in their dark deels, their hands folded at their waists. His chief officers, their faces hardened by years of service, followed in silence. The tomb loomed ahead, a layered stone structure built according to Mar Yanqa's decree. It sat alone on the steppe, its stones stacked with precision, its entrance narrow and dark like the gaping mouth of a beast waiting to swallow the corpse. The ground around it had been stamped flat by the feet of those who had labored to build it, an amazing feat accomplished in only three days. As the procession neared, the shamans broke their silence. It was now their turn to sing their sacred mantras. Their chants rose in the cold air, the low hum of their voices mixing with the sound of the wind. They burned juniper, and the scent of the smoke, sharp and acrid, curled into the sky, carrying with it the last vestiges of Qatun's name.

Alan-Ko did not look at the litter as the men lowered it and carried it through the narrow opening into the tomb. She did not step forward as the shamans anointed the wrapped body with mare's milk. Her hands remained still at her sides; the fingers curled only slightly against the fabric of her robe. She had stood at the side of her father in life, a figure to be adorned and displayed, and now she stood at the edge of his death, a silent figure as the stone door of the tomb yawned open before them. The litter bearers carried Qatun's body into the darkness of the tomb. Inside, the air was cool, untouched by the heat of the steppe. The walls were lined with stone carvings listing his victories—battles won, cities burned, enemies broken beneath the hooves of his cavalry. But they were mere echoes of a life spent in pursuit of total domination that was always beyond his reach. He had conquered, but he had not been loved. He had ruled, but now it was evident he would not be mourned.

They laid him against the western wall, once again according to Mar Yanqa's instruction , so that the ancient glory of Yahweh's holy city would shine upon him. His weapons were placed beside him, though they would never be wielded again. A bronze bowl, filled with fermented milk, was set at his feet, a final drink for the journey to the next world. The shamans whispered prayers, their voices hushed as if speaking too loudly might wake him.

Alan-Ko watched without expression. When her mother had died, she had wept until her ribs ached. When her husband had been cut down in battle, she had torn her clothes and screamed her grief into the wind, not because she loved him but because now his sons would be fatherless. As the heavy stones were lifted, and the tomb was sealed securely, she felt nothing but the wind at her back and the vast, empty steppe stretching before her. When the last stone was set into place, the chants of the shamans faded. The banners of the procession lowered. And Alan-Ko turned, walking away from the tomb without looking back, stepping into the vastness of the endless plains, where the living still had choices to make.

Those people that remained in the funeral procession marched around the tomb three times in a clockwise direction, a demonstration of both honour and respect. Having done that, it was time for everyone to disperse, while family members returned to family yurt, careful not to make the mistake of looking back at the tomb as it was said that the spirit of the dead may attempt to beckon them to return, trapping their souls within the tomb if they did so. Once back at the yurt, the family members were treated to tea and food for the rest of the week, but those that were the immediate family of Qatun, they were not permitted to partake in the feast, forced to remain in another room where they would be kept separated from the rest of the clan for seven weeks, unable to socialize and forbidden to cut their hair during that entire duration.

Still, there was one question on everyone's mind, 'Where was Mar Yanqa? Why did he not attend?' As the newly declared Qagan of the entire Khitan nation, his absence from such a significant event could not be easily overlooked.

Some saw it as an insult that he did not come to claim his prize for ascending to the position of supreme chieftain, the hand of Alan-Ko, as Qatun had wagered. If this was a sign that he was rejecting her as his bride, then not only was it an affront to the woman considered to be the Borjigin queen, but a betrayal of his oath to Qatun when he accepted his challenge. Mulling upon the matter, the people became restless and not long after they became boisterous, demanding to know the whereabouts of their new leader. The reaction had been anticipated and it was when they surrounded and pressed Tamerlan for an answer, that he promised to make it clear to them. Tamerlan, who had attended the funeral as Mar Yanqa's chief representative attempted to explain the reasoning as it related to Mar Yanqa's religious beliefs, but these beliefs were still strange to Tamerlan, despite their close relationship, and explaining them he knew was going to be a challenge. He knew he had to sound knowledgeable, even though he lacked the theological reasoning to back up his statements' He began by saying that Mar Yanqa could not take Alan-Ko to wife until she had mourned at least six months for her father. He attempted to repeat the reasoning exactly as Mar Yanqa had explained it but even as he was telling the crowd what he had been told, it made little sense to any of the people listening.

"If a parent dies, then a child must mourn that parent for an entire year, before they can participate in a ceremony that would celebrate a joyous occasion. But," he clarified, "If that ceremony had been planned prior to the death, then the event only needs to be postponed for thirty days."

Hence, the question that Mar Yanqa pondered was whether or not the wager of their daughter's hand in marriage should they lose the death match constituted a planned ceremony prior to the parent's death. Not even the priests that constantly advised Mar Yanqa could resolve this particular riddle. As such, Mar Yanqa arrived at his own decision that the mourning period must be somewhere in the middle and he proposed six months. Difficult as that may have been for the people to understand and accept, it still did not explain Mar Yanqa's absence from Qatun's funeral.

Tamerlan was prepared with an explanation for that question as well, knowing that it would arise. "To see Alan-Ko before then and witness her extraordinary beauty that was known throughout the land, might be enough for him to break this religious commandment to which he and his betrothed must ascribe to. To break this commandment, he feared would result in a terrible disaster due to their offense to God. For the sake of his people, he could not risk bringing down Yahweh's wrath upon them."

Tamerlan had tried to dissuade Mar Yanqa from this position, knowing that the people would find his failure to attend the funeral nothing but the dishonoring of a great chieftain. The explanation for Mar Yanqa's reluctance to immediately fulfil the promise of marrying the Khitan Queen he was satisfied would appease a significant portion of the people, but Mar Yanqa's failure to attend the funeral he knew would not sit well with the majority. He had sought Mar Yanqa to reconsider.

"This may be the way of the land from which Mar Yanqa came, but it is not our way" the crowd grumbled. The explanation that upon seeing Alan-Ko's beauty, it might ignite desires in Mar Yanqa's heart that would make him break his vow not to interfere with her mourning period appeared too contrived and unrealistic. It certainly did not explain why he could not at least attend parts of the funeral rites for his rival whom he had slain. Soon it was an affront that had become obvious to everyone and those surrounding Tamerlan were becoming verbally aggressive.

Tamerlan sensed the crowd's mood shifting, a rising tide of anger sweeping over those congregated in the valley. They had not rehearsed for this contingency and Tamerlan attempted to assemble a logical sequence of facts that would support the decision not to attend but his usual glib tongue was suddenly at a loss for words. He stared out the assembled crowd that had gathered beneath the shadow of the sacred hill where their Chieftain Qatun now lay entombed, sensing a restless sea of warriors, elders, and clansmen who were now murmuring with more intensity. The air bristled not just with grief—but with an angered sense of betrayal.

Tamerlan, tall and lean with a face carved like weathered stone, tried to still the crowd once again by repeating the words that he had rehearsed with Mar Yanqa. His voice remained steady, as he again explained that Mar Yanqa could not come, for he was pledged to Alan-Ko, the jewel of the Borjigin realm but to behold her now, in the bloom of her mourning, would ignite a fire in him too powerful for him to resist and it would compel him to break his sacred vow to God that he would lay no hand upon her until six moons had passed in grief.

But repeating the words was not enough to still the rising tide of bitterness. Religious oaths lacked the logic intended to be the balm for a warrior's pride. Nor was it comfort for mothers whose sons had died over the years for Qatun, nor the elders whose loyalty had aged into the man's legend. A low growl of discontent passed through those assembled, like wolves on the scent of blood. Men spat into the dust. Old women wept with heads bowed. Fingers curled around the hilts of blades. Murmurs of insult rose like the evening star.

Shouts were hurled in Tamerlan's direction.

"He dishonors our dead Chieftain!"

"How can a coward that fears the sight of a woman rule over us?"

"A chieftain who sends his dog to bark for him has no right to rule!"

Tamerlan was beginning to fear for his life, and then, she appeared. From the mouth of the tent of mourning, where she was to remain for seven weeks, Alan-Ko stepped into the fading light of the afternoon. She was still dressed in the full white garb of grief—the color of bones and spirits—draped in fine Khitan linen that fluttered like the wings of a ghost. Her hair was braided tightly, each braid adorned with thin white ribbons, falling like rivers of snow down her back. Her face was bare of paint or jewelry, and yet it shone with a light so radiant that even the most hardened soldier felt his breath catch.

She did not speak at once. She did not need to. A hush fell over the gathering. Every man, woman, and child felt it; the silence that comes when a hawk casts its shadow over the plain, or when lightning touches the edge of the world. They had all heard of her beauty, passed down in songs and whispered in the hush of tents, but it was more than beauty that held them now. It was a presence so overpowering that it was without description.

Her voice, when it came, was low. Measured. It carried not on force, but on music. A voice shaped by poetry and sharpened by grief.

"My people," she said. "Sons and daughters of the plains. Followers of Qatun, my father, the great lion of the East. I have come before you not as a princess, not as a bride, but as a daughter who grieves with you." She paused, and the crowd bent forward, aching to hear more. "I, too, felt the fire of fury when Mar Yanqa did not appear. I, too, wanted to cast down his standard and cry to the sky that the man who slew my father now hides from his corpse. But I did not. I could not. For my father taught me something greater than vengeance."

Her hands folded at her waist. Her eyes swept the crowd. Many there would say, later, that she had looked directly into their hearts.

"He taught me that a true leader does not stoke rage. He bends it. He tempers it into steel. He transforms it into a vision."

The murmurs stilled. The blades were lowered.

"Tamerlan spoke true. Mar Yanqa keeps away not out of cowardice, but out of fear, not for himself, but for you. He fears the wrath of heaven. I do not know his god, but He must be truly powerful if he invested Mar Yanqa with the strength to overpower my father. If his god is that powerful, then I will accept him as my God as well. As must we all! Mar Yanqa fears that in laying hands on me before my mourning is complete, that his God will bring ruin down upon us all. Such is the strength of his belief that he dares suffer your scorn in silence."

She let that truth hang in the air like incense over a fire.

"I have never seen this man. I have never touched his hand. But I have heard the stories. He fought my father in single combat and he won. Not through treachery. Not through poison. But through strength. Courage. Resolve."

She stepped forward, just a pace. "Do you not see the signs? The great wheel turns. The old gives way to the new. But the blood of Qatun does not end today. It lives in me. It lives in you. And it will live in the child I will one day bear with the man who now leads us."

A ripple of emotion passed through the crowd like wind over grass.

"Let there be no more talk of resistance. No more insult thrown like stones at men who have shown us only reverence. Mar Yanqa is not your enemy. He is your future. And I, Alan-Ko, will walk into that future beside him. Not as a widow or a daughter in grief, but as a queen reborn from mourning, carrying the spirit of Qatun forward into glory."

She raised her arms, not in supplication, but in strength. "The steppe is wide, but our hearts must be wider still. Our sorrow is deep, but our hope must be deeper. Let this be the last day we speak of division. From this hour forward, we prepare for greatness."

The wind lifted her ribbons, casting them into the sky like white flames.

Silence. Then a single voice cried out: "For Alan-Ko!"

And another: "For Qatun!"

Then a roar. "For Mar Yanqa!"

They raised their fists, their spears, their grief now made clean by the promise of a future shaped by beauty, by fire, by the will of a daughter whose voice could calm the storm. Tamerlan bowed his head in reverence and respect to the woman that would be his queen, awed by her oratory and strength of personality. And as Alan-Ko turned and disappeared back into the tent, the steppe was stilled. Not by power, nor by fear, but by a dream of future greatness.

Chapter 14: 515 AD

The wedding day dawned under a sky of endless blue, swept clean by the night winds. All the Khitan tribes had gathered like stars fallen to earth, their yurts arranged in concentric rings, a living mandala of horsehair, silk, and smoke. There were banners flying with hawks and wolves, drums echoing from the far hills, and bonfires being stacked chest-high in anticipation of the night to come. The Steppe itself seemed to stir, restless and breathless, waiting for this marriage of fate and fire. This was a day of celebration and tension, to be followed by a night intended to seal the fate of two great peoples. The Khitan and the eastern steppe tribes under their new Qagan, Mar Yanqa Kahana, the young lad they all referred to as the Glittering Man, and the Borjigin, fiercely loyal to their queen and his wife to be, Alan-Ko.

During those months that intervened, the Glittering Man, had already become a legendary figure among the Khitan clans. Across the steppes, stories were told of a warrior of unmatched prowess and strength, a leader of exceptional wisdom. Some said he had descended from the stars, while others claimed that it was his very own skin that fractured the light in such a way that it dazzled his enemies and inspired his followers to victory. There were tales that claimed he was a giant of a man, so tall that his head was in the clouds, while others said he was gifted with immortality, marching across the continent and engaged in battle for over a thousand years, subjugating all in his path as he spread the word of his God. Even those stories which were more accurate, that spoke of his emerald, green eyes and red hair were enough to fill the people with wonder, having never seen anyone their entire lives with anything other than brown eyes and coal black hair.

As word of the tremendous event about to take place spread across the vastness of this desolate land, the inhabitants came by the hundreds, the thousands, even the tens of thousands, to witness the birth of what was being hailed as the Khitan nation. For the first time they would be united, not merely as nomads that shared a common heritage but as a nation that shared a common purpose and were now in possession of a common goal. This was the day when Mar Yanqa would be no longer just their anointed chieftain but on this particular night he would soon be a husband of the woman many had already considered as their queen, Alan-Ko, her beauty matched only by her fierce spirit. Alan-Ko was no mere pawn in the political games once played by her father; she would be a force to be reckoned with, all on her own. A skilled rider, a master of the bow, and a woman who had earned the respect of her people through her own deeds, some wondered if Mar Yanqa had finally met his match.

In the center of it all, behind silk curtains of white and crimson, sat Alan-Ko. The bride was calm, but her heart was not. She wore the mourning white no longer. Her robes were layered in cream and gold brocade, trimmed with otter fur, her sleeves stitched with the crescent moons of the Borjigin. Her long black hair had been undone, washed with milk and honey, then rebraided with red ribbons and bells that chimed when she moved. Gold earrings framed her cheeks, but no paint touched her face. She needed none. The maids had whispered it all morning that no woman born of man had ever looked so regal nor as stunningly beautiful.

She turned from the mirror, gripping the lacquered armrest of the bridal bench. "He is only a man," she murmured aloud. "They say a good man. A good man cannot take sons from a mother." But her self-assurances rang hollow.

As if summoned by her thoughts, a rustle came at the tent's door. A herald's voice murmured, "Princess She-Ping of the Imperial House of Northern Wei requests an audience."

Alan-Ko blinked. "His mother? Let her enter."

The curtain parted, and in stepped the exiled Chinese princess. Her gown was of Han silk, modest and elegant, trimmed in pearls. Her face, though marked by years of exile, bore the unmistakable beauty of the Eastern court; almond-shaped eyes, high cheekbones, and full lips trained in silence. But what struck Alan-Ko most was the look of sadness. It clung to the woman like perfume.

She-Ping bowed, not deeply but respectfully. "My lady," she said in fluent Khitan. "We are to become family. I thought it time we met."

Alan-Ko stood to greet her. "Princess. It is an honor."

They regarded each other in silence. Two women bound by duty, yet both strangers to the choice being forced upon them. She-Ping could immediately sense the tension that had been weighing down Alan-Ko.

"I know what you fear," She-Ping said softly.

Alan-Ko's brow lifted.

"You fear for your sons. You fear that my son, Yanqa, will do as conquerors often do; clear the bloodlines. End your first husband's legacy. Take only what is his and burn the rest."

Alan-Ko said nothing, but her gaze sharpened. She-Ping smiled, though it was tinged with sorrow.

"He will not harm them. You have my oath."

"How can you be so certain. Oaths are easy to make and just as easy to break," Alan-Ko replied. "It is fear that stokes bloodshed. Not malice. Fear of what might grow. What might challenge the future."

"My son is not like other men. He is a good boy."

Her last comment caught Alan-Ko by surprise. "I guess to a mother, no matter how old the son, he will always be a boy."

"You do not know?" She-Ping sounded surprised.

"Know what?"

The older woman drew closer. "My son is only sixteen. Still a boy as far as I am concerned, but to the warriors that follow him into battle, he is a man far beyond their own years. It is his soul that is old. He does not kill for pride. He fights for honor. And for his unswerving faith. He believes you are a blessing sent by God. He prays three times a day not for victory, but for wisdom. And when he learned that he was to marry you, he wept. Not with fear. With a feeling of being honored."

Alan-Ko's breath caught. "He is only sixteen..." she repeated. "How am I to address him? To call him 'my Lord' when he is four years my younger would feel awkward."

"He is merely Yanqa," his mother responded. "Though the son of a king, he is much like his father was, without pretenses. His father preferred the simple 'Mar' meaning Lord, rather than have anyone call him 'your majesty' My son needs a good wife, not someone to praise him with honors and titles. To you he will always be Yanqa, as he is to me."

She-Ping took her hands. "But in that matter of being a wife, I fear he is not ready for you. He knows that. But he will grow. He will learn from you. And you, if you are willing, can help him become more than any warlord can. Only you can make him a true king!"

Alan-Ko looked down at their joined hands, one set small and pale, the other darker, stronger. "And if I refuse? If I flee from this marriage?"

"You will not. You are Bojigin. You are your father's daughter. You do not flee."

Alan-Ko looked up. And for the first time, she smiled. "No. I do not. I was a mere child myself when my father married me off to Dobun Mergen. I knew nothing of being a woman at thirteen. By fourteen I was already delivering my first child. We are Khitan by spirit and I must learn these things quickly. I will not flee. You have my word."

Across the encampment, in a tent that stank of goat leather and sweat, Mar Yanqa stood stiffly as Tamerlan adjusted the ceremonial belt around his waist. The boy chieftain was exceedingly tall for his age, lean and muscular, with the thick eyebrows and high nose of his Hebrew ancestors. His red hair had been shaved on the sides and left long at the top, braided with eagle feathers. He wore the robe handed down from his father, the bejeweled glittering robe which made him a legend, with its gold embroidery and multicolored jewels. But now there was an addition, the left chest marked with a wolf's head in white thread, emblem of the Borjigin.

"She will laugh at me," he muttered.

Tamerlan snorted. "If she laughs, you will be the luckiest man alive. A laughing wife is a forgiving wife."

Mar Yanqa frowned. "What if she doesn't like me? What if she thinks me a child?"

"You are a child."

"Not helping!"

Tamerlan shrugged. "She's twenty. She's had children. She buried her husband. She led a tribe through war. She's fire and fury wrapped in silk. And you? You're sixteen, barely kissed a mare, and still think goats can't swim."

The boy scowled. "I don't even know what that last part means."

"My point is this, you won't win her heart by pretending to be older than you are. You win her by being honest. Strong. Humble. Be the warrior you were on the field, not in the mirror."

Mar Yanqa looked down at his hands. "She's...beautiful, isn't she?"

"Like the moon mated with the wind and gave birth to a storm," Tamerlan said, far too poetically.

"Is that a yes or a no?"

"A yes. Her beauty is unquestionable. She's a goddess!"

"That doesn't help either."

"No. But it's true."

A silence settled between them, broken only when Tamerlan leaned in and added in a conspiratorial whisper, "Now, on the wedding night... things might move faster than you think."

Mar Yanqa's eyes widened.

Tamerlan lifted a brow. "You know what to do, yes?"

"I've...read poems."

"Poems?" Tamerlan stared at him, aghast. "Boy, you don't recite Li Bai when she's naked. You—"

"I said I've read poems, not that I'm going to recite one."

"Still, let me give you some advice: start slow. Very slow. Don't jab at her like you're spearing a wild goat. Ease in, like you're bathing in hot milk."

"That is disgusting."

"Effective."

The two stared at each other. Then Mar Yanqa sighed.

"I am not ready."

"No one ever is. But fate doesn't wait."

Mar Yanqa sat hunched on a carved wooden stool, staring at the floor. He looked like he might buckle under the weight of his worries. His fingers trembled against his knee, and he had not spoken in several minutes.

Tamerlan sat down beside him, his weathered face calm, his hands folded across his lap. He studied the young man; not with a gaze that had seen decades of war and loss, but with something gentler.

"Yes, I know you're afraid," Tamerlan said softly.

"No. I mean...maybe. I don't know what I'm doing."

Tamerlan chuckled. "I'll let you in on a secret...none of us do. Not at first."

There was a pause. Then, the old warrior sighed and leaned back slightly, gazing up at the hide-lined ceiling of the tent as if trying to summon something from memory. "I have served two other Qagans in my life," he began. "Each great in their own way. Each flawed. Each of them believed they were the center of the world, chosen by the spirits, born to command. And maybe they were. Because of them, I thought I would be next in line to be Qagan. But not one of them made me kneel the way you did."

Mar Yanqa looked at him in confusion. "I haven't done anything yet."

Tamerlan smiled. "Exactly. You didn't have to. I saw it the first time you stood before me in the Korean general's tent, barely able to hold a spear, and yet unwilling to yield. I saw the fire in your eyes."

He paused again, then his voice dropped, tender now, almost broken. "You are the son I never had, Yanqa."

Mar Yanqa blinked, startled.

Tamerlan continued, not letting him interrupt. "I could have claimed the right to rule. I had the lineage. The loyalty of the elders. It was my tribe to command. I had ruled over them for years. But what is the point of leading one or even a hundred tribes if the one who truly deserves to rule is sitting in your shadow, waiting for his time?"

He reached out, placing a strong, calloused hand on the boy's shoulder. "You are my legacy, whether or not the blood says so. I would give up ten crowns, a hundred kingdoms, to see you rise. And not because of duty or prophecy, but because I believe in you. More than I've ever believed in myself."

Mar Yanqa's eyes began to glisten.

Tamerlan looked down for a moment, gathering himself, then spoke again, quieter, the edge of something deeper in his voice. "I once hoped your mother would marry me," he said. "I thought, in some foolish corner of my heart, that I could heal the wound left by your father's death. That I could be enough. And through our marriage I would legitimize my claim to be Qagan." He smiled sadly. "But you can't compete with ghosts. And no man, not even me, can ever replace what she lost when your father died. I can only assume the greatness I see in you is exactly what she saw in your father. I learned that we all must accept our place in life and I let her go."

The tent was very still now, the fire in the brazier crackling softly across from them.

"But even so," he went on, "I never stopped loving her. Not once. And if she gave me nothing else in this life, she gave me you to fill the emptiness that was in my life. That's more than any marriage, more than any crown."

He stood then, heavy with years but tall as ever, and looked down at Mar Yanqa. "I would be proud to call you son. Not out of obligation. Not for politics. But because you are the best of us, Yanqa. And when you stand before the tribe today, under that marriage canopy, when the banners fly and the vows are spoken, remember this..."

His voice grew firm.

"You are the best of us and I believe in you. When the time comes, you will know what to do."

Mar Yanqa rose slowly, unsure if he was trembling from nerves or from the weight of the love poured over him. He looked up at Tamerlan, then did something he had never done before.   He embraced him.

The old warrior stiffened at first, caught off guard but then, with a breath like a sigh of decades unburdened, he folded his arms around the boy and held him tight.

Outside, the drums began to beat.   It was the signal that the bride was approaching and the time had come.

The wedding was held under the open sky.   An arch had been constructed of shed antlers and white birch, strung with woven grasses and horsehair. Beneath it, the elders of six of the tribes stood in ceremonial garb, their staffs crowned with ivory. To one side, the fire drums beat. On the other, musicians played long-necked lutes and flutes carved of bone. Tens of thousands had gathered. Riders from the north. Shamans from the desert. Even emissaries from the Song court, enemies of Northen Wei, veiled and stiff with suspicion but seeing an opportunity to gain an important ally.
As the sun reached its zenith, the procession began.

Alan-Ko emerged on horseback, riding a white mare. Her veil was of silk, trailing like smoke, and the crowd gasped when they saw her.   Every eye watched her. Every heart beat a little faster.   She was to everyone watching, the most beautiful woman they had ever laid eyes upon.

Mar Yanqa waited nervously under the arch, his boyish face wearing a false mask of calm but pale as the moon. When he saw her, he forgot to breathe.

When their eyes met for the first time, the world stood still.

She approached slowly, dismounted without help, and stepped beside him under the covered arch.

The chief shaman intoned the rites of fire and earth, of sky and womb. The head priest recited from the Tanach how God had created woman because man needed a companion.   Combining Hebrew prayers with Khitan traditions, milk was poured on the flames. A strip of horsehide bound their hands together.   They circled each other three times. And when the rites were done, the priest raised his voice. They drank from a cup of fermented goat's milk which they then crushed under their feet.

"In the eyes of the tribes, in the ears of the sky, and in the breath of God, you are now husband and wife."

The cheers were deafening.

Spirits were spilled.   Horns were blown.   Dancers began their spinning. Horses were loosed in races down the hill.   The fires roared to life.   And through it all, Alan-Ko stood beside her husband, who was not yet a man, and nodded to the crowd with dignity.

She leaned to him at last.   "You look younger than I imagined."

He swallowed. "I am taller than I look."

She almost laughed. Almost.

"You will not harm my sons."

"I would rather lose my life."

And with that, she took his hand. Firmly. As the people feasted, the stars began to rise. The marriage ceremony had been a grand affair, with Khitan from all the tribes and clans coming together to witness the union. Songs had been sung, toasts had been made, and the night had echoed with the sounds of merriment. But as the celebrations began to wind down, the moment that both Mar Yanqa and Alan-Ko had been silently anticipating, and dreading, drew near.

The wedding tent stood at the center of the camp, its entrance adorned with symbols of Mar Yanqa's tribe's power and his personal victories. Inside, the tent was warm and inviting, a stark contrast to the now cold wind blowing outside. Soft furs covered the ground, and the air was thick with the scent of incense and the faint, metallic tang of the warrior's armor perched in the corner. A large bed, draped in rich fabrics and furs, dominated the space, a silent reminder of what was to come.

Alan-Ko stood at the entrance of the tent, her heart pounding in her chest. She had faced enemies in battle, had led men into the fray, but this was a different kind of challenge. She had been trained to be a leader, a warrior, and a daughter of the steppes, but since the passing of her first husband she had not been with another man. Dobun Mergan had been much older, well experienced having had numerous woman before her and so he took control of their encounters, sometimes forcibly, but almost always without concern of whether or not his wife took pleasure from their union. But now, this was an entirely different matter and it was clear to Alan-Ko that she must assume the dominant position and it was not a role in which she had any prior experience. Whatever she did, she knew and understood would leave a lasting impression upon her youthful husband, and that was not necessarily for the best.

Mar Yanqa's imposing figure was silhouetted against the warm glow of the firelight. He had removed his robe; his broad shoulders and muscular frame still clad in the finely woven undergarments. His face was now unreadable, his dark green eyes watching her with an intensity that sent a shiver down her spine because she sensed that he expected her to make the next move.

Taking a deep breath, Alan-Ko stepped towards the conjugal bed. The flap of the yurt fell shut behind her, cutting off the sounds of the camp outside. It was just the two of them now, alone in the quiet intimacy of the night. She met his gaze, refusing to show any sign of fear or hesitation. Mar Yanqa inclined his head slightly, a gesture that spoke volumes that was not lost on Alan-Ko, as if he had verbally asked, 'what's next?'

'The next', she knew depended entirely on what she would say and do at that moment. She thought back to that first night as a young girl lying in Dobun Mergan's bed and what he said to her that helped her overcome her fears. It was one of the few times he had ever shown any empathy and compassion for her, raising her level of confidence through a stream of complements tinged with a trace of humor.

She patted the bed for him to come and sit beside her. As he sat, her hand stroked his bicep tenderly as she looked directly into his emerald, green eyes. "These are the muscles of a man that has raised a sword through decades of battle. How is it even possible that one so young has been gifted with a body so magnificent? It is a shame that I am not permitted to see all of it because you still wear your undergarments." She smiled with a small ripple of laughter, a gentle tease that encouraged him to shed his final bits of clothing. As he did so, her hands brushed against the hard muscles of his chest and traced the deep demarcations that defined his abdomen. "Such a body must be carved from stone, chiseled by the hands of the God you speak of, because such perfection is not natural." Alan-Ko found the words flowing easily, realizing they were the truth and she couldn't help but to admire his beauty and form as her hands sensed the incredible power beneath her fingertips.

Mar Yanqa found himself relaxing and responding to her touch. He couldn't stop looking at her. For months he had heard the stories of her strength and her astonishing beauty, but seeing her now, in the soft light of the tent, he realized that none of the stories even came close to the truth. There was a fire in her eyes, that illuminated the radiance of her almond skin. Every curve and feature of her face was sheer perfection. A statue carved from marble and completely flawless. You are far more beautiful than they say," he said, his voice low and resonant, a definite trace of adoration in his tone.

She found herself melting as she ran her fingers through his red hair. "And you are as strong and handsome as the tales on the steppes have claimed," she replied, her voice steady, though she could feel her heart racing in her chest. "But strength alone does not make a man worthy of a princess," Alan-Ko teased him further, sensing that he was growing more confident and relaxed in her presence.

Mar Yanqa allowed a small smile to play at the corners of his mouth. He was enjoying this banter between them, "Nor does beauty alone make a woman worthy of a warrior." It was his turn to tease her back in the same manner that she had used.

The smile that spread across her face spoke volumes. And if it was possible for a simple smile to make her appear even more beautiful than he had already seen, then it certainly did so, captivating him completely. There was a moment of silence between them, a charged stillness that bound them together. They were both aware of the roles they were expected to play, the duties they had to fulfill. But there was now something far greater than their respective roles as leaders of the Khitan. There was now mutual respect, an understanding that they were both more than just symbols of their peoples. There was genuine affection and without any doubt it would blossom into love.

Alan-Ko knew that it was time. Her movements were careful, deliberate. She could feel the tension in his posture, the way his hands were clenched at his sides, afraid to offend if he let them loose to explore her body. She reached out, gently taking one of his hands in hers and placing it upon her breast. Her skin was cool to the touch, but there was a warmth that radiated along his arm and across the entirety of his body as he gently fondled her nipple.

"We are bound by more than just duty tonight," she said softly, her thumb brushing over his lips. "This alliance is not just for our peoples, but for us as well. We are partners now, in war and in life."

Mar Yanqa studied his face, searching for any sign of deceit or insincerity. But all he saw was honesty and a determination that mirrored his own. He nodded slowly, as his fingers explored the curves of her upper torso.

"I will not be a mere ornament by your side," she warned, her voice adopting a firmness that told him she would not compromise. "I will fight with you, lead with you, and stand as your equal."

Mar Yanqa nodded, his fondness for her growing as if that was even possible. "And I would not have it any other way." He reached out, brushing a strand of her hair away from her face, his fingers lingering against her cheek.

Alan-Ko met his gaze, her eyes steady, her breath increasing as she knew the time was rapidly approaching. They began moving together, tossing aside the layers of furs and fabric that were strewn across the bed, until there was nothing left but the two of them, bare and vulnerable in the quiet of the night. The firelight from the hearth danced across their skin, casting long shadows on the walls of the tent as they came together. The intensity of their consummation was a union not just of bodies but of spirits, a merging of two powerful forces into one. Whatever concerns either may have had regarding their differences were quickly swept away in a tide of pure emotion.

As the night wore on and the fire burned low, they lay together in the warmth of the furs, their breaths mingling in the cool air. Outside, the wind still howled, but inside the tent, there was only the quiet aftermath of their union, a silence filled with the promise of what was to come. And as sleep began to claim them both, Mar Yanqa found himself feeling something unexpected, a sense of peace. For the first time that night, he allowed himself to close his eyes and rest, knowing that whatever challenges lay ahead, he would not face them alone.

Chapter 15: 515 AD

Their days together soon rolled into months, and before long, no one would mention the name Mar Yanqa without appending the name of Alan-Ko to it. They had become inseparable, stronger together than either of them had ever been apart. The remaining tribes of the steppes flocked to them, acknowledging Mar Yanqa as their Qagan and Alan-Ko as their queen, but not quite all of them. As promised, the leader of the Tuoba, Liwei Guo, arrived with his elite force and took a knee before the pair of royal Khitan. Relinquishing one's rule over a tribe and delivering it to some foreigner from the west that laid claim to the Khitan crown was not an easy thing to do for some of the younger chieftains that had only recently assumed the role of leadership and were now being asked to give up their authority to someone they barely even knew.

That night, as the fire crackled softly in the hearth, the atmosphere in the tent shifted from one of tension to one of shared purpose. They spoke in low tones, their conversation touching on their respective peoples, their hopes for the future, and the battles they had fought. There was no need for false modesty or pretenses; they were both warriors, both leaders, and they understood the burdens that came with those roles. Alan-Ko spoke first. "I am pregnant Yanqa," she stated without showing any emotion other than perhaps trepidation.

In contrast, Mar Yanqa appeared overjoyed by the news. "How can you be certain?" he asked.

"A woman knows these things, plus two moons have passed and I have not bled," she responded, her voice still sedate.

"I did not notice," he confessed.

"Why would you; you're a man." She jabbed him with her finger in order to make her point.

"This is wonderful news," he rejoiced. "So why do you seem reluctant to tell me this?" he was confused by her somewhat detached attitude.

The expression on her face became very serious. "Because I need to know that if it is a boy, that you will not harm my other two sons."

"You mean our sons," Mar Yanqa's tone was tinged with hint of disappointment. "Have I not cared for the two boys as if they were my own flesh and blood? Did I not already tell you that I would never harm them? Why would you doubt me?"

"Because it has always been the way of kings to remove any threat to their own offspring," she defended her concern.

"And in the time we have been together I had assumed that you would have seen that I am not like any other man. You have wounded me deeply to think that I was capable of such a thing." He lowered his head so that his gaze no longer looked upon her. "The slaughter of children is not my way. It is not the Lord's way. It pains me to think that you could consider me capable of such a thing."

"Forgive me my love," she pleaded as she draped her body over his frame from behind. "It was foolish of me to consider such a thing but as their mother, it is only natural to worry about one's children. Can you forgive me, my love?"

"I will have to think about it," he paused. "You did wound me, accusing me to be no different from those other men."

"How could a little thing like me wound such a big and powerful man?" she teased him as she playfully punched his shoulder.

Yanqa reacted by twisting his torso so that he could grab her wrists and throw her back onto the pile of furs that made up their bed.

"Careful now," she laughed. "After all, I'm pregnant."

Changing tactics, Yanqa began to tickle his wife, driving her into a fit of frenzied laughter.

"Stop it, stop it," she could barely get the words out as he continued his onslaught. "You're killing me," she laughed. "Stop it! We have to discuss some serious matters."

"Having a baby isn't a serious matter," Mar Yanqa sounded confused.

"Other serious matters," she corrected herself.

"Such as…" Yanqa was having too much fun to think seriously at that moment.

"Such as what shall we call this child?" she inquired.

"You mean this child who is a blessing from God but instead provided you with so much worry," Mar Yanqa reiterated their prior discussion in a single phrase."

"Yes, that child with whom you are now making fun of me," Alan-Ko replied.

"That is what we will name him," he said without hesitation. "In the language of my religion, 'Brucha Hadagi', My Worried Blessing."

"You know I cannot make those sounds common to your language," his wife complained. "You chose that name just to hear me embarrass myself every time I would call him," she laughed. "I will simply call him Bukha Khatagi in my language. Because you thought my concerns were ridiculous and amusing, then he will be known by the name 'Source of Laughter."

"You were laughing pretty hard yourself," he reminded her.

"Only because you wouldn't stop tickling me."

Well, it sounds almost the same as the Hebrew and the child will always remind us of how you were being foolish, judging me to be like other men. But now we can laugh at it together." Mar Yanqa nodded his head, confirming that they had settled upon an appropriate name.

"But what if it's a girl?" Alan-Ko suddenly raised the other possibility. "Hardly an appropriate name for a girl to bear all of her life."

"I wouldn't worry about that," Mar Yanqa dismissed the possibility. "It's definitely going to be a boy. I know it."

"And you know this because…"

"In time you will come to realize that Yahweh has gifted my family with certain attributes. We can often see that which will be."

"Well then," Alan-Ko smirked, "If you can see the future then tell me how this other matter will be dealt with. Our marriage alone is not enough to unite all the tribes. There still remains several chieftains that need to be convinced that unity is their only path to survival and prosperity. What does Yahweh have to say about that?" she chided him.

"He says we are to embark on a journey across the steppes and visit each clan that has thus far refused to join with us," Yanqa responded.

"And does He also tell us what we are to say to these chieftains when we meet with them," Alan-Ko sounded skeptical.

"We are to say that together we can be a Khitan nation that would be strong enough to defend its people, rich enough to trade with the greatest empires, and wise enough to govern justly."

"I hear the voice of my husband, rather than the voice of God," she still remained doubtful. "After all, you have been telling me the benefits of our unity for some time now."

"Only because Yahweh has set me upon this path right from the beginning. It has always been His plan for me to unite all of the tribes. I am just the means by which to carry out His intentions," Yanqa explained, confident that any success he had enjoyed thus far was gifted from God."

"But does your God understand the nature of the Khitan people?" she questioned. "Clearly those chieftains that have refused to join our camp are stubborn, clinging to their independence and fearing for the loss of their power. And though I personally know better, some are wary of you, Yanqa, seeing you still as a foreigner and an outsider."

"Then they will be shown that they are in error when we talk to them," Yanqa insisted. "They will be made to understand that this is the will of God!"

"They will not come to believe so easily," Alan-Ko advised, as she rested her hand upon his. "The chieftains in the south swear that the will not kneel to a boy, no matter how many visions he claims to have. And Abaoji—he says he'd rather die in the mountains than yoke his tribe to the banner of another."

Mar Yanqa did not flinch. "They will come over to us," he replied assuredly. "We must go to them. Yahweh has made that clear. Each reluctant tribe must be approached in person, face to face, as brothers."

Alan-Ko looked up at him, her brows drawn. "And you insist that God has told you this?"

He nodded without hesitation. "He speaks in the dark hours, in dreams, in the moments before waking. He has shown me paths, names, even words. Believe me when I say that I am mercly the vessel."

"You are young," she said gently, though her tone carried steel. "And dreams are tricky things. I've seen wise men destroyed by voices they thought divine. What if it is not God speaking to you? What if it is your own will; clever, burning, ambitious, cloaked in holiness? Would you be so eager to place your life in danger by riding into your enemies' domain if it was not the will of your God to do so?"

A silence arose between them, long and uncertain. Outside, the wind picked up, rattling the flaps of the yurt.

Mar Yanqa's eyes did not waver. "You think I would lie about such a thing?"

She exhaled, not with anger but weariness. "No. But I think even the pure of heart can mistake their own fire for heaven's flame. I am your wife; I fear for your life."

He reduced the space between their bodies and rested his hands on her knees. "My love, I have never asked you to follow the whims of a dreamer. I have only asked you to follow the will of the one God who thus far has led our people through the ice valleys, who scattered our enemies on the battle fields, and who will make the ravens circle thrice before our first son's birth. You believe in Him. I know you do."

"I do," she admitted, softer now. "But I also believe He does not speak so frequently to men. And never so clearly. Why you?"

He turned his gaze downward, as if searching within the furs for words that would suffice. "Because I do not desire it. I do not deserve it. That is why He chose me."

She blinked, her head tilting to suggest she did not understand,

"I did not seek a crown. I did not chase the alliance. I would have been content living in exile and keeping my father's life nothing but a memory. But He came to me, first in fire, then in wind, and finally in the stillness of silence. He told me, 'Unite them. Or they will all die at the hands of your enemy.'"

Alan-Ko's throat tightened. She had felt that same premonition in her bones. A sense of closing shadows. Of disunity breeding destruction. "And this enemy being…?"

Mar Yanqa continued, voice low but resolute: "My uncle, the Emperor. The Khitan must become one people, not scattered clans. That the time of raids and rivalries is over. My greatest enemy coming—his blood lust will not be satiated, until all those that have bound themselves to me have died by the edge of his sword. Our only hope is through unity."

She studied him, trying to find the man-child she first met many moons ago, the boy whose ears blushed at crude jokes, The young man who playfully ran around the yurt on all fours, chasing her two sons with clashing teeth and snarls, pretending to be a tiger. But that boy was buried beneath something else now. Not just command—but a calling. And she saw then, not certainty, but obedience in him. That was what moved her. Not a boy's hunger for glory, but a prophet's fear of failing something larger than himself.

"Say again what your God told you," she said finally.

Mar Yanqa took a breath. "He said, 'Speak to each man as if he were your brother, and tell him not what he fears, but what he hopes. The tribes will follow not out of fear, but the promise of belonging. Tell them they will not lose their names in the union, but find them again; stronger, louder.'"

Alan-Ko was still. The words struck something deep. Not because of their power, but because they echoed something she herself had once told her own people, when fleeing the burning plain after her husband's death. Perhaps this was how God worked, threading voices through many lives until His own could be heard.

She reached forward and placed her hand over his. "Then we will ride together, Mar Yanqa. To every chieftain. To every forgotten corner. If God speaks through you, let me be there to hear it."

He smiled, and it was the first time that she noticed that his appearance now exceeded his age. "We will bind them all together," she said confidently.

Chapter 16: 516 AD

They had been travelling across the steppes for weeks now, encouraging those few clans that had not sworn allegiance to the new Qagan, to do so. At each village, as they waited by the gates, the horns were blown, their horses stamped impatiently but they would not enter until the village masters invited them in. It was Mar Yanqa's way of showing that even with twenty thousand men at his back, he would not take that which is not freely given. To the villagers, it was a sign of respect, humility and integrity. It was their guarantee that he would not take what he considered his by force and this in turn earned him their respect.

It was a shrewd strategy that worked well with the nomads of this wilderness, assuring that they were seen as equals and not forced labor as others that called themselves the Qagan had done in the past. He asked of them only that they provide his troops with what provisions they could spare. Often that meant leaving their village empty handed but neither Mar Yanqa nor Alan-Ko held that again them. Instead, they would leave behind any meats or vegetables that were possibly surplus to their own needs, thereby aiding the villagers battle against the harsh, bone-chilling natural elements of their lands.

One by one the head of each clan swore they would heed Mar Yanqa's call in times of need and times of war. For the first time in their history, it appeared that the Khitan would be united into a nation with common purpose and shared goals. A true miracle to those that had adhered to a nomadic lifestyle that intentionally separated the people into small groups so that they could survive on the sparse resources that the land provided.

Alan-Ko realized that Mar Yanqa was achieving the impossible, convincing her that this invisible God that her husband was devoted to, most assuredly was providing the guidance and desired outcome. How else could she explain a people that for hundreds of years had fought, stolen and killed each other, suddenly swearing off their inborn natural behaviour and be seen embracing members of other tribes and clans that they had been warring with, not even a year ago. It wasn't natural, and she knew for certain it wasn't magic as her husband had prohibited the practice of witchcraft among his followers. Witchcraft from then on would be punishable by death. Those that sought guidance from a witch would be severely punished as well.

She realized his success could only be through Yahweh, and for the first time, the thought that Mar Yanqa might actually be in direct communication with the supreme deity, terrified her. How could one man dare to survive being face to face with such awesome power?

There was one final challenge that awaited them: the most difficult one of all. The chieftain of the Kiyat, known as Abaoji, had sworn his large and formidable tribe would follow no other man but himself. Abaoji was a fierce warrior and a cunning leader, and he viewed Alan-Ko's and Mar Yanq's efforts as a threat to his own ambitions. He had already sent word to their encampment, days earlier, refusing to join their cause, and vowing that he would have his own men assembled to engage them should they still continue to ride in his direction.

Alan-Ko knew that without Abaoji's support, her husband's dream of a united Khitan nation would never come to pass. Everything he had built thus far would begin to disintegrate as Abaoji's opposition would begin to draw some of the other tribes to his own side. What would have begun as a mission to unite a people would end up as a civil war. Even though she was beginning to believe in Mar Yanqa's divine inspiration, she felt she had to do something to protect the dream. She decided she would confront Abaoji directly, traveling to his camp alone, with only a small escort, leaving Mar Yanqa and his army of warriors behind. Abaoji had warned them he would attack if he saw the main body of their forces approaching but said nothing about refusing to engage the Queen of the Khitan if she came alone.

When she first approached Mar Yanqa with her idea, he became terribly upset, fearing for her life and did not even want to hear her defense of such a plan. But Alan-Ko could be just as headstrong as her mate and she would not back down, slowly explaining her logic and reasoning bit by bit until even Mar Yanqa had to admit it was an acceptable strategy to avoid the confrontation that Abaoji had threatened. Though she would be escorted by only a small party of riders, he insisted they had to be twenty of his best warriors. Within that party there would be Tamerlan, Valentius and Shiqan, the newly appointed leader of the Tuoba tribe, which Mar Yanqa calculated would make Abaoji think twice about engaging in battle, once he saw the extent of his coalition as evidenced by the presence of these three very different leaders.

The valley ahead curled into the rising hills like a clenched fist, framed by pine-draped ridges and streams that danced to the whispered song of the wind. Beneath the overcast sky, the banners of the Khitan fluttered, azure eagles embroidered in silver thread, riding in orderly silence toward the borderlands claimed by Abaoji, the unbowed warlord of the largest eastern tribe, known as the Kiyat.

At the front of this tide of hooves and steel rode Alan-Ko, her sable robes flaring behind her like wings as they approached. Behind her, the three most feared men in the Khitan army followed: the tall and aged tactician Tamerlan, Valentius with eyes like burning coals and armor from a past western civilization, and the broad-shouldered Tuoba war-chief, Shiqan, whose armor bore the glyphs of a dozen dead rivals. They rode under the banner of parlay, and every hoofbeat as they approached echoed louder than the last.

Abaoji's scouts, watching from the rocks, raced back to their chieftain. Word spread quickly through Abaoji's camp. Most were taken aback by the Khitan Queen's exhibition of boldness, but when they saw the three general's that rode by her side, they had their first revelation as to the size and threat of the opposing force as represented by these three renown leaders. Mar Yanqa had speculated that their presence would have such an effect on Abaoji's men, spreading both awe and fear and he was not wrong.

Bound by tradition, Abaoji had no other recourse than to invite Alan-Ko and the three generals into his tent to offer them the customary tea and seasoned meats to be followed by parlay. Inside the black-and-red striped tent at the foot of a ridge, Abaoji sat like a boulder in a stream, unmoving even as his advisors shifted nervously around him.

"Clever," he muttered, mostly to himself.

"They are baiting you," whispered Bolkar, his second. "Kill them now and their army will hesitate. Mar Yanqa will rage, but—"

"No," Abaoji cut him off. "Tradition binds me. I must honor the banner of parlay. That woman is cunning. She has cornered me with civility."

The tent flaps opened with a gust of cold air and foreign perfume. Alan-Ko stepped in first. The men of Abaoji's court fell silent as the three generals stood tall like statues behind her. The Queen's presence was understated, but commanding. Her eyes swept the room like the wind before a storm.

"Chieftain Abaoji," she said, bowing respectfully. "Thank you for honoring the rites of the land."

"I have no choice," Abaoji growled, gesturing toward the thick cushions. "Sit, speak. Let us exchange words now. We can always exchange arrows later."

Servants brought drinks of red tea and fermented mare's milk, along with roasted roots, and strips of cured meat. Alan-Ko touched none of it.

"My husband," she began, her voice calm but firm, "does not wish to bring war to Khitan soil. The tribes are tired, the old enemies in Wei stir again, and our sons are growing up without peace. You know this."

Abaoji didn't speak, his penetrating stare never falling away from Alan-Ko.

"You're a leader of men, Abaoji. But you know as well as I do, Khitan cannot survive divided. You command fierce loyalty, and your lands are harsh and hard. You've made warriors out of herdsmen. But what if your legacy could be more than defiance?"

She stood slowly, walking toward the map, painted onto a stretched deer hide hanging behind Abaoji's seat. "This," she pointed, "could be ours. Not yours, not mine. But ours. A union of fire and steel. You see an invasion. I offer you alliance."

Abaoji laughed, but the sound was bitter and hollow.

"You come with three wolves at your back and call it a friendly visit. You say 'ours' as if your armies have not crossed into my territory. Speak plainly, woman." Abaoji had not anticipated that his adversaries would take such a bold and risky approach, anticipating Mar Yanqa to be like every other would-be-king to parade his massive miliary might first before his enemies with the intent to frighten them into submission. Abaoji had already drawn his battle strategy taking advantage of his men's knowledge of the land to strip Mar Yanqa of his manpower advantage. This unexpected intrusion into how he had viewed the sequence of events to follow would require a rethinking of that strategy. The feeling of being outmaneuvered at the onset did not sit well with Abaoji.

Alan-Ko did not flinch. "Then I will. Right now, you're thinking that you still have an advantage of knowing the lay of the land and that will somehow overcome our superior numbers. It won't. If we fight, you will lose, though not without spilling plenty of my people's blood too. We will still be standing as the last of your army is buried beneath our boots. Your dream of ruling all Khitan will die with your first rider. You will be remembered not as a unifier, but a fool who resisted too long. The woman and children of your tribe will spit and curse when they hear your name."

Abaoji's jaw tightened. The tent was silent save for the sputtering of the firepit.

"You think you are clever," he said. "But I see what this is. Mar Yanqa sends his wife because he knows I won't spill a woman's blood in my tent. He sends his war-dogs to glower behind you while you sweeten your poison with honcyed words." He leaned forward, eyes sharp with calculation. "But I will not be shamed into bowing. Not yet. If your vision is truly one of greatness, then prove your worth. Not with words. With deeds."

Alan-Ko narrowed her eyes. "What are you suggesting?"

"Your husband became Qagan through a test of the old ways, is that not so? He killed your father wrestling in single combat according to the stories."

"You want a test," Alan-Ko was surprised to hear his suggestion. "You want to wrestle my husband?"

"Do not take me for a fool," Abaoji shot back. "What chance would I have wrestling against the man that could defeat a monster like Qatun?"

Alan-Ko failed to respond to Abaoji's deliberate attempt to unnerve her by referring to her father as less than human.

"No, I propose three tests. If you and your husband succeed in all three, then I will swear fealty, bring my men to your cause, and kneel before your banner."

Valentius shifted his weight, and Shiqan's knuckles cracked like ice splitting. Alan-Ko gave no sign of discomfort even though it was clear that Abaoji was setting a trap.

"And if we fail?"

"Then you leave my lands and never return. Not a single Khitan and Xianbei boot of your people will enter into my land. Otherwise, we meet in war."

She tilted her head slightly. "Name your tests."

"The first archery; on horseback," he said. "You, Alan-Ko, will ride against me. Ten targets. Ten arrows. Speed and precision."

Alan-Ko's mouth twitched. She had trained since her youth with the best riders. Her aim was as sharp as her tongue. "Why against me? Why not my husband."

"Do you not claim to be the Khitan queen," Abaoji asked. "If I am to kneel before you, then you must also prove you are worthy."

"Agreed."

"The second, your husband will fight me. Sword to sword. No tricks, no armor. We fight until one of us can fight no longer or yields. In swordplay, the gods still smile on whichever of us has clever hands."

He was planning something. Alan-Ko could sense it. Perhaps he was fast with a blade, yes but Mar Yanqa's skill was forged in blood. Everyone knew Mar Yanqa to be a master swordsman. "And the third?" she asked.

"We both have our trained pets. Our tribal mascots" he said, smiling now. "Mar Yanqa's eagle. My wolf. They will be released at dawn to hunt. The one who returns with prey worthy of a chieftain's table wins."

Tamerlan scoffed. "A wolf against an eagle? That's no fair match."

"Why?" Abaoji sneered. "Is the eagle not swift? Do you not boast that it hunts even snakes in the sky? Do you have no faith in your own clan's mascot?"

Alan-Ko's mind raced. This last test was not random. Abaoji must have trained his wolf to hunt on command just as Tamerlan's people trained their eagles. The terrain would favor it. And if the eagle failed, no matter the previous victories, the entire contest would count as a loss.

"And who will judge which prey would be the preferred offering," Tamerlan demanded to know. "On what criteria will the decision be made?"

"To be fair, let a shaman decide not only which would be the best offering for ensuring bountiful meals but which may also serve as an omen for the future," Abaoji offered.

Before Tamerlan could reply, Alan-Ko had already turned to answer. "Very well. All three tests. But you will not interfere with any test."

"I swear it," Abaoji said, smiling like a man who had just set a trap. "Let the gods decide our fate."

Alan-Ko and her escort rode slowly back to the camp where Mar Yanqa would be waiting.

"He is willing to lose the first two," Tamerlan muttered beside her. "To make the third decisive."

"Possibly," she replied. "Perhaps he is better archer than we are aware. Or a finer swordsman than my husband."

"Unlikely," Valentius offered his opinion.

"There is some trick he will try involving that third test," Tamerlan continue".

"I know," she agreed. "He has likely trained his wolf to find something specific. Perhaps the bait has already been laid and the wolf merely needs to retrieve it."

Tamerlan's thoughts were even more malevolent. "Perhaps he will find a way to see that the eagle does not return at all."

Shiqan grunted. "Then we must cheat."

"No," Alan-Ko said. "We win at his game. And we do it in plain sight."

Valentius leaned in. "How?"

Alan-Ko looked east, where the moon rose over the hills. "He will not be able to influence the shaman. The shaman is bound to speak the truth. The eagle must hunt not for meat. But for meaning."

"And how do you propose that Mar Yanqa trains his eagle tonight to hunt in such a manner?"

"I do not know," Alan-Ko admitted, "But my husband will find a way. You will see."

Chapter 17: 516 AD

The sun rose behind a curtain of haze, spilling golden fire over the sweeping valley that lay between the two mighty encampments. On the western ridge stood the banners of Abaoji, wolf-skin standards snapping in the mountain winds, his warriors massed in dark clusters, faces grim beneath helms of bone and iron. To the east, where the grass dipped into shadow, Mar Yanqa's black-lacquered spears and bronze standards with golden eagles against a black background shimmered like obsidian flame in the light.

Between them, a swath of neutral ground had been marked. Forty paces across, with white stones delineating the sacred space of the trial. In its center, a high wooden platform had been hastily erected, adorned with carved totems, sacred blades, and bowls of offering smoke.

A horn was sounded.

From the east, Mar Yanqa emerged, cloaked in his robe of glittering gems, a wolf-fang necklace resting on his bare chest. Beside him rode Alan-Ko, her silver-studded armor catching the sun in flashes.

From the west, Abaoji strode in full view, flanked by his blood-bound general Bolkar and the shaman known as Lady Tse, who held a smoking censer of juniper and ash. Abaoji wore a half-mask of carved bone and a deep crimson cloak. His wolf, Shaar, loped silently beside him.

A hush settled as the two parties met at the dais.

Abaoji's voice rang out first, strong and theatrical, meant for all to hear.

"Before blood is spilled and steel drawn, let all tribes bear witness: This is not war. Not yet. This is judgment. Judgment by test, by skill, by strength, and by the spirit of the earth and sky."

Lady Tse stepped forward, raising a bone staff topped with feathers and bells.

"Let the rules be known and bound by oath!" she cried.

She turned slowly, her words echoing across the valley. "Three trials shall decide the fate of the Khitan clans for an eternity. The first is the Trial of the Wind, a contest of archery on horseback, between Alan-Ko and Abaoji. The second will be a trial of Iron, a duel of blades between Mar Yanqa and Abaoji. The third will be the Trial of Spirit, in which each clan's beast shall hunt and return with an offering that will be judged on its meaning and contribution. If Mar Yanqa's house wins all three, then Abaoji shall lay down his arms, swear loyalty to the kingdom of Mar Yanqa and Alan-Ko, and lead his warriors under their banner, unified and indivisible.

But if even one trial is lost, the union is broken. Abaoji's clan will remain sovereign, and Mar Yanqa must retreat beyond the Urgun Steppe, never to return. No pursuit shall be made, but neither shall aid be offered. Let no spear be raised against the outcome. Let no vengeance follow."

The crowd on both sides murmured, tension rising like storm winds. Lady Tse lifted a bowl of sacred fermented milk, handing it first to Mar Yanqa. He took it and drank. Then to Alan-Ko, who followed solemnly. Then to Abaoji, who drank deeply, his jaw clenched.

The shaman held up a dagger and sliced a small cut across her palm, letting three drops of blood fall into the bowl. "The gods have tasted this oath," she intoned. "Breach it, and the land will remember. Break it, and the ancestors will turn their backs."

Then she turned, eyes blazing, and bellowed into the wind. "Do you, Mar Yanqa, Qagan of the Khitan and Xianbei, swear upon your name and your blood to uphold this trial's verdict?"

Mar Yanqa raised his blade. "By Almighty Yahweh, I swear."

"And you, Alan-Ko, Queen of the Khitan, do you swear?"

Alan-Ko nodded. "I swear it, by the memory of my mother and the breath of my sons."

The shaman turned to the other side.

"Abaoji, son of the Grey Hills, chieftain of the Kiyat's nine banners, do you swear?"

Abaoji's voice was flat and cold. "I swear it, by the bones of my father and the eyes of my wolf."

The crowd roared. The oaths had been mad. The trials would begin.

In the narrow field marked upon the valley, a circle of flags marked the arena.

At the edge of the arena, Alan-Ko tightened the leather straps on her forearm guard. Her horse, a lean black mare with white socks, tossed its head anxiously. The targets—ten wooden disks hung from poles at irregular intervals, spaced unevenly across the even more uneven terrain. Some half-shrouded by brush, others swaying slightly in the breeze.

Abaoji mounted a roan stallion with calm ease. He wore a deep red cloak and carried a bow made from birch and horn. His eyes gleamed. This was not a contest of death, but dominance, and he knew how to perform but seemingly unworried if he won or lost.

The herald lifted his horn and blew a low, droning note.

Alan-Ko kicked her heels and charged. Her mare lunged forward like a shadow, galloping with wild grace as she drew her first arrow. She passed the first target and loosed, thunk, a clean hit dead center. She didn't stop. The second came up faster, at an awkward angle. She twisted, fired. Another solid hit, though closer to the edge. The third and fourth flew by like ghosts. She struck both, but barely. Sweat beaded on her brow.

Abaoji was riding on a parallel course. His stallion moved confidently, with deliberate, almost theatrical ease. He struck the first with ease. Then landed the second perfectly. He was matching her shot for shot. She understood now. He only needed to match her. It all served to create drama by claiming a tie, which would not constitute a win and therefore Mar Yanqa would fail in the task of winning all three, even if they did win the other two trials.

But Alan-Ko had no intention of letting there be a tie. She kicked her heels into the side of her mare, quickening the pace. A they both approached the final target; a gust of wind bent them both swinging sideways. Any archer would have hesitated and waited for the target to swing back into position. Abaoji waited. Alan-Ko instead, dropped low in the saddle, leaned into the motion of the mare and the swinging target, and fired without looking. Her arrow sang through the air and buried itself in the target's heart before Abaoji even aimed his final arrow.

The crowd roared its approval of her marksmanship. Even Abaoji's men shouted despite themselves.

The herald declared the scores. Alan-Ko: ten of ten. Abaoji: ten of ten. Completion in the shortest time goes to Alan-Ko. She had won. There would be no argument regarding the determination of a tie.

An hour later, Mar Yanqa stood in the center of the ring, stripped to his waist, his curved sword gleaming in the mid-morning sun. Across from him stood Abaoji, also without armor but arm heavily wrapped, sword in hand, confidence oozing from every movement.

They circled each other. No words. No boasts. Then they struck.

Steel clanged against steel. Abaoji was faster than expected. Wily, slippery, trying to feint and dance around Mar Yanqa's power. He struck low, fast. Mar Yanqa blocked. Abaoji pivoted, struck high. Mar Yanqa leaned back, let the blade whistle past his face, and countered with a bone-rattling swing that nearly split the air open.

For several minutes, they traded blows like men possessed. Abaoji tried every trick—sand kicked at the eyes, sudden lunges, fake slips. Yanqa was a wall. Patient. Measured. Every step placed perfectly. Every strike economical.

Finally, Abaoji overreached. He lunged, desperately trying to jab into Mar Yanqa's ribs. But Mar Yanqa turned his body just enough to slip the blow and smashed his hilt across Abaoji's jaw. The warlord stumbled backward. Mar Yanqa stepped in and twisted his sword from his hand with a savage jerk. Abaoji dropped to one knee. A kick to the side had Abaoji on the ground, and Mar Yanqa's sword at his throat. Mar Yanqa chose not to draw blood, instead demanding that Abaoji declare defeat. "There is no need for bloodshed between us," Mar Yanqa said. "Say that you yield and rise as a brother."

At first Abaoji refused to make the declaration.

Mar Yanqa pressed the point of his sword a little more firmly into Abaoji's flesh, drawing a droplet of blood.

"I yield," he cried out.

Silence fell. Then cheers exploded from both sides.

By mid-afternoon, all eyes turned to the edge of the forest. Abaoji stood beside his massive gray wolf, Shaar, a beast that reached to his hip. The wolf's yellow eyes darted, muscles twitching beneath its thick coat.

The herald lifted a black cloth and let it fall. The hunt had begun.

Abaoji whispered to his wolf, sending it running into the forest. Shaar vanished into the underbrush like smoke. As suspected, somewhere deep in the woods, small prey had been placed by Abaoji's men to provide Shaar with easy pickings. Several fat hares, a few penned game birds, even a tethered ewe. Abaoji was confident that there was no way he would lose this time.

Mar Yanqa whistled sharply, and from his gauntleted arm his golden eagle took flight. It rose into the wind, wings spread wide, shrieking once before soaring toward the trees and out of sight.

As soon as he could no longer follow his trail, Mar Yanqa retreated to a quiet spot where he bowed his head and prayed quietly. "Lord, if you still have faith in me, now is the time I need you to show it and deliver a victory that will convince everyone that you are the one and only God. My wife says that the eagle must return with an item that has far more meaning than a mere meal offering. I don't know what that might be. But I do know that you will be able to master that riddle. You will know. For you are the God of Abraham, Isaac and Jacob, the God of my forefathers and I believe in you."

Alan-Ko watched the eagle's shrinking form in the sky, heart pounding. It circled once, twice, then veered sharply east, as trained. Whether he returned and what it returned with was out of their hands now. Seeing Mar Yanqa in a quiet corner off the arena, she strode quietly over and saw that he was praying. She waited until he raised his head and completed his prayer. "Did God hear you my love?"

"We won't know until Sepor returns," his answer was tinged by the unknown. "I am but a servant of God and the servant cannot guess the mind of his master."

"He will hear you Yanqa, I know He will," she tried to reassure him.

Time dragged on like a funeral drum. Minutes turned into hours. Then, a howl. Shaar came loping back, fur bloodied, a hare dangling from its jaws. The Kiyat soldiers cheered. The meat was fresh, and the kill clean. Abaoji grinned, arms crossed. Abaoji laid the hare before the shaman to receive her judgement.

Lady Tse examined the animal corpse closely. "I see nothing more than a single meal for two, perhaps three men. It has no other meaning that I can visualize."

Not long afterwards, a sharp cry came from above. Sepor dove from the sky, then flared his wings with talons extended, dropping a silver tipped wolf cub into Mar Yanqa's outstretched arms. The cub cried loudly for its mother but otherwise appeared completely unharmed. The eagle had not even made a single scratch or cut when it seized its prey. Alan-Ko took the cub from her husband and it immediately stopped howling, finding comfort in her arms. Sepor landed on his master's gauntleted arm.

The shaman looked over the strong, healthy cub and made her pronouncement, while everyone stared on in amazed silence. This wolf cub represents many meals in the future for the family that raises it. As long as it lives it will provide but its meaning is far more significant.

Abaoji finally found his voice and objected. "This is not how the trial was intended. The were to bring back prey. That was clearly stipulated!"

"No!" Lady Tse corrected him. "It was said that the third will be the Trial of Spirit, in which each clan's beast shall hunt and return with an offering that will be judged on its meaning and contribution. The meaning of this offering should be obvious to all. The eagle was clutching a wolf, meaning it is dominant. The cub was unharmed, indicating that it is to serve the eagle. The cub was delivered to Mar Yanqa, demonstrating that he is its master. The omen is clear, Mar Yanqa is truly the Qagan to rule over all of the Khitan.

There was silence once again.

Then murmurs.

Abaoji looked stunned. He turned to Bolkar, who whispered furiously, "It is impossible. I have never seen an eagle grip an animal in its talons without killing it, let alone a wolf cub. The cub would be in its den. Eagles don't dig."

Abaoji stepped towards Alan-Ko, examining the cub in her arms. "Where did he find it?"

Alan-Ko looked him in the eye. "What are you trying to say?"

"It's not natural. Eagles don't have the opportunity to hunt wolf cubs. Either someone placed this cub so the bird could grab it gently or this…"

"Or what exactly," Mar Yanqa urged Abaoji to complete his sentence.

"Or this…this…would be an act of that god of yours!"

"Praise the god of Mar Yanqa," Lady Tse shouted for all to hear, "For He has delivered a miracle." The shaman had ended any further discussion.

The crowd erupted. What had begun as a trial for leadership was now a tale to be told for generations. A new legend had been born.

Abaoji, face red, fists clenched, turned to his men. But there were no cheers for him. They were already stepping forward, heads bowed, not in shame, but in awe of their new chieftain.

Mar Yanqa took Alan-Ko's hand.

Abaoji looked at them both. "You have won. By the will of your god, by the eyes of the clans, and by the beating of my own heart."

He knelt. Then one by one, his warriors followed. And in that moment, the Khitan nation began to rise.

Chapter 18: 517 AD

Having finally united the nomadic tribes of the steppes; it was time to conduct the grand ceremony where all the Khitan tribes would openly pledge their loyalty to their new leader. The celebration was intended to be more than a conveyance of rituals, speeches, and the forging of a powerful alliance. It would be about the forging of a new nation. The vast steppes of Mongolia had witnessed countless gatherings of nomadic tribes in the past, but none would be as significant as the unification ceremony of the Khitan. For the first time they would unite under a single banner.

The wind stirred gently through the sacred valley of the steppes, providing a hushed murmur across the endless grassland. Here, in the cradle of their ancestors' bones and blessings, a fire waited to be born; a fire that would not only pierce the night sky but kindle a new era in Khitan history. By twilight, the valley had come alive with the thunder of hooves, the clinking of leather plated armor, and the distant calls of flutes and throat singers echoing against the granite cliffs. Tribes arrived from every corner of the plains, their horse-borne banners fluttering on the breeze, heralding their presence. The clans people huddled together, flanked by proud warriors and solemn elders, as they streamed into the valley. Their camps formed a ring around the ceremonial grounds, and above them, the sky blushed with anticipation.

The valley vibrated with the voices of the hundred or so thousand that had gathered in the sacred valley, surrounded by towering mountains and threaded by a crystal-clear river. As deafening as the sound was, it immediately fell silent as Mar Yanqa emerged from the tent of preparation followed by his wife, the beautiful Alan-Ko. In his right hand, he held the ceremonial staff, carved long ago by a master artisan from the high mountains of Barkul. It bore the history of the Khitan, its origin, migrations, battles, and chieftains from centuries before, all etched in sacred lines and curled motifs. He raised the staff high, and all eyes transfixed upon the carved masterpiece.

"Brothers and sisters," he began, his voice carrying the weight of leadership, "today, we stand in this valley united as one people. Our strength lies in our unity, and together, we shall overcome any challenge. Tonight, we will celebrate that unity and bind ourselves together for an eternity. Let us light up the night with a sacred fire that will serve as a beacon to all the world that never again we will let others exploit the weakness of a fractured people."

Mar Yanqa and Alan-Ko stepped towards the towering bonfire, which thus far had remained unlit but crowned in a lattice of dry tamarisk branches, ready to receive the spark. A priest emerged from behind and offered each a flaming torch. Mar Yanqa and Alan-Ko accepted them solemnly and then each touched their torches to the base of the wood pyre. It caught immediately, as if the fire had been waiting for this very moment. The flames surged upward with a crackling roar. It was then that everyone saw that Mar Yanqa was wearing his legendary robe that earned him the name of the 'glittering man.' The robe shimmered in the flames like a river of light; threads of silver, gold, with the dazzling jewels embroidered into the folds. Every movement he made caught the firelight as though stars had come to rest upon his body, shattering them into rays of a brilliant colored prism. The crowd immediately responded with a cacophony of 'oohs' and 'ahhhs' as they were bathed in the colored beams of light emitted by the robe.

Then their attention returned to the massive bonfire. The flames danced and crackled, casting a warm glow over the assembled tribes. The fire symbolized the spirit of the Khitan, a beacon of hope and resilience. With every crackle that released a flare of sparks, the Khitan would show their approval with a raucous cheer. The chieftains, one by one, approached the bonfire and placed offerings of food, drink, and precious items into the flames. These offerings were a tribute to the new Qagan and his queen, a gesture of gratitude and respect for their guidance and protection. The flames consumed the offerings greedily, sending pillars of smoke spiraling into the sky.

Once again cheers erupted, but these were quickly silenced by the sharp beat of a kettle drum. Mar Yanqa raised his hand, commanding silence. His voice rang out clear over the crowd, rich and youthful, yet steeped in reverence:

"Sons and daughters of the steppe, hear me! Under the gaze of our ancestors, we have come to do what our forefathers only dreamed might happen. Today, we are no longer scattered tribes. Today, we are one people. One fire. One spirit."

Cheers of raw emotion rippled through the gathering.

"The Khitan tribes have pledged their strength to a single cause. As have the clans of the Borjigin, Yelü, the Xiao, the Zubu, the Tuoba, the Xianbei and the Kiyat. All of you have gathered into this one place, not as enemies but as one family. No longer shall our blood feud with our blood. No longer shall the steppes be ruled by division and distrust. This valley, this flame, marks the beginning of a new day!"

Mar Yanqa raised the ceremonial staff, glowing intensely from the firelight, signaling for the first chieftain to approach. The elder carried his banner, then knelt as he tied his banner to the ceremonial staff and stood with a satisfied gleam in his eyes. One by one, the other leaders followed. Each approached with solemn dignity, tying their tribal banner to the previous one that had been tied to the staff. The staff was then planted into the earth. At its top, the many clan banners now hung as one, tied and bound, a single emblem of unity. The crowd roared their approval, and elders wept openly.

With the unified banner flapping in the wind, Mar Yanqa spoke once more. "Let this banner forged from many be a symbol of our unity and our strength. As long as we stand together, no force can break us. We are the Khitan, and our spirit is unyielding."

Upon completing those words, the shamans gathered around the ceremonial staff, and began chanting and drumming, invoking the protection and favor of the ancestors. The shamans then anointed the banner with sacred oils and herbs, imbuing it with spiritual power.

Alan-Ko stood nearby, veiled in the flickering light. She stepped forward, the roundness of her pregnant belly obvious to all. Her two sons watched from the inner circle: their young eyes wide. Her voice was quiet at first, measured, but grew in intensity with each breath:

"I came to you as a widow, a woman without protection. You called me queen and I was shown kindness, but also suspicion. For how can a queen rule a divided people that bristles at the thought of being ruled over like a horse that has not yet been broken. I doubted it would ever be possible to bring unity to these steppes. But then I was wed to Mar Yanqa, and I found not only hope but courage as well. Through his eyes I could see the hope in all of you. I found a true home. May this fire burn away all doubt and suspicion that any of you may still harbor. May our daughters walk proudly. May our sons not know the sting of cousin killing cousin. Today, I know for a fact that we are one people!

Together we shall raise villages where once there were only tents. Laws where there was only vengeance. Peace where there was only a pause between raids. We carry in our hearts not just the future but the memory of those who fell. We call upon the spirits of the ancestors: guide us, guard us, and grant us your favor."

The applause erupted spontaneously and then came the music. A wild, layered sound consisting of deep drumbeats and strings plucked from morin khuur, flutes and gongs, voices raised in overtones of harmony. Dancers whirled, warriors from each tribe leaping into the ring in succession, displaying feats of blade, bow, and bare-handed skill. The dances told stories of bravery, sacrifice, and the enduring spirit of the Khitan people. There was no competition involved, only celebration. The movement of each dancer reflected the distinct flavor of their clan, but together they became a tapestry of defiance and glory. The rhythmic beats of the drums and the haunting melodies of flutes filled the air, creating an atmosphere of celebration and reverence.

Then the shamans emerged, dressed in bear skins and beads, their faces painted with ash and ochre. They moved in trance, spinning and stamping as if to stir the very bones of the earth. One collapsed to his knees, eyes rolled back. He began to speak in tongues, translated by a second shaman:

"The ancestors are pleased. The wolves will run beside your herds. The rivers will not forget your names."

The priests that the Princess She-Ping had brought with her when she returned from Persia followed next. They were cloaked in pale blue silk, embroidered with water patterns created by folds of white linen. From among them, one stepped forward holding a book—not made from paper, but thin, flexible wood sheets, bound in black lacquered leather. Clearly it was intended for this book to have a level of permanence. To exist as long as the Khitan people existed.

Mar Yanqa took the book in his hands, reverently.

As soon as he began to speak the music stopped and the crowd fell silent. His presence commanded respect, and his eyes shone with determination. The chieftains and their clans formed a circle around him, their faces reflecting a mix of anticipation and admiration.

"It is not enough for us to stand here and say that we are united through a bond of brotherhood for even family are known to turn one against the other. It is not enough that we share traditions to claim that we are united since every tradition varies with every hundred leagues travelled. There is only one way to establish and ensure unity and that is only possible when we are ruled by one faith and one set of laws. You may have heard that I worship a foreign god that I brought back from the west but that is wrong. I worship the one and only God and He has blessed me and guided me to the point that I am standing before you as your leader and unifier. But my God is not foreign to you. You just did not know his name. This is the Book of YahSu…Yahweh's Water. These are the waters that do not dry. Within this book are the laws of justice, the stories of exile and return, the visions of wise kings, and the covenant of fire and mercy taken from the holy books of my ancestors and presented in the Tartaric-Mongolian tongue, so that you all will recognize them as universal. From our Xianbei elders and our Hebrew kin, we draw this wisdom, not to dominate the spirit, but to direct the heart."

At that moment, Mar Yanqa opened the book and read:

"In the beginning, there was only the breadth of the heaven, and the silence between the stars. And the heavens became aware and said: I am not one name but many winds. I spoke to the mountain tribes, and they called me Tengri. I spoke to the desert wanderers, and they called me Yahweh. But I am not divided. I am the breath of all things, the riderless horse that gallops across the heavens. I am one and I am all that I am.

Call me YahSu, if you will, for I am the water that falls from the sky to the earth and returns again. I am the living water that provides for all life. I am beyond temples, images, or names, dwelling in the infinite blue of the heavens, which can neither be owned nor conquered. Make no idols because I will not tolerate your attempts to make me dwell within a piece of wood or stone for I am boundless.

Do not attempt to house me in a centralized temple but let my priests wander freely through the steppes and carry the wisdom from yurt to yurt, from oasis to mountain. The day you choose to emulate your neighbors and live in cities of stone and asphalt is the day you will start turning away from Yah and begin following their false gods and pursuing sin. On that day I will turn my back on you and your existence will come to an end.

The stranger is not your enemy; remember, you were once a stranger in the land of your ancestors. Do not spill blood where words can heal. Do not forget the widow or the orphan. And do not build greatness on the backs of slaves. A king's worth is weighed by how he treats the lowest of his people. It is your duty to protect the weak, speak truth, and live in balance with the world I have given you."

The wind picked up again, as though responding to the reading. The people remained entranced, holding on to every word.

"There is a time for war, and a time for peace. Let this be the valley where peace was born. No weapon shall be raised in anger, no life taken unless in defense.

Oh Yah, whose eye is the sun and whose tears fall as rain, teach us to ride with justice in our hearts and the truth on our tongues.

Let not the strong trample the weak, nor the hunter kill without thanks, nor the elder speak lies to the young lest the young no longer respect their elders.

Bless the rivers, that they may sing peace. Bless the winds, that they may carry truth. Let them be evidence of your oneness and I worship no other.

Let our yurts be open to the stranger, and our swords remain sheathed until all words are spoken and no lies remain uncovered.

You shall not hoard what the Earth gives. For the sky gives freely, and so shall you.

Let us not covet anything that another may have but to be satisfied with our lot in life.

If a tree gives you shade, give it your song. If a beast gives you meat, return its bones to the earth with thanks.

All things live by giving, and so shall you be kept alive by your faith in Yah.

Oh YahSu, this is the harmony You command, and in it shall we walk."

Closing the book, Mar Yanqa ended the reading with a blessing for the one God, the great unifier of the Khitan. "There is much more written in the book but this will be for your chieftains to unveil once they have read the book themselves. We will share this faith in common but the enforcements of its requirements and institution of its guidelines I will leave in the hands of your clan and tribal leaders. Now let us feast together and celebrate this glorious night."

The eating followed, long into the night: roasted lambs, goat stew, horse milk wine, dried fruits soaked in honey, barley cakes. Children ran between fires, without a care. Storytellers held court beneath trees, recounting how the Khitan had survived the ancient winters, outwitted the Jin emperors, and endured the harsh and impenetrable migration storms.

In the darkness beyond the firelight, some wept not from sorrow but relief. A sense that something ancient had just been repaired, a fracture that had divided the people for generations now stitched with flame and faith.

Near dawn, the elders formed a circle around Mar Yanqa and Alan-Ko. One by one, they placed their left hands on the staff and their right hands on the book of YahSu, repeating the oath:

"We will not break what YahSu has bound. We are one. We are Khitan!"

Mar Yanqa then approached the shamans to receive their blessing. The head shaman, an elder with deep-set eyes and a commanding presence, placed his hands on Yanqa's shoulders. "May the spirits guide you and grant you the strength to lead our people," he intoned. "With their blessing, the Khitan shall stand united and unyielding."

The shamans' blessing was a moment of profound significance, symbolizing the spiritual unity of the Khitan tribes. The warriors and chieftains, inspired by the shamans' rituals, felt a renewed sense of purpose and determination. Although Mar Yanqa had little to no belief in the spiritual world, he knew the presence of the shamans and their supposed connection to the spirit world reinforced the sacred nature of the unification ceremony. This was evident as the night fell and the shamans remained vigilant, ensuring that the spiritual balance was maintained by offering prayers and performing rituals throughout the night to the gratification of the people. The unification ceremony had not only brought the Khitan tribes together but had also strengthened their bond with the ancestors and the spirit world through the incessant work of the shamans.

As the night deepened, an elder shaman known as Qorchi, entered a trance-like state, seeking guidance from the spirit world.

Qorchi's eyes glazed over, and his body swayed to the rhythm of the drums. The other shamans continued their chants, their voices rising and falling in a mesmerizing cadence. The air was thick with the scent of sacred herbs, and the flames of the bonfire flickered and danced, casting eerie shadows across the valley.

In his trance, Qorchi found himself transported to a realm beyond the physical world. He stood in a vast, open plain, the sky above him a swirling tapestry of colors. The spirits of the ancestors appeared before him, their forms shimmering with ethereal light. They were the guardians of the Khitan, the wise and powerful souls who had guided their people through countless generations.

An ancient spirit warrior with a stern yet compassionate gaze, stepped forward. "Qorchi," the spirit intoned, "you have called upon us in this time of great need. The Khitan stand at a crossroads, and the path they choose will shape their destiny."

Qorchi bowed his head in reverence. "Great ancestor, we seek your guidance and blessings. The tribes have united, but we face many challenges ahead. How can we ensure the strength and prosperity of our people? What are the crossroads of which you speak?"

The spirit raised a hand, and the swirling colors of the sky coalesced into a series of visions. Qorchi saw the Khitan warriors, their banners flying high, riding across the steppes with unmatched speed and precision. He saw them forging alliances with neighboring tribes, their unity bringing strength and stability. He saw the Khitan people thriving, their yurts dotting the landscape, their herds flourishing. But then his visions changed and he witnessed the death of the emperor of Northern Wei, followed by fierce battles, the clash of blades and the cries of war. He saw the Khitan seizing the palaces of the Wei kingdom, adopting their customs and abandoning their way of life on the steppes. Not long after the Khitan began facing powerful enemies, their resolve tested time and again, until finally they succumbed to the onslaught and the Khitan were no longer, being absorbed into an even greater empire whose ways were foreign to them.

The ancient warrior spoke again. "The path to greatness is fraught with challenges, but the Khitan's strength comes from living the life they are accustomed to. Stray from that path and what you perceive as strength will only seal your doom. Remember this: unity is your greatest weapon. Stand together and honor the spirits of your ancestors. With guidance from Yah's waters, you shall prevail."

The vision began to fade, and Qorchi found himself back in the physical world, the chants and drums still resonating in the air. He opened his eyes, and the gathered tribes fell silent, sensing that the shaman had received a profound message.

Qorchi raised his hands, his voice strong and clear. "The spirit world has spoken. They have shown us two paths to greatness. One is to live the life we have always lived and our kingdom will be eternal. The other is to seize greatness when it is offered and assume the life and power of our enemy but our world will burn out quickly like a flaming candle. To choose the eternal path requires unity, strength, and unwavering resolve. We must accept the lessons from this book of YahSu and we must not waver from it."

Turning towards Mar Yanqa, Qorchi delivered one last message, "Great one, Qagan of all the Khitan, the emperor Hsuan Wu Ti is dead. The spirits have spoken but now the decision is yours to make alone."

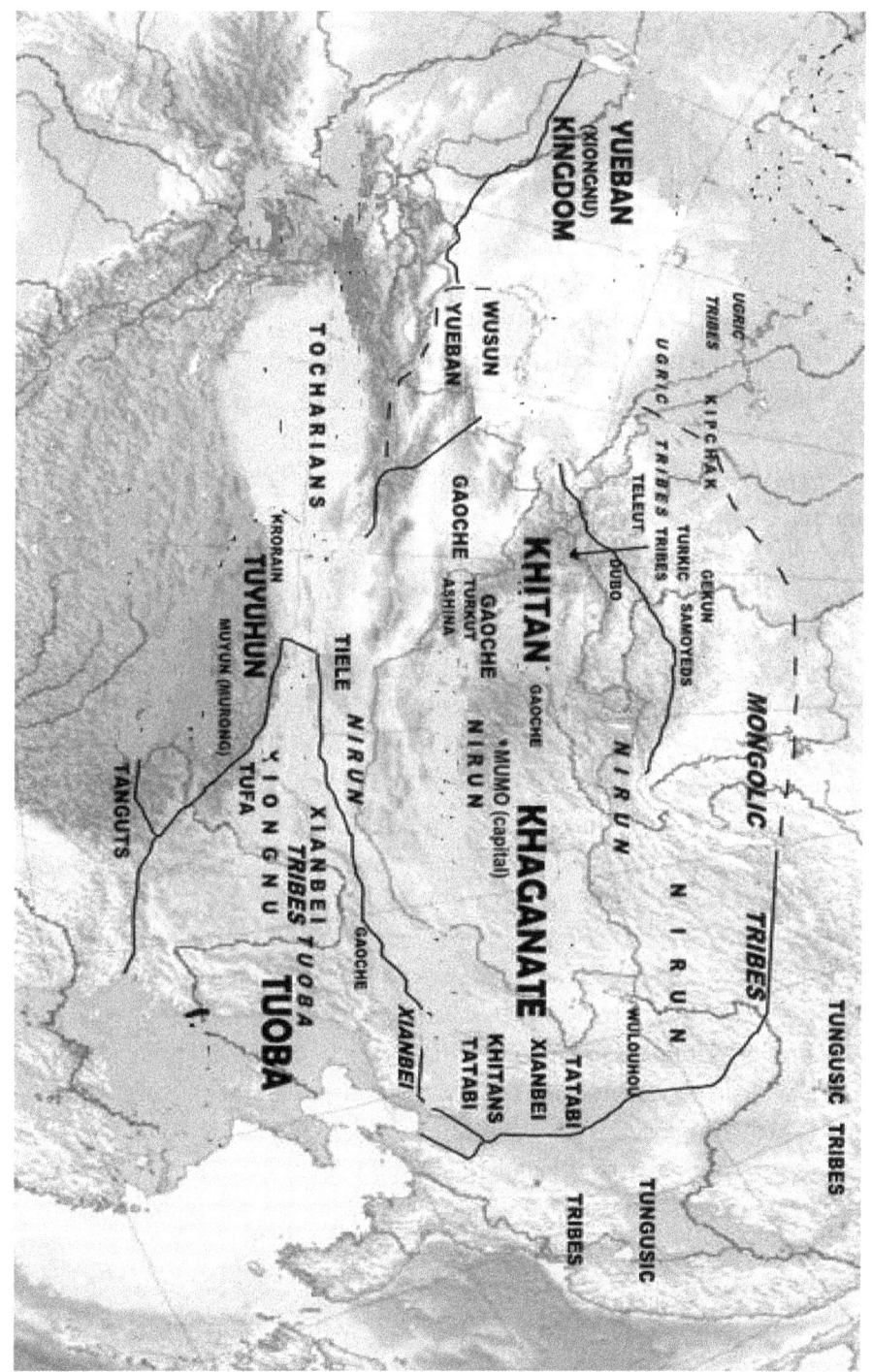

The Khitan Clans and Tribes

Chapter 19: 517 AD

As reluctant as Mar Yanqa remained regarding the spirit world, he could not shake the words that Qorchi had spoken to him. To allay any doubts, he sent several spies into Northern Wei to discover if his uncle was truly dead. If such an event were true then it would certainly change the future for the many peoples that populated his region of the world. He was well aware of the resulting chaos that occurs every time an emperor died, leading to numerous changes in the existing power structures, some for the better, but most often for the worse. The beginning of one power struggle often led to outbreaks of insurrection and attempts to seize power in all the surrounding territories. His young coalition of the Khitan tribes would be ripe for such a power play. He was only a young child when such changes occurred in Mahoza, propelling his father from merely a city king to practically being the ruler of the Sassanid Empire, but he would never forget every catastrophic event that eventually tore apart his family. He understood that the death of Hsuan Wu Ti, if it was true would be no different. He would need to hold a council of the elders as soon as he received confirmation.

A week later the braziers burned with pungent cedar and juniper, thick smoke curling through the great yurt of assembly like an omen. Outside, the northern wind howled across the steppe, rattling the leather walls. Inside, it was hotter than a furnace. The blood of warriors boiled. The circular council hall, built from thick yak hide and reinforced timber, trembled with the angry voices of men not used to being told "no." Tribal chieftains, swathed in wolf pelts and feathered braids, leaned across the wooden council table, fists slamming, words like daggers flying. Mar Yanqa sat at the head of the table, flanked by the Book of YahSu and the brass eagle and wolf standards of the Khitan Confederacy. His face was calm—but his knuckles whitened on the carved armrests of his throne as the room descended into chaos.

"The Northern Wei is broken!" cried Chagan Bor, chief of the Western Tümen. His thick arm struck the table. "Their Emperor lies dead. An eight-year-old boy sits on the throne, his widow-mother pulling his strings like a puppeteer. We could be at Luoyang by the end of spring!"

"We wait?" thundered Abaoji, veins bulging on his thick neck. "Wait? Like cowards? Like eunuchs? The Emperor is dead! A woman rules, hiding behind her child like a turtle beneath its shell!"

"Why stop there?" roared Shiqan, the bear-like chief of the Tuoba. "We could claim the Yellow River! The rice fields! Let the Khitan ride golden in the Middle Kingdom!"

Several elders banged their drinking horns against the table in support; their faces flushed with the intoxicating scent of conquest. But others frowned, their eyes cautious and dark with memory.

"Do not be fools," came a soft voice, silken but cold as frost. "The boy is nothing. The mother is the venom," Princess She-Ping said, her voice hard as tempered metal. "Dowager Hu commands the Imperial Guard and the secret courts. She weaves her power in silence, and lets others take the blame when knives are drawn." She-ping's black hair was bound in a single plait that coiled like a serpent around her shoulders. "You do not know the Dowager Hu as I do. She may wear a veil of mourning, but beneath it is a dagger sharper than any your smiths have ever forged."

"She is but a woman!" snapped Yelü Daran.

"A woman who most likely arranged the death of her own husband, I would suspect," She-Ping replied, her words laced with venom. "And she did it without lifting a blade. Do you think she will hesitate to poison a thousand Khitan hearts if it secures her rule? No... she will crush any threat with the subtlety of a silk rope around the neck."

"A snake!" growled Abaoji. "All the more reason to strike now, before she coils tighter. Every day we hesitate is another day she wraps her coils around the garrisons!"

"You'd like that, wouldn't you, Abaoji?" sneered Tamerlan, still unable to forgive the latter's challenge for power against Mar Yanqa. "Ride down from your western fortresses and seize the loot before the rest of us lift a sword."

Abaoji shoved back his chair, pointing a calloused finger. "Say that again, dog-son, and I'll rip your tongue out myself!"

"You've always been hungry for Chinese gold," said Yelü Daran. "We all know it. Don't talk to us of patriotism. You married a Han concubine and wear silk under your wolfskin."

"Careful, Daran," Abaoji said, eyes narrowing. "The last man who insulted my wife now eats soup through a reed."

The table shook as Shiqan slammed his fist on it. "Enough! If we had any balls left in this tent, we would already be marching south! The Wei are weak, their gods are dead, their generals squabble. What do we wait for...Yahweh to give us a written invitation?"

"Do not blaspheme," Mar Yanqa said quietly, never raising his voice as his three words were more than a suggestion but a warning.

The murmuring resumed, now tinged with unease. Across the chamber, Mar Yanqa sat unmoving, eyes locked on the Book of YahSu placed reverently before him. The sheepskin cover was already worn, the edges stained by the fingers of all that read it. Though it may age, its voice still spoke to him as clearly as the day his priests presented it to him. "My lords," he began, rising. "What you seek is glory. What I fear is ruin." His voice, though young, carried weight. The son of an ancient king and the daughter of an empire, now the supreme commander of the horse lords, Mar Yanqa bore the gravity of three worlds and his mere presence commanded respect.

"It was my hope by now that all of you would have read the Book. If you had, you would realize the book already speaks of this day. The book warns us of what will happen next. When Israel chose to abandon its semi-nomadic ways, ruled by judges and prophets, just as we are, in order to choose a king and seize a kingdom, they turned from the desert toward the city of Jerusalem. Toward palaces, tax collectors, conscription and a census of the people. And in so doing, they turned from God. Their kingdom, like any built on pride and greed, was fractured. Within three generations they were torn in two. In five, scattered like dust in the wind. What had once been great, was reduced to rubble."

He looked out at them, eyes now as dark as the green of the ocean and solemn.

"Do you not see? We are not meant to rule from golden thrones. Just as that was not the path of the Israelites, that is not the path of the Khitan."

Chagan Bor rounded on him. "You quote that book as though it were law! But our fathers followed the blade, not the page. The Khitan were feared, not pious! Shall we tremble before cities while our horses eat bark?" he snarled. "Would you have us kneel to a child emperor while their garrisons raid our borderlands?"

"That book is the law," Mar Yanqa thundered in a voice that made Chagan Bor recoil. "The child is not the danger," Mar Yanqa said. "His mother is. And the mother's ministers. They will bait us into pride and punish us with war. Ignore the child. He is nothing more than a lure to lull us into a false sense of security."

The storm was rising again—some muttered oaths, others shouted.

"The Khitan," came a deep voice from the shadows, "will be nothing but dust if we forget what made us endure."

All turned. It was old Qorchi, the ancient shaman, rising unsteadily on his carved staff. His face was lined like a riverbed. He had seen it all before, surviving three Wei armies and living to spit on their banners.

"Every empire falls," he said. "Not from spears but from internal rot. From pride. That is what the boy-king's court reeks of. Let it rot. We need not hurl our sons onto their walls. The walls will crumble of their own accord."

"Words of the weak," scoffed Yelü Daran. "You want to wait until we're surrounded?"

"Better to wait than to bleed for vanity!" Qorchi snapped.

The room broke again into a shouting match. Spittle flew, and blades were half-drawn from scabbards. Accusations resurfaced; ancient betrayals, broken truces, blood-feuds barely buried beneath the surface. Brothers once united by the vows they made in the sacred valley now stood nose to nose, fury burning behind their eyes.

"Enough!" The voice sliced through the air like a sudden thunderclap. They turned again but this time it was Alan-Ko, Queen of the Khitan who demanded their silence. She stood tall, her hair braided with blue river-jade, in her violet robes, the tribal belt of her father hanging from her waist. She looked at each man in turn, and each man, chieftain or not bowed his head, if only slightly.

"I have borne the death of my first husband. I have buried a father, and seen my land swallowed by fire. But I have also borne sons, and I will see them live."

Her hand touched the Book beneath her husband's hand. "I did not believe, at first. This Yahweh… this God of winds and warnings. But I have read His words. I have seen what happens when the strong forget that strength is not wisdom. And I believe now." She stepped forward, her voice steady, unshaken. "Yahweh sees into the hearts of men and knows their weaknesses. If we ride to war, we must ride not for pride, but for purpose. You say the Empire is weak. Good. Let the people of the Wei see it too. Let rebellion rise in the garrisons. Let us feed that flame with gold, with whispers, not with our sons' blood and bones."

She looked at each man in turn. "Make no mistake. The Empress Dowager Hu will not yield to fear. She will not break because a dozen Khitan banners appear on her border. She will strike from the shadows. She will send whisperers into your yurts, turn brother against brother."

She looked to Abaoji. "Your Han concubine…do you not think the dowager knows her name? Her family? She will twist that knife and turn her against you. Perhaps to cut your throat in the middle of the night."

To Yelü Daran. "Your sons train in the foothills near Wei lands. If you fall, they fall with you."

To Shiqan. "And your people…brave, yes, but few. You would throw them into siege engines, and for what? A golden chair that you, yourself will never sit in?"

She then spoke to all the assembled chieftains. "You want to destroy Luoyang? Good. Then make the people destroy it themselves. The lion eats the wounded, not the fighting stag. This book speaks not only of war, but of waiting. Of discernment. The Israelites had strength, and yet it was their kings who led them to ruin. Their temple fell because pride devoured their faith."

She looked out at the room, her voice solemn and clear. "We are a people either on the edge of greatness or extinction. If we become like those we seek to conquer, then we will lose our souls before we ever take their cities."

There was silence, long and pulsing.

Mar Yanqa scanned the faces of all the leaders once more. The firelight danced in the eyes of old warriors and young brutes alike, flickering across the scars of battles long past. Finally, he spoke again, his voice still low but resonating. "There will be no war. We will not march! Not yet. We will wait, and watch. We will send in the shadow first; agents, gold, whispers. Let the Empire crack from within. Let the people of Wei rise up. And when the walls of Luoyang tremble, not from our swords, but their own rot many generations from now, when they have no resistance to offer, then perhaps we ride. But only then."

Some cursed beneath their breath. Others nodded slowly. The tension did not vanish but it bowed, for now, to the wisdom expounded by their Qagan.

The fire cracked and flared.

The war hawks had been leashed but they had not been silenced. The council adjourned. But as they left, the chieftains still avoided one another's eyes. The storm had not passed.

Chapter 20: 518 AD

The road to Wuchuan ran through black pine forests and fields of frost. Morning mist clung low, curling around the hooves of the riders as they crossed into Wei territory. Khitan cloaks fluttered beneath brown merchant coats, their sabers hidden beneath bolts of silk. There were five of them—not warriors, but whisperers. Spies. Agitators. Flames sent to ignite the Empire from within.

At their head rode Ninbo-Li, son of Gao-Chi, a hawk-eyed man with narrow shoulders and a tongue sharper than any sword. Once a scribe in the court of Luoyang, now a loyal vassal of Mar Yanqa as he had been to the Princess She-Ping prior. Beside him rode Lashi, a former slave who'd once escaped Luoyang's hellish jade mines. Her body bore scars deeper than any confession, and her soul carried a hatred that burned steady and cold. Her and Ninbo-Li had become lovers. They moved in silence. The Khitan did not wage war with noise now. They had come to plant seeds.

Wuchuan was a garrison town wedged between the coastal mountains and the Jian River in the south, a crossroads of imperial commerce and military supplies. The Wei had fortified it well. But like any stone, it could crack when the fault lines were properly tapped.

Ninbo-Li and his agents arrived as traveling traders from the steppes, bearing dyed wool, fine horsehair ropes, and spirits brewed in the mountains. The markets welcomed them. The garrison commanders paid no mind. They were but just one of hundreds of merchant caravans passing through before the harvest.

But each night, behind closed doors, Ninbo-Li and Lashi worked. In the taverns, they spread tales that could not be easily ignored.

"Did you hear the latest? Another grain tax from Luoyang. The dowager is bleeding us dry for her son's palace gardens." It was not far from the truth. The palace in Luoyang was famous for its luxurious gardens.

"They say the Empress's cousin has taken command of the southern armies, a mere boy! An unbloodied incompetent whelp that wouldn't know the first thing about war. Meanwhile, the north is shivering under frequent attacks by those rebel ghosts. How long before they are attacking us here in the south?"

Another favorite tale mocked the dowager empress for the numerous affairs she was rumored to have. "Did you hear? The imperial courier was dragged off his horse near Anyang. Locals say he screamed her name like a lover concealed in the bed chamber."

Most certainly the people listened. All that were within earshot listened. The butchers and weavers. The ox-drivers. The widows of dead conscripts. The veterans who returned from the last northern campaign with missing body parts. The impoverished, that lost family members because they could not afford medicine to stave off the diseases that afflicted them. They all listened and grew angry, needing only a single spark to ignite an inferno.

In the garrison barracks, there was discontent as well. Lieutenant Peng Zhao, a seasoned officer of twenty years, stood at the wall, watching the smoke rise over homes in the distance. He had served well under Emperor Hsuan Wu Ti, awarded several medals for his dedicated service and displays of bravery. He had commanded and watched good men die in the cold mountain passes while court nobles plotted and planned from the safety of their marble palaces. Now the Emperor that he had admired was dead and in his stead, a woman ruled. He bore no angst against women. He did not fear women. But he did fear ambition wrapped in silk and perfume and he certainly recognized the dowager empress bore each of these items in excess.

"Captain," came a whisper from behind. It was Sergeant Jun Sung, young and lean, eyes darting. "I'm afraid there's something's stirring in the slums."

"Another drunken brawl?"

"No. This is different. There's talk of foreigners causing a disturbance. Possibly agitators from the north. Khitan, some of them say."

Peng Zhao narrowed his eyes. "Khitan? This far south? Hardly likely. Bring me one of them... alive!"

With their orders declared, his troops spread out over the city in search of the agitators.

Ninbo-Li sat in the corner of an ale house, scribbling on a scrap of parchment and not paying attention to the movement swirling around him. Had he been more attentive, he would have seen the signal passing between several men sitting at the table across from him. By the time he looked up from his writing, they were on top of him and he had no chance of escape. The three plainly clothed guards seized him by the arms and dragged him into the street.

Lashi saw it all but there was nothing she could do. She exited through the back of the tavern and vanished into the shadows, her face blank.

Ninbo-Li's hands and feet were bound with rope and then he was forcibly heaved into the back of a waiting cart. The three men climbed onto the wagon and with a snap of a whip, the two mules began pulling the cart down the road, toward he garrison tower. It only took a few minutes before Ninbo-Li found himself kneeling before the garrison commander, his limbs still bound.

"What are you? A trader? A thief? Perhaps a spy?" Peng Zhao questioned the man in front of him.

"None of them," Ninbo-Li remained relatively calm. "Just a man that was trying to enjoy a quiet drink in a tavern before being rudely interrupted."

"Oh, I think we both know that you are far more than that," Zhao insisted. "You're obviously not from around here."

"I didn't know that being from out of town had become a crime," Ninbo-Li mocked his adversary.

The comment earned him a whack across the back of the head with the butt end of a spear.

"Let me rephrase my question," Peng Zhao smiled sinisterly. "What is your purpose in the city? It is obvious you are not a trader. Why are you here?"

"I did have dry goods when I arrived," Ninbo-Li began his explanation, "But I sold those immediately and now I'm just enjoying some relaxation before I return home."

"Since when is fomenting rumors of revolt considered to be relaxation?" the commander made it clear that he knew Ninbo-Li was lying. "Yes! You have been observed for some time and we know exactly what you were doing."

"Well, if you know so much, then why even bother asking me the question?" His insolence earned him another caning to the head with the spear.

"I was merely trying to provide you with an opportunity to speak," Commander Zhao explained without having to beat the answers out of you. It looks like that's not going to be possible."

"Perhaps if you had been more direct with your questions, I could have provided better answers," Ninbo-Li defended his failure to respond properly.

Zhao shook his head. "No, I don't think that was the problem. I think you don't want me to know why you're here. I believe there are others here with you and you're trying to protect them."

"Which part of your men abducting me from the tavern where I was sitting all alone, did they fail to mention? Was it the part that I was writing poetry at the time they interrupted me before I could finish my poem? Does that sound like a man that was waiting upon others to design some nefarious plot?"

The commander shook his head. "It sounds like a man that is too well educated and too well versed in the arts to be a mere peddler of dry goods."

"So, I had an education prior to accepting my lot in life as a merchant. Since when is that considered a crime as well?"

"A very good education from the sound of your diction," the commander commented. "Let's put an end to this charade and just tell me what was your purpose at the tavern."

"I'm a listener," Ninbo-Li said with a crooked smile.

"And exactly what is it you listen for," Zhao was curious.

"I listen for those things that one can hear whispered in the streets that you should be very afraid of."

Peng Zhao waved his hand to the guard and immediately Ninbo-Li was struck again to the back of the head. The force of the blow forced him to fall forward on his face.

"I believe you are the one doing all the whispering," the commander commented. "Do you really think you could turn the people under my control against the ruling house of Wei?"

Ninbo-Li struggled to raise himself back into a sitting position but with his hand and legs tied, he was unable to do so. "I don't have to turn anyone," he replied from his recumbent position. "Your own people are doing that on their own. They know the truth when they hear it. If I whisper, it is only to pass on the truth."

The commander kicked him hard enough in the side to crack a rib. "Enough. We'll see if you still enjoy your whispering after I put you to the fire. Tell me who else are you working with and I will give you a quick death without the flames."

Despite coughing up blood from the force of the kick, Ninbo-Li still managed to laugh. "Don't you know that fire does not silence a whisper. It only manages to carry it farther upon the flames."

"You still wish to recite poetry," Zhao had reached the end of his tolerance. "Then you might as well write your epitaph."

By dawn, Ninbo-Li was lashed to a post that had been erected in the town square. The crowd gathered even at this early hour. They had seen the victims of the beatings before but they sensed that this time it would be different. This time they could sense the fear emanating from Zhao's men, fearing their execution of Ninbo-Li would light the fuse of rebellion across the land.

Lashi watched horrified from the rooftop above the baker's house. She feared that if she came any closer that she would attempt something foolish to free her lover. If she did, then Commander Zhao would have two fish to fry that morning

When the flames touched Ninbo-Li's tunic, he did not scream. He recited from the poem he had been working on at the time he was apprehended. "The seed that falls on cracked earth shall bloom in thunder."

The crowd began to murmur, expressing their discontent, as those fallen seeds germinated in rich soil.

By sunset, they tore down the post and buried his ashes with a martyr's rites. By dusk, graffiti began to appear on the city walls: The south remembers, it never forgives and it never forgets. A veiled threat but sufficient enough that four soldiers deserted from the garrison that very night, or so the official report said.

Far away, in the palace halls of Luoyang, Dowager Hu received the report concerning the events in Wuchuan. She read it slowly, absorbing the information regarding the garrison unrest, the spreading of rumors and the burning of the visiting merchant that had now become the symbol of the resistance. A poet that had been killed for the words of freedom he had written. The Dowager Hu knew a dead poet was far more dangerous than one ignored and alive. "Send word to General Bao," she said. "Double the patrols in all the provinces. Interrogate every merchant who does not carry a letter of Luoyang authorization."

Her steward bowed. "And the people of Wuchuan?"

Dowager Hu stared out the window. "Have the garrison build a shrine in honor of the dead Emperor. That should remind them of whose blood runs in the veins of the new child-emperor." And then, she added coldly: "Burn the quarter where the graffiti was found. Let us eliminate any thoughts of insurrection before they can take hold. That should remind everyone to not seek to elevate their standing beyond what they can actually reach."

Back in the Khitan lands, Mar Yanqa received word of Ninbo-Li's death and a shadow of guilt enshrouded his heart and mind, for he felt responsible. He took the scroll advising him of what happened in Wuchuan and placed it squarely on the table, while he sat trapped in his own silence.

Alan-Ko entered into the yurt and easily sensed the distress that occupied her husband's mind. "He died well," she said, attempting to allay any feelings of guilt.

"He died because of me."

"Yes, he did," she didn't deny it, knowing the truth was the only way to deal with his feelings of guilt. "You commanded him, he followed that order, and in so doing, he died. And anyone else under your command would have been willing to do the same for you. You are their king and they would willingly give their lives for you if you asked it of them."

"But I did not wish for his death," Mar Yanqa responded.

"Nor did Ninbo-Li, but he did not shy away from it either. He knew the inherent dangers of his mission. Everyone did. And he would do it again if he had the opportunity. You instructed him to sow the seeds of rebellion in the empire and he willingly did so. And he did it magnificently. He is to be glorified, not to be mourned with pity. He accomplished his mission with great success."

"And the people are listening," Mar Yanqa commented, emphasizing Ninbo-Li's success, now that he thought about it more clearly. "Six major garrison towns are dealing with similar events."

"Yes," Alan-Ko confirmed, emphasizing Ninbo-Li's success.

He looked at the fire burning at the center of the yurt. "This is how the fall of an empire begins. Not with war drums, but with embers; the ashes of a dying civilization. It crumbles from within, leaving a vacuum that others will eventually fill."

Alan-Ko placed her hand on his shoulder. "Ninbo-Li was the spark. And we remain nothing more than the wind to fan the flames he started."

"As long as we can convince our people not to attempt to fill that vacuum. The day the Khitan enter the empire's cities to live behind the gold and ivory walls of palaces is the day that we as a people will begin to crumble as well. We must try to prevent that day from ever happening."

"Then find a way to do so, my love. Don't let Ninbo-Li's death be in vain."

Chapter 21: 520 AD

In the valley of the sacred steppe, the Khitan pitched their great silken pavilions that shimmered in the early spring sun like sails on a celestial sea. The mountains echoed with the cry of hunting eagles, and smoke from roast yak and mare's milk fires coiled into the sky like prayers. It was the season of renewal, of foalings and calvings, and the season of birth among men.

Alan-Ko, veiled in a robe of ivory wool, emerged from the birthing tent, cradling their second son in her arms. A great cheer rose from the gathered tribes as Mar Yanqa, her husband, lifted the newborn high for all to see. "I have son," he shouted to the heavens, to the cheers and applause of everyone that had waited anxiously outside the tent.

The boy blinked against the sunlight falling upon his eyes. His hair, like that of his elder brother, burned with the fire of the west, an uncanny copper-red, his eyes a piercing blend of blue and green, like frozen jade. The elders murmured with awe, for the Khitan believed in signs, and two red-haired sons were not by chance, they were omens of the flames that would eventually burn down the empire in the East.

Dancers erupted into movement, arms slicing the air like the wings of cranes. Drums thundered. Horses whinnied. The horns of the high herds were sounded in great spirals, and men came forward to smear the child's lips with fermented mare's milk, the first taste of life on the steppes.

Mar Yanqa stood beside Alan-Ko, his rough fingers entwined with hers. He recalled how a mere four years ago he had not known how to be a husband when they first wed. But now, there was no doubt in anyone's eyes, he had become a man. His eyes were wise, his decisions measured. The presence of his children, and of Alan-Ko, had remade him into something more, something greater. "I am Mar Yanqa Kahana!" he shouted over the assemble masses, "And let the world shake before my son, the next generation of the warriors of Khitan!"

"Yanqa Khan, Yanqa Khan," the people erupted in jubilation as they shouted their version of his name. It seemed like their voices would never stop, as they shouted "Yanqa Khan," over and over again.

Elsewhere, across the thousand-mile shadow of the Altai and Taihang

Mountains, the north of China burned. In Luoyang, the capital of the Wei Empire, fires smoldered in the alleyways of the southern quarters. Dust coated the once-marble courtyards. The Grand Canal was silting up, trade had slowed to a crawl, and discontent had blossomed like mold on the walls of the crumbling palace.

Dowager Hu sat on the Phoenix Throne, wrapped in robes of crimson silk and lined with sable. She held a jade scepter in her left hand, but the real power was clenched in her right; the execution warrants she signed daily; green seals pressed deep into wax with merciless precision.

"Another rebellion in Nanyang?" she asked, not looking up.

"Yes, Majesty," said the Minister of Punishment, bowing low. "And another in Shandong. The peasants are organizing under a self-proclaimed sage. He calls himself the 'Son of Straw' and claims visions from the Mountain God."

"Send General Fan," she instructed. "Burn their villages. Salt their fields. Hang every tenth man and send the rest to the river barges."

The boy emperor, Xiaoming, sat beside her, just twelve years old, draped in robes far too large for his frame. His eyes flitted nervously from face to face, trying to discern meaning, trying to be a ruler. But he was a reed in a storm, bending to the gale like force that was his mother.

Dowager Hu leaned toward him. "You must look stern when we give orders, my son. The Empire must believe you are strong."

He nodded, trying to mirror her face, but could not mimic the tightness of her jaw, a look that would send shivers down a man's spine.

She had much to clench her jaw about. The garrison rebellions that had been instigated by Mar Yanqa continued to fester and spread along the northern border of the empire. They had already torn at the fabric of the empire for years and there was no indication that they'd be extinguished any time soon. The Dowager Empress continued her strategy of fighting fire with fire, burning neighborhoods to the ground, whenever and wherever her forces found an enclave of rebels. It only served to make her even more despised by the people.

To the north, the Rouran tribes were suffering from a major famine due to successive years of drought without any aid or relief provided by the government in Luoyang. Rouran forces raided the Wei territory in search of food and rather than defend against the Rouran, the people of the towns that were raided rose up and slaughtered the garrison commanders in an attempt to appease the Rouran and persuade them to leave off their devastation. But starving people are only appeased when they have full bellies. The Rouran would not be satiated with anything less.

In contrast, back on the steppe, strength was not hidden behind veils and courtly masks. It thundered in the hooves of horses and sang in the throats of warriors. The Khitan gathered for the Naming Rites beneath the great Sky Banner, a sheet of eagle feathers and blue-dyed silk that only flew when a son was born to the ruling house. It was now the second time it had been unfurled to honor a son of Mar Yanqa, and that called for an even greater celebration than the first time.

Tamerlan, chief advisor to Mar Yanqa on this day was now steward of traditions, as he intoned the ancient blessings now that the baby had survived the first week of life. "What shall you name your son?' he directed the question to Mar Yanqa and Alan-Ko, who carried their second born on a silver tray.

"Bukhatu-Salji!" Mar Yanqa roared, his voice cutting across the highland wind. "He who has the strength of a bull to walk apart!" Once again the name was a compromise, because the Hebrew version was too difficult for Alan-Ko and her people to pronounce. Mar Yanqa had selected a name that would be a reminder of his failings due to both his pride and hubris. Pride which made him desire to bring down the Wei empire and hubris of willingly sending others like Ninbo-Li to their death in order to achieve that goal, readily accepting the danger his spies would face. He saw the birth of his second son as a sign that Yahweh had forgiven him for his manifestation of pride. In the language of his father, Mar Yanqa named the child Bruch-atah Salagi, in which he blessed Yahweh for forgiving his abundance of pride. The Khitan version may have been more suitable, for at nine pounds the baby was built like a bull.

Tamerlan continued the ceremony. "Under the Eternal Blue Sky where Yahweh dwells, we name this child today. May the spirits of your ancestors walk beside you. May your path be long, your heart strong and your name said with honor. May Bukhatu-Salji grow as the grass in spring, fast and deep-rooted. May he hunt the stag in the mountains and speak to the spirits of his fathers. May your spirit be free like the steppe winds and like he wild horse, may your strength know no bounds. May your voice be true, your hands bring peace and may our eternal God in Heaven smile upon your life. Grow tall like the larch, stand firm like the mountain and shine like the stars of your lineage."

Mar Yanqa removed his son from the tray and then held the boy firmly between his legs while a priest knelt down and with a sharp blade and steady hand, circumcised the child. Bukhatu-Salji cried out but as soon as he did, fermented mare's milk was placed to his lips and the tears and cries ceased almost immediately.

The cheers rang out from those assembled as they shouted out the name of their new prince.

Offerings were made. A wild goat was loosed and then brought down in a ceremonial hunt. Its heart was removed, still steaming, and along with the child's foreskin, burned in the sacred fire. It's smoke drifted over those that participated in the hunt, bestowing them with Yahweh, the great sky-god's blessing.

Farther south, smoke of a different kind billowed over the walls of the imperial cities. In Guangling, the Yellow River had broken its banks, flooding half the province. Refugees crowded the roads, heading north, bringing plague and famine in their wake. Bandits struck at will, no longer fearing the name of the Wei. Everywhere one turned within the empire, disaster appeared to strike.

Within the imperial observatory, Dowager Hu consulted her astrologers. The chamber was dark, except for the flickering light of oil lamps set along the curved, lacquered walls, their smoke curling up into the perfumed shadows like silent prayers. A faint scent of burnt juniper clung to the air, mingling with ink and old silk scrolls. At the center stood the bronze celestial globe, its rings turned just hours ago to record the rare conjunction in the eastern sky.

The Dowager Empress Hu, robed in layers of black and gold brocade, stood motionless before the globe, her expression unreadable. Behind her, eunuchs kept their distance, their heads bowed. The three court astrologers knelt low before her on embroidered cushions, their foreheads nearly touching the floor.

"The heavens are disturbed," said the chief star-reader. "There is a conjunction of Mars and the Ghost Star. The north rises. The dragon star dims."

She said nothing at first and then erupted into a vicious diatribe of these so-called seers of the heavens. "Rise and speak plainly to me. You tell me nothing more of what I can see outside the window for myself," she shouted. "Tell me exactly the meaning of these signs or I'll have you all tossed into prison where you can rot for the rest of your miserable lives."

The senior astrologer shuddered as she demanded an explanation. He had hoped to avoid saying anything further and thus avoid inflaming the dowager. Now it could not be avoided. "There is unrest in the spiritual world, your Majesty. The fiery star of Mars will bring war, bloodshed and chaos."

Dowager Hu picked up a vase and hurled it at her chief astrologer, striking him forcefully in the side of his head. "Tell me something I don't already know, you fool!" she screamed.

"When it aligns with the Ghost Star," he stuttered nervously, "The barriers between the living and the dead will be weakened. The ancestors are wrought with anger and there will be a great betrayal followed by assassination. Civil war is unavoidable."

"Do you see who will try to betray me?" she demanded to know, ignoring everything else he said and focusing on that single point.

The head astrologer feared to say anything further but he knew he had no choice; his life depended upon it. It hung in the balance either way. Zhenlong, the dragon star is dimming," he could barely get the words out of his mouth. "It is the star of imperial lineage and reflects the divine authority of the emperor."

"You are suggesting my son is dying?" her face became a mask of raw anger.

The astrologer shook his head. "No…no," he insisted. "It is his vitality that is waning. The child-emperor is weak and his authority is being over-shadowed. The moral order has been disrupted and the heavens are no longer pleased."

As soon as he said those words, his fellow astrologers shuffled nervously and mumbled endlessly, feeling the imaginary ropes tightening around their necks.

The silence that followed was like a held breath in the imperial tombs.

Dowager Hu turned slowly to face them. Her expression was sculpted in ice. Her words were as deliberate as falling stones.

"Say it plainly Master Zuo, if you have the spine."

Master Zuo bowed his head lower. "Your Majesty… we beg forgiveness, but the alignment suggests that the Dragon is hidden, overshadowed. That the Heavenly Mandate, which must rest upon the Son of Heaven, may be obscured… because he does not sit in his rightful strength."

Dowager Hu stepped down from the dais, the hem of her robe sweeping like storm clouds over the jade inlay floor. She stood over them now, looming like a carved goddess.

"You speak of my son as if he were a man. He is a child. You would see the realm placed in the hands of a boy, while wolves claw at every border? While generals drink rebellion and eunuchs sell gold for whispers?

Master Zuo choked on the saliva in his mouth as he tried to swallow. His voice cracked. "Forgive us, Your Majesty. We speak only what the heavens write."

"I have preserved the empire with blood and silence. The court eats because I starved the traitors. And now you dare…you dare…to say Heaven withdraws its favor because I have kept the throne from ruin?" Her voice rose, not loud but sharp enough to make the eunuchs flinch. "Do not mistake stars for truth. They shine alike for emperors and beggars."

"But the message remains the same for both," Master Zuo attempted to defend his craft.

She turned from them abruptly, her silk sleeves flaring like wings. A long silence followed as she looked up at the painted ceiling, toward the blue dome representing the Eternal Sky.

"Then the heavens are mistaken." She paused. Her voice lowered and as dangerous as a drawn blade. Her mind could be seen filling with other thoughts. "Or perhaps, Master Zuo, they are being purposely misinterpreted."

Master Zuo froze on the spot. He knew that his days were numbered.

One of the other astrologers collapsed into a deeper bow. "Your Majesty, if I may. There are ritual offerings that may yet restore harmony. A ceremony at the ancestral temple. A symbolic return of authority to the Son of Heaven, witnessed by the court. It would appease Heaven without…"

Dowager Hu cut him off with a raised hand.

"Enough!" she commanded. Turning to the head eunuch she hatched a plan. "Have a decree prepared. A public rite will be held at the Temple of Supreme Harmony. Let it be seen. Let it be heard that the Empress Dowager places her trust in her son. But the reins of state shall remain where they are, until he is fit to hold them without bringing down the heavens."

She looked once more to the astrologers. "You may speak to the Ghost Star directly, gentlemen. You should have remembered to tread more carefully when you speak to dragons."

Turning to her waiting officers, she passed on her orders with a final flick of her sleeve. "Find me a new set of astrologers. These three have performed their final reading." The officers knew exactly what she meant. She then swept from the room, leaving behind the trembling astrologers and the cold silence of the stars.

To the northwest, under the argent moon, as the sun had not yet broken the spine of the eastern hills, the pale light slipped into the felt folds of the ger through the smoke hole above. Inside, the air was still, the smell of ash and milk mixing with the faint scent of horsehair and leather. A low fire smoldered in the hearth. Alan-Ko sat cross-legged on the felt mat, her robe half-loosened, nursing Bukhatu-Salji at her breast. Their eldest, Bukha-Khatagi, dozed beside her, with a hand resting protectively on her arm. Mar Yanqa sat nearby, sharpening his blade, a morning habit whether he needed to or not.

The baby suckled contentedly; his tiny hand splayed across her breast. Alan-Ko's gaze lingered on him, his downy copper hair, his warm cheek pressed into her arm. Outside, the sounds of the camp were beginning to stir, with the sharp whinny of horses, and men's voices faint in the distance.

"They say there is war in the south," Alan-Ko said as she looked at her husband. "There is talk in the women's tent. Some of the elders say it is time."

He did not look up. "Time for what?"

"To ride south," she said softly. "To rise while the empire tears itself apart. Woye has erupted. Rebel force have taken the garrisons at Taiyuan. Huaishuo has crossed the Fen River. The Dowager's armies are pinned, scattered across a thousand li. The imperial roads are unguarded. The heart of the phoenix throne is exposed."

"Let it be," Mar Yanqa replied. "We are united now. If we find them on our doorstep we are prepared. But we will not set foot on their land nor fight in a war that does not concern us. Let the Empire tremble in the wake of its own insurrections."

The fire cracked, and sparks spiraled into the sky. The boy with red hair suckled quietly.

"You know there are those on the council that say we should attack and destroy the empire once and for all," Alan-Ko mentioned somewhat sheepishly, already knowing what her husband's reaction would be. "They believe it is destiny. That the tribes have been united for such a long time. That we are the hammer Heaven waits to swing."

Mar Yanqa looked at her then. Not with anger, but with something older. Grief, perhaps. The grief of foreknowledge. "And you?" he asked quietly. "Is that what you believe?"

Alan-Ko hesitated. Bukhatu-Salji let go of her breast with a satisfied sigh, curling into her lap. She pulled her robe closed. "I believe we have been quiet for too long. And I believe we are strong now. The banners have never flown higher. The men are eager. The prophecies says the tyrant queen will fall. Perhaps it is we who bring her low."

Mar Yanqa stood. His shadow fell long against the ger wall, swallowing the dancing light. "The Book of YahSu also says we will forget our God in the Sky when we set foot in the palaces of our enemy."

He paced once around the hearth, then knelt beside her and the child, lowering his voice. "I have seen what happens when our people taste silk and sugar and gold. I have seen warriors become lords, and lords become merchants. I have seen the bow abandoned for a brush, the horse for sedan chairs. My father died because of it. My mother was widowed because of it. And I was left homeless because of it."

He paused. His hand brushed gently across Bukhatu-Salji's tiny forehead. "They do not even bury their dead with the wind at their backs. They seal them in stone and forget the smell of the open sky."

Alan-Ko's eyes brimmed with emotion, but she did not interrupt him.

"If we take the war into the empire, it will not end with victory. It will end with forgetting. We will conquer the phoenix throne and then sit upon it until we rot. And in time, our sons will bow like courtiers and debate the laws of selfish men instead of looking upwards to God in Heaven for guidance. Our daughters will bind their feet and burn incense to gods made of paint and wood. Everything we have achieved to unite our people will be lost."

He looked at her, deeply sensing that she still had doubts. "You think that I am choosing not to fight. But I am fighting for something greater than a throne. I am fighting for the preservation of our world, our way of life."

Alan-Ko swallowed. Her voice came smaller than before. "But if the empire conquers us first…"

"It will not happen but even if it did come to pass, then we die as Khitan," he interrupted, calm but immovable. "Not as ghosts of what we once were, dressed in silk robes."

Silence settled again, heavy with the weight of futures not yet chosen.

Alan took his hand. She placed it on the sleeping form of their son. "Will he understand when he is older? Will our children accept that we let the world pass us by?"

Mar Yanqa shook his head slowly.

"They will understand that we kept this way of life available to them. That they are given a choice to master their own destinies and choose which path to follow in their own lifetimes."

Outside, a gust of cold wind howled across the steppe, the sound reminding them that this was their reality. That there would be a cost to answering the call of destiny, as well as a cost of denying it.

Alan-Ko nodded, slowly, her eyes wet but steady. "We will let those others chase shadows. We will remain as one people beneath the open sky."

And there, in the pale hush of dawn, two parents sat together beside the fire, not as rulers, but as keepers of a faith, unwilling to sacrifice their greatest possessions, no matter how bright the phoenix burned.

Chapter 22: 523 AD

In Luoyang, a different fire burned. Dowager Hu stood alone in the Hall of Radiant Virtue, her back to the dragon screen. She whispered to her advisors on the other side of the screen, "Let them rise, these barbarians. I will answer with iron and shadow."

She refused to believe that her empire was already crumbling from within. She ignored the fact that in Woye, a man by the name of Poliuhan Baling had become the leader and symbol of the revolt there. His followers quickly took the town of Woye and he was now laying siege to Wuchuan, which had suffered unrest for years. Elsewhere in Qinzhou, the Qiang leader, Mozhe Dati had laid waste to the government. In Gaoping, Hu Chen rebelled and titled himself the King of Gaoping. In Hebei, the military officer, Ge Rong seized power and proclaimed himself the Emperor of Qi.

It was not long until city after city broke loose from the tightening fist of Empress Dowager Hu's brittle regency. Each rebel leader believed themselves to be unique, a savior, a rightful heir, a divine instrument of retribution. Their voices blurred together into a resounding cacophony of treason. In fields and mountains and deserts, torches were lit, banners raised, oaths sworn on blood and jade. The empire was disintegrating and by the winter of 523, all of China was burning.

Poliuhan Baling, who first rose in Woye succeeded in taking Wuchuan and then the warlord-turned-mystic managed to take Shuo Province in a single night through a clever ruse. His men infiltrated the garrison dressed as traders and then slaughtered the city guard in their sleep. His banners bore the image of the black sun and behind it followed a growing cult of peasants, monks, and dispossessed soldiers fueling his designs on even a greater prize, the Phoenix Throne.

In the floodplains of the Yellow River, Shuo Lin, a former court eunuch amassed an army from pirates and farmers, declaring himself to be the "Son of Heaven Restored" and he swore to cleanse the throne of its womanly corruption.

By the end of the year there were thirteen self-declared kings, six regional alliances, and over fifty armed revolts. Many cities changed hands not once but five, ten, even fifteen times. Scribes could not keep pace with the betrayals. Armies defected overnight. Roads became corridors of war, and no traveler moved without an armed escort. It had reached a point where the Empress Dowager Hu could no longer ignore that the Empire was crumbling.

From within her palace, the Dowager ruled like a spider in a web unraveling thread by thread. Her hair, once lacquered into regal coils, now hung wild and graying. She no longer dressed in silks but in black riding robes, her hands callused from the reins of war. She held court at midnight; her generals weary and sunken-eyed as she paced before them like a lioness in heat. The war council chamber was once a place of measured counsel, its sandalwood walls carved with dragons, phoenixes, and the inscriptions of emperors past. But at the midnight hour of these days, it echoed only with fear, exhaustion, and the rasping voice of a woman consumed by unrestrained wrath.

"Kill the root, and the tree will rot," she hissed. "Kill their leaders. Put their mothers in chains. Let every rebel choke on his own blood. I don't care if you need to kill thousands in order to bring an end bout. Just do it!"

Around the strategy table, the generals remained standing. Not one dared speak first. They had seen too much, heard too much. These were not green officers but hardened men, veterans of the frontier, commanders of campaigns that stretched back decades. And yet now, they stood like whipped dogs, watching their ruler unravel before them.

"Do you fools understand nothing? I told you to crush the rebellions. Not to contain them. Not to beg for terms. Crush them! Burn the cities if you must. Drown them in the rivers. Let every traitor's head rot on a spike."

General Xun bowed slightly. He was young but the most tactful. "Your Majesty, our forces are stretched thin. There are uprisings in Jizhou, Weizhou, Shandong. We cannot march in all directions at once."

"Then you will choose the worst of them and make an example so severe the others piss themselves at the thought of defying me!"

She reached across the table, seized a jug of wine meant for ceremonial toasts, and hurled it against the stone wall. It exploded, the shards clattering to the ground like bones.

"How many self-declared kings now? Twenty? Thirty? A hundred? Each one calls himself Heaven's favorite while I still breathe. While I still sit upon the phoenix throne!"

General Ma, whose white beard stretched down to his chest, spoke. "We would ride, my lady. We would slay a thousand rebels each if we could. But we are drowning in fires. Every time we put one out, three more rise."

"Then drown them in return! Drown them all!" she screamed, banging both hands flat on the table. "Kill every soul in the province if you must. Burn their fields. Salt their wells. I want whole prefectures silenced…permanently."

The generals exchanged glances. None dared say what they thought: that the empire was lost, and their Empress was mad.

She turned her wild eyes on General He, whose son had recently been executed on her orders for fleeing a losing battle. "You. You still have men. Why do you not ride? Why do you sit here like a eunuch playing court games while the empire slips into the abyss?"

Never one to avoid battle, General He stiffened, holding back on what he truly wished to say. "We have ridden, Majesty. My army took back two cities last month. We held them for five days. Then rebels returned in force. The people inside rose up against us. My men were butchered by those they protected."

"Then do I have to say the obvious? Kill the people too," she screamed, eyes unblinking. "Kill the towns, the villages, the children. Let the earth itself fear rebellion. Let the rivers run red until Heaven relents." Her voice broke. She trembled, not with fear but rage; an animal fury born of years of holding power by blood and terror. Then she laughed, a rasping, broken sound.

"Do they think me weak because I am a woman? Do they think they can take my crown with slogans and smoke? Well, let them choke on fire!"

General Ma cleared his throat. "Your Majesty, if we commit to a scorched earth strategy, the countryside will starve. We may survive the rebels, but famine will do what they could not. We will all die in the end."

She turned on him so fast he flinched. "I do not care if a million peasants starve. I do not care if the rivers turn to ash. I will rule what remains, even if it is a city of corpses!"

There was a long silence. The candlelight flickered, shadows trembling on the walls like spirits writhing.

Finally, General Xun spoke softly. "We will do as you command, your Majesty. But we cannot be everywhere at once. We must prioritize."

"No," she snapped. "You will be everywhere. You will divide your men. You will ride day and night. And you will silence these rats. No more excuses. No more failures. Or I will make towers of your skulls and burn Luoyang myself to mark your failure."

She turned her back on them, pacing to the open window. There was smoke in the distance marking another lost town. Or another slaughter. It was hard to tell the difference anymore.

"Leave me," she commanded. "Go. Kill. Burn. Return only when the empire is whole again."

The generals nodded. "Let it be done," the generals shouted in unison as the bowed and left her presence. One by one, they turned and left, their faces pale. As the doors shut behind them, no one uttered a word. They no longer strategized. They no longer planned. They only obeyed, afraid that their ruler was now nothing more than a specter of wrath with nothing left but vengeance.

In the silence of the war room, Empress Dowager Hu stood alone, gripping the window ledge as if it might keep her tethered to the earth. Her breath came ragged, her eyes searching the darkness. "I will not fall. I will not be forgotten. Let them call me monster, if only they remember my name."

The great General Yu Liang went west to crush Woye, but never arrived, having vanished into the desert. His body was never found.

General Shan of Jiangxia betrayed his oath and joined the rebellion, taking with him the entire 3rd Southern Army.

Reports came that bandits now controlled the Grand Canal, pillaging grain ships and flooding cities. An earthquake destroyed half of Changan's wall. Even nature was rising up against Dowager Hu.

In some towns, cannibalism broke out. In others, militia lords boiled dissenters alive in iron pots, sending their charred heads to Luoyang as offerings. No peace could be made. No surrender lasted. It was not a rebellion. It was the shattering of an empire.

In the rice paddies near Yingzhou, soldiers marched through mud littered with the bones of previous battles. Crows circled overhead, fat and fearless. A child wandered between corpses, her face painted with ash to avoid notice, picking over the dead for food.

On the banks of the Fen River, the river ran red for days. Thousands had been slain, their bodies heaped like fallen wheat. The stink of blood clung to the air for weeks. Mothers could not find their sons among the remains but the wolves did.

Soldiers went mad. One captain slit his own men's throats at night, whispering about ghosts in the trees. Men deserted in droves, forming warlord bands that pillaged as they pleased. A city under siege collapsed when its own defenders opened the gates to the enemy, begging to be spared. They were not.

Women hung themselves with their dead husband's belts. Monks climbed towers and threw themselves into pits of flaming fire below. Everywhere one looked, hope had died. But as everyone knew, a dragon dying is often when it is most dangerous.

In the southern mountains of the Empire, towns once loyal now flew black banners. The rebellion was no longer an uprising. It had become a civil war.

Armies clashed by torchlight, brother killing brother. The imperial army conscripted farmers and children. Entire regions bled.

Several weeks later the Ministers of the Imperial Palace in Luoyang stood before the Dowager Empress, shaking with fear. Viceroy Zhou Lin reported that another grain shipment had been taken by rebels before reaching the Yellow River. Meanwhile, Emperor Xiaoming, still under the control of his mother, was secluded in his study, surrounded by eunuchs and scrolls, learning about a country that was bleeding out beneath him, that he may never live to rule.

The Dowager Empress once considered a brilliant politician in her own right filled with ambition, snapped at her officials like a rabid dog. "Where are the northern tribes to come to our defenses? They must be planning something. Send more spies. Offer them gold and gifts. If they do not comply, then burn their villages. Do something!"

The ministers exchanged weary glances. Threaten what trade? The Khitan no longer came to barter. They no longer sent envoys. They had their own kingdom and other nations came to them to offer alliances. Silence, once a sign of peace on the northern border, now screamed of dread. Why would they prod a bear asleep in its den. If the Khitan were nowhere to be seen, that should be taken as a good sign. Approaching them now might shift the balance and definitely not in the favor of the Empire.

Some within the court, still loyal to the Dowager Empress, argued not to even bother trying to negotiate with the Khitan but to strike first and burn their grasslands, thereby starving the tribes into submission. In their minds it was better to use the element of surprise and attack the sleeping bear before it had a chance to awaken. They knew if the Khitan ever did decide to attack, then the Empire's days were over. They had their orders. Nothing they could do but discuss the options with the generals and let fate take its course. The madness had finally taken control.

Chapter 23: 523 AD

While Luoyang trembled in fear, in contrast Mar Yanqa's encampment stood orderly and calm. Too calm for the likes of the more seasoned Khitan warriors. Banners fluttered lazily in the breeze. Herds of horses grazed on the open steppe. Children ran among felt tents with painted walls, and women sang lullabies while weaving cloth by hand. There was no smoke, no blood in the dirt, no cries of the dying. Instead, there was a quiet celebration. Alan-Ko had given birth again; her third son with Mar Yanqa. The midwife announced the news in a tired but reverent tone: "The child lives. Strong lungs. A boy."

This time they finally agreed on a name that they could both pronounce, Bodonchar-Munkhag. In Mar Yanqa's father's tongue, the name held layers of meaning: Rejoice, Sigh, Suffer, and Celebrate. It was a name born of contradiction. It captured the mood perfectly of the Khitan nation that he currently ruled over. This time the people clapped, but softly. There were smiles, but they were short-lived. The drums were struck, but without passion. The heart of Khitan was fraying.

Alan-Ko, resting under thick furs beside her two older sons, studied the child's face. He had her eyes, dark and deep, but his nose and brow already belonged to Mar Yanqa. His hair was a ruddy brown, unlike the red hair of his brothers. As the midwife handed her the child, she whispered in Mongolian, "Bodonchar... one who endures." As far as Mar Yanqa was concerned, the name had the same meaning in both languages. But to Alan-Ko, she felt it had another meaning as well. Realizing how wise her husband had been to keep their people out of the endless bloody wars erupting in the south, she could no longer tolerate those among the council that continued war mongering. For them, the name would mean something else: 'He who survives among fools.' She had chosen it with both irony and hope.

Mar Yanqa sat at the edge of the celebration, his expression unreadable. He was not dressed in his usual ceremonial robes, nor did he ride through the camp announcing the birth as he had done for his other sons. When his first two sons arrived, the valley had erupted in joy, warriors sparred in his honor and great vats of fermented mare's milk had been emptied, while songs were sung deep into the night.

Now? Now he merely nodded as each well-wisher approached. The elder priest that performed the circumcision, Ben-Elekh, noticed it. He leaned near the Qagan and murmured, "They want more than peace, Yanqa. They have grown tired of living in a land of milk and honey."

The young Qagan's jaw tightened. "They want glory. But they don't understand that glory comes with a heavy price."

"They want purpose," the old priest corrected him. "The man that has too much Heaven often searches for a bit of Hell."

"Until they have had too much Hell and then they find it is too late and they are locked out of Heaven."

Ben-Elekh laughed. "That has always been the nature of the rivalry between God and man. Yahweh offers paradise and man always finds a way to have himself thrown out. Did you actually believe you could change the nature of mankind?"

"I had hoped," Mar Yanqa replied.

The old priest patted him on the shoulder. "I have known both you and your father, since he was a little boy back in Mahoza. Like you, he was a dreamer. He could always find the better nature of a man. Perhaps it is time to see us for what we are, the same way Yahweh sees us. Disobedient, stiff-necked, stubborn children that always find a way to disappoint Him. That is why he loves us so. For no matter how many times he disciplines us, He knows he will never break our independent spirit."

Mar Yanqa cast his gaze over the people assembled at the encampment. Riders from distant clans had gathered, not to witness the birth but to plead their case as to why they should go to battle against the Empire. Some had ridden for weeks, risking snowcapped mountains and hungry wolves, just to deliver the same message. Perhaps it was time to listen. But not today. Today he would rejoice with his wife the birth of their third son.

The fires burned low in the Khitan gers. A few strings of beads decorated the main yurt belonging to the Qagan. Within their home a small feast was laid out, but it was modest. The head of a goat, fresh milk, and roasted roots. Bukhatu-Salji, now two and a half years old, tugged at his father's cloak. He wanted to be lifted up, thrown high in the air, as he had been when he was younger. But Mar Yanqa only patted his head. Bukha-Katagi, now seven, played in the corner with his carved wooden horses. His mind was wandering over too many places, trying to solve too many problems at once. He knew that they all were watching him, condemning him for his hesitation. But it wasn't hesitation, it was wisdom and he could not fathom how they could not see it.

He turned to Alan-Ko, who sat pale and quiet, the newborn at her breast. She offered him no encouragement, no assurance. She too was watching, gauging. She knew the clans were shifting, restless. She knew the birth was both a miracle and a reason for delaying any decision. How much longer would their people wait.

"They want war," she said softly. "They want to ride."

"I know."

"Will you let them?"

Mar Yanqa did not answer.

Later that night, when the stars hung low and the wind was quiet, Alan-Ko took her newborn and walked beyond the circle of the tents. She watched the fires of other camps flicker on the horizon. Each was a clan. Each held men who wanted to ride south, to reclaim ancient glories, to avenge old wounds. But she also saw the women. The children. The herds. The tents. The life they had built. Would war preserve it, or end it?

She whispered to the child, "Bodonchar-Munkhag. Remember this peace. Remember your father's sigh."

Behind her, Mar Yanqa stepped silently. "They'll leave without my command. If I keep denying them."

"Then let them go," she said. "But do not follow."

He looked at her, studying her face as if he had not seen it before. Her face was softer, worn. But still as beautiful as ever. But the war in the Empire had aged them both.

"You don't want me to fight."

"I want you to live."

"And what about all of them?"

She glanced back toward the fires. "Let them find out what the Empire really is. How miserable their lives will become if they forsake all that we have here."

He wrapped his arm around her and the child, and for a moment, just a moment, they stood in silence, suspended between two worlds, one torn by fire, and one waiting for the spark.

"What will you do," she asked.

There was a sudden sparkle that flashed across his emerald, green eyes. "I will pray to Yahweh and he will answer me. I will do as He commands. He will send me an answer to this problem."

"I wish my faith was as strong as yours," she sighed.

"Do not despair. I have a feeling that very soon it will be," he smiled for the first time that day, sensing that God would come to his aid.

The next day, a group of young warriors approached Mar Yanqa's tent. He had been waiting for them. In fact, Mar Yanqa had been sitting outside his ger all morning expecting visitors. He nodded his head, letting them approach.

Their armor was polished; their eyes were fierce. As soon as they were within several feet of where he sat the all bowed and then knelt at his feet. "Great Khan," their spokesperson said, bowing low so that his forehead actually touched the ground. "We wish to go south."

"Then you wish to fight," Mar Yanqa acknowledged their request.

"Yes, great Khan. It is time that we bloodied our swords in battle. We are Khitan and the fact that we have not tasted battle is a shame upon us. You and our fathers may be content to sit around a fire and tell stories of the wars in which you were engaged, but we have no stories to tell."

Mar Yanqa simply nodded as if he had not actually heard their need for personal glory.

"It is our way, great Khan," the boy pressed further.

"And when you go south, who will you fight?" Mar Yanqa asked.

"Whoever stands in our way," he answered spontaneously.

"There is the empire's army, the rebels, the townspeople, the robbers and the rogues. Do you intend to fight against all of them?"

"If we must," came the reply.

"Then you will be entering into a war without end, a battle without purpose," he cautioned them. "That is a war that you cannot win."

"Even so, great Khan, we will die with honor."

Mar Yanqa rubbed the stubble on his chin. "Let me propose a different strategy. I will call a meeting of the council for this afternoon. We will come to a decision and we will provide you with a strategic plan of attack. Will you agree to provide me with enough time to arrange this and not leave the encampment until a decision is made."

They talked it over quickly and nodded their head in agreement. "We will extend you the time to summon the council, great Khan and await their response."

"Good," Mar Yanqa responded. "You will have goal and mission defined before the sun sets. I promise you this. Now go back to your tents and await the call."

The group of young warriors rose from the ground and bowed courteously once again as they backed from his presence. Alan-Ko emerged from the ger, having been listening intently behind the leather flaps of the domicile.

"What exactly do you think will be different if you wait until his afternoon and summon the council." She sounded confused by the request he had made of the youths.

"There will be a surprise," he remained obscure, not offering any details. "But I promise it will be the answer to our current situation,:

Alan-Ko's curiosity was piqued. "Does this have anything to do with what you said last night? Did Yahweh speak to you last night?"

"Let me assemble the council and all will be explained." He was unwilling to say any more.

The Council of Elders met in the massive yurt that was reserved for such purpose. The old men and women of the tribes sat cross-legged in a ring around the stones that contained the fire at the center of the tent. Each elder bore the mark of their clan, sewn onto thick woolen cloaks. Smoke from the fire curled into the spiraling column that swirled up and out the center hole in the roof, like the ghosts of the ancestors, listening.

The next circle comprised all the chieftains and clan leaders that had sworn allegiance to Mar Yanqa. As their Qagan, he stood at the center beside the fire, dressed simply in a white linen robe as he faced the Circle of Iron, as the council was known. Alan-Ko sat nearby, holding Bodonchar-Munkhag against her chest, her expression guarded. Around the outer perimeter of the yurt, the younger captains and selected warriors watched in uneasy silence. Those that had come to visit that morning were among those standing in the outer perimeter.

Mar Yanqa raised his hand, it was time to speak. "You ask me to go to war," Mar Yanqa said, his voice calm but firm. "But I tell you: we are a people of peace now. Our flocks are fat, our sons are strong, and our women no longer weep at night for husbands who do not return."

A rumble of protest moved through the chieftains.

"War is in our blood!" growled Ochir of the Eastern Ridge. "You forget who we are. We do not barter for peace like merchants...we take it with steel!"

"Aye!" shouted another. "Our ancestors thundered across the steppes like storm gods! Shall we now sit and braid each other's hair like milk-drinkers from the valleys?"

Mar Yanqa raised a hand, and silence fell. "I will not lead us to war...unless we are attacked. Then, and only then, shall we rise. And when we do, the heavens will tremble."

The murmurs turned to outrage. A few stood, pacing. One even spat near the fire. Chieftain Chagan Bor of the Western Tümen Clan rose to speak. His beard was white as hoarfrost and hung down to his chest. His voice was worn like cured leather.

"You have heard the stars, Mar Yanqa. You have seen the omens. The empire cracks like old lacquer. Rebels ride through Taiyuan unchallenged. The phoenix bleeds. Why do you sheathe our blades?"

Elder Altani of the Three Rivers, her face lined as mountain stone, tapped her cane once upon the earth. "We have waited. Held back as you commanded. Married, united, watched the storms of the south boil over. But if we wait too long, we will be left with nothing but scraps again."

A murmur of discord passed through the circle.

Mar Yanqa met their eyes without flinching. "You speak of conquest as if it were hunting. But this prey is cursed. The empire is not merely land; it is a way of life. A way of life that we must not covet. It lulls you into a trap of forgetting who you are. And I will not trade the sky for a roof made of gold."

There was silence, then a sharper voice.

Elder Darga, the Hawk-Eyed, leaned forward, his eyes sparkling from the flames. "Is this the voice of a khan, or a monk?"

A few elders chuckled bitterly.

Darga continued, "Our sons train. Our daughters bear sons for war. And yet the Lion of the North speaks of memory, of wind and ghosts. If Yahweh is God in the Sky and has set us apart, as the Book of YahSu says, then why keep us idle while the world burns?"

Mar Yanqa stepped towards the elder. "If you understood what was written in the Book of YahSu then you know that the God in the Sky does not desire cities. He desires people who remember who He is and who they are." He let his words hang there for the moment. "Conquer the empire, and before long we will become it. We will feast in its halls and call it victory. Until we wake one morning speaking their tongue and kneeling to their gods. That is not conquest. That is capitulation by another name."

Tarkhan's eyes narrowed. "And if they come for us? If the Dowager survives and remembers who watched while her throne burned, deciding to punish us for her own failure?"

"Then we will meet her armies on the field as Khitan. In open war. We will fight to defend our freedom, not hidden conquest. Our blades will shine beneath the same sky our fathers died under. And we will still be us."

A long silence fell.

Alan-Ko looked around the circle. Some elders looked down, conflicted.

Others leaned back, withholding judgment. But it was Elder Altani who finally spoke, voice low and rasping.

"You fear the sickness of civilization. But war is its own sickness. Are you so certain we will be untouched by it, whether we go south or not?"

"No, I am certain we will be touched by it and that is why I have summoned all of you to this tent today. I must confess that I have not told you everything."

"Do you wait for your enemy to burn your tent before drawing your sword?" an old war chief bellowed.

But Mar Yanqa did not flinch. Because he knew what they did not, that the enemy was already near. "Let me make it clear to all of you. It is not the fear of war that taints me but the fear of the consequences of winning such a war. To defend that which we possess, there should be no doubt in your minds that mine will be the first sword in battle, but to consume that which is theirs, I see as a poison and I will see that we avoid it with my dying breath. As I said, I have not told you everything. This morning, long before dawn, a dream had come to me. A voice like wind and thunder had spoken. I knew instantly that it was Yahweh that spoke to me saying, 'A thousand spears hide in the forest, a hundred leagues hence. The serpent comes with gifts in one hand and poison in the other. Choose wisely Kahana, as your father chose for me.' That is exactly what I intend to do."

The shamans in the tent broke into a series of chants upon hearing that the Sky God had spoken to his servant. Most of the elders didn't know what to make of the prophecy but then the tent flaps stirred. As they slowly peeled back, Tamerlan entered.

He was mud-caked and breathless, flanked by a dozen riders. If that wasn't enough to surprise the council, it was what followed behind them that was certainly unexpected. Golden-armored, wrapped in silks, bearing lacquered boxes and scrolls, a delegation from Northern Wei consisting of some of their top ministers and generals were suddenly standing in the great yurt. Faces paled on either side from the sudden intrusion that crossed two worlds. The representatives of Northern Wei entered under a flag of truce, heads high, uncertain of the events they'd just walked into.

The tent exploded in shouts and curses. No one knew what to make of these envoys. "Spies!" some shouted. "Give us leave to kill them where they stand!" greeted the visitors.

Mar Yanqa raised his arm and the uproar died slowly, like thunder retreating across the plain. "They come under a flag of truce. Did I not tell you that Yahweh told me that they were here. Did He not talk of gifts and poison?

He told me to listen and to choose and I will honor that. After all, we are not barbarians. Let them speak," he commanded. "They came to parlay. We are bound to hear the voice of the Empire before we answer it."

The delegation's leader, Yu Wei, an old minister with trembling fingers, stepped forward. "We come in peace, mighty Khan, may you rein over the Khian last a thousand moons. Dowager Hu sends her blessings and her tokens of appreciation if you honor her request. Gold, jade, and titles await those who stand with the Empire against the southern rebellion."

"And if we refuse?" asked Mar Yanqa.

"You cannot refuse. You are bound to us. Our treaties and agreements say that we are your overlords and the tribes must come to our defense in our time of need."

"Agreements that also made promises to all the tribes of food and medicine in our times of need, plus a guarantee that you would never expand and encroach on our lands. That part of the bargain has never been carried out. You have never honored your end of the agreement. Why would your promise of gold and titles be any different? What was signed long ago in the past I now declare revoked and expired."

Minister Yu's tone hardened. "Then the Empire will secure its northern flank. Clearly you have disavowed your loyalty. We will remedy that by any means necessary." Clearly it was a threat.

There was a moment of stillness, like the eye of a storm. Then Mar Yanqa's lips curled into a smile that bore no warmth. "You speak of loyalty," he said, "But to whom? A boy-king with no voice? Or the barking woman who holds his leash?"

"To the royal family," Yu responded. "Our Empress Dowager has only the Empire's stability in mind."

"You don't recognize me, do you?" Mar Yanqa teased the delegation.

"Of course, you are the Khan," Minister Yu responded, while his delegation nodded in agreement. "We have said as much and praised you as such."

"I suggest you take a closer look, since you are obviously blind to the past," Mar Yanqa moved closer so that he occupied the minister's entire frame of vision.

The delegation still shook their heads failing to recognize Mar Yanqa from before.

"Then allow me to help refresh your memories," Mar Yanqa interrupted their train of thought as he turned toward the back of the tent, "Someone find my mother and bring her here at once."

It took only minutes to retrieve the princess. Gasps followed as She-Ping stepped forward, her veil falling away like morning mist. The delegation fell back in shock, the color draining from their faces.

"You say you are loyal only to the royal family, then here is your true Empress," Mar Yanqa shouted. "Show her your loyalty!"

"You... the generals stammered. "We thought you... the court declared you dead."

"Your court," She-Ping responded, her voice regal and icy, "Declares many things. Truth among any of what they declare is rare."

Mar Yanqa stepped beside her. "Bow," he commanded, "Before your sovereign. Kneel before the blood of the Heavenly Line. You stand not before rebels but heirs."

The delegation stood frozen, caught between orders and oaths. "We are loyal to Emperor Xiaoming..."

"You should be loyal to the Emperor Xiaowen, father of both Emperor Hsuan Wu Ti and Princess She-Ping. She carries his blood. With the death of her brother, she is the rightful empress if the boy is unfit to sit on the throne."

"We are pledged to Xiaoming," Minister Wei declared.

"Who suckles at the teat of a throne hijacked by a regent," Mar Yanqa snapped. "I give you one last opportunity. Bow and kneel before your rightful empress or consider your business here concluded.

"We cannot," they responded though some of the generals appeared hesitant.

"If it is war you threaten in return, then know this: the Khitan do not tremble. They do not kneel. And they do not forget."

Mar Yanqa signaled for the tent flaps to be parted.

"You may go," he said coldly. "But be warned. Our arrows fly faster than your messengers, and our riders travel light. Let your legion that lies hidden in the woods know that I am already aware of their presence. You should also make them aware that the land will drink their blood as well."

The delegation looked back and forth between them, wondering who the traitor was. How else did the Khan know of their hidden legion. They turned and fled, white-faced and trembling.

As the flaps fell closed behind them, the silence broke. First with murmurs. Then with shouts. A wild, howling cheer rose from the chieftains. Spears clashed against shields; fists slammed into chests. War had come.

"You played us!" one chieftain cried gleefully. "You tricked us into waiting! But you knew of this moment all along."

"None of you should ever doubt the authority of Yah ever again. He will tell you when it is time for war and time for peace and you will listen!" Mar Yanqa warned them.

"You've learned well from your mother!" laughed Ochir, tears in his eyes.

Mar Yanqa raised both arms. "This day, you doubted me. Those men have dishonored my mother. But most of all, they have dishonored our ancestors. The Khitan are servants to no one. Today you doubted me but tomorrow you will ride with me. Let no one ever say that the Khitan do not honor the old ways. That Mar Yanqa does not honor the Khitan way!"

He turned to the circle of young warriors who had come to his ger shortly after dawn. "You came to me begging for a chance to go to war. But now I must tell you there is far more to war than the clash of blades and the pounding of hooves across the plains. Those are merely the outcome of a wise strategy. Now what is most important is tracking that delegation back to where they have hidden their legion. Stealth is essential. Like a wolf pack you will follow their scent without ever being seen. Like eagles you will see their entire compound and assess their true strength. You will listen to Tamerlan who will lead you and most importantly, you will not engage the enemy. As soon as you have completed your tasks, you will return to us and report. We will then make our plan and ride as one. Have I made myself clear?"

"Yes, Great Khan," they replied in unison.

As Tamerlan left the tent with the seven youths in tow, the council tent erupted with howls of delight. The peace was finally over.

Chapter 24: 523 AD

The scouts departed before the fire in the Council Tent had even cooled. The seven young warriors that had visited Mar Yanqa that morning were already known for their degree of cunning, and unmatched horsemanship. Tamerlan rode at their head, his lean frame bent low against his stallion's neck as they galloped eastward toward the thick pinewood forests. The trees had once marked the boundary between Khitan lands and Wei territory, but with the Empire in disarray, those lines had blurred significantly. There were no more maps, only threats.

Each rider was silent, their expressions grim, their minds fixed on the task. The Northern Wei delegation would not have traveled alone, not in a time like this. Their path would lead them back to the hidden legion that was revealed to the great Khan in a dream. How was that even possible, they pondered in the silence of their own thoughts but there could be no doubt that there had to be a force large enough that the delegation felt safe in making their threat. The shadow force had been revealed to Mar Yanqa in a vision and it was their responsibility to find it, mark it, determine its size and return before the storm broke.

The wind howled through the valley like a mourning spirit. Dry grasses whispered across the barren plain, and above them, vultures circled as if they knew death was coming. The Khitan scouts crouched among a line of ridges, eyes fixed on the meadow below. Far off in the golden light of dawn, the dust trail of the departing caravan of the delegation curled like smoke from an extinguished fire.

Turugen, eldest of the scouts, spat into the dirt. "They've moved again. They run like terrified mice. Same as before. Never straight, always angling west and doubling back."

"Do not be fooled," Tameran advised. "It is a well-known tactic. It's as if the know we're up here and they're trying to fool us into thinking they have no destination."

Beside him, Otchigin nodded. His sharp eyes never left the caravan. "Are you suggesting they are laying a decoy trail? Keeping us occupied while their army is already marching against our camp."

Tamerlan narrowed his eyes, drawing out a worn map of the region and unfurling it. "It's a possibility. They left our camp three days ago. First headed south, as if returning to Luoyang. Then north, toward the river, and now west again into the Ghost Hills. If I were hiding at least five thousand soldiers, that's where I would hide them. I don't think they know we are following them, but just in case they want to ensure they throw anyone off the trail."

"Or they're just a decoy leading us on a wild goose chase and their army is already marching," Otchigin said darkly, repeating his previous speculation.

But Tamerlan was already rolling up the map. "Saddle up. We follow until they stop again. Then we wait for nightfall."

The Khitan riders moved like whispers on the wind. Each man was clad in light leathers with dark scarves wound around his face. They avoided the ridgelines, tracked the wind, and let their ponies drink only at night. What they chased was not merely a delegation from the Empire, they were the Dowager's ministers and generals. Men that she would not be willing to risk so easily unless there was a hidden force concealed somewhere in this forest. Tamerlan was certain of it.

By the fourth day of tracking, Tamerlan's suspicions were taking root. They were heading in the direction of the Ghost Hills and there were signs of larger movements; hoofprints more typical of war ponies, broken shrubs, food caches buried in shallow pits. All signs of a large force having passed through the area.

That evening, Turugen returned from a solo sweep with eyes wide and breath tight. "I found their fire pits. Hidden beneath overhanging stone, behind the fifth bend of the eastern ridge. They've been burning pinecones and dried goat dung. It burns hot and fast but produces little smoke."

"How many?" Tamerlan asked.

Turugen hesitated. "Too many to count. Forty, maybe more."

"Fires?"

Turugen nodded. "At least."

Tamerlan did a quick calculation and then stared at the young scouts. "Usually thirty men around a fire. Forty or fifty fires and were looking at around fifteen hundred soldiers just up ahead. It makes sense that they would have split their force into smaller groups. More manageable that way and harder to spot."

"So do we head back now," Bortei, another of the young warriors asked.

"Not until we have seen everything," Tamerlan informed the group. "Part of fighting a war is knowing everything there is about the enemy in advance."

On the sixth day, they found the main body of the Northern Wei legion. It was not through sight or sound but smell. The odorous fumes of burnt metal, old blood, and boiled rice. The air was thick with it. They circled down through a narrow canyon where the shadows lasted longer than the day, and the ground had been eroded by a spring rivulet that was now dry as if it had never existed.

Below, nestled in the crags of the Ghost Hills, was a vast encampment hidden beneath a canopy of camouflage tarps dyed to match the vegetation. Painted wagons and bundled weapons were packed in orderly rows. No banners flew. There was no singing. These were soldiers who had come with no other purpose but to strike stealthily against the heart of the Khitan encampment.

Tamerlan, stared down from a crevice above and muttered, "Five thousand men… possibly more. Engineers. Archers. Supply caravans. They've obviously come for a long stay."

Otchigin whispered, "Why didn't they cross the border openly?"

"Because this isn't war yet," Tamerlan said grimly. "They had to wait for the delegation to return with Mar Yanqa's answer. They had no knowledge that Mar Yanqa was already aware of their presence from a dream. But now they are aware it's war."

They remained watching until evening, taking turns. They would begin their journey home under the cover of darkness so as not to be spotted by the camp's sentries. At the twilight, a commotion stirred in the camp. A column of men filed toward a cave in the eastern cliff. Guards attempted to block the entrance to whomever it was that arrived, but only briefly, as the torchlight revealed a figure emerging from the cavern. It was a ranking officer wearing armor but from the body shape, definitely a woman.

"The Dowager's own daughter?" Turugen guessed in a whisper.

"I don't think she has one," Bortei responded,

"Or a priestess?" Otchigin guessed.

"A priestess in armor," Turugen scoffed at the suggestion.

"Or something far worse," Tamerlan muttered. "Get the horses ready. We ride now!"

But just as they began their descent from the ridge, a twig snapped.

A cry echoed from the forest below. "Spies!"

Shouts rose in the Wei tongue. Horns began to sound.

"Ride!" Tamerlan shouted, and the young warriors leapt on to their mounts and plunged into the trees.

The hunters suddenly became the hunted, their horses racing through the dark, foreboding forest, as images danced between shadows and torches began to light across the hills. Arrows flew all around them. One grazed the young warrior Yegun's shoulder. Another embedded in a tree near Tamerlan's head. They had missed discovering on their approach that the enemy had cavalry stationed in the forest; light riders whose sole purpose was to flush out spies. The Wei cavalry pursued fiercely, but the Khitan riders knew the landscape well and managed to evade their pursuit.

Tamerlan veered west, guiding them toward the river. The water would mask their scent, confuse anyone following their trail. They rode until their lungs burned and the hooves of their horses were slick with sweat. Only when they reached the shallow river ford did they stop.

They were seven now.

"Where is Otchigin?" gasped Tamerlan as he caught his breath.

No one spoke. The silence said enough.

They crossed and doubled back once, leaving another false trail. It was another three days before they saw the Sacred Valley again. Smoke from the council fires drifted into the sky. Horns sounded from the hills, not in alarm, but in welcome.

By the time they reached the yurt of the Council of Elders, the sky was dark with storm clouds. Mar Yanqa met them at the opening of the yurt.

"Well?" he asked before Tamerlan had even dismounted.

"They're here. Easily five thousand. Possibly more. Hidden in the Ghost Hills. Supplies for months, engineers, calvary, archers and foot soldiers. Looks like they plan on staying a while or at least until they think they can finish us off."

Mar Yanqa turned to the others to see if they had anything further to add.

"And a woman of rank leading them. In armor," Bortei thought it might be important. "She passed into a cavern beneath the cliff. We did not follow."

"Good...but," there was a long silence from Mar Yanqa. "One of you is missing." He ignored the mention of the woman as if it was irrelevant.

"We lost Otchigin," Tamerlan bowed his head.

"I instructed you not to engage," Mar Yanqa sounded angry.

"We didn't," Tamerlan explained. "They had men in the forest. They discovered us. We were lucky that the rest of us made it."

Turning to the remaining young warriors, Mar Yanqa expressed his condolences. "I am sorry for the loss of your friend. I sent you all on this mission in order to learn that there was far more to warfare than trading blows on the battlefield. Instead, I think you learned the most important lesson of all. In war there is a higher likelihood that you will die than survive. Whatever glory you earn may be fleeting. We will recognize Otchigin as a hero, but given time, few will remember him. That is a fact. That is the reality of war. If we must fight, then we must learn the only reason to fight is to survive. Now go through the camp and summon all the chieftains and elders and have them meet here at the council tent. Tamerlan, walk with me and tell me everything you saw."

As soon as the council had assembled, Mar Yanqa reappeared in the yurt, standing tall in his lacquered and jeweled armor, his emerald eyes appearing fierce beneath his fox-fur lined helm. He addressed them from the center firepit. "Our enemies will not knock at the gate," Mar Yanqa said, voice echoing through the dome. "They do not intend to announce their arrival. They bury themselves in our earth and wait for us to strike. They wish for us to knock over the ant hill."

"Let us attack now," one of the chieftains yelled.

"That is exactly what they want," Mar Yanqa dismissed the suggestion. "One only sees the top of the ant hill and tries to squash it with a foot. But as soon as he does, those beneath the ground swarm from the nest and cover him in death. We know the lay of the land, we can use that to our advantage. Tamerlan and seven of our brave young warriors scouted out the enemy for us. He returned with only six. Otchigin has been lost. May his soul find rest in paradise. We will avenge him!"

"Otchigin, Otchigin," everyone shouted over and over again as they pounded their right fists against their chests.

After around thirty seconds, Mar Yanqa raised his hand, calling for silence. "He did not die in vain. We know their strength, we know their strategy and we know where to find them."

"Then we should attack," Abaoji shouted. "We have far more men and as you said, we know this land better than they do. It is all to our advantage." Many of the other chieftains grunted their approval, sharing the same sentiment.

"We do out number them ten to one," Mar Yanqa admitted but they have dug themselves into the Ghost Hills and that actually provides them with an advantage that we must overcome. Apparently engineers have fortified their position and Tamerlan suggests they would easily repulse any frontal attack. We must be just as cunning and find a way to draw them out into the open field where we have the advantage." He looked to the ring of seated warlords for suggestions.

The murmuring began almost instantly.

Chagan Bor of the Western Tümen, his beard stained with wine, slammed a fist against the low table. "Then we bury them! Wave after wave of ten thousand men trampling their trenches, day and night! We grind them into dust!"

Some of the chieftains banged their drinking horns in agreement.

"That is not a strategy," Mar Yanqa dismissed the idea.

Kharbak the Grey, the oldest among them, shook his head slowly. "The Khan is right. You'd lose half your strength before reaching their fortifications. You'd feed their cannons with Khitan blood." By the end of the day, we'd lose twenty-five thousand men and they'd still be wedged solidly in the Ghost Hills."

Ochir, the Eastern Ridge chieftain, sneered. "Are we not the masters of this land? We hold the valleys, the rivers, the sacred places. Let them rot in their ghost-hole! Cut off their supply lines. Wait a month or two and they'll begin eating their own dead."

"And if they don't?" growled Ujin Baatar, a broad-shouldered warrior with a golden sash. "Wei engineers can tunnel. What if they're digging even now beneath our feet? What if they break out into our flanks like moles, or blow fire from beneath?"

Laughter broke out thinking Ujin's concerns ridiculous, but a nervous laughter just in case he was not.

Mar Yanqa raised a hand. "I too have thought about starving them out, but Tamerlan has informed me they have at least three months of provisions. I know us. We lack the patience to lay siege for three months. They count on the fact that over time our unity will fray. We need a way to draw them out. That is the only means by which we can have a decisive victory."

"Their commander is smart," Tamerlan commented. "I think it might be General Yang Zhen, but I could not see him clearly. He built his reputation defending the passes in the Qinling Mountains. He is a master of defensive strategy. He wants us to attack. He knows it would be a Khitan massacre."

There was silence.

"Then don't attack," Alan-Ko said softly. "Make them believe we have fled."

All turned to listen to the Queen who sat in a corner and remained silent all this time.

"Advance and then withdraw from the western ridge. Let their scouts report it. Burn your own tents in the forest. Leave behind broken wagons, fallen standards. Make it look like disorder and collapse. A feint of retreat as if we were in disarray and gave up any hope of attacking. Then, as they rise to pursue, close the trap behind them."

"And what if they don't take the bait?" asked Yelü Daran.

"We make certain that they don't have a choice," she argued. "We make the bait so enticing that they have no other option."

"What are you suggesting?" Mar Yanqa inquired of his wife, not understanding where she was going with this plan of hers.

"You saw their reaction when the delegation saw your mother. They panicked. They were so terrified that she'd be able to convince them to betray the Dowager Empress that they decided to flee from the tent rather than negotiate further. What effect do you think she would have on the regular soldiers if she called out to them to come to her as the true and only Empress of Northern Wei, promising them clemency."

"She would definitely confuse them," Mar Yanqa admitted. "There must be some officers that regret serving the Dowager Empress. It only would take one to cross over and their generals would be terrified of that happening. Tamerlan, bring my mother here. I would like to hear what she thinks of this plan."

Without hesitation Tamerlan left the council to retrieve the princess.

"They would come," Alan-Ko seemed certain. "Perhaps only in the hundreds, but enough deserters that their generals would become worried. Do that for several days, let them see that the deserters are well taken care of when they cross over to our lines and no general can withstand the thought of mutiny if it continues. And then we scatter as if we abandon our plan of attack. Their generals would see that as an opportunity to strike."

Chagan Bor spat into the brazier. "Too clever by half."

"Does that mean you agree or disagree, Chagan," Mar Yanqa didn't understand his response.

"It means what it says. A clever idea but faulty as well. Only those at the forefront of their troop will even see or hear the Princess. The others will be oblivious to her existence."

"Who could possibly be oblivious to my existence?" She-Ping said somewhat jokingly, overhearing part of the discussion as she returned with Tamerlan at her side.

The elders bowed their head in reverence as she moved to the front of the circle. Mar Yanqa quickly repeated the plan that Alan-Ko had devised, coming one again to the part where Chagan doubted the Princess would be able to extend her reach to affect more than a handful of the Wei soldiers.

Alan-Ko had not finished. "They don't all have to see the Princess. We send riders to the edges of their camp. Spread rumors. Whisper that the Princess She-Ping is alive, that she walks among the so-called savages of the steppes. That she calls the Dowager Empire a traitor to the throne. We destroy their morale from within. A whisper will often cut deeper than a blade."

The mention of affecting morale immediately triggered a response from Tamerlan. His voice wavered as he recalled more of what he saw on the scouting mission. "Forgive me my fellow lords but I have ben derelict in revealing all that I witnessed in their camp. There is a woman among the enemy dressed in command armor."

"I mentioned that," Bortei raised the point searching for some acknowledgement.

"Yes you did," Tamerlan gave him the credit of disclosing the fact earlier to Mar Yanqa. "And I think now, I failed to take it as serious as I should have. She moved among the men like a dragon in silk. They deferred to her without hesitation. Not as if they feared her, but more like they revered her. At the time, I believe she was leading a column that was concealed in a cavern. Her eyes were as cold as jade, sharp as a hawk's. I believe from the style of her armor, she must command at least part of the vanguard."

A murmur swept the room, darker than before. Elder chiefs shifted uneasily in their cloaks. Then one of them stood. It was Sartaq, the Bear of the Qorchin.

"I know of this woman," he growled. "From my cousins beyond the Khingan. They call her a witch."

"A witch?" Mar Yanqa asked with a raised brow, more curious than dismissive.

Sartaq nodded. "Her name is Hua Mulan. She fights like a man, rides like a hawk flies, and commands the wind itself, or so they say. She's never lost a battle. Enemy soldiers desert just hearing her voice on the wind. Others throw down their swords and kneel in fear as she approaches. The Wei believe she is sent by their ancestors as an avenging spirit. She wears a red plume when she rides into battle. When the Wei soldiers see it, they say the tide turns. Always."

A shiver rippled through the circle of warriors as Sartaq told the story.

"Yes, I've heard of her too. She brings luck," said another chieftain, a younger man named Temuk, the Vulture of the Hulunbuir. "Or blessing. Whatever it is, she changes the tide of battle. I've heard even the Wei generals defer to her tactics. If she is here, we must prepare not just for men and steel, but for the magic she spins. The enemy will rally behind her like she's a divine banner. Her presence will even outweigh that of the Princess."

Mar Yanqa listened, eyes narrowed, his knuckles white against the table's edge. One thing he could not tolerate was superstition blinding a man to reality. He held his tongue, waiting for cooler minds to prevail. Meanwhile, his mother She-Ping sat in silent reflection, chin poised in one hand. The light from the fire gilded the fine threads of her silk robes, casting her in a soft imperial glow.

Mar Yanqa turned to her. "Mother," he said, "You are still a Princess of the Empire. What power might your presence wield against this woman they call a witch?"

She looked up, blinking slowly. "Hua Mulan is no sorceress," She-Ping said calmly. "She is merely a symbol. I know of her from my brother. A living legend he called her. But symbols are not invincible. They are vulnerable when you expose the myth behind them."

Alan-Ko stepped forward. "How do we expose her myth?"

"She is revered because she embodies purity," She-Ping said. "Loyalty. Filial piety. The obedient daughter who took her father's place. A paragon of the Confucian ideal. She is the Empire's mask of honor and sacrifice. But masks can be removed."

"Go on," Mar Yanqa urged. "Tell us more."

"If she is a daughter of the Empire," She-Ping said, rising now, "then I am her true mother. Even if I'm its discarded, exiled, humiliated mother. I will not fight her with a sword. But I can speak to her with words. I can stand on the battlefield where she can see me, where her soldiers can see me and I will strip the mask from her face. If I can break her in front of the Wei army, then your hoax of a retreat will not even be necessary. The spirit of the enemy will be crushed before a single blow is exchanged."

Temuk frowned. "With words?"

"With truth," She-Ping said sharply. "She fights for an Empire that discarded its own blood. That left me to die in the wilderness with my young son. I will remind her and the Wei troops that their glory was built on treachery and dishonor. That their so-called heroine is fighting for a lie and a woman who sits on the phoenix throne that is not worthy to even be my handmaid. That is something that Hua Mulan will understand."

Alan-Ko nodded slowly. "And if this Huo Mulan hesitates, if even a shadow of doubt creeps into her spirit, then it may be enough to disrupt their entire command structure."

She-Ping raised a hand. "I will do more than just speak to the troops. Let me speak to her. Face-to-face. Let me seal her fate by direct confrontation."

There was a hush.

"You would parley?" asked Mar Yanqa.

"I would summon her," She-Ping replied. "To speak like daughters of the Empire. If she refuses, it makes her look afraid. She will lose respect and I believe she fears loss of respect above all else. If she accepts, I can sow the seeds of her undoing directly."

Mar Yanqa turned to warlords. "This will work. We will prepare a rider to deliver the summons. Under a flag of truce, he is to make the request for parley public. We will direct it to all of the officers but especially to her. An invitation from one noblewoman of the Empire to another. I expect the other officers to refuse to meet, but she won't. There's too much honor at stake."

Sartaq scowled. "She may not answer." He still had his doubts.

"She will," She-Ping answered. "A daughter of the Empire cannot refuse the call of her princess, especially not in front of her men. If she does, as Mar Yanqa said, she concedes honor and loses face. As Khitan you may not appreciate face, but in the Wei empire, face is everything. And when she comes, I will shatter her."

Alan-Ko looked at She-Ping and felt a strange unease for her mother-in-law; pride, yes, as well as awe, but also the chill of something far more ancient. The Princess She-Ping still possessed the conscience of a rotting Empire.

"We strike at the myth," Mar Yanqa explained. "We pull the veil from their warrior goddess and show her humanity. And while they watch the illusion crumble, we will strike. No more feigned retreat," he turned to his wife as he dismissed that original idea. "We'll use a hidden horn division to flank from the east as soon as she falters. Between the whispers we spread and the effects of the parley, I doubt there will remain any morale left to manifest into a fighting spirit on their part."

"It's still a risk," said Kharbak the Grey.

"All plans are risk," Mar Yanqa responded. "But we increase our odds of success by defeating both mind and body. We will have split our men and Tamerlan and Valentius will take ten thousand with them north through the Pine Vale. I calculate it will take them roughly four days to reach the Ghost Hills from the east at which time my mother will already be engaged in this parley. You will lie in wait and we will sound the horns when I'm certain the results of the parley have spread like an infection through their troops. Their generals will be so focused on the meeting and confident that our force in its entirety is spread over the plains to the west, they will never notice our penetration from behind. Be ready to attack by the next day," He directed that last instruction to Valentius and Tamerlan, his two most trusted officers.

Some clapped. Others grunted. The elders looked at one another with satisfaction. They had a plan. An unusual one, but one they steadily gained confidence in.

Only one voice remained. It was Alan-Ko's.

"My sons will not grow beneath imperial chains. My husband will march, and I will bless his sword."

With a quiet gesture, she produced a curved blade wrapped in white silk that she had kept hidden beneath her robe all this time. "This is the blade of Oboq Khan," she said. "Buried with the Ancestors. Taken from underneath the shrine beneath the burial mound. You will carry it into battle, Yanqa. If she is a witch, then the power of this blade will overcome her."

Mar Yanqa was not aware that his wife had secured such a precious item. He stepped forward. He took the blade, and for a moment, all were still. "She is only a woman, I have no doubt," he refused to believe in witches, "But this blade will sing with victory nevertheless."

Chapter 25: 523 AD

At midday, when the wind lay still and the steppe shimmered like beaten brass, the two women rode with their escorts into the valley beyond the Ghost Hills from opposite directions. She-Ping dismounted first. She wore no armor, only the robes of a Xianbei princess long believed dead, crimson and jade thread, a phoenix pattern embroidered across its entire length with wings aflame. Her black hair was coiled like a crown, pinned with a single gold phoenix feather.

Across the clearing, the Wei banner hung loose in the windless air. Hua Mulan appeared like a blade from mist, astride a white stallion that stepped carefully across the cracked ground. Her armor gleamed beneath a red cloak, stiff with battle-dust. A red plume fluttered from her helm, which she removed as she approached, revealing a face both beautiful and unyielding—sharp cheekbones, with dark eyes ringed in shadow, and a mouth that had not smiled in years.

They stood facing each other, neither bowing.

"You are the Princess She-Ping," Mulan said.

"I am," She-Ping replied. "And you are Mulan. They say you turn the tide of battle."

"They say you died."

"I was forgotten," She-Ping said coldly. "There is a difference."

Mulan's gaze flicked over her robes, her bearing. "You still wear the trappings of the Court."

"I was born in the palace you believe you fight for," She-Ping replied. "I nursed at the breast of its grandeur and choked on the bitterness it left behind. My father was a man of honor. He commanded respect as emperor. Where is that respect now?"

Mulan said nothing. Her hand rested lightly on the hilt of her saber.

"Tell me," She-Ping continued, stepping closer, "how long will you wear their glory like borrowed armor? How long before you realize you are a ghost like me. Only they haven't buried you yet?"

"I fight for the people," Mulan replied, voice low. "For the farmers who bleed in silence. For the fathers who limp home from barbarian raids. The empire is flawed but it still protects."

"Protects?" She-Ping laughed once, sharp as flint. "As it protected myself and my son by attempting to poison our wine. As it protected the rights of my family by erasing our names from the records of the living. You speak of fathers; what of mothers? What of daughters traded like silks, discarded like common straw? You carry the weight of honor, Mulan. But do you know whose honor it is?"

"I carry my own," Mulan said.

"No," She-Ping said, stepping even closer, her voice like coiled silk. "You carry only an illusion. A name. A tale they needed. A myth. You are not their hero, Hua Mulan. You are their mask to conceal their ugliness. A shroud to wrap around the rotting body of an empire that willingly slaughters its own people. They hide behind your decency and when you fall, another girl will take your place, until she breaks too. You know the Dowager Empress is evil and malevolent. You know she probably had my brother killed. Her heart is black and yet you fight for her."

A long silence followed.

The wind finally stirred.

"I did not come here to be attacked by words," Mulan said.

"Then why did you come?"

Mulan did not answer right away. "I don't know."

"Yes you do," She-Ping insisted. "You came seeking the truth. You want to hear the truth and that is why you are standing here."

"More words."

"No," She-Ping replied. "You came to look into the mirror. I am what waits in your future. When the empire is done with your body and your legend. I am what you become when you are no longer useful to them. Discarded and dismissed as dead."

Mulan's jaw clenched. Her saber remained sheathed, but her shoulders were taut with unreadable tension.

"I am not afraid of becoming you," she said finally.

"You should be," She-Ping whispered. "No one should wish to be a ghost before they die."

Another silence.

Then, unexpectedly, Mulan bowed. A crisp, mechanical motion. A formality.

"I honor your past, Princess. But my path is chosen."

"You believe that. But you don't believe it enough."

Mulan began to turn in order to return to her waiting escort. Her movements were stiff. She paused once more, turning back. "When next we meet, it will be on the battlefield."

"I welcome it," She-Ping replied. "But I only ask that you choose your battles wisely."

And in that moment, something passed between them. Not hatred. Not even rivalry. But recognition. They were not enemies. They were the same fire forced to burn on the same candle from both ends.

As Mulan rode away, the wind shifted, and the sun slipped behind a curtain of cloud.

She-Ping stood alone in the valley, her robes rippling faintly before returning to her own escort.

The tent of General Yang Zhen was carved from imperial silk and propped with red lacquered poles. Its gilded dragons snarled at the wind, but inside the tent, the air was thick and sour.

Hua Mulan entered in silence, having been summoned, dust still clinging to her boots from her visit to the valley. Her face was unreadable; her hands unclenched at her sides. She gave no ceremonial greeting, only removed her red-plumed helm and placed it gently on the table.

General Zhen stood stiffly behind his desk, flanked by two junior officers and a pale looking eunuch scribe. The general's polished breastplate was untouched by dust, his manicured hands gripping the edge of the campaign table as if holding down the very map of the steppe.

"You went to see that woman without my permission," he said flatly.

"I went to answer the summons of a princess," Mulan replied coldly.

"A traitorous princess."

"A daughter of the dynasty."

General Zhen's nostrils flared. "You were sent here to command the vanguard. Instead, you play diplomat with exiled vipers and return without even demanding her surrender."

"She offered no surrender," Mulan replied.

"Then you should have taken her head."

"We met under the terms of parley. I honored those terms," Mulan defended her lack of taking any action.

"Then you are a fool," the general snapped.

Mulan stepped forward. "You think she's a blade to break? She's truth, General. And truth cannot be killed like a pig in the field."

Zhen slammed his fist against the desk. "Enough of your philosophy and pride. She is a traitor and you are not a hero! You are a tool, and I am telling you now, in case such thoughts have entered your mind, if you do not ride with the vanguard tomorrow, then I will relieve you of your command."

There was silence.

The junior officers exchanged glances, suddenly uncomfortable.

Mulan's voice, when it came, was cool and clear. "Then relieve me."

"What?" Zhen acted as if he didn't hear.'

"I said relive me."

Zhen stared. "You defy a direct order from the Son of Heaven's representative?"

"I do not defy Heaven," Mulan said. "I defy you. I don't hear the young emperor giving any orders thus far. Do you?"

Zhen's mouth trembled in rage, but she was already turning. She picked up her helm and turned to the tent flaps.

"I have not dismissed you," Zhen yelled.

"I have dismissed myself." At the threshold, she paused. "I will not fight for an empire that uses its daughters and discards them like husks. I will not lift a sword while the Court poisons its own blood and calls it justice. And if I am nothing but a sword," she added, "then I choose to be sheathed."

She left before he could say another word. Outside, the camp stirred. Rumors flew like wildfire on the wind. The whispering campaign at the edges of the camp had already taken effect.

By dusk, the Red Plume column was silent. Five hundred cavalry, the most elite riders of the eastern command, waited silently without sharpening a single weapon. Their tents remained unrolled. Cooking fires burned, but no armor gleamed by the light. They had seen Mulan return to her campsite in the cavern. They had watched her walk past their ranks, saying nothing, her face cold as winter stone. And they had understood.

Mulan sat alone beneath a bannerless pole, her blade resting across her lap. Her horse was unsaddled outside the cave opening, tethered loosely. A thousand eyes watched her from the shadows and firelight. Talk of desertion began to spread like wildfire.

They waited for her to rise.

She did not.

By morning, the infection had spread like a plague.

The Iron Crane detachment refused to move out of formation without the Red Plume's lead. The archers refused a scouting order from a general known to have supported Zhen's humiliation of Mulan. One by one, small fractures deepened into chasms.

Yang Zhen stormed from tent to tent, screaming of insubordination, of honor and empire and sacred duty. But his words rang hollow. The soldiers had seen something in Mulan's silence…conviction. Something the generals, with all their brocade and lineage, could not match.

A sergeant said it best in a whisper overheard at the latrines, "If she won't fight… maybe we shouldn't either."

It was then that the Khitan horns split the sky. A low, droning summons like the voice of a thousand mountains trembled across the plains. It came not from one direction but from everywhere. The distinct banners of the northern clans snapped to life on the ridgelines.

From his vantage point on the central plain, Mar Yanqa sat mounted on his warhorse, a dark bay giant clad in iron scales that resemble his own jeweled armor shimmering in the morning light, his eyes sharp beneath his war helm. He could see that the Wei army had not made any preparations that morning and knew instantly that their morale had been broken.

Concealed in the positions in the Ghost Hills the Northern Wei army seethed like an ant nest upturned. Their ranks, already unstable from disobedience and rumor, now fumbled for formation. Officers shouted over clashing orders. Drums pounded without rhythm. Columns buckled.

Mar Yanqa, with the main body of Khitan behind him flew across the plain like thunder given form. Hooves drummed across the ground in waves, black, brown, and gray horses tearing through the tall golden grass, eyes wild and ears back as if they too had a score to settle with the Middle Kingdom. The first wave hit the Chinese flanks, where light infantry had hastily repositioned to defend against envelopment but they were left partially exposed due to the configuration of the hills. Khitan horsemen with recurved bows rode in tight rings, loosing arrows with pinpoint accuracy. Each draw was a snap, a whistle, a death. The Empire's soldiers dropped clutching eyes, throats, and groins, as arrows skipped and spun through the gaps between the rocks. Their horses passed within feet of the Chinese front line and never slowed as mounted archers circled and fired in a murderous ballet.

Mar Yanqa pulled his riders back and then came the second wave consisting of the Khitan lancers and axe-riders who hurled themselves headlong into the western perimeter. The impact was like lightning splitting a tree. Shields crumpled. Bodies flew. Khitan blades hooked past shields and dragged men from behind the rock formations, so that they could be trampled under iron hooves or gutted by dismounted spearmen. Blood sprayed high into the air, catching the light like a red mist.

From the east, where their rear had lain unguarded, a second force appeared. Tamerlan with his ten thousand riders surged like an avalanche from the shadow of the higher hills, their approach masked by a midnight march and the silence of sand-covered hooves. They struck like a blade through silk.

The enemy camp exploded in chaos.

The first to fall were the supply lines. Fires roared through the stores of grain consuming everything and everyone in close distance. Screaming horses trampled the medics and the scribes. Tamerlan's cavalry broke through the rear, their lances splintering into meat and steel. The Wei captains screamed for archers and the crossbowmen atop a small embankment loosed volley after volley, but the Khitan rode low and fast, weaving between shots. A cluster of Khitan riders peeled away, drawing the fire, while from behind a sand-colored ridge came Valentius with the men he held in reserve.

Now the Wei soldiers turned to fight in two directions, as Mar Yanqa led a second charge from the west, only to find themselves completely encircled. General Yang Zhen tried to rally his men but was pulled from his horse and trampled beneath his own banner. All across the battlefield, the Chinese soldiers began to break. The center collapsed into chaos. Horses rolled over bodies. Wounded men crawled through the gore, screaming for their mothers and for gods that would never hear them. The grass turned black with blood. Fire arrows lit the tents, and the remaining wagons exploded into bursts of flame and charred timber, sending trails of smoke high into the sky. The scent of burning flesh spread across the valley.

The Red Plume column, still untouched at the far edge of the camp, stood mounted in formation but did not move.

"Mulan!" cried one of her officers, pointing toward the slaughter. "What do we do?"

She did not answer.

All around her, the wind was thick with smoke and cries. The smell of blood was heavy like incense. Her horse reared beneath her, sensing her personal conflict.

"Captain," the man pleaded again. "Your orders!"

Mulan looked across the burning field. This was the failure she had feared. Not death but her own dishonor. The loss of every man who had believed in her. The shame of paralysis while others bled. She had sworn to protect them. And in the end, she had done nothing. Tears stung her eyes.

"I was wrong," she whispered. "I should have died before shaming them."

And then the horns blew again.

But this time, the Khitan forces appeared to be riding from the south. Approaching from the high plain but suddenly a different banner rose. Not of the Khitan but of the ancient Tang. It was the banner of the burning phoenix. Red and gold on white silk. A forgotten flag, thought to have been long lost. At its head, rode She-Ping, followed by Alan-Ko and her Borjigin clan. They descended upon the Khitan right flank with a fury that surprised even the most hardened of he Khitan warriors.

"Shield Mulan's column!" She-Ping cried. "Hold the line! Save the Red Plume!"

The rest of the Khitan were momentarily stunned, unsure whether this apparition of the Tang was some omen or trick. They looked to Mar Yanqa as to what they should do. In that moment of hesitation, She-Ping and the Borjigin warriors drove a wedge between the Khitan main force and the Red Plume column, giving them precious space, but more importantly, time.

"Move, Mulan!" She-Ping called out to her. "Get your soldiers out of here! My son will not hesitate to slaughter all of you."

"I failed..."

"You still breathe. That is not failure."

"They will never follow me again."

"They already are, you fool. They need you now to lead them."

Mulan turned and it was true. The Red Plume had not broken. They had waited. Obedient only to her. Even as the Wei army collapsed, even as the fires raged, they had waited for her command.

She looked at She-Ping, her eyes wild. "Why? Why save me?"

"Because this battle is not about the Wei, nor the Khitan," She-Ping said fiercely. "It's about what comes afterwards. You are not their pawn anymore. You can be the sword of the people, not of a corrupt and evil Court. Now take this banner and ride."

And in that moment, something cracked in Mulan. She had been freed. She mounted her horse, raised her saber, held the banner of the Tang and let out a cry that cut through the battlefield like lightning. "Red Plume…with me!"

They charged. Not into battle but to carve a path that led away from the conflict and back to the northern boundary of the empire. Some may have called it desertion, others a judicious retreat, but only if the Khitan had left any survivors of the Wei legion would anyone have called her traitor. The battle was over in a matter of hours.

By nightfall, the last of the Wei army was gone. Slaughtered, scattered, or taken in chains. Those that had scattered were pursued by Khitan riders for miles, cutting down the stragglers, loosing arrows into their backs as they ran, laughing like wolves drunk on blood. General Zheng's head was hung on a Khitan spear and proudly displayed back at the encampment.

But Mulan's column, protected by She-Ping's timely intervention, had escaped the worst. Bloodied, yes. Dishonored, yes. But alive. Intact but now without a country and all alone. Except for her platoon. Her men followed no empire now. Only her. And she had but one mission, to fight for the people and free them from tyranny.

Later that night, Mulan knelt before the phoenix banner of the Tang that She-Ping had given her. "I have no right to lead them," she said to herself.

In her mind she could hear She-Ping's voice. "They do not care about your right. Only your truth. Serve the people with honor."

Mulan looked into the fire and pondered her destiny.

Chapter 26: 523 AD

When the wind died, the plain lay dormant but for the buzzing of flies and the fading moans of the dying. Smoke curled endlessly into the purple dusk. Crows circled overhead, their cries falling on deafened ears. The red earth of the ravine had turned to mud beneath the thousands of footprints, soaked with blood and trampled flesh.

Mar Yanqa rode through the aftermath with his saber sheathed, his eyes distant. His horse picked its way between corpses. Around him, warriors raised the Dowager's banners on upside-down poles and set them on fire. One Khitan boy, no more than twelve, dragged a broken Chinese helmet behind him like a toy, grinning wide, as he showed off his prize.

The blood was not yet dry on the battlefield when the true storm broke loose. Receiving the summons. Mar Yanqa returned, to now stand in the yurt that served as the Great Hall, awaiting the Council of Elders to hold court. Here, the victor of the battle of Ghost Hills, now free of his armor but draped in wolf-pelt was about to face an even greater battle. There was no triumph in his face. His brow was drawn tight, his voice cracking with emotion as he restrained his anger.

"You could have died," he said. "Both of you. What were you even thinking, wedging yourself between my men and the enemy?"

Alan-Ko sat opposite him, regal and calm, her face lacking any emotion but her eyes glittering with something sharp.

Beside her sat the Princess She-Ping, radiant as ever, her chin lifted. No shame touched her posture; no regret plagued her soul.

"We rode to save the Red Plume," Alan-Ko replied softly. "And we succeeded."

"They were our enemy!" Mar Yanqa barked. "You, my mother," he pointed at She-Ping, "And you, my wife," gazing upon Alan-Ko, "Rushed into a slaughter to defend a woman who defied the empire and dishonored her own general! She probably would have preferred death rather than dishonor."

"Whose empire?" She-Ping shot back. "You forget that I was once princess of that Empire."

"The same empire that cast us both out," Mar Yanqa reminded her, unable to fathom how she could overlook how ruthless her brother had been to the both of them.

"I have not forgotten," she immediately fired back. "It is the same empire that called my exile treason. That used Mulan like a warhorse and left her to rot? I saw in her the last breath of honor left in the Wei. The same last vestige of honor of a crumbling empire that survives in me. I am still a part of its royal house and I chose to keep it alive."

Mar Yanqa stepped forward, his voice low, but full of heat. "You gambled your life and my wife's, for one soldier! Does that make any sense? Now look where you are. Sitting in front of the council to explain your actions and plead for their forgiveness."

"We plead to no one. She was not just a soldier," Alan-Ko spoke, her voice rising. "She was and still is a symbol. A symbol to the people. A hope to all the women that fear and need to hide in the shadows. A reminder to every soldier who wonders what they fight for, that they have the right to choose their own destiny."

Mar Yanqa's hand fell on the hilt of his sword. "This must be a woman thing. I don't understand either of you," he shook his head. "And what of the Borjigin men who followed you, Alan-Ko? What of those who left their positions and abandoned my command to follow your banner? Have you not made me look like a fool before my own chieftains?"

"You may be their Khan but I am their queen," she answered. "They will always be my people. The Khitan know that about the Borjigin. We are one but we are not the same."

Mar Yanqa didn't know if he should be furious or ashamed that he could ever question his wife's intentions. At that moment, the tent fell to silence as the flaps were pulled open. The elders entered.

Wrinkled and stone-faced, these were the voices of law, of custom. Veterans of a hundred migrations and a thousand feuds with the power of deciding life or death with a wave of their hands. They seated themselves in the crescent of the council, and the senior among them, Elder Oshun, whose right eye had been put out at the Battle of the Sul River spoke.

"The matter is grave. Two women of our royal house acted without leave and without concern to the danger they imposed on our warriors through their recklessness. One is born of our blood; the other, of exile. Both now stand accused of endangering the unity of the Khitan nation. Let them speak."

She-Ping rose first. She wore no crown, only a riding coat stained with smoke and ash from the battle. But when she spoke, her voice could have cracked the spine of the mountain.

"Had I stayed in camp, the Red Plume would have been annihilated. And with it, the most disciplined force left in a crumbling Wei Empire. You see only the enemy on a map but I see the horizon. And on that horizon, new wars will come. Rebellions, refugees, starvation. If we do not absolve those that are willing to live in peace with us from suffering the fate of their evil masters, then someone else will. And that someone else may not be friendly to our cause. Hua Mulan is not a woman. She is a banner. And now she flies under her own and will no longer threaten us."

The elders murmured. Some nodded their understanding but it did not signal their agreement.

Alan-Ko stepped forward next. "I am not Khitan simply by blood. I am Khitan by vow. I married your Qagan. I bore you warriors. I ride in your battles. And I say this as one of you: this war is not just swords and horses. It is for the soul of this world. The people are watching. If we become as ruthless and as cruel as those we defeat, then we will inherit only ashes. I saved the Red Plume because one day, they may save us."

The tent remained silent.

Then Elder Oshun stood. He looked to Mar Yanqa. "Do you deny that your mother and your wife betrayed our nation on the battlefield?"

Mar Yanqa's mouth tightened. He could not lie. "No."

"Do you deny that their actions may strengthen our enemies by leaving those that might fight against us in the future?"

"No. It is a possibility, but…"

The elder interrupted him before he could continue. "Then you agree that this council should punish those who acted in this manner and defied your command."

Mar Yanqa's jaw clenched. "No. I do not." He refused to yield.

"How can you deny their guilt," Oshun demanded to know.

"I do not deny they did as accused" Mar Yanqa responded. His voice was strong and firm, sending a murmur rippling through the elders. "They acted without orders and on their own accord. They defied me. And by the letter of our laws, they betrayed the Khitan. There is no denying that is what happened."

There was silence. Alan-Ko closed her eyes. She-Ping drew a slow breath. The fire at the center of the yurt crackled.

"But," Mar Yanqa said, as his voice changed, growing rich like the low call of a mountain drum, "I am the law! And I decide what is right or wrong." His hand rested firmly on the hilt of his sword.

His answer caused the elders to growl spontaneously.

Mar Yanqa did not wait for their permission to explain. "Yes, the Council of Elders is responsible for making judgements and carrying out the law, but it the right of every Qagan to make the laws that you enforce. There is no black and white to the law. Each law is to be tempered by the situation from which it arose. That is how I rule and I dare anyone to question my authority. Now, I ask you, in your wisdom, what is betrayal? Is it the merely the breaking of some law as you understand it, or is it the breaking of faith with our future?"

He turned slowly, meeting the eyes of each elder, sending a shiver down each one's spine.

"Did She-Ping act to weaken us? The answer is no. She saved the Red Plume, the only Wei force with the courage and discipline to abandon a misplaced cause. Did Alan-Ko seek glory? Once again I tell you no. She rode to save lives, knowing full well that hers might be forfeit by her action."

He turned back to Oshun.

"They disobeyed but not for ambition. Not for gold. Not even for glory or even love. They disobeyed for a vision. A vision of what the Khitan can become. They did it for mercy."

One of the elders grunted. "Mercy is the weakness of women."

"No," said Mar Yanqa, stepping forward. "That is where you are wrong. Mercy is the strength of those that wield greatness. Only those that hold the power can grant mercy. Mercy is what separates conquerors from butchers. If I had ordered the annihilation of Mulan and her Red Plume, the Wei would have fought to the death for decades to come because of a false ideal they held regarding her. They would never have let us live in peace again. Instead, the people of a rotting empire now know that we can be merciful and that they need not always be fearful of us. Many will come to us as a result and ensue for peace. After all, it is that fear of us that makes them fight in the Dowager's army. Without that fear, they have no reason to take up arms."

Mar Yanqa paused. "So, tell me in your wisdom, if I had done what custom demands, and slain all our enemies, would you now be sitting in a tent of victory or waiting on the hills to see what force next comes to oppose us? Never knowing peace. Never having rest."

No one answered.

"Look at this map," he continued, unrolling a crimson silk and laying it at their feet. "Here lies the Wei, bleeding. To the north, the Mongols stir. To the west, the Yueban remnants still dream of their own empire. You think we are finished fighting? No. We have only begun. And when the next fire rises, it will be these very women…these 'traitors' as you would define them, who will save us again by finding a way to turn the hate and fear in our enemies' hearts towards peace and friendship."

He turned toward the elders and then slowly knelt. Not in submission, but in defiant grace. "She-Ping is my mother. Alan-Ko is my wife. I would willingly give my life for either. If you choose to take their lives, then you must take mine also. Raise your swords now and I will bare my neck."

Oshun appeared shocked by Mar Yanqa's statement. "You are not on trial," he coughed nervously.

"And neither are they," Mar Yanqa remained defiant. "I grant all my chieftains to make their own decisions on the battlefield. So, I ask you not to see these two as women but as leaders in my army. They are warriors. Visionaries. Entitled to make their own decisions no different from any of my other warlords. Their courage defied my original orders but it saved a nation by maintaining something even more precious…our humanity. We are not savages as others would paint us. We are not barbarians. We do not murder those that willfully do not take up arms against us. It is only through the actions of these two women that we may have saved our frailest of all traits…our dignity."

A deep silence followed. The flames of the hearth flickered, casting the faces of the elders in stark relief.

"Condemn them," Mar Yanqa stated, "and we make a lesson that our laws are cruel and immoral. Spare them and we make a possible future of loyalty earned through mutual respect and honor. You think mercy is undignified. I would rather conquer the world with mercy than rule it through fear. I will not be that monster that mothers make their children afraid of, in the dark!"

The tent was so silent a child's breath could be heard.

And then, slowly, one by one, the elders stood. Not to condemn. But in an act of unity and respect.

Elder Oshun took a deep breath and nodded once. "It is clear we have chosen our Qagan wisely. She-Ping. Alan-Ko. You are found... not guilty. By the strength of your actions and by the word of a man who understands that even emperors must learn from those who love enough to defy them, you are free to go."

Alan-Ko placed her hand gently over her chest. She-Ping, for once, had no words, only tears that gleamed but did not fall.

Mar Yanqa felt the tremendous weight lift from his body.

And as he took his wife's hand and then his mother's, he whispered, not for the council but for them alone: "You have given me more than an empire. You have given me the heart and soul to rule it."

Later that night, beside his moonlit yurt, Mar Yanqa stood outside alone as Alan-Ko approached quietly from behind. "You hate that we disobeyed you," she said, searching into his concealed thoughts.

"I hate that I needed you to."

She smiled faintly. "Then we are even."

"Even?" Mar Yanqa said somewhat surprised. "When have I ever disobeyed you?"

"Whenever I ask you to take care of the children," she answered.

"That's not the same thing."

"Then we agree to disagree," she laughed.

"And now whenever I go to war am I supposed to take you with me so that the Borjigin don't defy my orders?" he questioned.

"I thought that was already settled," she answered. "Of course I will be there by your side.

His eyes rested upon her softly. "They will follow you now. I presume you'll be more than my wife; they will probably see you as my commander."

"I already am," she whispered.

He did not argue.

From the hills beyond, the sound of a flute rose, playing a sweet melody of happy times.

Chapter 27: 524 AD

The bronze bells of the Palace of Ten Thousand Autumns tolled only at death. On that morning, they rang without pause.

In the Hall of Primal Light, beneath a gilded dome of dragons and phoenixes, the court of Emperor Xiaoming assembled while silk robed ministers whispered behind jade-inlaid screens. The eunuchs stood as still as statues. Only the incense moved, curling in the air like ghostly fingers.

General Zhao Bao, the Supreme Commander of the Empire's legions, stood rigid before the throne. He was not in his usual armor. He had been made to wear the black linen robes of mourning. His lips trembled, though he dared not show it.

"Speak it," came the brittle voice from the Dragon Throne.

The boy emperor, almost fifteen, looked small, sitting inside a sea of cushions and brocade. But the clawlike hand resting on his armrest belonged to his mother, the Empress Dowager Hu. Claws that refused to release the seat of power from her grasp.

Bao bowed lower. "The Khitan prince...Mar Yanqa...attacked our delegation and the forces in the north. . Their horns sounded from the west but they struck from both east and west. Our legion was encircled before they knew what was happening."

A murmur moved randomly through the court.

"How?" hissed Viceroy Zhou Lin. "How could a barbarian outflank a mighty Wei host?"

Bao closed his eyes. "Apparently Mulan's column refused to fight. They were... ashamed. Demoralized. It spread like disease through the ranks. Discipline crumbled. By sunset, there were no lines; only fires and screams."

The Empress Dowager's fingers tapped once on the jade tiger beside her. "And Mulan?"

"She lives. Spared by the Khitan Queen Mother and her daughter-in-law from what I understand."

"The traitresses," the Dowager spat.

The word struck the court like thunder.

"Spared?" croaked Zhou Lin, his eyes bulging. "Spared and kept alive?"

"Yes. And we have heard rumors…she has pledged to fight no longer for the throne, but instead she will lead a people's army…against us."

The silence was complete now. Even the bells stopped.

Then, the Dowager Hu stood. "Bring me her portrait."

A eunuch scurried forward with a painted scroll; Mulan in her crimson-plumed helmet, one hand on the hilt of her sword, the other raised as if to command the wind itself.

The Empress Dowager stared at the portrait as if it were a poisonous serpent.

"She was our talisman. Our saint of the spear. And you let her fall into the barbarian's hands."

"No, Majesty," Bao whispered. "They say she chose to surrender to them."

A gasp. Dowager Hu did not speak for a long moment. When she did, it was with frost in her breath. "Seal the city. Send word to every provincial governor. Anyone with ties to Mulan is to be arrested. Burn every image of her. Her family, her former officers, even her stable boys. Their names wiped from the rolls. Their homes burned. Her legend… must be unwritten."

"Majesty," said Grand Tutor Liang with trembling hands, "that may cause unrest. She is still beloved in the northern provinces."

"Then they will learn to love someone else," Dowager Hu snarled.

The boy emperor shrank deeper into his robes. He did not speak. He had not spoken since the bells began.

"And the army?" asked Viceroy Zhou Lin.

"We will raise another," Hu snapped. "The Xiangnan conscripts are coming of age, are they not? We will bribe the Turkic mercenaries. Rebuild the legions."

A second eunuch ran in with a sealed dispatch from the border.

Dowager Hu took it. Her face paled as she read it. "They have entered the Yellow River Basin," she said. "Rebels march for Luoyang."

A silence fell again…this time heavier, darker, as though the very heavens had dipped lower with doom.

Minister Zhao collapsed to his knees. "We are not ready. The walls are strong, but the people…"

"The people believe in Mulan," Hu said slowly.

The Dowager's voice turned acid. "And she now rides as our enemy."

General Zhao Bao's voice rose with trembling rage. He could contain himself no longer. "She was your weapon." He pointed an angry finger at he

Dowager. "You cloaked her in ritual. You turned her into a myth. And when the myth woke up and saw the rot in this court, she turned from you!"

Guards moved toward him, but Hu raised a hand.

"Let him speak."

Bao's eyes glittered with tears and fury. "You lost the war not on the field but here, in this court of spies and shadows. The Red Plume was loyal. Until you made loyalty into a lie. She fought for the people, you told her. And now that is exactly what she does, realizing that ou fight only for your own selfish greed and the pursuit of power."

He ripped off his mourning robe and cast it at the emperor's feet.

"I served this Empire all of my life. But the Empire is dead. Long live the truth. Long live Mulan!"

And he walked away. No one even tried to stop him. Even the guards turned their faces aside, knowing that he had spoken the truth.

Dowager Hu stood frozen, her painted face unreadable. Then she turned to the portrait of Mulan and tore it in half. "Then let her truth burn with her," she screamed. "And someone see to it that General Zhao never speaks to anyone again!"

By the end of 524, the Dowager rarely slept. Her chambers stank of incense and burnt parchment. She had taken to wearing her son's robes, claiming they gave her some supernatural strength. She held court alone, speaking to the spirits of emperors long since dead.

"They fear me," she muttered. "The ghosts of heaven envy me. I held the dragon throne together with thread and fire, and still, they tear at it like dogs."

Her son, Emperor Xiaoming, now fifteen, dared to speak once during one of the council meetings. "Mother, perhaps if we open terms…"

She struck him hard with the scepter. "You will never speak of surrender while I breathe!"

After that, he kept to his rooms. Rumors swirled that he was kept drugged, or perhaps even castrated.

She had three of her ministers drowned for advising her to make concessions and seek an agreement with the rebel forces. General Ma, loyal to her since the beginning, asked only to see his family before returning to the front and instead she had his family executed, claiming it would make him fight harder. Insanity had taken over the rule of the kingdom.

Even her own guards whispered that she had gone mad. The signs were quite obvious. She scrawled curses on banners in her own blood, ordering them flown upon every city wall. She commissioned a tower of skulls, made from the heads of traitors, raised outside Luoyang's eastern gate. She forbade mourning rites, declaring that grief only served to weaken the soul of the nation.

"Let them die in silence," she said. "Let Heaven see that I am not moved by their tears."

But Heaven was the only place remaining silent. The stars turned. The days passed and the rebellions multiplied. The mobs shouting in the streets were not silent at all.

The imperial army was fragmented beyond repair. Their only success was that they finally put down the Poliuhan Baling rebellion that had been going on for years. The Dowager's elite guard was down to fewer than two thousand men. Grain was in short supply. The treasury was nothing but a memory. Spies reported that even loyal prefectures were no longer enforcing her decrees. The people refused to pay their taxes.

New rebellions broke out in Hebei and Guangzhou. In the south, a boy of fourteen declared himself to be the Emperor of a new dynasty. In the west, monks set fire to imperial tax offices and crowned a blind shepherd as king.

Meanwhile the Khitan nation continued to thrive, their strength and unity a testament to the vision and courage of a Qagan and Queen who had dared to dream of a better future, and a leader who had the strength to make that dream a reality. The Khitan watched. And waited. The Empire of Northern Wei was no longer a threat. They would let it drown in its own blood a little longer.

Dowager Hu stood before one of her last remaining generals, General Xun, a man of seventy-three with no heirs and little love left in him.

"Will you ride for me one more time?"

The old general bowed his consent.

"I will ride, my lady. But when I fall, there will be no one left."

She nodded, eyes hollow.

"Then let us ride into ruin with our heads held high."

That night, she stood atop the walls of Luoyang and looked west. Fires glowed in the distance, like a second horizon. The city was quiet, too quiet. Even the dogs had stopped barking.

She turned to her maidservant and asked, "Do you think the gods will remember me as strong?"

The girl withheld her answer. She had seen too much. She only knelt and pressed her head to the floor.

"Get up," the Dowager ordered. "You foolish, stupid girl. There are no gods left. Only women like me. And I'm not about to let my empire fall into the hands of the filth and scum that are burning my kingdom. I will find a general that knows how to deal with the masses properly. Someone who will teach them a lesson once and for all!"

The Empire was already bleeding from a thousand wounds, but Dowager Hu was prepared to rule over the dead husk of a corpse. And it was as if her threat against heaven somehow stirred what few gods may have been remaining from the pantheon she prayed to, because without any fanfare, one general, by the name of Erzhu Rong arrived at the palace in Luoyang and swore to restore the Empire on behalf of the Dowager Empress.

He arrived not as a supplicant, but as a warlord draped in wolf pelts, the snow of Bingzhou still clinging to his boots. His retinue was small, only twenty horsemen, no more, but they bore with them the heads of three rebellious governors. Erzhu tossed the burlap sack of skulls before the Dragon Throne and knelt with a predator's grin.

"Your enemies are scattered like bones in the wind, Your Majesty. I bring you peace."

Peace. A poisoned word in a nest of vipers.

Dowager Hu had known many killers, but Erzhu was different. He made no pretense of loyalty, no fawning proclamations of fealty. He looked at her not as a subject but as a rival and that, curiously, earned her respect.

For weeks, Erzhu made Luoyang his hunting ground. He dined with the ministers he did not trust, gambled with the princes he would later betray, and found allies among the discontented lords of the southern provinces. At night, he walked the Hall of Bronze Mirrors with the boy emperor, Xiaoming, whispering secrets that twisted the youth's heart against his mother.

"She rules in your name," Erzhu told him. "But she does not let you rule. She has no intention to let you do so."

Xiaoming, barely fifteen, burned with the desperation of a caged falcon. He had grown weak beneath her shadow. He was bright, clever, but most of all, resentful. Erzhu fed his hunger with promises of battle, of command, and a throne he would no longer have to share. The young Emperor Xiaoming began to change. His voice sharpened. His steps no longer echoed hers. He walked with Erzhu through the bronze gardens and spoke of power, not patience. Of thrones, not regency.

In the shadows of the Vermilion Hall, they wove their lies like spider silk. Whispers and blades flashed everywhere. The eunuch Sun Bao fell first. He had long been Dowager Hu's whisperer, her silk-robed enforcer who knew every secret passage of the palace. His fingers had held many knives, and his lips had sealed the fate for many in the court. One dawn, his body was found hanging from the Cypress Gate, flayed and painted with lime. Erzhu left no note, only a blood-stained phrase carved into the palace stone: "A serpent cannot serve two masters."

Dowager Hu said nothing of it. She walked through the gardens as if Sun Bao had never existed. But behind closed doors, she summoned old allies from the far west; men whose loyalty came not from blood, but from shared crimes. They brought poison brewed in turquoise bowls and black scrolls sealed with wax.

Erzhu's wine turned sour that month. Several of his captains fell ill. One choked on a fishbone, though he hadn't eaten any fish that day.

In retaliation, Erzhu stormed the Ministry of Rites and drowned the Grand Censor in a vat of ink. He accused him of treason. None questioned it.

Erzhu then held a series of feasts to charm the court. At one, he invited the young emperor to preside and presented him with a blade forged from the iron taken from a rebel's shackles. "A prince must never be unarmed," Erzhu said, pressing the weapon into Xiaoming's hands. "Especially in the Hall of His Ancestors."

The gesture shocked the court. No one had ever armed the emperor before.

Dowager Hu watched from behind her veil, her face unreadable. But that night, she summoned the astrologers and burned incense until dawn.

"The boy will be the death of me," she murmured, "or I will be his." The line between mother and sovereign had begun to blur.

Chapter 28: 528 AD

In the cellar of the palace, where slabs of pork and venison hung from iron hooks, Erzhu and Xiaoming made their pact. The cold silenced their breath.

"You will be emperor in truth," Erzhu said. "But you must first give me the sword arm of the realm."

Xiaoming's eyes shone with rebellion. "But my mother controls the army…how?"

"You make the announcement in court," Erzhu instructed.

"Perhaps I should do it quietly, without announcing it?" the young emperor was already panicking at the thought of going up against his mother.

"No. I do not whisper behind curtains. I command in the open. I strike first. You must learn to lead in that manner as well."

"But my mother?"

Erzhu leaned closer. "You must bring about her end. Not with ink, but with will. I will see it done. But it must be your name that seals her fate. It is the only way!"

Xiaoming hesitated. "She raised me."

"And caged you. Princes are not born to kneel. You were born to rule!"

"How am I supposed to do it?" the boy was scared but enticed by the thought of being free of his mother.

"You are aware that more rebellions are breaking out in the south. I will declare that there be a notice of a grand campaign against the rebels. That will force your mother to conduct a ceremonial send-off at the Temple of Nine Heavens, according to our tradition. She can't refuse. You will attend as well and once you've ascended the stairs, you'll declare your mother as a traitor to the mandate."

"What does that even mean," the boy was confused.

"It means you be carrying an imperial edict that you signed which says that Dowager Empress Hu is hereby stripped of regency. That she has defiled the throne and conspired against the Son of Heaven."

"But she'll stop me."

"No. As soon as you announce the edict, I will have my men surge forward, seize the old ministers, take out anyone who resists, and then lock your mother away in the Jade Tower prison. It's actually quite simple."

"I can do that," Xiaoming agreed to the plan.

"But tell no one. You can trust no one. Do you understand?"

The young emperor nodded his head but he really didn't understand. Having not been permitted by his mother to participate in any manner of governance, he had no concept of how to write an imperial edict. Naturally he inquired from his servants if any of them knew how to properly write an edict or know of someone that could, unaware that some of the servants were loyal to his mother and not towards him.

"The boy speaks like a dragon now," the Emperor's valet said, eyes cast downward. "But his tail is still soft. He follows Erzhu. He says… the time of regents is over. He is plotting something your Majesty. I am certain of it!"

Dowager Hu paid her loyal servant and sent him back to her son's quarters. She then ordered her spies to confirm the presence of a plot and what her son and Erzhu intended to do. It wasn't long until her spies had gathered everything she needed. Letters. Witnesses. A knife hidden in Xiaoming's drawer, engraved with Erzhu's family crest. A secret oath that someone overheard when the two of them were conspiring in the cellar.

She wept in private. Not out of sorrow, but out of fury. "They would unseat me," she cursed. "My own son. My own blood."

Knowing exactly when her son was going to make an announcement at a council meeting that he was making Erzhu Rong the Supreme Commander of all of Northern Wei's forces, she pre-empted that event by ordering Erzhu to immediately quash the rebellions in the south while still under her command. No announcement of promotion, no ceremonial send-off, she managed to evade their plot expertly without alerting them to the fact she had uncovered their plot.

While Erzhu rode south with ten thousand troops, the Empress Dowager prepared for a feast. A note was sent to Xiaoming's quarters, penned in her own hand, sent with love.

My son,
Let us put aside the shadows that have gathered between us.
Come to dinner. Let us dine as family.
No titles. No politics.
Just mother and son.
—Your Loving Mother

The boy never hesitated. For all his pride, he had never stopped yearning for his mother's approval. Perhaps this would be a reconciliation. Perhaps she had relented. Now that Erzhu was gone, he could afford the illusion of peace.

They dined alone in the Vermilion Chamber. The air was thick with lotus oil and the scent of roasted duck. The servants, all women loyal to the Dowager, moved about the room in silence. The table shimmered with delicacies, such as steamed carp, plum wine, boiled millet, and ginger broth.

Dowager Hu wore a robe of soft lavender, with golden embroidery at the hem. Her hair was pinned in a simple coil, a gesture of humility. Her voice was gentle, her eyes exceedingly warm.

"You have grown, my son," she said softly, pouring his wine. "Soon, the realm will belong to you."

"It already does," Xiaoming said, with a sharp edge to his tone.

She smiled. "Then let us drink to your reign."

He raised the jade cup.

She raised hers.

They drank.

It began with a twitch at the corner of his mouth. A sudden wince. Then his limbs stiffened, and the cup fell from his hand. He gasped, clutching his throat, knocking over a tray of dumplings.

"Mother… what…?"

She rose calmly, stepping around the fallen dishes.

"I taught you many things, Xiaoming," she said, her voice cold now. "How to speak to ministers. How to read the stars. But I did not teach you the fine art of patience. And now you have learned the cost of haste. This is your own fault."

His fingers clawed at the lacquered floor. Foam bubbled from his lips.

"You were my son. And I would have given you everything. But you let a dog teach you ambition."

He tried to rise…tried to crawl. He could do neither as his eyes rolled back into his skull.

"You will sleep now with your ancestors," she whispered. "And I will continue to rule."

By morning the announcement was being spread through the empire that Emperor Xiaoming was dead. The proclamation was brief: The Son of Heaven passed peacefully in his sleep. The gods have taken him into their embrace.

A new child emperor, Yuan Zhao, a distant cousin of the royal line, was declared in his place. Another puppet, barely six years old. Dowager Hu resumed the regency, her power iron-clad once more. Those who knew the truth dared not speak it.   Some fled. Others simply vanished.

When Erzhu Rong rode back through the northern gates, triumphant from his campaign in the south, he waited to hear the victory drum as he approached but he was met with nothing but silence. In the distance he could see the outline of the palace, laying silent under a shroud of pale mist, its walls rimmed with the mildewed breath of an early spring. The mighty Yellow River rolled nearby, its waters dark and sluggish.

General Erzhu Rong arrived before the palace gates not to the cheers and accolades for a returning hero but as a god filled with vengeance. His campaign in the south had been swift and brutal, crushing the insurgents like insects beneath an iron boot. Yet that victory which should have earned him glory was hollow when one of his palace spies rode hard to meet him on the road beyond the palace walls. 'Dowager Empress Hu had murdered her own son, the young Emperor Xiaoming, poisoning him in his chambers and seizing the throne for a puppet child named Yuan Zhao,' the spy reported.   Erzhu Rong had no knowledge of the boy but it was easy to immediately picture a six-year-old marionette with sticky fingers and a pasty face with the perfumed talons of the Dowager Empress coiled tightly around his neck.

Erzhu Rong turned to his captains and said, "Now the serpent has bared its fangs. Let us tear out her tongue."   He dismounted before the palace, not waiting for any ceremony. His armor was still streaked with mud and blood; his eyes set like stone beneath the leather trim of his helmet. Flanked by three thousand of his loyal soldiers, he gave a single nod. Battering rams slammed into the gates. Screams began before the doors even cracked.

The palace guards, once loyal to Xiaoming hesitated, then fled or were cut down in droves.   Erzhu's forces poured through the gates like a tide of steel. Courtiers in silken robes ran like rats in the corridors. Eunuchs dropped their scrolls and begged for mercy. There was none to be given.

Making his way to the throne room, Erzhu announced that he was installing a new emperor, to be chosen by an ancient Xianbei method of casting bronze figures, while summoning all the officials of Luoyang to come to the great hall and meet their new emperor.   Upon their arrival, the doors to the hall were slammed shut   and sealed.   There was no escape.   The main hall became a slaughterhouse.   Scribes were skewered where they stood. Ministers were beheaded on the lacquered steps of the throne.   Blood sprayed over the dragon carvings and soaked the golden tapestries. The room was thick with the smell of perfumed incense mingled with the reek of opened entrails and scorched parchment.

In the women's quarters, palace maids wept and scattered. Dowager Empress Hu, her hair unbound, fled barefoot through secret corridors. Erzhu hunted her like a hound on the scent. He grinned ferally when he found her. As he approached, she clutched a jade comb to fend him off, while screaming obscenities. She was dragged through the halls by her hair, stripped of her jewels and her dignity, then brought before the shattered remains of her usurped throne.

As the child, Yuan Zhao, cried in the arms of his care-giver, Erzhu gave the order. The boy was flung down the stone stairs like a rag doll. The Dowager watched, shrieking, her eyes wide as bowls, before Erzhu lifted her by the throat and crushed the last breath from her windpipe with his bare hands. Her body convulsed, twitched, and stilled. He let it drop to the floor like a rag doll.

But Erzhu Rong was far from finished. The executions began that night and lasted for three days. Over two thousand courtiers, ministers, scholars, clerks, and servants, all those who had conspired, consented, or even hesitated during the coup were rounded up. The air reeked of bile and terror. Men screamed the names of their ancestors, their wives, the gods, but all in vain. No one listened. None came to save them. The general remained unmoved.

One by one, they were bound, stabbed, and hurled into the Yellow River until the banks turned red. Corpses floated for miles like broken offerings. The river moaned for days afterward, swollen with the weight of the bloated bodies. The thirteenth day of the second month was etched into history as the Heyin Massacre, a tale of such horror that mothers would cover their children's ears when the story was retold.

On the morning of the fourth day, Erzhu Rong summoned the remaining nobles to the Grand Hall. The throne room stank of vomit and dried blood. In the center stood a thin youth, his eyes cast downward. It was Yuan Ziyou, a grandson of the late Emperor Xiaowen, plucked from obscurity like a blade drawn from its scabbard. Erzhu raised his hand. "This," he said, his voice cold as the northern wind, "is your new emperor. He will take the throne name Xiaozhuang. Remember him. And remember what happens when loyalty breaks."

The nobles knelt. The sun pierced through the shattered stained glass above the throne, casting shards of colored light across Erzhu Rong's armor. For that one moment, he seemed not a man, but a reincarnate carved as the avenging god of war. An unrelenting fist of retribution that had fallen upon Luoyang without mercy.

Chapter 29: 529 AD

Far to the north, Mar Yanqa sat in a ring of firelight, surrounded by the elders and the gathering of tribal leaders. The air within the tent was thick with the scent of burning yak fat. Outside, the wind howled over the ridges, carrying with it the news of a distant war.

As their Qagan, he stood in order to speak, while wrapped in wolfskin, his red beard a constant reminder that he was different, originally from another world. Behind his eyes burned the keen awareness of the shifting of power within their universe. He gestured toward the crackling central fire, where a map of the Wei Empire had been painted on rawhide and pinned to the ground with iron daggers, where it could be seen by all.

"Luoyang burns," he said, his voice slow and deliberate. "The Dowager is dead. The emperor, the real emperor, Hsuan Wu Ti's son, murdered soon after reaching his eighteenth birthday. Not long afterwards, another child-king is thrown from the throne down a flight of stairs. And now General Erzhu Rong plays emperor-maker with blood-soaked hands and chooses another boy to sit the Phoenix Throne."

Grumbles and whispers rippled through the tent. Derga the elder with his braided hair and clouded eyes leaned forward. "A tyrant is dangerous, yes. But an unstable tyrant is to be considered even worse. What does this mean for us, my lord?"

Mar Yanqa looked around the circle. "The Empire is not only wounded; it is diseased. It is rotting from the core and a diseased beast, especially when cornered, will bite even its own kin. Today, it slaughters itself. Tomorrow, it may lunge at us."

Chieftain Ujin Baatar, fiery-eyed and draped in a bear hide, thumped the hilt of his blade against the floor. "Then we strike while it is blind and bleeding! We take the border cities, ride all the way to Luoyang and pull the palace down brick by brick!"

Mar Yanqa shook his head. "Not yet. Let the sickness spread. Let Erzhu exhaust his strength keeping the cities in line. Let the Yellow River run until it overflows it banks with Wei blood. We must let the disease run its course lest it infects the rest of us. When the body of their civilization is dead, then we will come to bury it forever."

A hush fell. Then the gray-bearded horse-lord, Kharbak muttered, "And if the disease should burn out before it consumes them all? What if a new emperor rises, one who can hold the realm together?"

Mar Yanqa stepped closer to the fire, his face lit orange in its glow. "Then we deal with him in that unlikely event. Whether he is an emperor or a demon, we will be ready. But we will not go to war blindly. That will never happen while I am Qagan."

He turned to Tamerlan. "Send riders south. Quiet ones. I want to know who holds what cities. I want to hear from the merchants, the monks, the wives of generals. If there is weakness in Erzhu's foundation, I want to find it."

The elders nodded, with some murmuring approval.

"And the people?" a blind elder asked.

Mar Yanqa gave a slow, grim smile. "If Erzhu Rong is feared, then let us be seen as their saviors. We will offer them grain, whereas the Empire offers them nothing but breadcrumbs. We will speak of peace while they watch as the Empire burns. Eventually they will come to us, and in time they will open their cities' gates and welcome us in."

Many of the tribal chieftains were still disgruntled. Offering food, waiting for open doors, that was not the warrior's way. But thus far Mar Yanqa had proven himself to be a powerful and capable leader and no one was ready to challenge him. To the last few stragglers to leave the yurt, Mar Yanqa voiced his final comments. "We will not knock on the Empire's gates," he said, almost to himself. "We will wait until they fall off their hinges. Let that be known by all."

At the edge of Mar Yanqa's great camp, the signal fires had been burning for weeks on end. Those riders that were sent to spy on the empire's health began to return after several months of gathering information, their mounts crusted with the dust from endless roads they travelled on. What these Khitan scouts saw disturbed even the boldest among them as they handed over their records and reported to Tamerlan.

In his family's ger, Mar Yanqa sat before a low lacquered table scattered with the dozen scrolls that Tamerlan had placed there. Tamerlan bowed. "Do you need time to read them all," he asked.

"Why don't you give me the shorter version of what your spies had to write," Mar Yanqa suggested.

"Essentially, they've started killing each other again," Tamerlan said grimly. "Chen Qingzhi struck first."

Mar Yanqa raised a brow, not familiar with the name and motioning for more information.

"Chen Qingzhi...a Liang general. Crossed the Huai River like a man possessed. Marched into Luoyang while Erzhu Rong was still consolidating his grip. He found the emperor undefended. The Emperor Xiaozhuang fled with his personal guard before Chen could catch him. In his place, Chen crowned Yuan Hao, another imperial grandson. It was a spectacularly brief reign. A candle in a gale."

"Because?"

"Erzhu returned like thunder rolling across the valley. Drove Chen out. Hauled Xiaozhuang back and seated him once again as the puppet on a broken throne."

Mar Yanqa exhaled. "So, the play begins again. The actors haven't changed, nor has the plot."

"Not exactly," Tamerlan corrected him. "The court from top to botttom belongs to the Erzhu clan now. He installed all of his relatives in key positions. They decide who eats, who dies, who breathes. Xiaozhuang reigns in name only. A prisoner with a crown."

From the shadows of the ger, Alan-Ko stepped forward, eyes narrow, arms folded inside a robe trimmed with wolf fur. She had been listening all this time. "Until Xiaozhuang decides to unsheathe his ambition, like Xioaming did. Every puppet dreams about the day when he can cut his strings"

Tamerlane nodded. "Another scroll will tell you that already happened. He grew tired of dancing while Erzhu pulled the strings. He called Erzhu Rong to the palace for a feast. Xiaozhuang concealed guards in the cloisters. They ambushed Erzhu. Cut him down where he stood. Head split open like a gourd."

There was silence in the tent. Even the night wind seemed to hold its breath.

"Bold," Mar Yanqa said finally. "But foolish."

"Braver than I expected," Alan-Ko muttered, "but not nearly ruthless enough I suspect."

"You're right," Tamerlan agreed. "The Erzhus struck back, hard. Take a look at this." Tamerlan unfurled a rough map of the Central Plain and placed ivory markers over the cities of Luoyang, Ye, and Pingcheng. He pointed to the different locations. "Erzhu Zhao, Erzhu Shilong, Erzhu Zhongyuan, all of Rong's nephews and cousins descended on the capital. They besieged it, stormed it, took it in a matter of weeks. Xiaozhuang tried to flce but was captured. They say he was strangled in his cell."

Mar Yanqa's eyes narrowed. "So, the dragon's head is severed, but I presume the tail still thrashes."

"The Erzhus rule openly now," Tamerlan said. "But the realm is cracking. One half doesn't recognize their legitimacy. Two generals have risen against them; Gao Huan in the northeast, and Yuwen Tai in the west. Both have gathered men, arms, and are launching attacks. I suspect they will be the new powers in the near future."

"Eastern Wei and Western Wei," Mar Yanqa murmured, already seeing the shape of the future as he stared down at the map. "And neither likely to kneel to the other or look to share their power."

Tamerlan tapped Gao Huan's name that he had written on the map. "This one…he's no fool. Military genius, very shrewd. Already commands the loyalty of the northeast. The common soldiers adore him. Yuwen Tai is clever too but perhaps not as ambitious. Sits quieter, but I can guarantee he's watching. Waiting. Collecting his strength in the west."

Mar Yanqa walked to the edge of the tent. The sky beyond was breaking into dawn. Red and purple fire lit the clouds like a bleeding tapestry.

"All this death," he said. "All this chaos... and still, no emperor with the spine to rule. Just puppets and generals with bloodied hands. This is the way it is going to be for a long time I fear. At some point someone will turn to us for help, while another turns on us, for no other reason than he needs an enemy."

"All the while the people suffer," Alan-Ko said. "Cities burned, sons lost, daughters stolen and fields left untended."

Mar Yanqa turned to her. "I know what you are thinking, that the Khitan must choose. Either to watch the world collapse and profit from its fall… or step into the center, before the pieces harden into new empires with new dangers."

"Is there another choice," Alan-Ko asked, thinking that none exists.

"The former troubles you because it entails a long term of inactivity on our part. We sit and wait only to collect the scraps left behind after they have destroyed themselves. It is not the Khitan way and therefore you inherently don't like it," Mar Yanqa attempted to read her thoughts.

"I don't like it," she corrected him, "Because watching the world burn without even raising a hand to try and save it, lacks the spirit of humanity that you once spoke of. Letting people suffer endlessly, even if they are not our people is devoid of any morality. It is not what good people do!"

"But to enter into the midst of the war that does not concern us directly, is not what a smart leader would do either," Mar Yanqa advised. "What would be gained except the deaths of our own people in numbers too high to record. How can you save that which is beyond saving. I agree that left on their own, a new empire may rise and perhaps it will be even more dangerous than what existed before. I will leave that in the hands of Yahweh. If He so decrees we must face an even more terrifying enemy in the future because we do nothing now, then I will accept that decision. It is better than making the wrong decision now."

"You mean... not to intervene?" Tamerlan asked. "To not do it now, while they tear each other apart?"

"Are you both that eager for war that you will send our boys into a battle that does not concern us at this moment in time?" Mar Yanqa questioned them both.

"But it will concern us eventually," Tamerlan attempted to defend his position.

"But not yet," Mar Yanqa said. "Eventually is not now. Let the fighting exhaust them. Let the court rot. Let the people starve. Then... we ride." He looked to Alan-Ko to see if she still disagreed. "You said to let the people suffer would be immoral. You said it would be immoral. But since the dawn of time, it has always been the way. There has always been suffering, people pathetically struggling to survive. I cannot save them all, but I can keep our people safe. They must be our focus and I need you to understand this."

"I understand," she responded. "But somehow part of me wishes that we could do more."

"For all your hardness in battle, my wife, you still have a soft side," Mar Yanqa smiled fondly. "Perhaps there is something I can do. A way to confuse all the parties in their war to be more apprehensive and therefore less likely to pursue slaughtering the innocents."

"What are you considering?" Alan-Ko couldn't imagine what he implied.

"Diplomacy," he grinned. "Is that not a way to show that I am not indifferent to the suffering of the people?"

"Diplomacy?" Tamerlan questioned which was echoed by Alan-Ko. "What do you know of diplomacy?

"Perhaps enough," Mar Yanqa suggested. "We will prepare a letter to Yuwen Tai. Speak to him of common enemies, and of the old wrongs. We offer no army to assist him but suggest understanding. Let him know that the Khitan are listening. And we remember who slaughters their own for a throne."

"And what about Gao Huan?" Alan-Ko asked.

Mar Yanqa smiled. "That one is too clever to trust. But perhaps... we'll send a gift along with a similar letter. Something to make him at least curious as to our true intentions."

"I am confused," Tamerlan admitted he did not see the point.

Mar Yanqa laughed. "Exactly! It will confuse both of them as well. Do I speak as a friend or do I come as a foe? It is hard to tell from the language of diplomacy. It will make them second guess their next step, afraid of overstepping the limitations that I have set for them. The mere implication of remembering those that slaughter their own can either be a deterrent or a threat. Either way, I do not believe they will wish to find out."

"So now we are diplomats," Tamerlan found the idea amusing.

"My husband is many things, Tamerlan, but calling him a diplomat may be giving him false credit."

"I am wounded," Mar Yanqa feigned being stabbed in the heart. "I believe the letters will cause hesitation. Hesitation will buy the people time to remove themselves from between opposing forces. It may not be as dramatic a showing as you made for Hua Mulan, my dear wife, but if it results in the saving of the life of at least one innocent then I will be satisfied that I have done all that I can at this time. This is my final word on the matter. We will strike only when the time is right."

There was no further discussion and Alan-Ko knew not to press her husband any further.

Chapter 30: 530 AD

A glint of metal caught the first rays of the sun outside. Tamerlan heard the sound of approaching hooves to see the returning scout, a boy no older than fifteen, breathless, bruised, his coat shredded from the thorns of the Taihang Mountains.

"He has been gone a long time," Tamerlan turned to Mar Yanqa who was standing beside him. "I had forgotten that I had sent him out many months ago."

The rider jumped off his horse and dropped to his knees before them.

"Great Khan! The Erzhus have begun fighting among themselves. Erzhu Shilong and Erzhu Zhao, each now claims to be regent!"

"Regent for whom?" Mar Yanqa was curious since Tamerlan had indicated from prior reports that they had deposed all the puppet emperors.

"A new emperor called Yuan Ye," the boy replied.

"Do we know who this Yuan Ye is?" Tamerlan questioned Mar Yanqa.

He shook his head. "I will have to ask my mother. It is probably some distant nephew or cousin. She might know."

"They are fighting within the court to see who stands behind the throne," the boy continued.

Mar Yanqa laughed. A sound like a rumble of distant thunder. "So, the lion cubs devour each other now," he said. "Good. Let them." He turned to Tamerlan. "Let us all be patient. The Empire of the North bleeds without our blades. Soon, they'll cry out for a new dawn. That is when we will let our sun rise over the empire."

"That may be a long time in coming," Tamerlan was still not pleased that the Khitan did not ride against Luoyang.

"We have nothing but time on our side," Mar Yanqa answered. "We wait, we watch and we act only when the time is right."

"And how will we know when that is?" he sounded somewhat impatient.

"We will know," he assured him. "When they manage to fracture the empire into a hundred little pieces, we will know that our time has come. They will leave us with no other choice. We will need to save them from their own destruction."

"That could still be years from now," Tamerlan complained.

Placing his hand on Tamerlan's shoulder, Mar Yanqa reassured him that it would happen. "We are still young," the Great Khan commented.

"Perhaps you forget that I am much older than you," Tamerlan did not find it reassuring.

"You will live forever, my friend," Mar Yanqa was not about to concede that Tamerlan was approaching sixty years of age. "I know this for a fact. What would I do without you?"

"From your lips to Yah's ears, I pray this is true," Tamerlan smiled, knowing well that time was no longer on his side.

It was as if Mar Yanqa had a crystal ball with which to divine the future concerning the impact his letters to the two generals would have. Neither one took the chance to make all out war with the Northern Wei Empire. As weak as the empire had become, the only deterrent that could explain why they held back had to be a fear that the Khitan would become involved. General Gao Huan, described as being ambitious as he was clever by Tamerlan, showed none of those traits as he restrained any intention of going to war completely. So much so that he made the decision to the capital and swear his allegiance to the current power structure. Beneath the scorched banners of the Erzhus, General Gao Huan knelt in his armor still bloodstained from battles fought in the name of men he was now obligated to bow before. Fighting for years on the northern frontier, where he had earned a massive reputation quelling the Rouran clans, he now was swearing his undying fealty to the very people he despised, fearing that if he did not, the Erzhu clan would see him as a potential rival and threat. He was not in a position to challenge them, not yet, especially if the Khitan would become involved. So, he bent the knee, thinking it prudent to abide his time.

By the time Genal Gap made it south to Luoyang, there was already a new emperor on the throne. No one even questioned what had happened to Yuan Ye. Almost two years since the death of Erzhu Rong, yet the corpse of his legacy still rotted in the capital with the infighting between the Erzhu cousins. Yuan Ye obviously did not appear impartial enough to satisfy all he factions, so they raised a new puppet, Emperor Jiemin, to the throne; a timid man with the eyes of a deer panicked by the hunt, and the spine of a worm. Now they had an emperor that would not say no to either party. Gao Huan had no other choice but to pledge loyalty, no matter how much he may have despised this new emperor. He managed to smile through clenched teeth as he swore the oath. With each passing day it became more and more difficult for him to command the city garrison for the Erzhus, hunting down their political enemies with deadly efficiency.

Meanwhile, in the West, Yuwen Tai also appeared to have taken Mar Yanqa's so-called letter of diplomacy as a veiled threat as well. Unlike General Huan, who saw no other choice but to capitulate to the existing powers, Yuwen Tai decided upon a different strategy. In the western provinces of Guanzhong, Liangzhou, and the mountain corridors of the upper Yellow River, he set in motion a gathering storm, steadily growing in intensity, doing so silently and methodically.

Yuwen Tai had grown wary of the court long before the Erzhu clan began tightening their grip, avoiding returning to Luoyang, even when summoned by claiming he was constantly engaged in putting down the insurrectionists, leaving no time to engage in the palace's social gatherings. Born of Xianbei and Han stock, hardened by frontier campaigns, Yuwen Tai understood the shifting tides of loyalty and knew that distance was the best way to keep one's head attached to their neck.

Instead, Yuwen Tai used the vacuum of power in the west to mold his forces into a blade loyal only to his hand. At first, he worked within the forms of imperial authority. Orders issued from Luoyang reached his headquarters in Chang'an but Yuwen Tai delayed, interpreted, and reworded them to his own advantage. He sent choice gifts to the Erzhu leaders, such as silks, horses, and jewels, buying time with flattery.

At the same time, the officers under his command, many who were Han, were quietly rotated and any whose loyalties were suspect found themselves facing early retirement or were posted to distant garrisons with names that no one ever heard of. New appointments were made personally, often among men who had fought beside Yuwen Tai against in prior rebellions. He demanded personal loyalty first, and by the autumn of 530, the western armies, on paper still identified as part of the Northern Wei's northern command, had become an autonomous force in all but name.

Knowing that the imperial court still claimed the Mandate of Heaven, Yuwen Tai staged grand ceremonies in Chang'an's military encampments. Shamans, carefully chosen, proclaimed that Heaven favored the strong and the just, not the corrupt and the bloody-handed. The Erzhu clan, they said, had defiled the Mandate.

During these ceremonies Yuwen Tai would take the opportunity to address his men personally. "You have fought for emperors. You have fought for generals. But now the fate of the people lies with those who defend them, not those who poison the court. Swear not to the throne, nor to silver-tongued eunuchs, but to your brothers beside you and then to me, who will lead you to glory and honor."

One by one, the squadrons, cohorts and legions knelt and pledged themselves anew to Yuwen Tai. While the capital still convulsed under Erzhu domination, Yuwen Tai turned his eyes outward, not toward Luoyang, and certainly not toward powerful Khitan under Mar Yanqa, whose letter of warning had certainly given Yuwen Tai reason to pause. Yuwen Tai had no wish to provoke a sleeping den of wolves. Instead, he ordered his banners west and northwest.

The Tocharians, scattered remnants of the Yuezhi, had settled in the oasis cities along the Tarim Basin where they controlled the Silk Road routes west of Dunhuang. Their rich caravans were ripe for plunder and therefore became Yuwen Tai's first targets. What they stole made it possible for Yuwen Tai to keep his army well fed and well paid. The two most important ingredients in sustaining loyalty.

Next, he went after the Yuebans, a confederation of steppe tribes descended from the Juqu Xiongnu, that were scattered across the Altai foothills and Dzungarian plains. They posed no alliance risk with Mar Yanqa, being totally unrelated to the Khitan and therefore could serve as excellent practice for Yuwen Tai's horse archers and heavy cavalry without violating any of the conditions that had been written in his letter of diplomacy.

In the summer of 531 AD, Yuwen Tai's general Dugu Xin led a lightning campaign against the Tocharian strongholds near Kucha and Karashahr. Fortresses were stormed, tribute was exacted, and prisoners were marched back to Chang'an to serve in Yuwen Tai's workshops and stables. The incident went unnoticed by Mar Yanqa and the Khitan. The Tocharians were not his people.

In the autumn of 531, Yuwen Tai personally led five thousand elite cavalry against the Yuebans encamped along the Irtysh River. The battle was swift and brutal. The Yuebans were unable to match Yuwen Tai's disciplined formations and tactical use of terrain. In the end, they were scattered, never to be heard from again. Mar Yanqa did not flinch; they were not his people.

By early 532, Yuwen Tai ordered his engineers to rebuild and expand Chang'an's western arsenals, incorporating Tocharian metalworking techniques into the new armor and arms production. It was then that Mar Yanqa finally paid attention. Through his series of small victories, Yuwen Tai had managed to enrich his coffers, permitting him to pay his soldiers directly from spoils rather than wait for imperial pay wagons that hardly ever came. The skirmishes blooded his troops in real combat, turning virgin recruits into actual killing machines. At that point Mar Yanqa knew that they'd be fighting for Yuwen Tai, rather than for the throne and a state that they didn't know.

Remarkably, the Erzhu clan did not intervene in Yuwen Tai's rise in power. Drunk on their own triumphs in the capital over their enemies by General Gao, it was easy to disregard the reports of Yuwen Tai's growing independence and consider them simply to be exaggerations. The west was distant, and so long as no challenge came from Yuwen Tai's banners, the Erzhu focused their paranoia on rivals closer to the throne.

While the Erzhu generals vied for court titles and clashed with those that had been loyal to one of the many prior emperors, Yuwen Tai's army hardened. His cavalry became a terror along the trade routes. His foot soldiers learned siegecraft in the mountains of Gansu. His commanders, Dugu Xin, Li Xian, and Zhao Gui, emerged as a new breed of officer: ruthlessly competent, personally loyal. These men were no longer the shield of the Peacock Throne but instead they had become the hammer with which to tear it down.

Chapter 31: 532 AD

Finally, in the winter of 532, Gao Huan could stand it no longer. His Han army, loyal and fearless, turned on the Erzhus in a sudden storm of steel and treachery. Fortress after fortress fell to him, most not by siege, but by betrayal, bribery, and the sheer force of Gao's rising reputation and status. In the capital, the cries of surrender rang out long before dawn arrived. Luoyang, blood-soaked and weary, fell into his grasp like a dying bird.

Emperor Jiemin, the last Erzhu puppet, was dragged from the palace in silken robes soiled with sweat. Gao Huan did not speak to him. He simply watched as the guards bound the emperor's hands and led him away into the beckoning silence. But even Jiemin's fall did not satisfy the general's ambition.

Across the realm, in the city of Yechang, Yuan Lang, another puppet ruler, placed on a throne by Gao, himself, trembled behind the court screens. Gao had raised Lang in desperation, needing a claim to legitimacy during his fight with the Erzhus but now that he had taken control of the capital, Emperor Lang was viewed more as an inconvenience made through a hasty choice. He had become expendable. Gao removed him just as easily, raising in his place, Yuan Xiu, a quiet, refined man, whom he heralded as Emperor Xiaowu. Gao believed Xiu would be pliable, in fact grateful for the opportunity to wear a crown, even if he was not permitted to wield the scepter. And for a period of time, it seemed so.

But General Gao had underestimated his new Emperor Xiaowu. Xiu had his own plan, and in Husi Chun, the military chief of Luoyang, he found a co-conspirator. The two of them were often seen whispering in corridors. They sent messages west, past the Yellow River, to the warlord Yuwen Tai, who was now the unofficial ruler of the Guanzhong region. Together they plotted to arrest Gao, to break his control, and restore imperial independence.

But for all Xiaowu's plotting, he failed to appreciate just how deeply integrated General Gao's spy network was within the palace walls. Almost immediately, Gao Huan heard the rumors. Like the series of emperors that had ruled briefly before him, Xiaowu was just another fool. The general simply smiled upon hearing the rumors. Then he marched again.

Before spring had thawed along the mountain roads, Gao's forces had returned to Luoyang like an avenging frost. Husi Chun's men scattered without putting up any resistance. and Emperor Xiaowu fled west beneath a heavy cloak and a woman's veil, crossing the river in darkness, and leaving the palace abandoned. He was received in Chang'an by Yuwen Tai, who promised protection to the now in exile emperor, but at the same time was carefully plotting his own rise to power.

Now that the throne was once again unoccupied, General Gao Huan arrived at a final decision. "Luoyang," he declared, "is a corrupt and evil city. It has tasted too much blood over the years and now bears the rancid stench of death and dishonor. From now on, the Imperial Court will be in the city of Ye." With the announcement that Yecheng would be the new capital, he dared to do what only a few rulers had ever done before. "The capitol buildings shall move. All families, all households loyal to the realm, shall leave Luoyang and come to Ye. You have three days or you will suffer the consequences!"

There was no debate. There were no petitions. There were no refusals. And so, the people moved. Over four hundred thousand families, clutching what little they could carry in their carts and wagons, abandoned their ancestral homes. The roads became rivers of humanity, with oxen dragging carts, children wailing, and old men stumbling through the last remaining snowdrifts. Winter's final breath crept into their bones and filled their lungs. Thousands perished along the way, their bodies left frozen in ditches as silent monuments to Gao's will.

By the winter of 532 AD, as rumors of a gathering Khitan horde filtered through the steppes, Yuwen Tai stood at the head of an army transformed. No longer a frontier garrison force, it was now a mobile, disciplined, and battle-tested host numbering nearly thirty thousand strong. By the waning days of 532, the same winter winds that punished the exiles to Yecheng, swept across the western plains, and the snow-blanketed all the roads out of Chang'an. The feared Khitan horde never arrived. Merely a rumor on the wind that whispered change.

For two years, General Yuwen Tai had built his force in the shadow of the empire. His men had bled on the steppes and returned seasoned, wealthier, and loyal only to him. The Tocharians and Yuebans had been humbled. The arsenals of Chang'an brimmed with captured steel. The treasury, swollen with silver and silk, kept the army content through the long winter nights. But Yuwen Tai was no fool. He knew the time for mere preparation was ending.

By the time the snows began to clear, Yuwen Tai's scouts on the steppes returned with other news: the Khitan Qagan, Mar Yanqa, was consolidating his own position to the northeast but had shown no signs of threatening the western passes. Nor was he seeking an alliance with any Chinese faction. This reassured

Yuwen Tai that he would not have to fight the Khitan, at least not yet.

But perhaps the most important news came from his own spies within Luoyang. "The people hate the Emperor Xiaowu. They fear General Gao. Something was brewing within the city guard under Husi Chun. The people hunger for a champion. Gao Huan's power is wavering, since he is a northern warlord and distrusted in the court. If you move now, General, the hearts of the west and south may be yours."

In early December of 532, Yuwen Tai summoned his most trusted commanders to his great hall in Chang'an. The braziers glowed red-hot against the cold. Around the long lacquered table sat some of the best that his army had to offer. Dugu Xin, his most daring cavalry general. Li Xian, a master of siegecraft and infantry command. And Zhao Gui, a wily diplomat and spy-master. All of them loyal to one man, Yuwen Tai.

Yuwen Tai spoke plainly. "We have honed our blade in the west. The east lies broken. If we wait, Gao Huan will seize the empire, and we shall forever be confined to the mountains. But if we move now, swiftly, decisively, then we can carve our own road to power. The Erzhu are finished. The court is begging for a savior. And the people will follow the strongest hand."

"True," Dugu Xin spoke out, "This may be the time for us to rescue Luoyang from the madness which cripples it, but time is a peculiar adversary. It will take time to prepare our strategy. Time to prepare our supply train for the march east. And time to cross the country all the way to the other side to reach Luoyang."

"We do not have the luxury of time," Yuwen Tai insisted.

"No, we don't," Xin agreed. "The one who has time is Gao Huan. As soon as he hears of our intent to march east, he will change the entire dynamics of the current scenario. Much can change in the time it would take us to reach Luoyang. We must be prepared for that inevitability."

"Are we prepared to march east?" their general asked.

"Given perhaps three months to prepare and the arrival of spring with better conditions to march, then yes." Dugu Xin was being brutally honest.

"We are forgetting one very important thing," Zhao Gui interrupted. "The Khitan may also think that it is time that they invade Wei and seize control."

"We have used the excuse of the Khitan horde to frighten our children to sleep for years now. Every few months I have a report that the Khitan are coming and each time it has turned out to be nothing more than smoke on the horizon," Yuwen Tai dismissed the threat.

Those around the table grumbled. They could not dismiss he Khitan so easily.

"I am not some reckless gambler," Yuwen Tai announced. "You all know me to be better than that. "I will not openly declare against the Erzhu or Gao Huan without first securing our rear and sounding out the court in Luoyang. Xin, you said we need time. I suggest we start securing the west immediately."

"How soon General," Li Xian asked.

"Immediately," he repeated. "I expect you to start tomorrow. I need the garrisons in Liangzhou and Longxi reinforced. Roads through the Qinling Mountains will need to be fortified. Promise the local Di and Qiang clans new lands and titles if they keep the western frontier quiet during the coming campaign."

"That will not be enough to stop the Khitan if the invade on our rear," Zhao Gui poured water on the plan.

"You're right," Yuwen agreed. "If I intended to stop them, it wouldn't be enough. I only wish to slow them down. Long enough that we can take Luoyang. We'll have control of the east. We can worry about winning back the west at a later time. The east is where the real power and the wealth lies. It is where the heart of the nation resides. Even if the Khitan were to take the west, I doubt they would stay very long. It would have little value to them and would spread their forces too thin."

The thinking was logical and the commanders nodded their heads, giving their consent to go ahead with the plan.

Yuwen Tai sent quietly dispatched several envoys to Luoyang with the explicit instruction to make contact with the beleaguered imperial court. They were to deliver the message to the Imperial Court that General Yuwen Tai will act to restore order, defend the throne, and punish the usurpers.

Emperor Xiaowu was ecstatic, thinking that General Yuwen would be coming to his aid. He knew that his city commander, Husi Chun, lacked the military strength to taken on Gao's forces directly, but now there was an opportunity to create several disturbances to keep Gao's army occupied while Yuwen Tai slipped across the border. Messages were sent back to General Yuwen Tai from the Emperor saying that he would be eternally grateful for his effort to liberate the empire. He urged him to come quickly and in the meantime he would be hatching a plan of how to arrest General Gao on charges of treason.

Yuwen Tai was equally delighted to hear that he would be welcomed in Luoyang as its savior by the Imperial Court and he did not hesitate in giving the order for three corps to begin moving out and begin the eastward march. Ten thousand elite cavalry under Dugu Xin would serve as the vanguard and strike deep into the Wei heartland. Twelve thousand infantry under Li Xian, would take and hold key passes and river crossings, while Yuwen Tai would command eight thousand auxiliary troops and the Qiang horsemen, to screen the flanks and harry the enemy's supply lines.

A last check on the Khitan forces reported that they were still far to the north and unaware of any activity taking place in the western lands of Wei. "He will not interfere…for now," Yuwen Tai told his generals. "But we must move swiftly, before the Khitan see opportunity in Chinese weakness. We cannot let ourselves be caught between two opposing forces."

As the year 532 rolled into 533, while winter skies and crisp mountain winds chilled their bones, Yuwen Tai's columns were marching east. At each river crossing and mountain pass, Yuwen Tai's envoys spread the word, "The western army comes to restore peace. We bring protection…not conquest…for the people." Pretty words to satisfy a disheartened people, suffering under the hand of a despotic, tyrannical government. Had they known Yuwen Tai's true intent, to seize the throne for his own purpose, they may have been less welcoming to his forces, to whom they gave food and shelter.

With the first thaw of spring approaching I the second month, Yuwen Tai's army was already on the border of the eastern provinces. The hammer was ready to fall. The long column of Yuwen Tai's soldiers wound eastward across the dusty roads of the Central Plain, their armor dulled by weeks of wear, banners limp under a gray, windless sky. The plan was to strike swiftly into the heart of the empire, seize Luoyang before General Gao could return and solidify his hold, and present himself to the people as their savior from the chaos being perpetrated by the emperor. Word was spread among the troops, not about the chance to restore the rightful order, but instead of the plunder and glory they would share in once they reached Luoyang. It was their general's destiny to shape the future of Wei and they were eager to receive the rewards for making it a reality.

They crossed the border into the eastern provinces one morning, the soldiers hungry and weary but buoyed by hope of future riches. The land here bore the scars of recent battles, abandoned farms, and burnt villages. Yet no great resistance appeared, and Yuwen Tai rode at the head of his forces with growing trepidation. It could only mean hat General Gao had already passed through this way and was already heading towards Luoyang.

By midday, as his army halted to rest and regroup by a shallow river, a dust cloud was seen rising in the distance. The advance scouts galloped back with strange news that a small contingent of riders was approaching under a white flag, escorting a single, covered wagon. Suspicion rippled through the ranks. Some feared a trap. Others whispered of imperial envoys, or perhaps just a welcoming committee from the emperor of Luoyang.

Yuwen Tai dismounted and stood waiting beneath a gnarled elm; his arms folded across his breastplate. His commanders gathered close, as a cloud of unease settled upon them.

The wagon rolled into camp under watchful eyes. Its wheels creaked, its canvas flap drawn tightly closed. Whoever was inside definitely wanted to keep their identity a secret. The escort captain dismounted and knelt before Yuwen Tai and his generals.

"My lord," his voice hoarse with exhaustion, "We bear the Emperor himself. He fled the city days ago and come to you for protection."

A stunned silence followed. Yuwen Tai's eyes narrowed. At his signal, the guards parted, and the flap was drawn back. There, huddled in the dim interior, was a slender figure swathed in a woman's cloak and heavy veil. The scent of sweat and fear filled the air. With trembling fingers, the figure pulled back the veil. It was Emperor Xiaowu, his face hollow with fatigue, eyes red-rimmed with grief. His hair was disheveled, his lips cracked.

"My lord Yuwen Tai," the Emperor rasped, "I come to you as my only hope."

Yuwen Tai stepped forward, still shocked by the emperor's sudden appearance. "What has happened?"

The words were bitter, often halting as the Emperor told his tale. How just two weeks before, General Gao Huan had returned stormed Luoyang and in a lightning strike took control of the city. The city guard under Husi Chun fled, barely putting up a fight. The people, weary of endless war, opened the gates to Gao's invading army. The general was now in control of the imperial city. His forces were numerous, dug in, already restoring order and securing allegiances. Unless he was to lay siege to the city, there'd be no way of retaking it. Yuwen Tai listened and his heart sank. He had anticipated the city to open the gates and welcome his troops, but now it was too late. It wasn't going to happen.

"I escaped only by disguising myself," Xiaowu finished, his voice breaking. "The city is lost to him. Now I need you to keep your promise to shield me and offer me refuge."

For a long moment, no one spoke. The chill wind seemed to die entirely. Yuwen Tai's commanders glanced at one another, faces pale but most of all confused as to what they should do next.

The news struck hard, dashing all of their hopes. There'd be no entering Luoyang to cheers, of claiming the mantle of defender. All that collapsed in an instant. They had marched for weeks through hardship and a hostile environment, only to find the city already beyond their grasp.

Yuwen Tai's shoulders seemed to sag beneath the weight of the news. His voice, when it came, was hoarse and choking. "We cannot fight Gao in Luoyang now. Not entrenched as he is. Not without the people's hearts. This is over."

A murmur of dismay rippled through all of the assembled officers. One commander swore under his breath. Another covered his face with a gauntleted hand so that his words could not be heard. The army's mood shifted visibly, like a wave breaking against unseen rocks close to the shore. Men who had marched with purpose now sat slumped by the roadside, staring at nothing. The clangor of sharpening swords ceased immediately. Silence and despair took hold of the camp.

Yuwen Tai looked the emperor up and down and began to have regrets for any promises he may have made. He felt trapped by his own words. "We welcome you Emperor Xiaowu. We pledge our service to restoring you to the throne that is rightfully yours." He didn't mean a word of it but had no other choice but to say what was expected of him.

At dusk, Yuwen Tai gathered his officers. "We must return west," he said grimly. "We cannot afford to be trapped here in this valley. We must return to a safe refuge. There will be another way. Another day. I promise you that this is not over."

But as the long column turned back beneath the leaden sky, a bitter truth settled over them: the war for Luoyang was over. It was lost before it had even begun. Their great hope had turned to dust. The road home seemed twice as long, each step a heavy burden of disappointment.

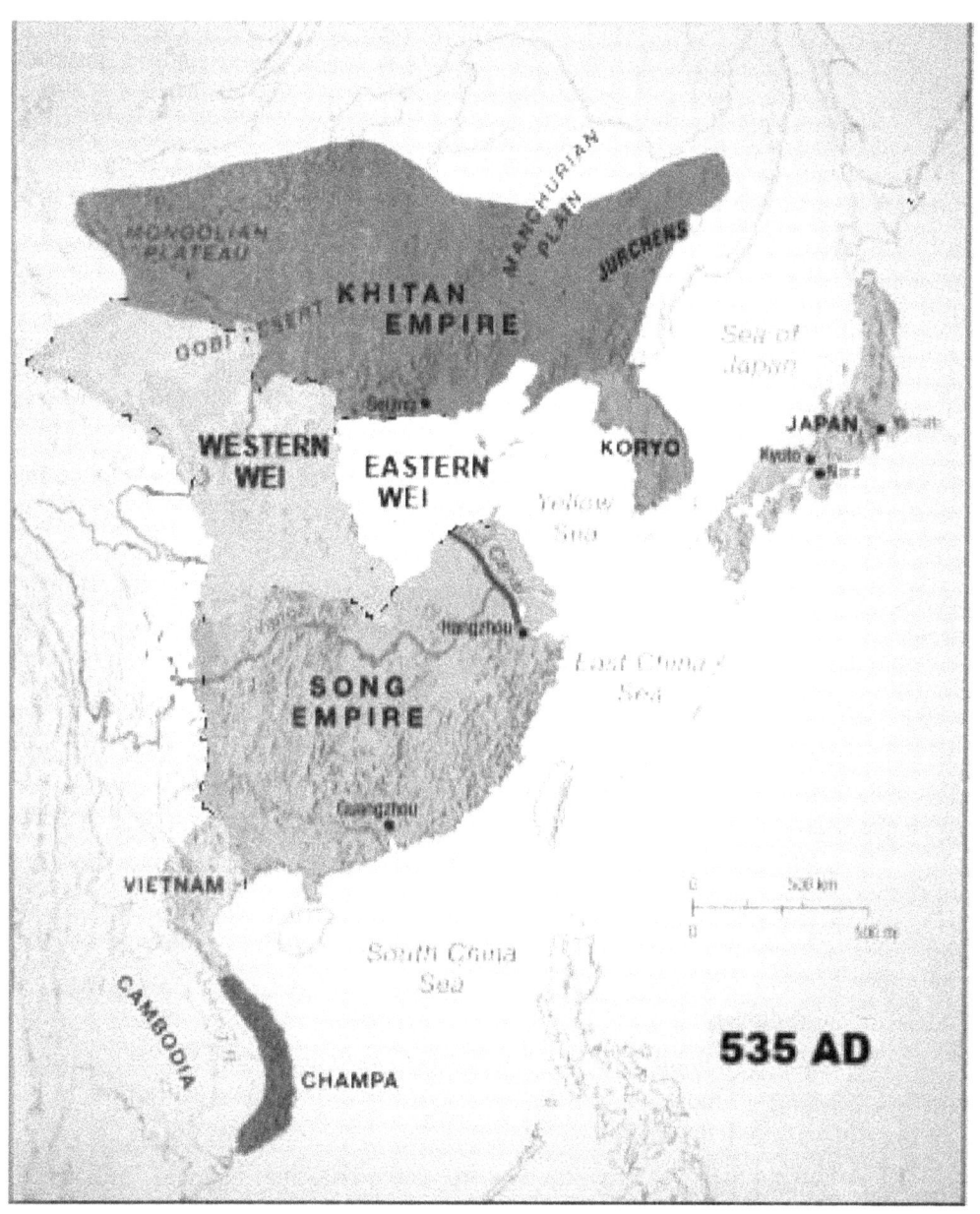

The Division of Northern Wei

Chapter 32: 535 AD

The empire was broken. In the west, Emperor Xiaowu, under Yuwen Tai's protection, proclaimed himself the true sovereign of Wei. He was the ruler of no one, trapped in a place that was nowhere. In the east, Gao Huan, master of Ye, raised his own dynasty in all but name. In the east, Wei was ruled through a new puppet appointed by Gao, the Emperor Xiaojing. Two emperors. Two capitals. But only one shattered crown. The split of the Empire of Northern Wei was now complete, and though neither side would admit to the division, Eastern and Western Wei were very much a reality.

The great yurt of the Khitan Council thundered with voices, the sound of clashing opinions echoing like war drums across the sacred valley. Under the golden canopy of stretched yak hide, each chieftain rose to express his opinion on the matter, while at the same time throwing insults at those that disagreed with them. A bronze brazier roared in the center, its smoke winding skyward, but its flames were not as hot as the tempers burning within that stifling yurt.

Mar Yanqa sat at the high dais, flanked by his wife Alan-Ko and his eldest son, Bukha-Khatagi. The young prince's emerald eyes, identical to those of his father, scanned the gathered elders, absorbing every gesture, every insult veiled as wisdom. Opposite him, the hawk-eyed Chief Chagan Bor of the Western Tumen tribe, his beard frosted with age and defiance, rose to speak.

"We all know that Yuwen Tai is no friend to our people," Chagan growled. "He probes our borders, steals our horses, tempts our warriors with silver, then sends them back broken or never at all. You ask us to side with a wolf wearing the robes of a fox. Gao Huan may be a conqueror, but he has not turned his eyes north and he fights with honor!"

Some grunted in agreement. Mar Yanqa did not answer immediately. He let the fire crackle. Let the wind beat against the tent walls. Let silence fall like snow before the avalanche.

"And what then?" Yanqa finally said, rising. His glittering robe shimmered, stitched with jewels that caught every flicker of the firelight. "Shall we wait until Gao Huan finishes with Yuwen Tai and then turns his eye upon us with his vast armies and eastern cunning? Shall we let our future be decided between two warlords while we remain fractured and afraid?"

"If that is the case, then it is only because we have been idle for over a year and a half, while those two generals were busy consolidating their land holdings and building their armies," Chagan Bor protested.

"Would you have had us take on both of their armies at the same time Chagan Bor? That would have been a recipe for disaster. We needed time to see which would be the better army to ally ourselves with. In making that assessment, we have been far from idle!"

Abaoji of the Grey Hills folded his arms. "You ask us to pick the lesser of two evils, Great Khan. But I have fought Yuwen Tai's regiments before. They know our language. They study our customs. I say this with respect: the man does not seek alliance. He seeks dominion over us."

The debate surged again, voices rising, fists pounding tables. Alan-Ko stood, her bearing as regal as any empress. "Then we name the danger and meet it on our terms. Do you not see? Yuwen Tai must accept our price for an alliance. We send our sons, my sons, as delegates. Not to be hostages but as the living contract of our joint will."

The murmuring paused. That was bold. Dangerous. But Mar Yanqa seized the moment. "You fear Yuwen Tai? Then make him fear us. Not just with our warriors, but with our unity. We send him our sons to show our strength, our future. He must treat with us as equals or not at all."

Some of the younger chieftains nodded. Bukha-Khatagi stepped forward. "Since when do we shrink from a clever enemy. No, we become cleverer still. He will know from the day that I set foot in his camp that I am not his hostage but instead, the bane of his existence should he dare violate any alliance."

"Gao Huan is a butcher!" bellowed Tamerlan, slamming his fist onto the oak council table, splintering a corner. "A Han with no honor! He betrayed the Wei court once already. He'll do it again. He cannot be trusted and that is why my vote is for an alliance with Yuwen Tai."

"But Yuwen Tai is a eunuch's whisker with no army that can match Gao's!" snarled Shiqan of the Tuoba, eyes wild beneath his ceremonial headband of elk hide. "He sits in the west with philosophers and drunk monks while Gao Huan feeds his army on conquest! Power follows the sword! We must ally ourselves with power! That is the way of the Khian!"

"The sword leads to ruin if the hand that holds it is blind!" Mar Yanqa's voice cut through the chaos like steel on mortal flesh. He rose, glittering under the torchlight in his gold-threaded robe, his hand resting lightly on the hilt of his curved blade. "Yuwen Tai is cautious, yes, I agree, but he has vision. Gao Huan burns everything he cannot control. Do you want to trade one dying dynasty for a tyrant of the north?"

"Piss on your vision!" shrieked Ujin Baatar, his beard matted with wine. He threw his horn cup at the ground, shattering it. "We follow the strong! Gao Huan has taken Ye! He controls the North China Plain! What does Yuwen Tai have but scrolls and ghost-loyalty to the Western Wei?"

"Yuwen Tai has the Mandate of Heaven!" roared Kharbak the Grey, an older chieftain and perhaps wiser. "And he treats allies like men, not dogs. One merely has to see how he has favored the Di and Qiang, to know that he is a man of at least some honor. Gao Huan will skin our sons for horse blankets and seize our daughters to warm his tents! Shiqan said his army is stronger, so why would any of you even think he has need of us."

"Enough!" Mar Yanqa's voice rose to a roar, and for the length of a single breath, the tent fell silent. He stepped forward, eyes blazing, teeth bared like a wolf's. "You think I do not know war? I have led you into battle after battle. I've watched men choke on their own bile after taking arrows in the gut. I will not send my people into slavery under Gao Huan's heel."

A murmur of agreement rippled from some, but others bristled.

"Where were you when Gao crushed Erzhu Rong!" sneered Yelü Daran, drawing his blade halfway from its sheath as a challenge. "How dare you speak of us as slaves to Gao when that was the time to attack!"

Metal whispered from scabbards almost instantly. The air shimmered with the heat of fury and Yelü Daran wisely resheathed his blade.

Mar Yanqa did not flinch. Instead, he reached into his robe and hurled a severed ear onto the table. It slapped wetly against the wood, drawing gasps and curses.

"You dare to draw a sword in this tent," he shamed him. "Here is what slavery under Gao will look like. Taken from one of my spies that I had infiltrate his ranks. Do not take me for a fool that I have done nothing to stop Gao Huan. I have been watching him closely for years. This is a present sent by Gao himself directly to my attention," he growled. "He calls us 'northern scum' in his letters. He promised to 'pacify the Khitan lands by putting us all in chains once he breaks the west.'"

"Is this true?" Yelü Daran asked, voice low and somewhat ashamed.

"Read it yourself," Mar Yanqa tossed a bloodstained scroll across the table.

As Yelü unraveled it, silence fell like a tomb's lid. "I cannot read," he admitted, holding it toward the other chieftains so that they could read it on his behalf. The chieftains gathered around, the firelight catching on the tight brushstrokes of Han script. As the words sank in, they became aware of Gao's plans to divide the Khitan tribes, to seize their herds, to replace their lords with Han generals. To have the Khitan woman serve as sex slaves to his soldiers. Suddenly their rage burst like thunder.

"DEATH TO GAO!" someone howled.

"DAMN HIM TO THE WORMS!"

"One day Yelü Daran you or one of your descendants may be a great leader of the Khitan, but today I am Qagan and I am aware of things that you have no knowledge of," Mar Yanqa quelled the fire in his adversary.

It was Alan-Ko who spoke next. She stepped beside her husband, placing a hand on his shoulder, and shouted loudly. "If you will not stand together now, you will die separately under Han chains. That is what Gao expects. That you will become divided as we once were in the past. But we are not that people that we once were. We are one people and one nation. We will not be divided ever again!"

The tent burst into shouting again, but this time with momentum, not chaos. Mar Yanqa turned, slowly raising his arm into the firelight and shouting, "Let it be Yuwen Tai. Let it be war. A war to preserve the freedom of the steppes. A war for the soul of the Khitan. I said we would fight when we are threatened. Gao Huan has sent us that threat!"

And one by one, the chieftains' arms rose to meet his.

By sundown, the votes were cast. Nine to three in favor of Mar Yanqa's proposal. The Khitan would march alongside the banner of Western Wei. A delegation would be sent consisting of Alan-Ko's sons from her late husband, Begunutei and Belgunutei, alongside her first two sons with Mar Yanqa: Bukha-Khatagi and Bukhatu-Salji. Four princes but with one mission.

The journey to Chang'an took three weeks, cutting across treacherous ridges and snow-laced passes. Even with their escort of two hundred men, the princes knew that their mission could be dangerous. There was no knowing how they would be received by Yuwen Tai. Technically, they were still enemies even though they rode under a flag of truce. They were relying on the fact that Yuwen Tai knew that he stood no chance against Gao's army unless he gained allies. Desperate times can make the worst of enemies the best of friends.

Yuwen Tai received them in his Jade Pavilion, surrounded by towering marble lions and flanked by a dozen silent guards. The four young men bowed in perfect unison. Begunutei, eldest and most composed, spoke first.

"The Khitan people offer you their strength in the coming storm. In return, we demand lands to settle near the Ordos bend, which will remain autonomous under our own laws, and shared spoils from your victories."

Yuwen Tai's dark eyes flicked from one brother to the next. He sat back, folding his hands beneath the long sleeves of his court robe.

"A generous offer but you ask a lot from me ," he said smoothly. "And what of loyalty? What of blood oaths? What of assurance that when the tide turns, you do not drift toward Gao Huan like so many others have?"

Begunutei replied with quiet confidence. "You have our word as the princes of the Khitan nation. And as many in your army are our kin, betrayal would only serve to cut our own throats."

Yuwen Tai rose and walked slowly toward the four.

"As the four princes of your people, and the Khitan I will remind you have over these past years raided my villages, attacked my convoys and stolen many a supply train. What makes you so confident I don't send your heads back to your father and thus remove any future your people might have?"

This time it was Bukha-Khatagi that spoke. "Three reasons why that would not be an option Yuwen Tai. The first is you have no chance to defeat General Gao's highly trained and disciplined troops. You know it, he knows it and we know it. Without our warriors by your side, you might as well surrender now. The second reason is that for every convoy and supply train we confiscated, your men have done the same to us. In that regard, we merely evened out our shared losses. But the third reason is the one that you should fear the most. You would have earned the wrath of our father. The Great Yanqa Khan would annihilate your army long before Gao Huan ever set foot on your territory. Yanqa Khan would show you no mercy! Of that, I can assure you, as we know our father well."

"Sons of Alan-Ko," Yuwen Tai emphasized the point that two of them were only half-brothers. "From different fathers yet still representing one blood. How interesting. Begunutei and Belgunutei born of the great warrior Dobun Mergen. And Bukha-Khatagi and Bukhatu-Salji, blood of Mar Yanqa, the infamous Glittering Man. Four stars shining brightly as one constellation. Or perhaps four arrows all pointed towards each other." His smile displayed the cunning of a fox.

He then slowly circled them like a wolf gauging its prey.

"Tell me, Bukha-Khatagi, if the Great Khan of the Khitan was to die in battle, which one of you would become ruler?"

"It is not up to us," he replied. "The Council of Elders chooses the next Qagan."

"And the Council may favor Dobun Mergen's sons, no? After all, he was one of them and Mar Yanqa truly is not of their blood."

"They will favor strength and leadership," Bukha-Khatagi answered.

"Of course they do," Yuwen Tai grinned broadly. "Indeed! They might even favor someone like me. I accept your offer. But each of you shall stay in my court for a time, to learn from our ways. To advise me and to remind me that we are one people."

Begunutei's jaw tightened slightly. Bukha-Khatagi remained calm. Bukhatu-Salji cast a sidelong glance at Bukha-Khatagi, who did not flinch.

"For the four of us to remain behind to learn your ways makes no sense, since two would suffice. We were sent here knowing that you would request some of to stay behind as collateral. I would suggest that Begunutei and I remain behind as we are the oldest and will be the best to learn. Our younger brothers must return in order to convince our father that this was a choice freely made by us according to our mother's original plan and not because you demanded our stay as captives. If none of his sons returned, I'm afraid that he would consider us to be your hostages and he would bring the full weight of our cavalry and legions against you. He would slaughter your forces based on a simple misunderstanding. We would not wish to see our alliance terminate under such an egregious error,"

"You are your father's son," Yuwen Tai complemented him. "Very astute and a point well taken," he added. "As the two eldest, you will be my guests. Your younger brothers may tell the Great Khan I am pleased to welcome and entertain you at my palace." Yuwen Tai returned to his throne, signaling the end of the meeting. As the brothers turned to leave, he spoke again, softly. "Let us hope blood remains thicker than ambition. Tomorrow the two of you…," he pointed at Bukhatu-Salji and Belgunutei, calling their attention once again, "…will return to your Qagan and let him know that we have an alliance.

That night, in the chamber allotted to them, the four brothers spoke little. The air was thick with unsaid thoughts. Begunutei, as the eldest, broke the silence. "He seeks to test us. To divide us."

"Let him try," Belgunutei said. "For we are Khitan. We are the sons of Alan-Ko. We bend to no one."

Bukha-Khatagi met his older half-brother's gaze. "We are the sons of Yanqa Khan. He is the only father any of us has ever known. By his hand he raised the five of us as equals. You have always been my brother and the same is true for Begunutei. We are more than just Khitan. We are the future of our people. Let Yuwen Tai play his games. We will play ours. And in the end, we will win"

Chapter 33: 536 AD

The Eastern Wei army, under General Gao Huan, advanced northwestward with confidence. Riding at the head of the army, the general had no fear in leading from the front. The soldiers were disciplined, their ranks unbroken as they marched across the plains. But the further they ventured into Khitan territory, the more they realized the challenges that lay ahead. The land was unfamiliar to them and that gave the Khitan the advantage of selecting the field of battle.

The first skirmishes were swift and brutal. Khitan horsemen appeared out of nowhere, their arrows raining down on the enemy soldiers before disappearing back into the vastness of the plains. The Wei archers tried to return fire, but the Khitan were too fast, their horses too agile. Gao's soldiers began to grow uneasy, their morale slowly eroding with each ambush and failure of their return fire to find any targets. It was as if the were fighting a ghost army that could appear and disappear at will.

General Gao Huan, however, was not a man easily rattled. He ordered his troops to tighten their formations and remain vigilant. He knew that the Khitan were trying to weaken them through attrition, but he also knew that the Khitan would eventually have to face them in a decisive battle if they wished to claim a victory.

The Khitan continued their hit-and-run tactics, striking at night, targeting supply wagons, and attacking isolated units. But despite their efforts, the Wei army pressed on, slowly but surely advancing deeper into Khitan territory.

Back at their encampment, the Khitan chieftains engaged in a strategy session to decide upon what they should do next. "We cannot face them head-on," said Yelü Daran. "Their numbers are too great, and they are well-equipped. We must use our knowledge of the land, our speed, and our surprise to our advantage."

Mar Yanqa nodded. He had fought in enough battles to recognize the overall strength of the Eastern Wei infantry and the tight discipline of their ranks. But he also knew that they were not invincible. Their heavy armor and cumbersome supply lines made them slow, and the vastness of the plains was a challenge for any invading force.

"For now, we will continue to harass them," Mar Yanqa declared, his voice firm. "We will keep striking their supply lines, ambush their scouting parties, and lead them into the wilderness where they will starve and freeze. We will lure them into a trap in one of the valleys where Yuwen Tai's army can engage them. In their weakened condition, Yuwen Tai should easily be victorious."

"As long as he shows up," an aged Valentius commented. "Thus far, we have been doing all the fighting and I haven't seed hide nor hair of his forces."

"Oh, I can assure you that he has had his scouts watching us. He is fox and the wiley fox will search for whatever scraps he can find after the bear and wolf have fought each other to the point of death." Mar Yanqa knew that the had pegged Yuwen Tai accurately.

The next confrontation arrived on a cold, wind-swept day. The Eastern Wei army had set up camp near a small river, its soldiers weary from the long march and the constant harassment. General Gao Huan knew that the Khitan would soon make their move, and he prepared his men for the battle to come.

As dawn broke, the Khitan appeared on the horizon, their banners fluttering in the wind. Mar Yanqa led his warriors, their numbers a fraction of Gao's army, but their spirits soared much higher. The Khitan had chosen this battlefield carefully, a flat plain that allowed their horsemen to maneuver freely, with the river at the enemy's back, limiting their ability to retreat.

The battle began with a thunderous charge by the Khitan cavalry. They swept down upon the enemy lines like a wave, their arrows darkening the sky. The Wei soldiers braced themselves, their shields raised, as the Khitan crashed into their ranks. The sound of clashing steel and the cries of the wounded filled the air.

But the soldiers of Eastern Wei were well-trained and well-prepared. General Gao had anticipated the Khitan's tactics, and he ordered his infantry to form a defensive line, their spears pointing forward and creating an impenetrable wall. The Khitan, unable to break through, circled around, looking for weaknesses, but the enemy line held firm.

Mar Yanqa realized that a direct assault would not succeed. He signaled for his warriors to pull back, feigning a retreat. The Eastern Wei soldiers, eager to end the battle, broke formation and pursued the fleeing Khitan. General Gao knew immediately it was a trap but it was too late. No matter how hard he ordered his signal men and trumpeters to call the men back into formation, they either could not hear or would not listen. It was the moment Mar Yanqa had been waiting for.

As the Wei soldiers charged, the Khitan wheeled around and counterattacked. The enemy charging forward were caught off guard. They became disoriented and disorganized and were soon overwhelmed by the sudden onslaught. The battle descended into chaos, with the Eastern Wei soldiers fighting desperately for their lives.

Despite the initial success of the Khitan counterattack, General Gao's superior numbers began to take their toll. Seeing his men in disarray, Gao was finally able to rally his forces. He ordered a detachment of archers to target the Khitan horses, ignoring the riders, while his infantry regrouped and formed a new defensive line.

The Khitan, now facing stiff resistance, began to falter. Mar Yanqa saw the tide turning against him, and knew if he persisted on the battlefield, all would be lost. He ordered a full retreat, his warriors reluctantly pulling back, leaving behind the bodies of their fallen comrades and thousands of the Eastern Wei soldiers.

Back in the tent of the war council, Mar Yanqa's chieftains were furious. "Where was Yuwen Tai with his army as promised?" They were well aware they had been set up to take he brunt of the damages to a point that both themselves, as well as the Eastern Wei army would be so weakened that both could be easily defeated by a well-rested force.

The air inside the war council tent was now thick with the smell of sweat, wet leather, and smoldering horse dung that burned slowly in the single brazier, casting long shadows that danced across the grim faces of the assembled Khitan chieftains. Each of them sat cross-legged on thick rugs, their armor still dusted with blood and mud from the retreat.

"He betrayed us!" growled Abaoji, slamming his iron-braced fist into the floor. "We had them in the valley. Gao Huan's forces were exposed, ripe for the taking. And where was Yuwen Tai? Nowhere."

"He never intended to come," spat Ujin Baatar. "He dangled your sons before us like baubles and then left us to bleed while he watched from behind his camp walls. We were fools to trust him."

All heads turned to Mar Yanqa, who stood at the far end of the tent, silent. His ceremonial helmet lay at his feet; the golden eagle crest smeared with dust. He looked older than his years, barely thirty-six, but his eyes held the weight of a lifetime of war.

"He knew we would not abandon the battle lightly," said Mar Yanqa at last, his voice like distant thunder. "He let us think he would strike. He let us believe he was an ally. But his army never stirred. That was his mistake, thinking we would remain to be slaughtered. Our losses were minimal. Our retreat strategic and that will be to his detriment."

Alan-Ko stood beside him; her eyes fixed on the floor. She had said little since the retreat. Her sons, Begunutei and Bukha-Khatagi, remained in Yuwen Tai's compound, safe or imprisoned, no one knew. It had been her plan to send her sons to his camp as a sign that the alliance they would forge would be unbreakable but he had not counted on Yuwen Tai breaking his oath.

"Then what now?" barked another chieftain. "Do we let this insult stand? Shall we grovel before a man who holds your children hostage?"

A low growl moved through the tent. The restrained anger began to seethe. Bows were unstrung and restrung with agitation.

"We march," said Mar Yanqa. "We do not draw blood... at least not yet. But we ride on Yuwen Tai's camp, surround it under the cover of night. We arrive in silence, in armor, our banners hidden until dawn. Then, when his men wake, they will find themselves penned like sheep."

Tamerlan raised an eyebrow. "We are to surround a Wei general's camp with a Khitan horde in the dark, and you think it will not end in slaughter?"

"It will not," said Mar Yanqa, "if they see we do not come to burn, but to shame. They will lay down their arms. Perhaps not Yuwen Tai but his men will understand. Remember, many of them share the blood of the steppes."

He looked to Alan-Ko. "And then we demand what is ours. Our sons. Our honor. Our price to be paid either with his honoring our alliance or with his blood."

The Khitan host moved with spectral silence beneath a moonless sky. Thousands of riders fanned across the grassy plateau where Yuwen Tai had established his camp. The banners were rolled tight. The campfires of the Western Wei flickered in the distance. There were too few guards, too much ease. Yuwen Tai did not expect vengeance. Once again he had underestimated the Khitan.

Mar Yanqa led from the front, wearing blackened armor laced with silver. His stallion made no sound but the breath of its nostrils. Every hoof fall was muffled with cloth. The Khitan surrounded the encampment like fog, tightening the noose as night deepened.

When dawn cracked the eastern sky, the Wei camp stirred.

And froze.

A sea of warriors ringed them. Khitan cavalry. Khitan infantry. Khitan archers on distant ridges. It was not a war cry that greeted them, but the sight of polished helms glinting in the morning light. Spears planted upright in silent menace. With a wave of his hand, Mar Yanqa could have slaughtered them all at that moment.

Confusion erupted. Officers shouted. Soldiers stumbled for their arms only to find that a large number of their swords had already been taken during the night.

No Khitan moved.

Then a single trumpet call split the air. The Khitan parted at the western edge of the camp. Mar Yanqa rode forward alone, his weapons sheathed.

Yuwen Tai emerged from his command tent, bleary-eyed, half-armored. He was tall, strong-jawed, a man of charisma and cunning. A man that always believed it was his destiny to rule.

Now, he was a prisoner in all but name.

"This," said Mar Yanqa, his voice pitched to carry, "is the honor you have earned. Either you fulfill your word or you find your eternal resting place in this valley."

He halted his horse before Yuwen Tai. The older man stood motionless.

"You hold my sons," said Mar Yanqa. "You held my trust. And you spent it like coin on the wind." Mar Yanqa spat, the spittle landing inches from Yuwen Tai's feet.

Yuwen Tai bristled. "You presume much. You come with numbers but no sanction to do so."

"I come with justice," Mar Yanqa answered. "Return my sons. Bow before me in sight of your army. Swear loyalty to the Khitan. In return, your men shall live. You shall live. And when Gao Huan is destroyed, you will be restored to your glory. But not until then."

"You seem to forget that your two sons are still my guests and even now are watched closely by some of my most loyal men," Yuwen Tai still believed he could bargain.

"I have not forgotten," Mar Yanqa acknowledged the truth of the statement. "I will be aggrieved to lose my children and I will mourn them deeply, but you seem to have forgotten that I have three other sons. I do not wish to lose any but if I was to lose them, as the price for your treachery, not a single one of your men will leave this valley alive. You have my word as a man of honor!"

The silence that followed was unbearable. Alan-Ko stepped forward. Her eyes met Yuwen Tai's. "I nursed those boys beneath the steppe stars," she said. "Do not make me mourn them. If you harm them in any way I will personally slice you into a thousand pieces and feed you to what will be left of your army just to make them choke on your lying stench."

Yuwen Tai looked past her to the encircling horsemen. He saw no wavering. No hesitation. None of this was merely posturing.

He turned, raised a hand. An aide darted away. Moments later, two young men emerged, Begunutei and Bakha-Khatagi, weary-eyed but unharmed.

Alan-Ko rushed to them.

Mar Yanqa pointed to the ground and Yuwen Tai knelt.

Gasps rippled through the Wei soldiers.

Dismounting, Mar Yanqa stepped forward, unsheathing his dagger. Not to strike, but to slice his palm which he held out to Yuwen Tai. He offered his blood. "Swear with blood, Yuwen Tai. Swear fealty, and you shall rise again."

Yuwen Tai took the blade and drew his own blood. mixing it with Mar Yanqa's.

"By heaven and earth," he intoned, his voice grave, "I, Yuwen Tai, pledge myself to the Khitan cause. Mar Yanqa is my master as long as this alliance reigns. Until Gao Huan is nothing more than ashes."

The soldiers of Western Wei all knelt in unison. The Khitan raised their horns and let out a single blast. The pact was sealed and was unbreakable under penalty of death.

Later, as the camps mingled and weapons were returned, Alan-Ko sat beside her sons beneath a flowering elm.

"He bowed to you," she spoke to Mar Yanqa when he approached. "Before all his men. I have never seen anything like it before. A Khitan chieftain would sooner die than grovel."

Mar Yanqa's face was unreadable. "He is no Khitan chieftain. Though he may be Xianbei, he is not one of us. He bowed to our strength," he reminded his wife. "But strength can be fleeting. We must strike Gao Huan before Yuwen Tai forgets the taste of fear."

Alan-Ko touched his arm. "Then let him not forget it. Let the earth remember."

As dusk settled and fires were lit, the Khitan and Western Wei dined side by side. But the mood was brittle, watchful. Peace held, but only just.

For now, Mar Yanqa had made Yuwen Tai kneel. But Mar Yanqa was well aware he had not gained an ally. It would only be a matter of time before Yuwen Tai or one of his descendants would seek revenge.

Chapter 34: 537 AD

Mar Yanqa gathered his warriors in a remote valley beyond the Shayuan plain, the air thick with the scent of pine and the sounds of horses pawing the half frozen ground. The Khitan warriors were a formidable sight, clad in leather armor and armed with bows, spears, and curved swords. They numbered only forty thousand, but their confidence was high, bolstered by their knowledge of the terrain and their belief in their cause.

Mar Yanqa addressed his warriors, his voice steady and resolute. "We have faced the might of China before, and we have always prevailed. They come with their numbers and their shining armor, but they do not know our land as we do. We will strike them where they are weak, where they least expect it. We struck them hard the last time and now it is time to finish what we started. We will show them that the Khitan are not a people to be trifled with."

In response, the Khitan warriors raised their weapons high above their heads, their faces grim with determination. They knew based on numbers, the odds may have favored the much larger army of General Gao, but they had something he didn't. An unbreakable bond with their land and their people. Mar Yanqa gave the order for them to ride out onto the plain beyond the valley.

The plain stretched out like a great bronze shield beneath the morning sun, a vast, unforgiving expanse of trampled wheat and loose shale. Across it, the banners of Eastern Wei snapped in the wind above the heads of rows upon rows of disciplined troops in serried formation, their armor glinting like fish scales in a sea of steel. Gao Huan's army was immense, ordered, confident. He had learned much from their last encounter. Fields once golden with wheat had turned to dust beneath the iron tread of armies. A wind from the northern mountains kicked up swirls of grit that stung the eyes and reminded them of the blood to come. Drums beat from their rear lines with the rhythm of a heartbeat that was slow, inevitable, and suffocating. A grim tempo that signaled death no matter which army one fought for.

Opposite them, the alliance of Western Wei and the Khitan had arrayed themselves in a much looser formation. Mar Yanqa sat atop his black warhorse, his silver and gold inlaid armor glinting with threads of jeweled beads, the red plume of his helm and a crimson cloak fluttering behind him like an eternal flame.

To his right, Alan-Ko rode in scale armor tooled in gold, her four eldest sons just behind her among the royal guard. To his left, Yuwen Tai remained silent, armored in blue lacquer, his honor at stake and his future tied now to the young Khitan chieftain. Mar Yanqa had claimed Yuwen Tai's allegiance with a masterstroke of political theatre, but this would be the proving ground. For the duration of the battle, Yuwen Tai would not be permitted to separate more than twenty feet from the Qagan's side. It was a way to ensure the leader of the Western Wei would not attempt any independent action that would place the Khitan hordes in danger.

Before them, the winds shifted.

There was a trumpet blast.

Gao Huan's army surged forward like a tidal wave, a thousand spears catching the rays of the sun. Cavalry thundered along the flanks. Archers unloosed volleys with machine-like precision. The arrows arced high into the sky, darkening it momentarily before falling with terrifying precision. The first clash was thunderous. The air filled with the whinny of dying horses, the scream of men pierced by pikes. The ground trembled.

Mar Yanqa raised his arm, and in that instant the Khitan appeared to vanish. Not so much vanished as shifted. Melting into the background, only to reappear as they split into two wings, after first feinting a withdrawal. The Eastern Wei cavalry pressed their advance, letting themselves be drawn into the hollow belly of a crescent formation. But General Gao was not about to let his men fall so easily into the trap of this maneuver a second time. He signaled for the cavalry stationed on either flank to attack each wing of Khitan horsemen head on. The Khitan riders only smiled as they saw the oncoming cavalry. They knew man for man they were the better horsemen.

The Khitan whirled around, their horse archers releasing black-fletched arrows into the exposed flanks. Each shot was delivered at full gallop, each arrow seemingly possessed of its own will. Volley after volley of arrows, slicing through armor gaps, striking unprotected necks. Screams pierced the din as the Eastern cavalry crumpled under the sudden rain of deadly missiles. With bone-chilling war cries, the Khitan charged, not in a line, but in spiraling formation, weaving around each other like serpents, hacking at riders, unseating officers, cutting through standard-bearers, until little was left of Gao's cavalry.

From the central hills, Yuwen Tai's generals unleashed the Western Wei heavy infantry in a staggered push, shield bearers first, halberdiers behind. The clamor of metal on metal roared like a hammer on anvil. Swords swung and bit. The battle raged for hours, the sounds of clashing steel and the cries of the wounded echoing across the plain. The Eastern Wei soldiers fought bravely, but the waves of the Khitan horde and the Western Wei tactics were taking their toll. Gao's army, so confident at the start of the campaign, was now struggling to hold its ground. The disciplined formations of the Eastern Wei began to contract under the pressure, being forced into a narrower front.

But Gao Huan had not risen to power through foolish blundering. He signaled his elite Tiger Guards, men who had trained since boyhood, to circle the Western Wei lines. Their black armor, edged with bone, gleamed with a dreadful symmetry. They cut into Yuwen Tai's flank with the cold efficiency of butchers. Heads rolled. Limbs severed. Morale faltered

Mar Yanqa saw the breach and charged. With two hundred of his finest riders, and Yuwen Tai in tow, he thundered down the slope, cutting into the exposed side of the Tiger Guard. With a sharp cry from the Khitan warriors, they descended upon the Eastern forces like a storm. Arrows rained down from every direction, striking soldiers and horses alike. Gao's soldiers raised their shields, trying to protect themselves from the onslaught, but the Khitan were relentless. They charged into the enemy ranks, their horses weaving through the chaos, cutting down the enemy with their curved swords. Mar Yanqa's sword hewed through helmets, his war cry a primal roar. It was madness. A pirouette of heroism laced with doom. The Tiger Guard faltered under the sudden pressure, distracted, just enough for Alan-Ko's Borjigin detachment to finish the rout. She swept in from the other side, her golden cavalry a spear of fire piercing the flank. The Tiger Guard broke. Some fell. Some fled. Others stood, surrounded, fearless, and died on their feet.

In the center, Eastern Wei soldiers pushed hard, trying to regroup. Arrows poured from their ranks in punishing volleys. Yuwen Tai's heavy infantry began to buckle. The ground beneath them slick with blood, churned by the dead. One Western Wei banner fell. Then another. "Reinforce the center!" Yuwen Tai shouted. The field had become a blur of dust, blood, banners and bodies. The Eastern Wei soldiers began to fall back, forming a new line along the edge of the river. Yuwen Tai, seizing the moment, signaled for his personal guard, the Iron Valiants, to charge, tearing through what remained of the Eastern Wei center. They struck with war hammers and spiked shields, battering Eastern Wei's soldiers into the dust. Every foot gained was earned with the death of a soldier.

Gao Huan attempted to rally his left, but by then, the battle had turned. The Eastern right had collapsed. The Khitan were merciless. They pressed forward like feral animals, their arrows falling in ceaseless arcs The center was now completely shattered.

On the northern ridge, Khitan horsemen found along the riverbank where the Eastern Wei had stationed their supply carts, hidden under canvas. With a cheer, they lit fire arrows and sent them arcing into the rear wagons. The carts went up in flames, exploding into sheets of fire. Smoke rose high, thick and choking.

The devastation was complete.

Gao Huan, perched atop his command hill, saw the shift. His lines sagged. His left was now collapsing. His center choked by smoke. His elite guard decimated. He drew his sword and prepared to charge. As he did so, he was severely wounded by an arcing spear. As he cried out, his horse reared and he fell. The general was dragged from the field by his remaining cavalry. The rout was complete.

The Eastern Wei ranks crumbled. Some ran. Others dropped weapons and fell to their knees begging for mercy. Mar Yanqa stood in the saddle, raising his sword high.

"Spare those who surrender!" he commanded. "This day he was feeling merciful, though once the survivors would see what was in store for them, death may have been preferable.

The Khitan rode among the broken ranks, collecting weapons, binding prisoners. Yuwen Tai's men moved in unison to form a perimeter. Alan-Ko, her cheek bloodied, saluted from her saddle. Her boys, now veterans, stood beside her.

As the sun dipped low and the cries of the dying faded into silence, the plain of Shayuan was carpeted with broken bodies twisted in the agony of their last breath. Smoke drifted across the plain. Dying horses twitched as their bodies shook from the death rattles. Blood pooled in low spots, making rivers in the dust. The banners of Eastern Wei lay trampled in the mud, while above them rose the dual standards of the Khitan and Western Wei. Both bloodied but unbroken.

Mar Yanqa dismounted, his boots sinking into the wet soil. He walked through the corpses, past shattered banners and broken helmets, toward a mound of bodies where his wife was standing. Mar Yanqa stood amid the ruin, his hair soaked in sweat, his sword dull with gore. Alan-Ko strode up beside him, her cheek slashed, but her eyes blazing.

"The victory is ours," she said.

"For now," Mar Yanqa murmured, scanning the horizon. "But we've awoken dragons. The remnants of the empire will not forget."

Yuwen Tai approached, his armor rent, but his posture proud. He knelt again before Mar Yanqa, placing his hand over his heart. Not in submission this time, but in solemn recognition.

"You are no mere warrior of the steppes," he said. "You are the hammer that forges empires.   You have done what few have dreamed."

The sun fell low. Shadows stretched like ghosts across the plain. Crows began to descend. And so, the Battle of Shayuan passed into legend. Not as the tale concerning the end of war, but as the day the Khitan rose to stand among the great powers of the age, and a young warlord named Mar Yanqa earned his place in the pantheon of warriors. The rivers would whisper of it. The winds would carry it. The souls of the dead would remember it.

Chapter 35: 537 AD

The sun did not rise quickly the next morning. It oozed across the plains like a dying ember, painting the battlefield in hues of rust and ruin. Smoke curled from the heaps of bodies that were now in piles to be cremated, mingling with the low mist, turning the air thick with a heavy metallic scent. Crows had gathered through the night and had now become their own formidable army. Early sentinels of what would become a banquet of rot and silence.

Mar Yanqa stood alone atop the ridge where his final charge had broken the Tiger Guard. The hill was black with scorched grass and blood that no longer steamed. His hands still felt as if they were red to the elbows. His sword was clean, having wiped it hours ago, but it still felt heavy with encrustation. He found it difficult to smile.

He knew that back at the encampment his warriors would be laughing and drinking, many who had started the previous night and never bothered to sleep. Their voices were raised in a chorus of victory songs. But beneath each chorus was a strange rhythm, a hesitation. Not all their brothers had returned. Not all their limbs were intact. Victory had a taste, sometimes sweet, sometimes bitter but always metallic and laced with ash.

Alan-Ko walked toward him, her step quiet, a sash of white tied around her arm in mourning for her cousin who had fallen in the second hour of the charge. "He was only sixteen," she said. She didn't have to name him. "He followed you like a shadow. I told him not to ride today."

Mar Yanqa said nothing. He could feel the ache of every fallen warrior like weights fastened to his ribs. The boy had died with a shout of joy on his lips. That was what made it worse.

"Yuwen Tai is calling our victory divine favor," she added. "He's already sent word to Chang'an. He calls you 'The Crescent Wolf.'"

Mar Yanqa gave a bitter laugh, almost a cough. "That's how they kill you," he said. "They make you into something you're not. A symbol. A myth. And then they expect you to keep becoming it. And when you can't do it any longer they become determined to slay the myth."

He turned to face the plains once again. Fires still burned where Gao Huan's supply trains had been torched. Khitan engineers had found the remains of burned children in a cart marked for grain. There were no innocent victories.

Returning with Alan-Ko to their encampment, he found the camp buzzing with the energy of victory. Fires crackled, casting a warm glow over the warriors as they recounted their feats in battle. Songs of triumph filled the air, and the aroma of roasted meat wafted through the camp. As far as the chieftains were concerned, the Khitan had not only defended their land but had also sent a powerful message to their enemies.

Elsewhere in the camp the Khitan warriors tended to their wounded and honored their fallen comrades. The battlefield had been partially cleared, and the spoils of war were being distributed among the warriors. The sense of unity and camaraderie was palpable, as each warrior knew they had played a crucial role in the triumph. Yet Mar Yanqa still felt at unease, despite his men's continuing celebrations.

Mar Yanqa took the opportunity to address his men. Standing atop a small hill, he spoke with a voice that carried the weight of leadership and the promise of a hopeful future. "Yesterday, we have shown the world the strength of the Khitan spirit," he declared. "But our journey is far from over. We must remain vigilant, for our enemies will seek revenge. But together, we will continue to protect our land and our way of life." Mar Yanqa knew that they needed to capitalize on this momentum. The Eastern Wei would not take this defeat lightly, therefore preparations for future conflicts were essential. "Take the time necessary to enjoy the fruits of victory today, because tomorrow we must begin preparing for the enemies return. It may not be for weeks, months, or even years, but most assuredly that day will be coming. We must fortify our positions, increase our scouting missions to monitor their movements, and we must forge alliances with the neighboring tribes to increase our strength. Only then will we be ready for the next battle."

The Khitan were inspired by their leader's words, as seen by their increase in commitment and efforts. Training sessions were intensified, and new strategies were devised. They were more determined than ever to defend their homeland against any threat. As the weeks turned into months, the Khitan continued to thrive. Their reputation as formidable warriors spread far and wide, and their influence grew. New trade routes would be established, bringing increased wealth to their people. Though Mar Yanqa had warned them of the pending return of their enemies, the victory over the Eastern Wei only appeared to be followed by a wave of prosperity, lulling them into a false sense of security regarding future threats.

In the Western Wei camp, Yuwen Tai sat inside his command tent, surrounded by trophies of war: captured banners, bronze helmets, scrolls looted from Gao Huan's command. His scribes were writing furiously, manufacturing accounts of the battle, proclamations, poetic declarations. His physician stood by with a tincture of roots and oil for the wound on his thigh.

He waved the man away.

"There is more pain in a treaty than in a spear," he muttered.

Yuwen Tai had won. But he had seen what it had cost. He had seen the Khitan ride like ghosts of the sky, turning the tide in a single maneuver no school of strategy could have ever taught. They were not men of discipline, but something older. Wilder. Even the way they burned the enemy's rear had not felt like war. It had felt like a ritual. A calling down of spirits. He wondered, not for the first time, if he had made a deal with something he did not understand, a pact with something far more evil. Something that would haunt him for the rest of his days unless he found a way to rectify it.

And in that flicker of unease, he reached for the incense burner and whispered an old northern prayer for balance. The wind outside howled once, low and long, as if it was laughing at him.

Far to the east, in the palace of Ye, Gao Huan sat in the darkness. He had survived. His face was bandaged; his ribs broken. The shoulder where the spear had pierced now rendering his left arm useless. The tiger sigil had been torn from his breastplate by an arrow. He clutched it in his hand like a relic, pressing it to his lips. Around him, the silence was deafening.

Messengers came and went. He dismissed them all.

Only one remained. A boy of nine, his youngest son, who stood beside him like a statue.

"They called him a messenger of his God," Gao Huan said at last, his voice soft and low. "A creature born of the steppes. He used us like pieces on a board. He used the fire, the mist, and the wind. He knew where and when our spirit would break. And he broke it."

The boy said nothing.

Gao Huan turned his head toward the window slit, where the gray dawn barely reached.

"This is not over," he murmured. "This was never going to be the end. We win battles, we lose them. But there are other ways to kill a wolf. You wait until winter. You take his pack."

He closed his eyes, feeding off his pain and suffering. And in the dark, he smiled a wicked smile.

Elsewhere, in the smoking remains of a ruined shrine on the battlefield, a hermit monk picked through the ash. He wore no shoes. His feet were cracked and bloody. His robes were scorched, yet he moved with purpose, his fingers brushing the broken icons, the shattered urns. He paused over the corpse of a Khitan boy, no older than fifteen, whose eyes had been pecked out by birds.

The monk knelt beside him and whispered an ancient phrase. The words were not Mandarin or Khitan. They were older. Forgotten. He took a shard of obsidian from the ground and pressed it to the boy's forehead. Then he stood.

Looking to the horizon, he spoke aloud. "The river runs red now. The gates of the underworld stir. Blood wakes the oldest sleepers."

He looked south, then west, then finally north.

"They will come now. Not kings. Not armies. Not men."

He turned and vanished into the smoke.

Several nights later, Mar Yanqa walked among the dead one last time. He passed a Khitan boy whose hands still gripped a broken bow. A Wei infantryman with his chest caved in, eyes open to the stars. He passed another boy. Alan-Ko's cousin who had ridden in secret among the scouts and been killed by a stray arrow to the spine. He saw no ghosts. But he certainly felt them.

The silence pressed on his ears like deep water. Every crackle of fire from the still burning supply train was too loud. Every breath too shallow. The stars above flickered like watching eyes.

He stopped at the hill's edge.

In the far distance, he saw torches—villagers, maybe, or looters. Perhaps something worse. He had heard the old tales: that where great battles were fought, the veil grew thin between the worlds of the living and the dead. He wondered if they had thinned it too much.

From behind him, Alan-Ko's voice came, gentle and low. "You should come back and get some sleep."

"You have been following me around all day," he commented.

"Because I am worried about you," she replied.

"I will be fine," he responded. "I just don't know if we achieved the desired end we wanted or created an entirely new set of challenges."

"Come sleep and you will be able to think clearer tomorrow."

"I can't," he explained.

"Neither can I," his wife admitted.

They stood together, saying nothing more. There was nothing sweet about this victory. It had left a taste in their mouths like vinegar and old bones.

"She reached out and touched his hand. "Promise me something."

"What?"

"When the next war comes, let it be worth fighting for."

He nodded as a tear rolled silently down his cheek.

Chapter 36: 540 AD

The battlefield had cooled over the three years that had passed but the air still trembled as if something evil had remained behind. It was said that the ghosts of those that died there could not be set free. For some reason they were still bound to the world of the living. Shayuan was on the one hand spoken of as a great victory but on the other hand people said that the plain was cursed and anyone that set foot there would suffer from madness. Mar Yanqa knew it from the very day his men shouted 'victory'. Since then, his dreams have been haunted by faces he did not know, events he could not have seen. Something was buried in that field that was beyond mortal explanation and he found himself drawn back to the battle site with regular frequency. Others seemed to suffer from the same strange phenomena and were also drawn to Shayuan.

South of the ridge where Mar Yanqa's charge had broken the Tiger Guard, a grove of old trees stood consisting of twisted elms and ash, gnarled like the hands of forgotten gods. Beneath their boughs, far from the songs of drunken warriors and generals counting trophies, a circle of Khitan women gathered in the moonlight.

In the center stood Lady Tse, the shaman priestess, draped in robes of black and vermilion, streaked with ash and wolf's blood. Her face was masked with ochre paint; her gray hair braided with bones and feathers. In her left hand she held a carved staff from the spine of a Siberian tiger, bound in rawhide. In her right, a shallow bronze bowl that was clearly ancient, dented, and blackened by centuries of use.

Around her, the women chanted. Not in song, but in series of rising and descending tones. Deep, rhythmic hums that seemed to come from some place buried deep within their souls. The ritual had begun at dusk. Now it was well past midnight.

Seven bundles of hair and teeth, taken from fallen warriors, Khitan and Wei alike, burned in a dish of cedar and bone. The air was now thick with smoke from the dish that curled unnaturally, as if alive and searching for ears to whisper in. A large horse skull had been mounted on a pike, staring eastward.

Lady Tse placed the bowl down and scattered powdered obsidian into the flame, causing it to spark with purple bursts. She lifted her staff and traced a circle in the air, her voice low and hoarse, the words ancient and scripted.

"Tengri, High Sky, open your breath. Ancestors, walk between our feet. Night spirits, stir from root and stream. We seek the truth behind the veil."

The fire snapped sharply. The humming stopped. Every woman turned inward with breath held.

Lady Tse lowered her staff and placed both palms into the flame.

It should have scorched her flesh but the fire bowed to her hands like an obedient servant. She scooped a handful of glowing coals and pressed them to her brow. Her eyes rolled white. Her body went rigid. Her lips parted. And she screamed. Not a scream of pain but of awakening. Like a door into the night bursting wide open, exposing secrets that should never be shared.

Her limbs jerked once, twice and then she fell still. Her mouth moved, but no sound came.

Then came a voice but it was not hers. Not human. It rippled through the grove like wind over glass, thick with malevolence.

"You have drunk blood not yours. You have opened a path you cannot close."

The fire flared tall and green.

"Your king rides high. His blade is moon-born. But in his shadow walks something with no face."

Lady Tse's face contorted, the bones in her neck popping as she tilted her head toward the sky.

"They will call him Savior. They will call him Wolf and Eagle. But he now carries the curse of the East. The dragon is not dead. It has only shed its skin."

The coals in her hands turned black. Her body slumped, then rose again like a puppet on strings.

"Do you want to see? Do you dare look, little witch?"

Lady Tse trembled but nodded.

The smoke turned black and roiled outward. The chanting women screamed and clutched their ears as visions pierced their minds. They were images flashing through their minds without mercy.

A child born beneath a blood moon, screaming not in fear but in command.

The Book of YahSu aflame, pages eaten by serpents whose eyes glowed like polished emeralds.

A battlefield of ice and stone where no grass grew, and warriors fought with weapons not made by men.

Mar Yanqa standing alone, aged and weary, surrounded by ash but his eyes were blank, his sword broken, his name whispered like a prayer and a curse at the same time.

And then came a woman's face, pale as bone, with lips like ink and eyes like shattered glass. She did not speak. But every heart in the grove heard her in the marrow of their bones:

"It will come from within. Not from the sky. Not from the gate. Not from the empire. But from within."

Then—darkness.

The fire extinguished and Lady Tse collapsed.

It took a full hour before she stirred. The other women had thought her to be dead.

When she finally sat up, her hands were blistered and her lips stained with black blood. She looked at the women or rather what was left of them. Three sat crying uncontrollably. One had bitten through her tongue and was weeping silently. The rest watched her, wide-eyed, mouths trembling.

She spoke only three words. "Burn the offerings."

They obeyed. The grove filled with ash.

Later, as the stars began to fade, Lady Tse hobbled to the edge of the battlefield. She stood beneath a lone tree where a sixteen year old Khitan boy had been buried. She planted her staff in the earth and whispered into the soil.

"I saw what comes. And it wears your brother's face."

The shaman returned several dawns later, wrapped in her black felt cloak and moving through the Khitan war-camp like a ghost from some buried age. Her skin was raw from fire burns, her fingers curled inward like scorched roots. Lady Tse said nothing, but her eyes, now nothing more than bone-white, grief-flecked orbs, spoke for her. And the women who had stood with her in the grove walked behind her in silence, their faces pale, their mouths tight with unspeakable memories.

Whispers rose all around her from those that saw her. Testimonials to her action and all of them in condemnation.

"The crone who drank fire."

"She peeked beyond the veil."

"She saw what should not be seen."

By the second hour, rumors of the ritual had spread from the horse corrals to the kitchens and into the ears of soldiers. Some called it madness, others recognized it for what it truly was, dark sorcery. A few knelt and prayed to their sky god, warding off what they called qara suul, the black spirits that trail behind seers who look too deep into the places they should not..

Alan-Ko heard the tale of Lady Tse before noon. And instead of calling for torches or soldiers, she sent for the shaman herself. Their yurt was quiet when Lady Tse entered. The air inside was thick with incense. Alan-Ko rose, wearing a robe of white wool. Her face still bearing the thin red slash she suffered from the battle, but her eyes were as sharp as any knife and her beauty never faded.

"Why did you go there," the queen demanded to know. "It is avoided by all now. Should my husband have made it forbidden to visit? It is a graveyard of thousands and should have remained undisturbed."

"For the very same reason that it still haunts the Great Khan's dreams," the shaman answered. "Where others found reason to celebrate, is it not true your husband has only felt portents of evils to come?"

Alan-Ko was shaking. "How do you know of this? He speaks to no one about those feelings save me."

"I know because the ghosts of Shayuan have told me."

"What ghosts?" she demanded to know.

"The ghosts of children. Children that should not have been there. Children by the supply wagons that were burnt alive on orders from the Great Khan. They scream his name. They want to know why."

Few knew of the children that had been killed that day. "It was an accident," Alan-Ko defended her husband. "No one knew they were there! No one other than General Gao probably even knows why they were there."

"They are trapped there now for an eternity," Lady Tze continued. "They want to rest. They seek justice."

"You will speak to my husband," she said. It was more of a command than a question.

"If he so wishes it." The shaman did not bow. She only nodded once, as though the decision had already been determined long ago.

Mar Yanqa sat alone, polishing the blade that was part of his daily ritual. A goblet of fermented mare's milk stood untouched beside him.

He looked up when Alan-Ko entered with the shaman. Then he stood.

" I have already heard that you led a forbidden rite," he said flatly.

"I did," she responded without any inflection of emotion.

"You called the dead." His words were formed as an accusation.

"I listened," she said. "They were already calling."

He stared at her for a long time. Then his voice hardened. "By law, I should flay you. Then burn you and the women who followed you for a sin against Yahweh. Scattering your ashes and your memory to the rivers."

"My fate is yours to command," the shaman responded without any sign of emotion.

Alan-Ko stepped between them. "But you won't. The calling was for you, Yanqa."

Nothing but silence followed. Then Mar Yanqa sat back down. Slowly. As though something ancient had just cracked open inside him. As if he had known all along that what haunted the plain was always intended for him. He knew the nightmares would only stop once he knew how to appease the spirits trapped on the plain.

"Tell me," he said. "And may God forgive me for what I have chosen to hear."

She told him everything. The circle. The horse skull. The smoke that turned to voices. The vision of a woman with eyes like shattered glass. The ash-filled battlefield. The broken sword in his own hand. When she spoke of the dragon shedding its skin, he flinched. When she described the unborn child screaming commands into the night, he clenched his fist. And when she said, "It will come from within", a shadow passed over his face like a curtain drawn too fast.

When she finished, she collapsed to her knees, exhausted.

Alan-Ko stepped forward and touched her shoulder but Mar Yanqa merely stood and turned away. He looked into the fire, and for a long time, said nothing.

Then he whispered, "I have sinned."

Alan-Ko's brow furrowed. "You only listened."

"No." He turned to her, his eyes hollow. "That was the sin."

That night, he rode out alone to the high priest's tent. Ben-Eleck, the Hebrew priest of Yahweh waited in silence while Mar Yanqa described everything he heard. Ben-Eleck wore his white linen robes, a square-cut beard, and eyes that had seen too much over the years. "Why," was all the priest said at first.

"I sought knowledge," Mar Yanqa said. "I sought truth in the shadows. I sought relief from my nightmares."

Ben-Eleck did not move. "Why did you not seek it from God?"

"He was not answering me, so I heard it from a witch."

Silence and then the priest sighed. "You know what Saul did. He sought the Witch of Endor. He too wanted answers that God would not give. And when he heard what he wanted… the Lord departed from him forever."

"I did not seek out the witch, she came to me unrequested," Mar Yanqa explained.

"And for that reason, you may not suffer to the degree that Saul did."

"But why did Yahweh not answer my prayers. Instead, I suffered a curse of seeing horrors from that battle night after night that I did not wish to see."

"Perhaps that was always Yahweh's plan. The greatest failing of a conqueror in the name of God is that they forget the value of life. Death and slaughter becomes meaningless to them and they no longer place value on the souls of their enemies. They forget that Yahweh infuses the soul into all men, whether they be ally or adversary. Your shame or guilt for taking all those lives would be a sign to God that he had made the right choice. The day you no longer shed a tear, even for your enemies, would be the day he would abandon you. What you perceived as punishment was His way of testing your worthiness."

Mar Yanqa paled. "What do I do now?"

"You wait," the priest said, voice like a tomb opening. "You wait for the One you have angered. He will come. And when He speaks, you will know your punishment. And there will be no sword, no child, no glory that can turn it back."

That night, Mar Yanqa did not sleep. The camp was quiet, save for the occasional snort of a restless horse and the murmur of guards. Yet in his tent, shadows moved unnaturally, and the oil lamps flickered though there was no wind.

At the third hour before dawn, the fire guttered and a presence entered. It had no form. No face. But it pressed against his soul like a hot iron. It felt like judgment. Mar Yanqa fell to his knees. His mouth opened but he could not speak. He wanted to scream for his wife but the words would not form in his throat.

And suddenly there was a voice. Not in the air, but in his head and it spoke. "You were chosen. A blade of the steppes. A light in the dark. And yet, you went to the dead for what was Mine to give. You asked the grave to guide you. And so, the grave shall have you."

Mar Yanqa wanted to deny the charge. He never sought out the shaman. She came to him; he wanted to say in his defense there was nothing he could say.

"You will win nations. You will command kings. But peace will forever flee from you. Your house will divide. And the sons of your sons will drink blood. In ten generations, your name will be forgotten. The book of YahSu will be hidden away forever. All that you tried to achieve will be washed away by one unborn yet to come from your wife's line. The dragon shall shed its skin and this unborn child will wear it. Everything you have tried to achieve, he will abandon. And so, your family's dominion will come to an end. The empire you forged shall crack at the roots."

"Because I let the witch speak?" Mar Yanqa was finally able to form the words.

"Because you listened."

Mar Yanqa collapsed, weeping, hands trembling as though the earth itself was shaking through them.

When Alan-Ko found him, he was still kneeling, eyes wide, whispering over and over, "Forgive me. Forgive me. Forgive me…"

But the heavens above were silent and the shadows had already begun to lengthen.

Chapter 37: 540 AD

The evening light washed over the sacred valley in amber and gold, the kind of light that made every blade of grass seem kissed by the heavens. The scent of pine and distant smoke mingled in the cooling air. Mar Yanqa summoned Alan-Ko's five children to the family tent. He felt an urgency to explain to them what the shaman, Lady Tze had exposed him to, and for which Yahweh had now condemned both he and his descendants. The matter weighed heavily upon his mind, as he had no doubt that God intended to carry out his threat but Mar Yanqa felt a need to make his sons understand why he had compromised their future.

Under a canopy of silken banners and weathered yak hides, Mar Yanqa sat cross-legged on a felt carpet, his broad shoulders cloaked in a robe of deep indigo threaded with silver runes. As they entered, he beckoned them to be seated in a half-circle with a wave of his right arm. There they sat, eager to hear what Mar Yanqa had to say. Begunutei, the eldest, wise beyond his years, now bloodied as a mighty warrior as marked by the wolf pelt across his shoulders. Belgunutei, both fierce and loyal, always around his older brother like a second shadow. Bukha-Khatagi, the quiet philosopher, showing much of his father's character. Bukhatu-Salji, the child of spring, born during a period of peace but savage on the field of battle. And finally, Bodonchar-Munkhag, seventeen, not yet wed like his four brothers, his eyes still full of the fire and unspent dreams of youth.

They had come at his summons, and now they waited for him to speak as cups of fermented mare's milk were handed to each of them by one of the family servants. Mar Yanqa's voice was soft at first, almost inaudible, forcing all the sons to lean forward. "Sons of Alan-Ko, branches of the blessed line... I must speak to you of a grief that has lived in my heart for several years now."

They watched him closely. He never spoke like this. Not in quiet tones. Not in such measured words and certainly not about matters that troubled him.

"Long ago," he said, "the sky god, Yahweh, the one and only God in the heavens promised our family an eternal blessing. We were to be the keepers of the valley, the defenders of the Book of YahSu, and the shepherds of a people not bound by the rot of cities or the pride of empires. But alas, I have sinned. And the blessing has been shortened. He said to my ancestors long ago, do not try to contain me within walls of stone. But they would not listen and they built for Him a magnificent temple. He said to them, do not place a king over yourselves, as I am your only king, but they would not listen. First they chose Saul, and then they chose David, my ancestor from long ago. Then He said to them, do not attempt to count my people, for I will make them like the stars in the heaven, beyond what any man can count, but these kings would not listen and they made a census so that they could collect taxes. That was then, and we suffered for our pride.

For the first time in fifteen hundred years, Yah gave us an opportunity once again to renew those pledges and promises to Him and correct the mistakes of the past. I have tried to do everything He asked of our ancestors. I refused to build Him a temple, choosing instead that we all worship Him in the open and in our common yurts and our own gers. I made no attempt to contain the sky within walls of stone.

And though many call me the Great Khan, I choose not to rule as a king, but instead rule by council, so that every chieftain has a voice, and the elders and the priests can guide us wisely so that we do not violate God's commandments. But most of all, I have spent the past twenty five years making us into a great nation, whose numbers are like the stars and at no time have I ever attempted to enumerate our population. All this I did, so that we would share in His blessing forever. But then in a moment of doubt, weakness and perhaps vanity, thinking only of my personal wellbeing, I threw it all away..."

The brothers stirred uneasily.

"Because I listened to the shaman, Lady Tse."

The name caused a hush. The witch-shaman whose whispers once slipped like oil through their tents. She had vanished soon after the revelation to Mar Yanqa, fearing retribution. Some claimed that she had died. Others, that she had turned into a fox and fled into the mountains. But it did not matter that she was gone, the damage had been done.

"I mistook her visions for wisdom. Her charms for prophecy. Her spells for a divine gift. But her counsel came not from Yahweh, but from another place... a much darker place. She was a necromancer and I listened to her!"

A long silence followed. Then, it was Bukha-Khatagi, his eldest son with the most penetrating eyes, who finally spoke. "Father... if Lady Tse had power, real power, then was it not given to her by Yahweh? Can anything in the world live or die without His will? Even if she was... a necromancer, perhaps God meant for you to use what she knew?"

Belgunutei nodded, crossing his arms. "She healed men in the war camps.

She spoke to the dead, and sometimes their answers helped us survive. Can truth come from such a woman and still be evil?"

Mar Yanqa didn't answer right away. He looked into the fire, watching the sparks leap up like tiny lost souls. Then he stood, hands behind his back, the lines on his youthful face deeper than ever.

"What you say is not foolish," he began. "Power is not always wicked. But it is not always holy either. God did not create Lady Tse's gift. He allowed it to manifest. Just as He allows locusts, or plague, or betrayal to occur. Yahweh permits evil to roam, but only for a time. He commands us to walk only by His light, not by whatever flickering torch we find in the dark." He looked up toward the night sky, its stars pulsing with an ancient calm.

"I still don't understand why Yah would have tempted you in this manner in the first place," Belgunutei still struggled with the answer.

"When you hunger, would you steal a loaf of bread? When you thirst, would you drink poison because it refreshes like water? I thought I was desperate. But I was not starving, and there were no droughts. There were no raids. Our people were victorious and not under threat. There were only dark dreams that would not leave me. Dreams that disturbed my sleep but could not harm me. And Lady Tse…she came with answers. Not prayers. Not patience. But sadly, answers that I did not need to know."

His voice thickened, his eyes glistening. "She told me what I wanted to hear. That my enemies could be silenced. That my ancestors could speak. That death could be… negotiated. But Yahweh is not the god of negotiation. HE IS THAT WHICH HE IS. The one sentence that he said to Moses that explains everything. The One who speaks once, and that is enough."

Begunutei frowned. "But you still won battles with her help."

"No!" Mar Yanqa corrected him. "The victory was God's judgment. She only saw what He was already committed to. That did not mean that she had His favor. The greatest punishment He gives is to let a man succeed in his sin, so he no longer hears the warning in his soul."

He turned to Bukha-Khatagi. "Do you know when I knew I had failed?"

His son shook his head.

"When I could no longer distinguish between the voice of Yahweh and the voice of a dead man speaking through her lips. When I wanted it to be Yah that was speaking to me… and no longer cared if it wasn't."

The wind suddenly picked up in the tent, brushing the banners above their heads.

"Surely Yah is merciful as the book says," Begunutei attempted to rationalize what was being said. "If a man sins once, does that mean he is condemned forever?"

"I should have known better. The Book of YahSu forbids necromancy. Not because God is cruel but because the dead are not ours to command. When we try, we step into a world which He has sealed shut for a reason. That was my sin. I opened a gate He wants to keep closed."

He turned and placed a hand on each son's shoulder in turn. "You ask if God would give power to one who means harm. Remember Pharaoh's magicians. Remember the whisperers of Babel. Yahweh does not share His glory. He tells us that He is a jealous god. We are not called to understand all power, only to obey the One who holds it rightly."

Bodonchar-Munkhag looked down at the blazing fire with some sadness. "Then the blessing… will it really end?"

Mar Yanqa didn't answer immediately. He pulled his sons close again and said, "You asked if Yah is merciful or not. His punishment to me is an act of mercy. He has not stripped me of my position, nor cast our people into slavery. He has not sent down plagues so that our crops do not grow nor turned our rivers to blood so that they would be undrinkable. All Yahweh has done is increase the threats and skirmishes with the kingdoms and tribes that surround us, but he still permits us be victorious, though our suffering and losses may have increased with each attack. And we will continue in this manner for ten generations before He abandons us completely."

"Unless the unborn one that is coming turns back…," Bukhatu-Salji suggested.

"Yes, but Yahweh has already said it will happen. The tenth generation will forget the mountain, the valley, and the sky. He will conceal the book of YahSu. He will speak only with the tongue of the empire. He will call wise counsel that which is foolishness. And the covenant will be broken with our family forever."

Mar Yanqa rose slowly and took five dry branches from a nearby bundle. He handed one to each son.

"Break it."

One by one, the sons did so, with a soft snap and splintered bark. Then he gathered five more, bound them tightly with horse sinew and twine, and gave the bundle to Bodonchar. "Now break these."

The youngest strained and struggled, but he could not break them.

Mar Yanq then passed them to Bukhati-Salji, who tried and failed. Next was Bukhatu-Khatagi, then Belgunutei, both who grunted in frustration, failing to break the bundle of branches. Finally, he gave the bundle to Begunutei, who no matter how hard he tried he could not break them.

"It cannot be done," he said.

Mar Yanqa smiled. "But alone, you can break them like straw. But bound together…" He looked into each son's eyes. "Bound together, you are unbreakable. Do you understand?"

They nodded their affirmation.

"There will be many that will attempt to turn you against each other. For no other reason to break you or bend you to their will. You must always be and act as one. If there is any chance that we can win back Yahweh's favor it will be by ensuring that your sons of each succeeding generation always act in unison and do not raise one of their own above the others. The day they forget this is the day that Yah becomes lost to us."

He sat again, sighing deeply, his fingers tracing the hem of his robe. He began to reminisce. "You do not yet know the full story of your grandfather. Mar Zutra. I have been derelict in telling you his story. It is time that I do so."

And so, for the first time, he told them the full story of Mar Zutra, the King of Mahoza. How he rode out with a fire in his heart, and his small army challenged the great kings of the earth with only the sky god and the Book of YahSu in his hand. How cities fell before his word. How he even captured the Emperor of Persia and was able to provide peace and prosperity for seven years to all the people of the empire. How even enemies came to love him. But also, how his strength began to crack the day he chose the wrong woman as second wife.

"She was beautiful," Mar Yanqa whispered. "As a young boy I still remember the Lady Avital. But her soul was wrapped and corrupted by secrets. She hated my mother, the Princess She-Ping. And she brought poison into the family. Not the kind that kills quickly, but the kind that takes its toll over a period of years."

His voice was nearly a growl now. "Remember this. A man's wife is not only the mother of his children. She is the hearthstone of his house. She sets the song in his children's hearts. Choose well as four of you have already done, and heaven smiles. Choose poorly…" He left the sentence hanging.

The brothers sat still, even the normally impatient Belgunutei, as if the weight of legacy had finally settled on their shoulders.

Mar Yanqa looked to Bodonchar-Munkhag. "You are not yet married. But soon you will be. I suggest you choose a daughter of your half-brothers. Keep the bloodline pure. Keep the blessing from fading. There is a shadow in the distance. I have already told you that a descendant will rise who forgets who we are. He will turn his back on Yahweh and the Book. He will embrace China, wear its silk, build its temples, and pray to its gods. And when that day comes, Yahweh will sever us from His covenant completely. But perhaps if we ensure that each generation marries within the family, we can cause the one that is still unborn to have a change of heart."

Uttering those words, a wind rose over the ridge, causing the tent flaps to flutter. For a moment, no one spoke.

Then Mar Yanqa smiled. A smile that melted years from his face. "But that day is not yet. For now, you are here. My five branches. My sons by adoption and my sons from my loins. From now on let your daughters wed each other's sons. Let your grandsons grow up in the same pastures, the same tents, under the same sacred sky. May your hearts beat with the same song."

The fire crackled low, and the stars above burned like a thousand silent witnesses. Mar Yanqa stood still, his hands resting on the shoulders of his youngest son, Bodonchar-Munkhag, who still held on to the bundle of five branches tightly in his hands.

Then, without being asked, Begunutei stepped forward. The eldest, tall and broad-shouldered, already bearing the voice of a chieftain. "Before Yahweh Most High, and before you, Father," he said, his voice steady as flint, "I vow to keep the Book of YahSu close to my heart. I will teach it to my sons, and I will not bow to the idols of empires or forget the ways of the mountain."

Belgunutei followed, quieter but no less fierce. He knelt briefly by the fire, then stood tall. "I pledge to honor Yahweh with every breath. I will not look to the dead for answers, nor bend my knee to the cities of silk and lies. I will raise my daughters to marry their kin, and keep the blood pure and the fire lit."

Bukha-Khatagi placed his hand on the branch bundle held by his youngest brother. "Let my house stand firm in the ways of the Book of YahSu. If my sword forgets Yah's law, may it shatter in my hand. If my heart turns from His word, may it cease to beat. I pledge my name, my seed, and my strength to the God of our forefathers."

Bukhatu-Salji stepped forward, his eyes glowing with quiet determination. "I will not trade our truth for their gold. I will keep the ancient path, even if I walk it alone. Yahweh is our banner, and the Book of YahSu our shield. I vow to guard them both with my life."

Finally, Bodonchar-Munkhag looked to his father. He said nothing at first. His hands trembled slightly as he held the branches close. Then, his voice, still youthful, rang out with clarity. "Though I am the youngest, I will not be the last. I vow to uphold our faith, to honor the wisdom of our mother, and to fear the mistake of our father's fall. I will marry within the line. I will teach the names of our ancestors. And when the one who turns comes… from my perch in the heavens, I will remember this fire."

Mar Yanqa's eyes glistened with tears. He placed a hand over his heart and bowed his head. "Then let the heavens record your words, my sons. And let the God of our forefathers stretch His hand over you… until the tenth."

And together, under the canopy of the tent, they stood in a circle, bound not just by blood, but by vow. Mar Yanqa opened his arms, and one by one, they came forward. He held them tightly, each in turn, as if they were still small boys clinging to his knees.

"I love you all," he said. "More than power, more than land, more than even my own breath. You are my greatest treasure. My last prayer. My only hope."

The fire burned low now, casting long shadows across their faces. The night air had turned still, as if even the wind held its breath for what was to come.

Mar Yanqa stepped into the center of the five. His cloak rustled softly as he drew forth a worn leather pouch from beneath his robe. From it, he removed a single object: a small, flat stone, etched with faded markings. It was the stone from the signet ring of his father, Mar Zutra.

He held it in both hands, lifted it heavenward, and began to chant softly. Not in Khitan, not in Persian, not even in the common Mongol tongue, but in the First Speech of his ancestors, a language passed from father to son for over two thousand years.

"El Elyon… Yahweh Tseba HaShemayim…Melech Ha-Oylum…Hear me."

The sons lowered their heads.

"I am Mar Yanqa, son of Zutra, grandson of Huna Mar, great-grandson of Zutra, the son of Huna, the son of Nathan, the son of Abba Mari, the son of Mar Ukba, the son of Nehemiah, the son of Huna, the son of Nathan Ukban, of the House of David and the tribe of Judah, servants of Yahweh. These are the ten generations of my heritage as taught to me and to be taught now to my sons."

He turned to each son, beginning with Begunutei. He pressed the seal to his forehead and intoned: "May your strength never fail. May your tents overflow. May the God of the sky, the rivers and the mountains walk beside you in battle and raise your sons like cedar trees."

He moved to Belgunutei: "May wisdom guide your steps. May your judgments be like clear like water. May you never be deceived by sweet words or pretty chains."

To Bukha-Khatagi: "May your eyes see truth, even in darkness. May your hand strike cleanly, and your heart remain unbroken, even when the world bends."

To Bukhatu-Salji: "May joy find you in the fields. May your daughters sing like doves, and your name be spoken with honor in every valley."

And finally, to Bodonchar-Munkhag: "May you remember. When others forget. When the world turns and the empire calls your name, may you remember this fire, this vow, this blood and rise up to defend your people with honor."

Then Mar Yanqa raised the seal high again. "Yahweh Most High, God of my forefathers, I place my sons beneath Your wing. If they stray, pursue them. If they fall, lift them. And if the destroyer rises from among them, let his name perish but spare the remnant."

A wind stirred, sudden and sharp, swirling through the tent and making the flames leap high into the air. The seal in Mar Yanqa's hand burned faintly with a pale golden glow, just for a moment, then faded.

He smiled. "It is done."

The sons embraced him, one by one. And though they did not speak again that night as they ate the meal presented to them, the silence between them was full of something deeper than words. Something ancient, binding, and divine.

Later that night, after they feasted, sang, and Mar Yanqa told tales of his youth, each of the sons finally returned to their own ger. Mar Yanqa stood outside the tent and inhaled the night air deeply, treasuring the silence before the dawn. He watched as the stars dimmed and the first mist rose from the valley floor. He faced southeast, toward China. Toward a future he feared he could no longer control. And as he pondered what would come to pass, a few silent tears escaped from the corners of his eyes.

Chapter 38: 553 AD

Neither Eastern Wei nor Western Wei were destined to be long-lived. In 550, Gao Huan's son Gao Yang forced Emperor Xiaojing of Eastern Wei to yield the throne to him, ending the existence of Eastern Wei and establishing what was then called Northern Qi. Similarly, Yuwen Tai's nephew Yuwen Hu not long afterwards forced Emperor Gong of Western Wei to give up the throne to Yuwen Tai's son Yuwen Jue, thus ending the Western Wei and establishing a new kingdom that they named Northern Zhou. The change of names made little difference as each kingdom still sought the destruction of the other. And just as before, each saw the conquest of the Khitan Empire as a steppingstone to achieving their final goal. Gaining control of the Khitan hordes was the ultimate strategy in finally having sufficient forces to conquer the other kingdom. But as they had encountered in the past, the major stumbling block to their plan was the one they referred to as the Great Khan, Mar Yanqa.

By the year 553 AD, Gao Yang finally felt his army had the strength of arms to attack the Khitans to the north. As for the Khitan tribes, they were still thriving under the leadership of their Qagan, Mar Yanqa. The steppes were their home, and though they still had their skirmishes with increasing frequency with neighboring tribes, their warriors were still known for their fierceness and unmatched horsemanship. To maintain their dominance in the region, the Khitans still entertained frequent raids along the Northern Qi border, procuring supplies and goods that they would then trade with other clans. The perpetration and presence of these raids was the pretense that Gao Yang used to raise and assemble a formidable army which he ordered north.

Khitan scouts brought word of the approaching force, and Mar Yanqa quickly gathered his warriors. He recalled the strategy he had used sixteen years earlier against Gao Yang's father, sensing that nothing much had changed regarding the Qi army's tactics. They would meet the Northern Qi on the open plains of the Juyan Steppe, just as they had done with the Eastern Wei, where their mobility and speed would give them a marked advantage. He trusted in the Khitan's superior maneuverability and their deep knowledge of the terrain. His plan was to lure the Qi army into the grass-choked ravines and false hills that veiled the steppe's true nature, then break them in an ambush with horse-archers and fire.

The two armies faced each other under a sky heavy with dark clouds. The thirty thousand Khitan warriors, mounted on their swift horses, formed a loose formation, ready to strike with their usual hit-and-run tactics. The Northern Qi soldiers, thirty-five thousand in total, clad in heavy armor and armed with long spears, stood in their disciplined ranks, their green and yellow banners fluttering in the wind above their heads. The Qi army consisted of heavy infantry, crossbow divisions, and thousands of disciplined cavalry drawn from the old Wei commanderies.

Mar Yanqa rode along the front lines, his voice carrying over the din of the battlefield. "Today, we defend our land, our families, and our way of life! Fight with the strength of our ancestors, and let the Northern Qi know the might of the Khitan!"

The Khitan strategy began brilliantly. Mar Yanqa divided his forces into three wings. With a thunderous roar, the Khitan cavalry charged. Their horses galloped across the field, kicking up dust as they closed the distance. The Northern Qi archers released a volley of arrows, but the Khitan riders skillfully dodged and weaved their way forward, their agility unmatched by any other cavalry.

But Gao Yang had anticipated this. The young Gao, a brutal yet brilliant tactician, turned the frontal attack into a feint of his own. He allowed his vanguard to be harried and broken, sacrificing his forward regiments to bait Mar Yanqa into full engagement. The clash of blades and the cries of battle filled the air as the Khitan cavalry crashed into the Northern Qi lines. Mar Yanqa led the charge, his sword cutting through enemy soldiers with deadly precision. The Khitan warriors fought with a ferocity that left the Northern Qi troops reeling. Their vanguard consisted of young recruits and they had never faced anything like the savagery of the Khitan before. It didn't matter; it was all as Gao Yang had planned.

Smashing through their front lines was easy, too easy as far as Mar Yanqa was concerned. There was no way that Gao Yang would be carelessly making the same fatal mistakes as his father. This had to be a trap. Before he could signal a retreat, the heavy infantry of the Northern Qi advanced from behind the front lines, using their long spears and pikes to dig deep into the flesh of the Khitan horses and their riders. As the Khitan right surged forward, they ran into the teeth of another hidden formation. The front lines of the Qi thinned in the middle then regrouped along the sides of the Khitan warriors, so that Mar Yanqa found his men repulsing attacks from three different directions. The Khitan's hit-and-run tactics, so effective against other foes, were suddenly ineffective against the disciplined ranks of the Northern Qi, as their freedom of movement became severely restricted.

As the battle raged on, the Northern Qi heavy cavalry, led by General Duan Shao, executed a flanking maneuver. The Qi cataphracts armored in lamellar iron, were fresh and had been waiting for this opportunity. The steppe thundered as these giants on horseback plowed into the lightly armored Khitan riders. Ujin Bataar's men were cut down before they could react, and he himself fell, pierced through by a double-headed lance. They struck the Khitan from the sides and the rear, causing chaos and confusion. Mar Yanqa tried to rally his troops, but the Northern Qi's superior tactics began to take their toll.

The Khitan warriors fought bravely, but they were gradually pushed back by the Northern Qi soldiers relentless advance. Gao Yang's army cut through the Khitan ranks easily. From the east, Gao Yang unleashed his elite crossbow corps, who had climbed during the night onto the rocky bluffs that flanked the battlefield. Thousands of bolts rained down onto Mar Yanqa's center, disrupting formations and killing his bannermen. Confusion spread like wildfire.

What had begun looking like an easy victory was now a battle to simply survive. The field that should have been a Khitan killing ground was now becoming their graveyard. Still, Mar Yanqa rallied his remaining horsemen and continued to ram the front lines. The Khitan sent arrows flying like a black rainstorm. They smashed into the Qi infantry, breaking the first two lines, and for a moment, the tide seemed to turn. Mar Yanqa himself led a wedge that shattered the center of Gao's ranks, his spear dripping blood, his face wild with fury.

But Gao Yang was not on the field. He had held himself back with three thousand heavy cavalry to be used as a final hammer. Once Mar Yanqa's wedge pushed too deep, the hammer fell. From both flanks, the reserve Qi cavalry struck. Surrounded, cut off, and exhausted, the Khitan elite were crushed. The field rang with screams, hooves, and the clash of steel.

Mar Yanqa, realizing the battle was lost, ordered a retreat. Responding to the sounding of the horn the Khitan fled across the plains, pursued by the Northern Qi. They had been routed, bested and the taste of defeat was bitter in their mouths. This was an experience many thought would never happen and they wanted to make certain that it never happened again. Someone needed to be held accountable.

The aftermath of the battle was devastating for the Khitan. Many of their warriors had fallen, and their once-unified tribes were scattered to the four winds as they made their escape from the battle. Those chieftains that were initially reluctant to join in the confederacy found an excuse to sever the ties and return to the old ways. Suspicions rose that Mar Yanqa no longer had the favor or protection of Yah and rumors spread that the Qagan had been cursed.

Following the battle, the army of the Northern Qi seized a large part of the Khitan livestock and raided the surrounding villages, enslaving many of the inhabitants, thereby further weakening their ability to retaliate.

Fingers pointed at Mar Yanqa claiming that he failed to anticipate the enemy's movements and charged in blindly, ignoring the consequences. What hurt Mar Yanqa most was that it was true. He had not calculated on Gao Yang being any different in his approach to open warfare than his father. That was a key mistake. Much had changed in almost two decades in how the Chinese empires conducted warfare. Equipment had improved, being more accurate and powerful, formations were radically different, and Chinese cavalrymen were no longer auxiliary to the battle but were now an essential component of the attack. Mar Yanqa had learned all this too late after giving the order to attack. The loss on the battlefield had emotionally wounded him but it was the desertion by some of the tribes from the confederacy that cut him the most deeply.

He was wounded but unbroken, and he vowed to rebuild. The Khitan had faced defeat before in their past, and they would rise again. But for now, the Northern Qi had dealt them a crushing blow, lessons had to be learned before contemplating engaging the Qi in battle again. For now, the steppes were silent, except for those mourning the loss of their brave warriors

Mar Yanqa recognized his first task was the preservation of their empire, the unity he had fought so hard for in order to create the first union of the Khitan tribal confederacy. He knew the Khitan were a resilient people, and from the ashes of defeat, they would certainly rebuild. He summoned those leaders that were still loyal to him, determined to restore their strength and reclaim their honor. Among them was Yelü Daran, one of the chieftains that he least expected would remain by his side. For years they had argued over almost every decision but during that time Yelü had gained tremendous respect for Mar Yanqa as Qagan.

Yelü Daran knew that the path to recovery would be long and arduous. For that reason, Mar Yanqa had to remain where the people could see him, leading, rebuilding and ultimately protecting those under his leadership. That would mean that as an elder, already in his fifties, Mar Yanqa could not spend all his time riding across the steppes in an effort to persuade those tribes that had left the union to return. Yelü Daran offered to take on that role, and as Mar Yanqa's ambassador, he began uniting the scattered tribes, reforging alliances, and fostering a renewed sense of unity among the people. These Khitan warriors, though battered and bruised, knew that they had acted on impulse following their defeat, and most were eager to reclaim their place on the steppes within the union.

The first step in their rebuilding process was to secure their borders. Mar Yanqa sent scouts to monitor enemy movements and established fortified camps to protect their territory. The loss of so many warriors in the battle against the Northern Qi had left the Khitan vulnerable. Mar Yanqa faced the challenge of rebuilding their military strength. He personally oversaw the training of new warriors, instilling in them the skills and discipline needed to defend their homeland. The memories of fallen comrades haunted him, but he used that pain to fuel his resolve.

The Northern Qi and other neighboring tribes saw the Khitan as weakened prey. Mar Yanqa had to remain ever vigilant, deploying scouts to monitor enemy movements and fortifying their defenses. There would be no more stealing of their chattel and enslavement of the people without resistance. Any place where Qi raiders were reported were immediately met by a squadron of Khitan riders. The arrival of the Khitan was usually enough to cause the Qi to return to their bases without entering into a skirmish.

Mar Yanqa knew that war with the Qi and perhaps even the Zhou was far from over. His punishment from Yahweh told him so. But that didn't mean they needed to face defeat again because they were poorly prepared. Under his watchful eyes, the new generation of Khitan warriors trained tirelessly, honing their skills, establishing appropriate defenses against their enemy's evolving tactics, and preparing their own equipment that would be necessary for a siege conflict. More importantly, they adapted their tactics, developing new strategies by which to counter their enemies.

Mar Yanqa was aware that they had to expand far more than their military expertise. The Northern Qi had seized a large part of their livestock, leaving the Khitan with limited resources. Therefore, he also focused on rebuilding their economy by establishing new trade routes with neighboring tribes and empires that they had been at odds with before, exchanging goods and resources to strengthen their overall position. His people, once desolate, began to thrive again as they worked together to rebuild their communities.

Meanwhile, Yelü Daran dealt with those tribes that were still reluctant to come together under a single banner. He traveled tirelessly across the steppes, meeting with tribal leaders and negotiating alliances. His charisma and determination gradually won them over, but it was a slow and arduous process. By the time he had finished, there were even more tribes in the confederacy than there had been before their defeat in battle at the hands of Gao Yang.

The emotional toll of leadership weighed heavily on Mar Yanqa. He had lost many friends and family members in the battle, such as Valentius, and the grief was a constant companion. Yet, he could not afford to show weakness. He buried his sorrow deep within, presenting a strong and unwavering front to his people. In private moments, he would visit the graves of the fallen, seeking solace in their memory and drawing strength from their sacrifice.

Despite the challenges, Mar Yanqa's leadership and resilience began to bear fruit. The Khitan Empire slowly regained its strength, its warriors becoming a formidable force once more. The economy stabilized, and the sense of unity and purpose grew stronger with each passing day

As the years passed, the Khitan grew even mightier than before. Their warriors, once scattered, now stood once again united under a common banner. The Khitan people, resilient and resourceful, had transformed their defeat into an opportunity for growth and renewal. Mar Yanqa knew that his efforts laid the foundation for future generations but the prophecy of only until the tenth generation made him wonder if all off his effort was worth the price. The defeat by the Northern Qi had been a turning point, but it had also been the catalyst for their rebirth, emerging stronger, with their spirit unbroken. He knew that other than his sons and closes circle of advisors, that no one else must ever know about the doomsday prophecy.

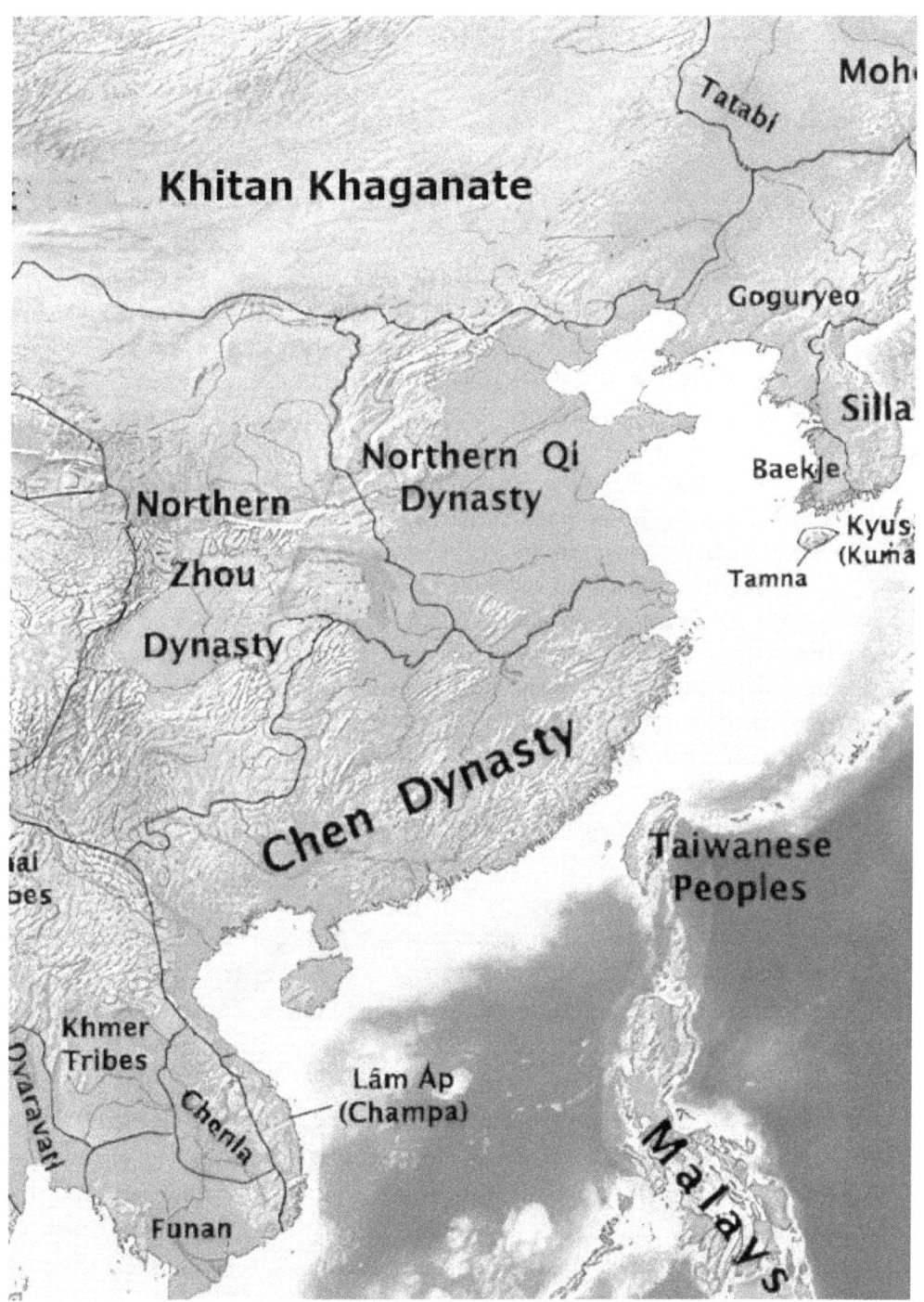

The Yuwen (Zhou) and Gao (Qi) Family Empires

Chapter 39: 560 AD

The sound of the wind blew through the valley like the ghosts of the ancestors, haunting, mournful, and restless. The morning mist curled around the mountain walls as the Khitan warriors took their positions in the gorge. Mar Yanqa sat astride his newest stallion, Khar Tal, draped in a coat of black felt sewn with bronze discs that shimmered like dying stars. His face, now hardened by the constant years of war bore the calm of a man who had already spoken to death and found no fear in its response. For seven years they had repulsed the Northern Qi invaders, until Gao Yang had decided he could tolerate it no longer. Originally the Khitan had come south to defend a mountain pass from Qi expansionists, but now this supposed raiding party they expected to find had turned into a full invasion force. Two days ago, scouts brought word that a Northern Qi column, of over four thousand strong, had crossed the frozen Yalu River under the banner of General Wei Kaixin, a man infamous for burning villages, torturing men and enslaving both women and children. Mar Yanqa had only ventured out initially with a thousand riders. He was caught unaware as to why the Qi would mount a significantly larger invasion at this time into the area around Liaodong. It made no sense: there was little of value in this region.

There were political factors that motivated Gao Yang towards this decision. In the opposing empire of Northern Zhou, Yuwen Yu, the son of Yuwen Tai, who went by the name of Emperor Ming had just been assassinated by his cousin Yuwen Hu. Yuwen Hu believed in a militarized Northern Zhou, and because of its strong Xianbei heritage, Gao Yang feared the enemy empire would ally itself with the Khitans against Northern Qi. He knew that if he could weaken the Khitan, then it would also reduce the likelihood that the Zhou arm would launch an attack on his empire.

The Khitan riders painted their faces with ashes, ochre, and blood. Their battle hymn rose in guttural harmony, an old song of the ancestors, sung before the encounter to announce to heaven that the sons of the steppes were ready to ride once more and many would soon be arriving at it gates. Mar Yanqa turned to look behind him. There, clutching a composite bow made from horn and bamboo that was nearly as tall as he was, sat Bodonchar-Munkhag, his youngest son, now thirty-seven years old. His face was streaked with dirt, ready for battle. Of all the sons, he was the only one not in command of his own squadron, having never demonstrated the strength of leadership that his brothers possessed. For that reason, he was assigned to his father's detail, so that he could learn from the best.

"Bodon," Mar Yanqa said quietly, reaching out to touch his cheek, "You will ride with me today, and you will see how Khitans face death." His son nodded in appreciation of the opportunity.

From the distal end of the gorge, General Wei Caixin's standard emerged, its red silk stamped with the imperial dragon waving in the wind. Behind it rolled the tidal wave of the Northern Qi, their spears gleaming, their drums pounding like a funeral dirge. Four thousand of them. Too many, even for a thousand Khitan riders but Mar Yanqa would never let his fears show.

"It is too bad Tamerlan is no longer with us to enjoy the sight. He would always laugh when an enemy paraded their forces as if they were invincible." Mar Yanqa closed his eyes to visualize his deceased friend and mentor.

Bodonchar spat. "They think they've already won."

Mar Yanqa smiled. "Then let them come find out what it means to bleed on Khitan soil." He raised his curved saber, and the Khitan line erupted into motion. A storm of hooves and screaming arrows, like a demonic horde charging from the bowels of the earth. Qi shields braced, but the gorge choked them. The Khitan rode low and struck hard, their arrows slicing like knives through lacquered armor. The gorge was a clever place to strike, where the Qi numbers meant little. The Khitan used the rocks, the trees, the sudden bends. The first wave of Qi infantry was shattered in the morning light, arrows turning the air into a shrieking storm.

Mar Yanqa rode through them like a spirit from the underworld, his saber dancing from left, then right, then plunging through a horseman's chest with such fury that the blade sang when it was pulled free. Qi infantry collapsed around him like sheaves of grain before the scythe.

Through the smoke and screams, he searched for Bodonchar, always scanning, his warrior's instinct being overridden by a father's concern. Along the side ridge, a Qi detachment broke through. It was a flanking manoeuvre, and it was heading directly towards his son. Five Qi cavalrymen at full gallop, clearly targeting Bodonchar. His son had let himself become separated from the rest of his father's detail and now he was, cornered. Bodonchar-Munkhag fumbled for an arrow, but his actions were too slow, and the Qi were upon him.

Mar Yanqa saw it. Time froze. He screamed. It was not so much a scream as it was the enraged roar of a lion. He then kicked Khar Tal into full gallop. Across the battlefield he flew. Arrows snapped past him like locusts, his cloak streaming, his teeth bared. He rode straight into the flanking party, like a living avalanche of fury.

The first Qi horseman fell to a thrown axe. The second he speared clean through the gut. But then a Qi captain, armored in iron scales, charged forward. His lance struck Khar Tal in the neck. The stallion shrieked and fell, and Mar

Yanqa flew from the saddle, crashing to the hard ground. He rolled, rose, and then staggered. His leg may have been broken. Blood poured from his mouth. But still, he managed to stand.

Bodonchar screamed, "Father!"

Mar Yanqa turned and looked at his son one last time. "I will always ride beside you," he said. "Now ride away from here!" Then he charged, practically dragging one leg behind. A long-curved dagger in his hand. A war cry in his throat. No shield. Just the fury of a father whose son was in danger.

The Qi soldiers froze for a moment. What they saw was not a man, but something beyond this world and far more dangerous. A legend. A raging storm in human form. A god of war made flesh. None of those descriptions came close to describing the human fury they were now facing.

Mar Yanqa buried the dagger in the captain's throat. He then pulled the sword from its scabbard and took another Qi soldier down with a single swing. But they kept coming. Five more approached. He fought like a roaring inferno, like pure lightning from a thunderstorm, striking with death everywhere he touched. Until at last he could stand no more.

Blades pierced him. One, two, three. They came from every direction.

Mar Yanqa was lifted under the arms, bleeding from a dozen wounds. General Caixin approached and the soldiers forcibly tried to bend his knees but Mar Yanqa almost dead, still refused to kneel. Caixin removed the sword from his belt. Spitting blood, Mar Yanqa shouted the names of his sons, calling for vengeance and then spoke six words in a language they did not understand. "Shemai Israel, Adonai Elohaynu, Adonai Ehud," completing the last word before General Caixing severed his head.

Only then did he drop to his knees. Then fell to the side. They left his body on the ridge to feed the crows.

The battle that day had been indecisive despite the overwhelming advantage of the Qi forces. Neither side could claim victory. Neither side could admit defeat. The battle would go unrecorded by the Chinese scribes. They would fight again some other day. After the Qi returned behind the boundary of their lands, Mar Yanqa's sons found his body, followed by his detached head a short time afterwards. They carefully washed both parts in the cold stream nearby and wrapped them in wolfskins, laying his sword which they found half buried in the gut of a Qi officer, across Mar Yanqa's chest. They placed him delicately on a litter, then they took him back to their encampment.

Bodonchar rode beside his father's litter, stone-faced, unmoving. Weighed down by feelings of overwhelming guilt.

"He would not want you to cry," Bukha-Khatagi said as he rode up beside his younger brother.

"He died because of me," Bodonchar fought to hold back the tears.

"He died for you," his brother replied. "There is a big difference. To father, there would be no greater honor than to sacrifice himself for the safety of one of his sons. You have honored him, and he has honored you. Remember that!"

Word of Mar Yanqa's death had reached the encampment long before they arrived with the body. By evening, the entire Khitan host sang the Song of the Black Wolf, an old lament for fallen heroes. Mothers wept. Warriors sharpened their blades with vengeance in their hearts.

The sun had just begun its descent behind the black slopes of the Altai Mountains when the Khitan squadrons returned. The hooves of their horses were muffled by the snow-matted grass, the kind of silence that did not signal peace but the approach of grief. They came in a long, mournful line, banners slack in the windless dusk, and at their center was a wooden litter draped in blue and gold, the colors of the Great Khan, the colors of a cherished husband and the father to a nation.

Alan-Ko stood at the edge of the sacred field, still beautiful at over sixty years of age. Her two sons by Dubun Merga stood to either side, the elder gripping her underneath her left shoulder, the younger clutching his mother's hand. They had not ridden out with the squadrons the day before, thinking it wasn't necessary. No one thought it was anything more than just another band of Qi raiders that had to be dealt with. The people gathered behind her, murmuring their prayers and shedding tears. None dared speak to her. Not now. Not as the litter came closer.

She was the queen of the Khitan, iron-hearted, serene as frost. She had watched her people go hungry and led them to full granaries. She had stood unflinching when emissaries spat at her feet. She had ridden into battle when the world had forgotten that a woman could bleed and still command men. But now she stepped forward, just one step, and for the first time in a lifetime, her shoulders trembled, her legs could barely hold her weight.

The litter stopped before her.

Mar Yanqa, her husband, her chieftain, the boy she wed turned legend, lay motionless beneath a covering of wolf-pelts, still dressed in his lacquered armor. His throat was bound with silk to hide the fatal wound. His hair, once wild and burning red like a brushfire, had been neatly combed. Someone had placed the ivory carving of a falcon, the first gift she'd ever given him, beneath his folded hands. She had no idea that he carried it with him into every battle. It had been his good luck charm.

Alan-Ko did not cry. She knelt beside him, slowly, like a dancer folding into a final pose. The ground was hard. Her knees bled. She reached out with both hands, one to cup his cheek, the other to unfasten the clasp at his neck. It was then that she realized to her horror that his head had been severed. She laid her brow against his and breathed a single breath, like she was trying to summon him back to life.

"My heart," she whispered. Not "husband." Not "king." Just that. "My heart."

And then, like a dam breached in spring, her body convulsed with a grief so raw that sound fled from it. Her mouth opened in a cry that had no voice, only silence. A silence deeper and wider than any scream could ever be. Her back arched, but no tears came. The Khitan do not cry in front of war horses. But she wept all the same. It was in the way that her face broke, in the way that her arms clutched his corpse as though it might warm him again.

Her sons began to sob and knelt beside her without lifting her head from his chest. She wrapped them in the folds of her robes as if they were still young children and spoke to them. Soft, broken Khitan words of love and war and the dead returning as stars. She told them of his first battle, of how he once trembled just to hold her hand, of how he loved the wind and feared no man, no beast, but only the thought of leaving them too soon.

They watched her there until moonrise. A queen collapsed over the ruin of her joy. And when the time came to prepare his body for its eternal rest, she rose not as a widow but as both a mother and monarch. She lifted his sword and kissed its hilt. She spoke no eulogy. Her silence said more than any poem could ever do.

Epilogue

They gathered in the dark, well before dawn broke over the eastern hills. There were no horns, no drums, no fire. Only the sound of hooves muffled by snow, and the low whispers of mourning voices carried from mouth to mouth: he is gone they appeared to say.

Mar Yanqa's body lay wrapped in soft, white wool and stitched wolf-hide, his sword placed beside him. A blade that would never be raised again. His face had not been painted with ochre or gold. No sacred beads adorned his arms. No blood-soaked trophies dangled from his funeral shroud. Because he had forbidden it. It was not the way of Yahweh.

"No stones piled on the steppe," he had once told Alan-Ko in a rare, quiet moment beneath the stars. "No shrine. No chants. No mourners with incense. I go where the sky takes me. And only where the wind should know." It was his last command.

So, they obeyed.

Six riders were chosen. Trusted men. Warriors who had once ridden into battle at his side and lived to tell tales of Mar Yanqa's bravery. They were given black veils, heavy cloaks, and one single order: take him beyond the lands of the living.

Alan-Ko and her sons did not go. Mar Yanqa had forbidden it. If they knew where he was buried, they would try to visit his grave and that meant others would follow and find out too. She watched from the ridge as the riders departed, her face pale with restraint, her five sons beside her. Bodonchar-Munkhag remained silent, lips pressed into a thin line, fists clenched around nothing.

Then suddenly the riders were out of sight.

They crossed the ice river. Climbed through the canyons. Entered the Hallowed Spine, a range of jagged mountains where the air grew thin and the sky pressed down like a god's gaze. There, in a hidden cleft between white cliffs and wind-cut stone, they found a hollow.

They dug into the frozen earth. They built no tomb of glory. The body was lowered in. Covered. A cairn consisting only of stones. Raw, rough, ancient stones. Each lifted in silence. Each placed with reverence.

Then the riders did what was required.

They descended from the cliff, their hearts heavier than the mountains. They erased their tracks with pine branches. They dismantled the sled. They threw their maps into a ravine. Each man swore a blood-oath to speak of the place to no one. Not even their wives. Not even in their dreams.

And as they heading back to the encampment, the sky wept snow.

When the riders returned, no one asked. Mar Yanqa said it was forbidden. They all listened to his final command. The people from all the confederated tribes gathered that evening under black tents under which no fires were lit. The multitude of their tents covered the entire plains. They shared no fermented milk. No meat was roasted.

Instead, one by one, they recited memories. Memories of the man that came to them as a stranger and rose to be their leader. Words passed from elder to child like an ember cupped in cold hands.

"I remember when he waited three days to ride, because one of the horses was limping," someone said. "He forbids any man from abusing his horse."

"He gave his water skin to the boy from the orphaned tribe," another recalled.

"Do you know that he never punished a warrior for fear. Only for cruelty," one of the warriors told the story.

By the end of the service, Bodonchar stood. He was the youngest at thirty-seven but when he spoke his voice was that of his father's. "He rode into battle not to conquer, but to protect. He lived to unite, and not to rule. And he died to save me when he did not have to. I will not weep. I will not build a shrine. Instead, I will build a world he would not be ashamed of."

Then he walked out alone and returned to his ger.

And the people remained in silence, knowing that their world had changed.

There was no stone marking his cairn that bore his name. There was no grave that drew pilgrims. Only the mountains knew, and they did not speak.

But as long as there were those that were alive that had known the man, they sang songs of Mar Yanqa's last stand. They were sung in every Khitan camp, on every firelit night. They called him the Storm-Father, the Black Wolf, the Golden Eagle and the Shield of Sons. And they swore that no man who died in such a way ever truly died. He simply rode on ahead.

Years later, songs would be sung of Mar Yanqa, though never mentioning where he fell, or where he lay. But after several generations they would forget his name, instead referring to him only as the Glittering Man. Parents would tell tale of his life, garnishing them with supernatural adventures upon each retelling.

Children would whisper that he had become the wind itself, causing the clouds to move fast across the steppes. He was the Ghost Chief racing his stallion through the sky. And before long the Glittering Man was said to have come from the sky itself, sharing Alan-Ko's bed each night and returning to his home in the sky each morning. He was no longer a man, no longer a legend, he had become a myth.

.

HISTORIC DETAILS BEHIND THE STORY

Early information on the Khitan is sparse and difficult to source. What we do know is that the Khitan were part of a broader nomadic world that included groups such as the Rouran, the Turkomen, and the Xianbei. These groups were often in competition for control of the steppes and the resources they provided. The Khitan's relations with these groups were marked by shifting alliances and conflicts, as each sought to expand their influence.

The Rouran Khaganate, which dominated the Mongolian Plateau at the beginning of the 6th century, was one of the Khitan's most formidable rivals. The Rouran were a powerful confederation of nomadic tribes, and their dominance posed a significant challenge to the Khitan. However, the Khitan were able to resist Rouran pressure through a combination of military strength and strategic alliances with other nomadic groups and on occasion, the northern Chinese states.

What we do know is that early in the 6th century, the Khitan underwent a radical change, becoming an organized confederacy that developed an enormous military almost solely reliant on cavalry and a strong economic structure through trading and control of the Silk Road. Eventually the Khitans were able to become the dominant power on the steppes. Exactly what caused this turn around can only be speculated, but the fact that a Chinese Princess with her half-breed son was exiled to the steppes by her brother, the emperor of Northern Wei, certainly cannot be discounted.

The rise of the Turkic Khaganate in the mid-6th century also had a profound impact on the Khitan. The Turkomen rapidly expanded their influence across Central Asia, and their emergence as a major power reshaped the political landscape of the steppes. The Khitan initially found themselves at odds with the Turkomen, but they eventually established a relationship of mutual respect and cooperation, recognizing the Turks' dominance while maintaining their own independence. This provided the Khitan with the years of relative peace as described in the story, permitting them to become a distinct northern empire on their own.

How this could all suddenly take place at the beginning of the 6th century, seemingly coming out of nowhere and defying the chaos that had permeated the lands north of the Wei Empire is the premise for the storyline behind The Glittering Man. Radical change only occurs when there is an individual that manages to rise into a position of power to make change happen. The allusion to such a person being the glittering man, although not historically proven, does have merit when individual and remote references are pieced together, even though initially they do not appear to share anything in common at firs glance.

Such is the case when certain events are examined that occurred as recorded in similar timeframes within Persian, Chinese and Jewish historical documents. We know from the Persian history at the end of the 5th century that the Sassanid Emperor Kavad was overthrown by a coalition of barons led by a relatively minor king of Mahoza, a city-state within his empire. We also know from the documents that this city king was the Jewish Exilarch, Mar Zutra II. Kavad's brother Jamasp, then sits on the throne of the Empire as a puppet ruler. There is very little else written other than seven years later, Kavad was able to take back his throne and Mar Zutra was put to death. Superficially, this minor historical footnote would appear to have no significance and would be easily overlooked. Until we look at stories from far outside the empire that seem to be connected to these events.

The first of these coincidental pieces comes from Chinese historical documents that correspond to the same period. At this point, the story becomes a little more factual. The Emperor Xiaowen of Northern Wei, in an effort to increase both his military alliances as well as trade exchange, commits his daughter, She-Ping, to marry a Persian King, who is unnamed in the Chinese history. We do know it wasn't the Sassani Emperor, so it must be one of the many satraps that rule over parts of Persia. The story is quite famous in China, not only because of this marriage between East and West, but also because he sent his daughter along with a trove of mulberry bushes and silkworms. The exportation of the manufacturing process of what was one of China's most valuable products, that being silk, was an enormous event, equivalent today to America's Silicone Valley giving up its domination of microchip manufacturing to Asian countries. For the emperor to do so willingly either says how important this marriage must have been or how desperate he was to seek military aid. Either way it was highly significant.

What is also quite fascinating is that this mission by the princess was painted on the cave walls of DanDan Uiliq, near Khotun, in western China. These paintings created by Buddhist monks, are interesting in the fact that one of them is a portrait of the particular king that She-Ping married. The gallery of paintings, covering a wide variety of religious and historical events were created between the

4th and 9th centuries, and researchers believe the events they portray were painted in real time or in other words, not long after the actual events occurred. Which would mean the portrait of the Persian satrap was painted from a real time source. Since it was the case that Princess She-Ping did not know the King she was being sent west to marry, then she could only have provided a description of him on a return journey. That matches the story from Mar Zutra's final days, that he sent both of his wives away from the city of Mahoza with their sons, each in the opposite direction. It would only be rational that the Princess She-Ping would take her son back to where she originated from, being Northern Wei.

Jewish documentation regarding Mar Zutra II is difficult to source as a strategic effort, most likely from orthodox circles has been made to remove almost every trace of his existence because they have labeled him as an embarrassment and heretic, when in reality it was the rabbinical council of Mahoza, desperate to hold on to power that was the real embarrassment. It started with his choice of wives, one being his step-mother and the other being a non-Jewish foreigner, the nation from which she came not being identified that riled the council in the first place. Accusing him of being a sinner, Mar Zutra responded by placing them all under arrest, but rather than go into the entire storyline which can be read in my book ***Zutra***, it is my goal only to point out that this foreign wife that he married was most likely the Princess She-Ping. One can only imagine the reaction of the Sassanid Emperor Kavad, when he found out that one of his subject kings actually married the daughter of another emperor without his knowledge nor approval. It would be tantamount to a rebellion and a declaration of war, which we know from the Persian records of the time, did happen.

As explained, when we consolidate this information from these three different sources, all recording events that were taking place at the same time, and eliminate any attempt to justify them as merely being a coincidence, then it is reasonable to say that they were all referring to the same people and the same series of events that took place in Mahoza between 497 and 506 AD.

Extrapolating outwards, that his son Mar Yanqa did find his way to the Mongolian Steppes along with his mother, the Princess She-Ping, then it can be assumed that the trigger that suddenly vaulted the Khitan from nomadic clans into an organized confederation of tribes that was equivalent to an empire, was the unexpected arrival of Mar Yanqa and the Princess She-Ping of Northern Wei on the Steppes.

As for the Glittering Man, our earliest tales of his existence only dates from what was written by the Persian historian Rashid-al-Din in 1307 as told to him by the 3rd great-grandson of Genghis Khan. Desperate to validate the Mongol rule over China, the members of the Yuan dynasty claimed the Glittering Man and Alan-Ko to be their direct ancestors and placing their existence in the 8th to 9th century to support their claim. There was no supporting evidence to this claim, nor did their claim that Genghis Khan was the tenth generation of the prophecy match up to the expectations for the prophesized conqueror of the legend. It was not uncommon for later Chinese dynasties to claim the achievements and accomplishments of earlier dynasties in order to enhance the legitimacy of their claim to the throne and this would appear to be exactly what the Yuan dynasty had done. If we ignore the Mongol claim and date the Glittering Man to a period three centuries earlier, then not only does this support that Mar Yanqa was the glittering man, but also the predicted events of the prophecy all appear to occur exactly as described, as will be explained in subsequent paragraphs.

So as stated, the only difficulty when attempting to identify the Glittering Man with Mar Yanqa occurs when credibility is given to what was recorded in the Mongol legends by Rashid-al-Din. In order to expose the Mongol Legend as being nothing more than cultural appropriation, it is necessary to examine as to how this error may have arisen in the first place. Genghis Khan claimed that he was the tenth generation from the Glittering Man, and as explained, that would mean his ancestor wasn't existing until around 800 AD or approximately three hundred years after Mar Yanqa was making a name for himself on the steppes. As such, the Mongol legend leads one to conclude that either Mar Yanqa wasn't the Glittering Man or that the prophecy of the ten generations was incorrect, and perhaps it was more like fifteen or sixteen. It must be remembered that Genghis Khan was desperate to claim the prophecy as his own because he required his followers to see him as much more than a barbaric warlord if he was to convince them that it was his destiny to conquer the world. He needed to be the subject of that prophecy in order to achieve his goals. That being said, he would have easily distorted the facts in order to make his case, where the end would be justified by the means. Exactly what those facts are can be found in the historical documents of the Liao.

The Liao documents provide us with the evidence to prove that ten generations after Mar Yanqa, one of his likely descendants did fulfill the prophecy and everything that Mar Yanqa feared would happen, did come to pass as was predicted. What historians know is that the Khitan officially became the Liao in the 10th century under the rule of the Yelu clan. Unfortunately, Liao documents from that time tell us their story moving forward and very little of their past. We do know that by 907 AD they had conquered the Northern Chinese empire and created the first Liao Dynasty to rule over China under Emperor Taizu. The Liao dynasty was in control of China until 1125 AD at which time the Jin rebelled against the Liao, defeating them and establishing what was known as the Jin Dynasty which ruled until 1211 AD at which time it was conquered by Genghis Khan. So, Genghis Khan, would have been very aware of how there was a Khitan ruler, fulfilling the prophecy, three hundred years earlier because his father would have been under the rule of the last Liao emperor.

To pinpoint exactly when the 10th generation would arise following Mar Yanqa's period as Qagan, without genealogical documentation is a difficult task. But if we use the standard assumption of 40 years to a generation, then the tenth generation would have been matured by the start of the 10th century, which coincides with the beginning of the Liao Dynasty. As Mar Yanqa had been warned, the day a Khitan Qagan conquered China and chose to rule over the empire, would be the day that they, as a people, would lose the culture and lifestyle that he fought so hard to preserve.

The rise of the Liao Dynasty (907–1125) marked a profound shift in the historical trajectory of the Khitan people, who as we see from the story were originally a nomadic confederation from the steppes of Manchuria and Inner Mongolia. The establishment of the Liao Dynasty not only elevated the Khitan to the ranks of imperial rulers over vast Chinese and non-Chinese populations but also challenged them to reconcile their nomadic heritage with the administrative, cultural, and ideological demands of ruling a sedentary, Sinicized civilization. To do so, the Khitan had to adopt the style and elements of Chinese governance, culture, and religion, at the cost of their own identity. It was not a cultural loss through total assimilation, but the result of a dualistic approach to empire-building. They referred to it as a "dual administration" though in reality, it was an absolute abandonment of the past.

Khitan society, as we can see from the storyline was organized along tribal lines, with a strong equestrian culture, both shamanistic and monotheistic Sky God beliefs, and a flexible, decentralized leadership structure. Mobility, kinship, and oral tradition formed the backbone of Khitan identity. This nomadic lifestyle allowed for military prowess, adaptability, and a unique worldview shaped by the open steppes, rather than the walled cities of China.

The founding of the Liao Dynasty by Yelü Abaoji in 907, who took on the throne name of Emperor Taizu, marked a radical departure from this tradition. Upon conquering agricultural regions and cities previously under Chinese control, the Khitan were faced with the challenge of managing a multi-ethnic, multi-cultural empire. Taizu did establish a dual administration system, which allowed the Khitan to govern both their own people and the conquered Chinese population according to two different systems. The Northern Administration, also known as Nomadic Law, preserved some of the more traditional Khitan tribal law and customs, including hereditary chieftainships, customary marriage practices, oral arbitration, and mobile encampments, but exposure to the Southern Administration or Chinese Law, which replicated Tang and later Song administrative models, such as employing Confucian scholars, written law codes, taxation systems, and civil service institutions to govern the largely Han-Chinese populations, resulted in a creeping infusion from the south into the northern administration.

It was a pragmatic and flexible approach to governance, avoiding the pitfalls of either full Sinicization or total rejection of Chinese institutions, but ultimately it resulted in gradual assimilation of the Khitan nation. No matter how careful the Liao tried to preserve the balance, full contact with Chinese civilization inevitably brought about change. The first noticeable change was the Khitan writing system, consisting of the Large Khitan Script (c. 920) and the Small Khitan Script (c. 925) both modeled in part after Chinese writing. This marked a complete departure from the oral-only traditions and was a significant step towards turning Khitan governance into a bureaucratic organization.

The next major change was in Khitan architecture and a shift of the population towards urbanization: Liao capital cities, such as Shangjing, were built using Chinese city-planning principles. Palaces, temples, and administrative buildings bore the distinct imprint of Chinese design. Art and ceremonial culture could not withstand the overwhelming Chinese influence. Liao ceramics, clothing, and court rituals reflected a fusion of Tang Chinese aesthetics but with some steppe artistry prese. The Khitan elite began to wear Chinese robes alongside traditional Khitan garb and commissioned Buddhist art and tombs that resembled Tang styles.

The one distinct feature that the Khitan populace had that maintained its separation from the Chinese empires over the past four centuries was the use and preservation of its own language. But now, Khitan remained in use only among some of the elite, Chinese became increasingly prominent in official records and communication with sedentary populations. Many Khitan nobles and royals were educated in Chinese classics. It is not hyperbole to state that when a population loses its language, it is not long before it also loses its distinct identity.

Numerous sub-plots within the story described the uniqueness of the Khitan religion of the period. The Sky God, or Yah, also known as Tengrin among the Mongols was the supreme being. But at the same time there was this belief in the one and only true god, there was still a strong influence of shamanism, with its belief in the spirits of nature and ancestral worship. The fact that these two religious practices could co-exist, even though they are naturally in conflict, was a unique feature of the Khitan during this time period. But with the conquest of Northern China by the Liao came Buddhism, and in particular Mahayana Buddhism. It was extensively promoted by the Liao Emperor, to the detriment and eventual loss of Khitan's dualistic religious practice of monotheism and shamanism. Buddhist temples and monasteries flourished in both northern and southern regions of the empire. Royal patronage of Buddhist relics, including the building of stupas and translation of Buddhist scriptures, legitimized the Liao as moral and civilized rulers in the eyes of their Chinese subjects, while promoting the practice and eventual loss of Khitan religion.

The practice of Mahayana Buddhism was exactly what Mar Yanqa feared would happen. It entailed the complete abandonment of monotheism and its belief in Yahweh. Where he saw reality as created and ruled by the singular divine will of Yah, Mahayana Buddhism as adopted by Emperor Taizu was impermanent, and empty of inherent existence. Where Mar Yanqa called for faith in a personal god, the Mahayana called for selfless insight and universal compassion. These views were not just different but they often negate each other at the philosophical root, making Mahayana Buddhism a profound counterpoint to monotheism. The fact that Mar Yanqa could see that the Khitan conquest and assumption of the throne of the Chinese Empire would immediately result in the abandonment of the religious structure that he introduced, showed phenomenal insight and what was unmistakably divine influence.

As if this wasn't enough to support Emperor Taizu as the howling unborn child that would be Mar Yanqa' curse, Mahayana Buddhism explicitly denies the existence of a creator deity, expounding that the universe is beginningless and governed by karma and dependent origination (pratītyasamutpāda), not by divine will or intervention. Reality unfolds through interdependent causes, not through the plan of any god. To someone whose entire life was built on his devotion to God, the denial of God's existence, would clearly explain why Mar Yanqa had become so distraught by the revelation from Lady Tse.

Contrary to the essential belief in Yah, the ultimate Sky God, Mahayana Buddhism upholds up the doctrine of "no-self." There is no permanent soul. Enlightenment comes from realizing this truth, not from salvation granted by an external deity. As an essential belief in God, that He infuses a soul into every human, the concept of a soulless religion would have been an anathema to Mar Yanqa.

The acceptance of Mahayana Buddhism of a vast cosmology with countless

Buddhas and bodhisattvas in multiple realms, though it claims such beings are not gods though they have power and sovereignty would have been viewed by Mar Yanqa as nothing more than paganism. Everything he had strived for in uniting the people was practically discarded in the blink of an eye, once the child of the tenth generation came to power.

Though it is true that the Khitan practices and shamanistic rites did not completely disappear under Emperor Taizu, they were increasingly syncretized with Buddhist imagery and rituals. This religious transformation by the Liao rulers was intentional, designed to eradicate how the Khitan saw their place in the world, no longer as isolated steppe warriors serving a supreme deity, but as rightful participants in the broader Eurasian spiritual and political order.

As the Khitan settled in cities, intermarried with Han elites, and participated in court culture, their social structures began to shift as well. A new elite class emerged that was neither wholly Chinese nor wholly nomadic, but a hybrid aristocracy comfortable in both worlds. Many Khitan nobles took Chinese surnames, read Chinese texts, and served as officials in southern bureaucracies.

Even the way that the Khitan fought their battles tended to give sway to the militarized style of Chinese armies. Even though it was the horse and compound bow that won them an empire, the Liao reliance on cavalry warfare gave way to mixed military strategies, such as permanent garrisons, fortifications, and supply depots, which were all signs of a growing integration into the sedentary infrastructure of a typical Chinese empire.

What the Liao Empire did retain was the relative equality of women. Perhaps the existence of someone like Alan-Ko as an ancestral figure contributed to this unique situation where Khitan women had more freedom than their Chinese counterparts, often participating in hunting, diplomacy, and politics. Liao empresses and princesses played prominent roles at court, reflecting the more egalitarian traditions of the steppe as was exhibited by Alan-Ko.

As Mar Yanqa had been forewarned, the conquest of the Chinese Empire by the Khitan ten generations later would involve surrendering their cultural and spiritual souls. Perhaps not completely, but to such a significant degree that it transformed the Khitan in profound ways that they were no longer the same people that he forged into a mighty tribal confederacy.

As stated previously, the legend of being the tenth generation from the Glittering Man may have been intentionally borrowed by Genghis Khan in order to support his ambitions. The history of Genghis Khan, the founder of the Mongol Empire, is rich with such legends and tales that have been passed down through generations. It has been commonly believed that the Mongols must be the generators of such legends because they were dictated by Temur Khan, Kublai Khan's grandson, to the Persian historian Rashid-al-Din in 1307. Recorded in his book, simply titled "Chronicles", he was told that the legendary "glittering man" ancestor of Genghis Khan was a tall, long-bearded, red-haired, and green-eyed man. This belief is reinforced when Rashid al-Din describes the first meeting of Genghis and Kublai Khan, where it is written that Genghis was shocked to find that Kublai had not inherited red hair. This in itself was a very interesting statement in that it suggests that perhaps Genghis Khan knew that his connection to the Glittering Man was tenuous at best, as nowhere is there a description of himself having red hair and blue-green eyes. The only comment recorded is that he had a ruddy complexion. It would have been impossible for any descendant to overlook and not remember their ancestor's uniqueness if he did have hair that wasn't black and eyes that weren't brown. In this telling of their meeting, it is almost as if Genghis hoped that his grandson, who did rule over the entire Chinese empire, would legitimize the legend to be true, so that he in turn could thereby prove he was the tenth generation by association.

According to al-Din, Genghis's Borjigin clan also had a legend involving their origins beginning as the result of an affair between Alan-Ko and a stranger to her land, referred to only as the glittering man, with the aforementioned striking appearance and mysterious origins. This story hase captivated historians and scholars alike but despite all their efforts they have never been able to identify him. Surprising since practically everything was recorded from the beginning of the 10th century onwards by the Liao who developed their own aforementioned writing script. To overlook such an important character affecting the balance of powers in the region from which they originated would have been unlikely. This again leads to the conclusion that the Glittering Man appeared on the scene long before this time period, when everything was passed down through oral tradition and very little, if anything was ever written.

This same legend regarding Alan-Ko is echoed in the Secret History of the Mongols (c. 1240), the oldest surviving literary work in the Mongolian language. In this chronicle, Alan-Ko is described as the wife of Dobun Mergen, with whom she had two sons. After her husband's death, she bore three more sons, whom she claimed were fathered by a radiant being of light who entered her yurt through the roof at night. The children of this mysterious union had an unusual appearance, having red hair and green eyes, which set them apart from their siblings and marked them as descendants of this other worldly figure. This myth served as a powerful legitimizing ideology, asserting that the Mongol rulers were not only descended from a noble lineage but were semi-divine, portraying them as chosen leaders with a unique and illustrious heritage. But at this same time, this Mongolian legend would suggest they had no knowledge of the real identity of the man, only hearing of the astonishing 'Glittering Man' from more ancient oral traditions and recording what little they could glean from the tale, adapting it, and then making it their own.

Alan-Ko's story emphasizes the importance of unity for the Mongol people, reflecting their values and beliefs. Her story has been passed down through generations and remains an integral part of Mongol cultural heritage. But the question that must be asked is, 'Was she truly the mother of all Mongols?"

Historians will tell you that there are no archaeological findings, inscriptions, or contemporaneous foreign accounts confirming her existence. They comment that her story parallels foundation myths found in many cultures (e.g., virgin births, divine ancestry), therefore serving a symbolic rather than factual role. They emphasize that Mongol oral tradition treated such ancestors as semi-mythical, combining historical memory with divine narrative to strengthen tribal cohesion and royal authority, hence, she may have existed but the truth has been fabricated and exaggerated, or generally what we simply refer to as folklore. What they may be failing to recognize is that they're looking in the wrong time period and dealing with someone whose Mongol connection may have been minimal, her existence being borrowed from the Khitan.

The perpetuation of the story that her children by the Glittering Man had red hair and blue or green eyes is significant. Because of the rarity of these genes in Asiatic populations, such an ancestor had to originate from outside the Asiatic community. The separation may have been over many generations, but Alan-Ko must have carried the alleles for these genes as a recessive in order to have children sharing those traits. The Glittering Man most definitely had to be a dominant carrier for these genes for all his children to display the same characteristics. The only way the phenotype would have carried on successively over the multiple generations between Alan-Ko and Genghis Khan is for there to have been consistent intermarriage within the family of cousins to cousins as suggested within the storyline. But this as discussed was not the case as neither Genghis Khan, nor his grandson Kublai Khan displayed these characteristics. This would imply that Genghis Khan believed the legend's prophecy was not something that automatically came about through inheritance but was achieved by fulfilling a specific set of tasks or requirements. Hence he was not genetically linked to the Glittering Man but believed it was possible to adopt the legend and prophecy for his own family if he completed a series of tasks as outlined in the prophecy.

So, how was Genghis Khan prepared to go about fulfilling these tasks and being in essence the Anti-Mar Yanqa. Fulfilling these tasks would mean eliminating all the rules and regulations that had been introduced into the Khitan culture by Mar Yanqa. Since his Mongols were now the overlords over the remnants of the steppe Khitan Empire, he had the power to do exactly that. But the only way he would know exactly what was introduced by Mar Yanqa would be if he was in possession of the YahSu. Fortunately, as the result of records written by Persian historians Juvayni and Rashid al-Din as well as the European traveler Marco Polo they confirm that Genghis Khan did have a copy of the YahSu, or the Yassa, as these chroniclers referred to it. Later writers have even attempted to credit Genghis as being the author of this book without any proof and overlooking the fact that he was illiterate. It was said that this book was intended to unify the Mongol Empire through strict discipline, efficiency, and loyalty. It reportedly covered everything from military discipline, governance, taxation, religious instruction and tolerance. social customs, historical legends and punishments, as well as the proper conduct of relationships with other nations. In fact, everything that was incorporated into the book of YahSu, based on the Hebrew Tanach. One would think this book would have been highly prized by the Yuan Dynasty, displayed to everyone as evidence of their moral and legal authority to rule the empire, yet at no time was it ever shown to anyone and at some point the Khans admitted they no longer had possession of the book, having lost it sometime in the past.

Remember that this book which magically appears in the possession of Genghis Khan, which it was said he may have even wrote himself, was in existence even though the Mongols first book that we have any knowledge of them writing was dated 1240 AD, or thirteen years after the death of Genghis. Therefore, the more likely probability is that Genghis Khan found the book in the Liao Imperial Library and simply claimed it as his own. Having it translated, he would have known there was enough detail in the book to prove to anyone that it was not a Mongol original and that the Khitan were the true inheritors of the Glittering Man's heritage and prophecy. Therefore, it was never published publicly by the Mongols. In fact, it was kept a secret, reportedly held in the Great Khan's court, likely in Karakorum and later in Khanbaliq (Beijing) during the Yuan Dynasty, and then at some point it became lost. No copy of the Yassa has ever been discovered. It certainly is known to have disappeared with the end of the Yuan (Mongol) dynasty, and the likelihood is that it will never be seen again. As the book would have challenged the legitimacy of the Mongols divine right to rule over China, it should be no surprise that one of the Khans simply made the decision to have the book disappear forever.

Therefore, the claim to have been both the authors and the original possessors of the book of YahSu or Yassa by the Khans was false. Chinese libraries have managed to preserve records for thousands of years until this day. The writings of Confucius have survived for over 2600 years. Books simply did not spontaneously combust or vanish from the Imperial library. Certainly, an important book such as the Book of Yassa should not only have been available at the time of the Yuan Dynasty, but also 700 years later in the 21st century, unless there was a deliberate attempt to destroy it.

What is possibly true is that Genghis Khan's ancestor was Bodonchar -Munkhag, who was a well-known tenth century chieftain and warlord of the Borjigin Clan. But this was as far back as Genghis Khan was able to trace his ancestry. As to the lineage that he memorized, in no place did it state that Bodonchar was the son of Alan-Ko. That information was added much later as the legends were repeated and added to over time. The existence of Bodonchar Munkhag in the tenth century can be firmly established. What is significant is his being ascribed to the Borjigin Clan. The Borjigin clan is not directly identified as being Khitan, but there is a connection between them and the Khitan. The Borjigin were a Mongol sub-clan that originated from the Kiyat clan, which was related to the Khitan. The fact that the Kiyat and Borjigin were two closely linked Mongolic clans among many tribal groups living under the shadow of Khitan supremacy during the 10th and 11th centuries, meant that they were directly influenced by Khitan governance and regulations on a daily basis.

At that time, these two clans were not politically unified; they were small, semi-nomadic groups scattered across the Onon, Kherlen, and Tuul river valleys, in what is now eastern and central Mongolia. During the height of the Liao Empire, the Khitan emperors claimed nominal suzerainty over these clans, treating them as frontier subjects, useful for defense, trade, and warfare. For all intents and purposes, the Kiyat and Borjigin were simply vassals within the Khitan hegemony. As such, the Kiyat and Borjigin were exposed to Kitan traditions, lore and legends. With the waning of the Liao Empire, these vassal client would have merely adopted the Khitan literature and legends as their own, later labeling them as being originally Mongolian.

With the embracing of the Khitan legends, folklore and literature, a young Temüjin, later to be known as Genghis Khan would have been infatuated by the prophecy of the tenth generation. He would have seen it as a blueprint for conquering the world. This child of the tenth generation merely needed to reverse and destroy everything that Mar Yanqa had put in place. The book of YahSu provided most of those details, therefore all he had to do was find out what it said and implement opposing actions. For the most part, that is exactly what Genghis Khan did. Where Mar Yanqa was the great uniter and negotiator, Genghis Khan was the great destroyer, eliminating and eradicating other tribes. Wherever Mar Yanqa introduced religious requirements, Genghis Khan would rescind them and make them illegal to practice.

The man that Hollywood has turned into a role model and hero, was nothing more than a brutal savage that was a scourge on humanity. In his attack on Zhongdu (modern day Beijing) he slaughtered hundreds of thousands of the population. His men looted, raped and happily burned palaces and temples. After the death of his son-in-law at Nishapur, Genghis Khan slaughtered as many as 300,000 of the population. Time and time again, any city that resisted his siege were annihilated completely. As an act of intimidation, he had his men stack the skulls of the dead into pyramids as a commemorative of his conquest. He starved populations, diverted river, used human shields from among captured civilians, all to demonstrate he was not the man that Mar Yanqa was.

The Mongols destroyed libraries, Confucian academies, Buddhist temples, and artistic centers during their conquests. Priceless texts and pieces of art were lost in the chaos. Often the women of those he conquered were taken as concubines or sex slaves. An entire slave force to be used as porters and laborers was created from the men he captured. He erased the entire Tangut civilization. Genghis Khan viewed previous resistance or future threat as reason enough to eliminate entire populations. By the time he was finished his barbaric slaughter, it has been estimated that he killed forty million people, or ten percent of the world's population at that time. This certainly earned him the honor of being the antithesis of Mar Yanqa, whose main effort was to unify all the people of the steppes into a peaceful and prosperous nation. Any of the laws in the YahSu against senseless killing, stealing, coveting possessions from other tribes and taking their woman were violated by Genghis Khan.

Whereas Mar Yanqa introduced the practice of circumcision as part of religious obligation, Genghis Khan banned its practice. Ritual slaughter was also banned and the restrictions on eating certain foods removed. Genghis Kahn claimed he sought uniformity of the populace and that justified his removal of any restrictions but considering the limited number of Jews and Muslims residing in his domain at that time, it would appear there was a far more sinister motive behind his ruling. As religious doctrine practiced by Mar Yanqa, in order to fulfil the prophecy, they had to go.

Despite all the anti-YahSu actions that Genghis Khan undertook, the reality is that the tenth generation prophecy had already been fulfilled by Yelu Abaoji, who established the Liao Empire as discussed previously. The dynasty, simply known as the Great Liao represented the end of everything that Mar Yanqa had fought for. And as can be seen in the timeline chart below, by the year 1218, with the elimination of the Qara Khitai, any remnant of Mar Yanqa's lineage had vanished. Genghis Khan, unlike the Liao did not win dominion over the Chinese empire as had been the prediction of the prophecy; the Liao did. Genghis Khan did not absorb the Chinese culture to the detriment of Khitan culture and its beliefs; the Liao did. Genghis Khan did not replace the Khitan monotheistic faith mixed with shamanism and replace it with a pagan philosophy of their being no god and no soul; the Liao did. Genghis Khan was not the author of the Yassa but most likely took possession of it when he raided the Imperial library or defeated the Qara Khitai; the Liao had it. Though Genghis Khan may have believed he fulfilled the prophecy and therefore had to be a descendant of the Glittering Man, the reality was that he only gained dominion over Central Asia because of his level of brutality, the likes of which had never been seen by the world before. He didn't fulfil a prophecy; he simply created his own savage and barbaric legacy.

Historical Timeline

Date	Event	Khitan	Kiyat/Borjigin
850s–900	Khitan tribes unite under the Yelü clan	Rise of Khitan tribal confederation	Mongolic tribes scattered across steppe; semi-nomadic
907	**Liao Dynasty founded** by leader Yelü Abaoji	Becomes regional power; controls parts of Mongolia	Kiyat & Borjigin under loose Khitan influence
930s–1000	Liao expansion north and west	Khitan rule extends into eastern Mongolia and steppe	Kiyat/Borjigin pay tribute or maintain low-profile autonomy
1000–1050	Stable Khitan rule over north China and steppe	High point of Liao power	Mongol clans (including Kiyat) remain decentralized
1050–1100	Growing pressure from Jurchens internal unrest in Liao territory	Liao power begins to decline	Kiyat/Borjigin involved in steppe skirmishes and alliances
c. 1120	**Yesugei**, a Kiyat-Borjigin leader is born (father of Temujin)	Liao near collapse due to Jurchen invasion	Kiyat/Borjigin gain more independence
1125	**Liao Dynasty falls** to the Jurchen Jin Dynasty	End of Khitan rule in East Asia	Mongol tribes begin to reassert local power
1130s–1150	**Qara Khitai (Western Liao)** founded by Khitan prince Yelü Dashi in Central Asia	Khitan elites flee west, form new state Qara Khitai	Kiyat-Borjigin begin to form tribal alliances
1162	**Temujin (Genghis Khan)** born to the Borjigin-Kiyat line	Khitan displaced, but legacy of empire remains	Temujin rises among Mongol clans, shaped by Khitan model
1189	Temujin named **Khan of the Mongols**	Qara Khitai still exists in Central Asia	Borjigin-Kiyat leadership consolidates Mongol tribes
1206	**Mongol Empire founded** under Genghis Khan	Khitan legacy absorbed into Mongol administrative model	Borjigin dynasty ascends; Kiyat roots form imperial base
1218	Genghis Khan defeats **Qara Khitai (Western Liao)**	Final fall of Khitan political power	Mongols inherit Central Asian dominion

About the Author

Author of the acclaimed *Kahana Chronicles* series of historical novels, **Allen E. Goldenthal** shines a light on forgotten empires and secret histories that have been buried for centuries. He brings the ancient world roaring back to life with vivid detail, emotional depth, and unflinching realism. Drawing on years of historical research, his work blends epic drama with haunting intrigue—challenging readers to see the past not as dead, but as dangerously alive.

Find out more about the author at https://authors.org.nz/author/kahana/

Other Books in This Series

Once A God
The Caiaphas Letters
Deliverance
Defiance
Dominance
Beneath A Falling Star
Zutra
Blood Royale
Shadows of Trinity
Blood of Trinity
Phantoms of Trinity
Vienna's Last Waltz

www.ingramcontent.com/pod-product-compliance
Lightning Source LLC
LaVergne TN
LVHW041609070426
835507LV00008B/177